Hiking Alabama

A Guide to the State's Greatest Hiking Adventures

Fourth Edition

Joe Cuhaj

FALCONGUIDES

GUILFORD, CONNECTICUT
HELENA, MONTANA

AN IMPRINT OF GLOBE PEQUOT PRESS

To Cora and Steven, find your own path, explore, and revel in life.

To buy books in quantity for corporate use
or incentives, call **(800) 962-0973**
or e-mail **premiums@GlobePequot.com.**

FALCONGUIDES®

FalconGuides is an imprint of Globe Pequot Press.
Falcon, FalconGuides, and Outfit Your Mind are registered trademarks of Morris Book Publishing, LLC.

Photos: Joe Cuhaj
Maps: Alena Joy Pearce © Morris Book Publishing, LLC
Acquisitions editor: Katie Benoit Cardoso
Project editor: Julie Marsh
Layout: Sue Murray

ISSN 1545-6080

ISBN 978-0-7627-8729-6

Printed in the United States of America

The author and Globe Pequot Press assume no liability for accidents happening to, or injuries sustained by, readers who engage in the activities described in this book.

Contents

Acknowledgments xi
Introduction 1
    Flora and Fauna 3
    Weather 4
    Restrictions and Regulations 5
    Getting around Alabama 6
How to Use This Guide 7
    How to Use the Maps 8
Trail Finder 9
Map Legend 12

The Hikes

Gulf Coast Region **13**
  1. Weeks Bay Nature Trail 15
  2. Pine Beach Trail 21
  3. Jeff Friend / Centennial Trail 26
  4. Gator Lake Trail 31
  5. Cotton Bayou Trail 36
  6. Blue Trail 41
  7. Perdido River Trail 46
  8. Village Point Park Preserve 53
  9. Historic Blakeley State Park 58
 10. Muddy Creek Interpretive Trail 64
 11. Cemetery Loop Trail 69
 12. Splinter Hill Bog 74
  Honorable Mentions
    A. Alligator Alley 79
    B. Trails of Gulf State Park 79
    C. Hugh Branyon Backcountry Trail 79

South Region **81**
 13. Gazebo Trail 83
 14. Bell/CCC Trail 88
 15. Old St. Stephens Historical Park 93
 16. Fort Toulouse / Fort Jackson Loop 97
 17. Five Runs Loop 102
 18. Nellie Pond Loop 108
 19. Perry Lake Loop 113
 20. Chewacla State Park Loop 118
 21. Wood Duck Trail 123
 22. Overlook Loop 129

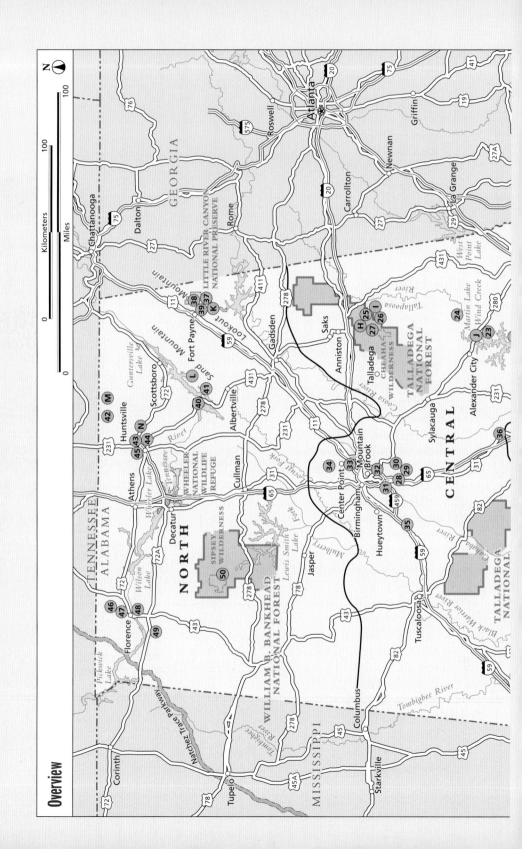

Overview

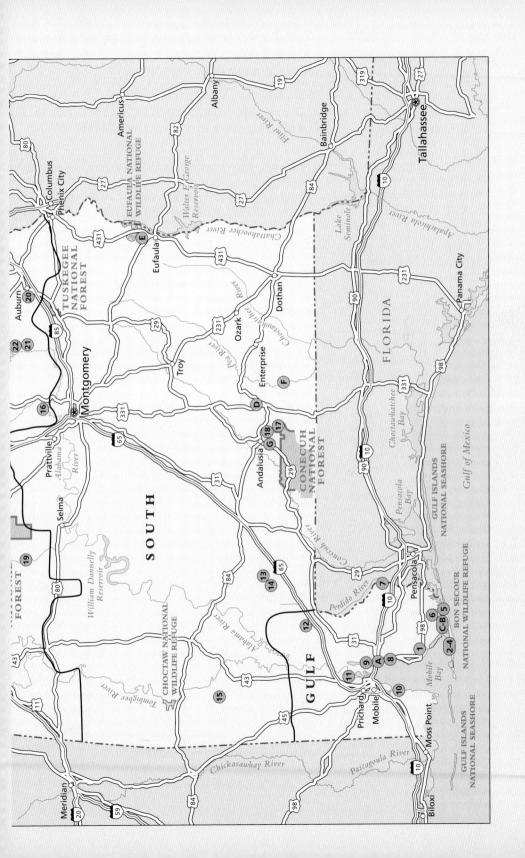

Honorable Mentions

D. Frank Jackson State Park 133
E. Eufaula Wildlife Refuge Nature Trail 133
F. Geneva State Forest 133
G. Conecuh Trail 134

Central Region

Central Region **135**
23. Smith Mountain Loop 137
24. Horseshoe Bend Nature Trail 141
25. Nubbin Creek Trail 146
26. Chinnabee Silent Trail 150
27. Pulpit Rock Trail 155
28. Maggie's Glen Loop 159
29. Treetop Trail 164
30. Peavine Falls Loop 168
31. Ike Maston–BMRR Loop 173
32. Tunnel Falls Loop 178
33. Quarry Trail 183
34. Turkey Creek Loop 188
35. Tannehill Ironworks Historic Trail 192
36. Confederate Memorial Park Nature Trail 197

Honorable Mentions

H. Rock Garden Trail 201
I. Bald Rock / Doug Ghee Boardwalk Trail 201
J. Deadening Trail 202

North Region

North Region **203**
37. DeSoto Scout Trail 205
38. Falls Loop 211
39. Beaver Pond Loop 217
40. Cave Mountain Loop 221
41. Waterfall Trail 225
42. Walls of Jericho 230
43. Monte Sano Nature Preserve Loop 234
44. South Plateau Loop 241
45. North Plateau Loop 246
46. Lawson Branch Loop 251
47. Jones Branch Loop 256
48. TVA Nature Trail 261
49. Cane Creek Canyon Nature Preserve 267
50. Borden Creek (Trail 200) 272

Honorable Mentions

K. Eberhart Trail.. 278
L. Point Rock Trail... 278
M. Russell Cave National Monument 279
N. Stone Cuts Trail... 279

Appendix A: Clubs and Trail Groups 280
Appendix B: Further Reading... 281
The Art of Hiking 282
Hike Index 304
Sidebar Index 305
About the Author 307

A blue spiderwort blooms along the Borden Creek Trail in the Sipsey Wilderness.

ACKNOWLEDGMENTS

First of all, I need to thank all of you, my readers, for the support you have shown me and *Hiking Alabama* over the years and for making the book so successful. I am truly humbled.

Once again it would be impossible for me to thank all of the hikers, clubs, organizations, agencies, and land managers for their help putting this edition together. Just know that I am very grateful for all of your support and input.

There are several people that I need to single out. They are Chris Smith with Alabama's Forever Wild (Alabama DCNR), Rob Grant with the Alabama Department of Economic and Community Affairs, Jim Felder and Debbie Quinn with the Alabama Trails Commission, Dr. Thomas Wilson at Perry Lakes Park, Judith Adams and Bob Harris with the Alabama State Port Authority, environmental manager for the City of Foley Leslie Gahagan, Julie Day with the Alabama Hiking Trail Society, and Jereme Phillips and Brittany Peterson with the Bon Secour National Wildlife Refuge. Thank you all for putting up with my bajillion questions.

And there is one other person that I cannot leave out. I have to thank my wife, Maggie, who hiked every mile of trail with me for this edition. I seriously couldn't have done it without her and couldn't have had better company.

◀ *The Cave Mountain Loop trail hugs the base of a tall bluff with a large tupelo swamp on the left (Hike 40).*

The DeSoto Scout Trail (Hike 37) gives you several chances to view Indian Falls.

INTRODUCTION

The last time we met, I mentioned that there was good news for hikers in Alabama, as the state's land protection agency, Forever Wild, was purchasing more and more land and turning it over for recreational use. This time there is even better news to report.

In a nutshell, Alabama has truly become a hiking destination. Through the efforts of Forever Wild and the new Alabama Trails Commission (see sidebars included with the hike descriptions) and the emergence of more volunteer trail-building organizations, the number of trails that are available to hike in Alabama has grown exponentially, so much so that it was really tough putting this edition together. Each weekend I would have a schedule of trails that I wanted to hike for the book, and inevitably I would discover a new one that I wanted to hike and include. I had to make some tough decisions, but that's a good problem to have—which trail to hike.

There is always a downside to everything, and once again weather plays into this edition. Last time it was the remarkable hurricane seasons of 2004–5 that ravaged the Gulf Coast. This time it's tornadoes. In April 2011 strong tornadoes ripped through the North and Central regions of the state. The 2011 storms actually spawned several twisters, including an EF5 that resulted in over 100 fatalities and almost 2,000 injuries. The destruction was devastating. A few major Alabama state parks suffered severe damage, forcing them to close hotels, restaurants, and campgrounds, and several trails were left barren.

But Alabamians are resilient people. The area is returning to normal. The state parks and national forests are back up and running again. Unfortunately, as I mentioned, a few of our favorite trails from the past weren't so lucky, and while they are open to hikers, it will take years for the land to recover.

On a brighter note, as I said before, Alabama has become a hiking destination for people from around the country and the world, with many new and exciting adventures available.

If this is your first outing on the trails of Alabama or if you are unfamiliar with the topography of the state, you're in for a surprise. There is literally something for everyone when it comes to hiking here.

The state is divided into four distinct regions: the Highland Rim, the Piedmont Plateau, the Black Belt, and the Coastal Plain. To the extreme north is the Highland Rim. Thousands of years ago the entire region was covered by a shallow ocean. As the waters receded and the land began to rise, ancient shell banks and coral reefs dried out and died, forming the limestone bedrock that makes up the mountains of north and northwest Alabama. Over the years the action of the elements on the soft rock created huge crags, cliffs, and caves. Areas such as Cane Creek Canyon Preserve in Tuscumbia and Borden Creek in the Sipsey Wilderness provide excellent opportunities to explore these mammoth outcroppings and rock shelters that usually come equipped with spectacular waterfalls.

Just as the receding ocean created the Highland Rim, so, too, did it unveil the Piedmont Plateau. As the land thrust upward, forming the southernmost end of the Appalachian mountain chain, it created the highest peaks in the state. It's in this region that you'll find Alabama's highest point, Cheaha Mountain, which stands just over 2,400 feet above sea level. You'll also encounter the largest canyon east of the Mississippi, Little River Canyon, carved by the Little River, the longest mountaintop river in the country.

The fertile Black Belt, the land from Montgomery to just above the coast, has gently rolling hills and notoriously rich soil that makes this region prime agricultural territory. Here rivers flow and create sanctuary for a multitude of birds and wildlife.

And finally there is the Coastal Plain. This region has some of the most pristine white beaches to be found along the Gulf of Mexico, as well as the second-largest river delta in the country. The Tensaw River Delta is one of the largest protected areas for wildlife in the state, with many endangered species calling the area home. Such locations as the Bon Secour National Wildlife Refuge, Weeks Bay National Estuarine Research Reserve, and Historic Blakeley State Park allow us to visit this wildlife firsthand.

The history of the state is just as remarkable. Native American history can be traced back to 7,000 BC. Europeans came to the region in the 1500s—first the Spanish, then the French, and then the British, much of which can be experienced at the Fort Toulouse–Fort Jackson Historic State Park in Wetumpka. The United States finally took control in the early 1800s, following such bloody engagements as the Battle of Horseshoe Bend, where General Andrew Jackson took down the last of the Creek Indian defenses.

Time and time again, the Civil War pops up in our travels. The last major battle of the war was fought near Mobile in what is today Historic Blakeley State Park. Tannehill State Historic Park is the site of a major foundry, rebuilt to its original condition, where munitions for the Confederacy were forged, and the state honored their veterans by establishing a retirement home at what is now the Confederate Memorial Park. But don't think that all of Alabama was behind the secession of the South: Winston County, where the Sipsey Wilderness is located, actually declared itself a free county and aligned itself with the Union.

History continues to be made in the state as humans reach for the stars. The city of Huntsville is home to NASA's Marshall Space Flight Center, where the Saturn V moon rocket was designed and the modules for the International Space Station were constructed, and where the new Space Launch System that will take us to Mars and beyond is being designed.

Since the first edition, I have been asked many questions about the book. One is why I chose to include some trails and leave others out. Many fantastic hiking experiences are available across the state, and it would be impossible to include them all. While the hikes within are day hikes, wherever possible I try to provide additional information to extend the length of the trip or to make it into an overnight (or two) backpacking trip.

The last dune before arriving at the Gulf of Mexico (Hike 2)

Another question I am asked is why the many rail trails that are being developed in the state were left out. These new trails are great and offer a new way to get out and enjoy the Alabama scenery and history, but they are multiuse trails. I have tried to narrow down the trips in this book to nonmotorized, nonpaved paths. There are a few that cross paths with bike and equestrian trails, but for the most part, I have tried to include strictly traditional hiking trails. I have also tried to present hikes that offer a wide variety of experiences throughout the state, hikes that should interest everybody from novices to more experienced hikers.

Finally, a question I know you will all be asking is what happened to this trail or that trail that was in the last edition? I did keep some of my favorites in this edition, but there were so many great new trails that I moved several to honorable mentions to make room for them. So there you are. It's time to hit the trail and explore Alabama the Beautiful!

Flora and Fauna

More than two-thirds of Alabama is covered in forest. On the whole these forests are southern yellow, red, white, loblolly, longleaf, and slash pine forests, though red cedar is also prevalent. Of the deciduous trees, you'll likely encounter hickory, sweet gum, and several varieties of oak, including live oak. Favorite aromatic and blooming trees in the state include the magnolia and dogwood.

Alabama is blessed with a wide variety of wildflowers along its trails and roadways. Some of the more interesting varieties include bellwort, also known as merry bells. These flowers are part of the lily family and bloom from April to June throughout the state. The plant has very thin and delicate stems topped with hay-yellow bells.

Along the marshes and streams, the trumpet honeysuckle blooms into bright scarlet from late spring to late summer. In early March the vines of the Carolina jasmine will be found clinging to fences and trees. These vines with yellow flowers can be found throughout the state.

Another common wildflower is the yellow orchid, which blooms late summer through early fall and can be found along just about any trail. From late July through September, the yellow fringed orchid can be found in roadside ditches, bogs, woods, and fields.

Mountain laurel and a variety of azaleas line most of the trails throughout the state, adding bright colors and fragrances to the hikes in springtime.

Alabama has a varied wildlife population. Although the hiker is more apt to find white-tailed deer and gray squirrels along the trail, the state hosts many other species. Black bears roam from one end of the state to the other, with the largest concentration found in the Tensaw River Delta of the Gulf Coast. Bobcat (or lynx) are also quite common throughout the state but are rarely seen.

From north to south, wild turkeys scurry along the trails. The turkey population was once on a dangerous decline but made an astounding recovery in the middle of the twentieth century. (Farmers used the eastern wild turkey to develop all current domestic varieties of turkeys.) Armadillos can frequently be seen foraging through the leaves along trails.

The American alligator, one of only two species of alligator in the world, can be found in the South and Gulf Coast regions. Alligators feed on fish, frogs, snakes, turtles, birds, and small mammals. Luckily they tend to be wary of humans, but feeding or harassing them in any manner changes the rules. The alligator was declared an endangered species in 1967 due to overhunting, but the species has made a strong comeback and some states, including Alabama, have reinstated alligator hunting seasons.

Several species of wildlife that are currently considered endangered have found sanctuary within the state, including the Alabama beach mouse, the loggerhead sea turtle, and the brown pelican. The American bald eagle has also found a new refuge in Alabama.

Weather

The range of weather in Alabama is striking—from its subtropical climate in the south to the cold and snowy winters of the north. In general, the weather for hiking Alabama is near perfect, except maybe for the dead of summer when you'd better be near a lake, river, stream, or the Gulf to cool off in. Even in the northern part of the state in the higher elevations, winters are generally short-lived, with frequent spring-like days scattered throughout January and February.

In the north, average temperatures range from 46°F in January to 80° in July. Colder temperatures are more frequent in the north, and, yes, significant accumulations of snow can occur, though rarely.

In the southern portion of the state, average temperatures range from 52° in January to 85° in July. Cold snaps of below 30°, even near zero, do occur, but they are seldom and only last a day or two.

Though the weather in Alabama is generally ideal for hiking, there are exceptions. The mix of heat and the 100 percent humidity of summer can make a deadly combination, with heat indexes that frequently soar well into the hundreds. On these days, outdoor activity of any kind is discouraged by weather services and state officials.

Also during the summer, extremely heavy and severe late-afternoon thunderstorms can pop up without warning. Although they are widely scattered and short in duration, the large amount of rain and dangerous lightning can make outdoor travel a challenge.

Finally, June through November is hurricane season. Though a hurricane will only hit a relatively small area with its full fury, areas hundreds of miles from the storm can still feel its effects. In fact, most injuries and deaths resulting from hurricanes come from flash flooding in areas that are not even in the storm's center, and tornadoes often accompany the storms as they push inland.

When hiking during hurricane season, especially in September when most of the storms in the Atlantic Ocean make their way into the Gulf of Mexico, check the weather and be alert for any tropical disturbances before heading out. If there are any storms reported, keep tabs on their progress to determine if hiking is a good idea at that time. There is typically plenty of advance warning to react to a storm, so don't let hurricane season discourage you from coming to Alabama to hike!

Restrictions and Regulations

Alabama has twenty-six state parks, five national forests, and a national monument and preserve. With the exception of high-altitude mountain climbing and desert hiking, these protected lands offer every type of hiking experience imaginable, from a short walk with endangered species through preserves to true wilderness hiking. As is the case across the country, the number of people hitting the trail is ever-increasing. Fortunately, state and federal agencies tasked with managing these facilities do an excellent job of maintaining the balance between use and preservation.

Alabama's state parks provide an ideal setting for families looking for a quick getaway to the great outdoors or for those seeking a bit more of an adventure. Several parks now allow trailside camping or "backcountry camping." Those that do are noted in the trail descriptions in this book. All state parks have primitive camping areas for tents and what are called "improved campsites" that have their own water spigot and electrical outlets.

Reservations are not required for primitive campsites at state parks. Reservations are recommended for improved sites and are accepted up to twelve months in advance. Generally up to eight people are allowed per site. Fees and additional regulations may apply, so be sure to check at the ranger station of each park for details or the website noted in the text.

Within the state's national forests, camping is permitted along the trails at no cost unless otherwise noted in the trail description. The rangers ask only that you follow the policy of dispersal camping in which campsites are spread far apart and at least 100 feet from the trail. In some areas, others have already set up campsites close to the trail. If this is the case, rangers suggest using these sites to minimize any further impact of camping on the location. Some of the national forests have recreation areas set up for camping. Again, these have both primitive and improved campsites and fees may apply.

Most of the trailheads described in this book at the national forests charge a small day-use fee. Since you'll almost always be within a stone's throw of a lake, river, or ocean, you may want to try your hand at fishing; visit www.outdooralabama.com for license information.

Dogs are usually welcomed on the trails, but a leash is required unless otherwise noted. Also keep in mind that hunting is allowed in national forests and Forever Wild properties. Contact the national forest, district forest ranger, or the Alabama Department of Conservation and Natural Resources (DCNR) for hunting seasons, which can restrict camping locations and hiking trails.

Getting around Alabama

Area codes: The area codes 256 and 938 cover Huntsville and northern Alabama. For the Birmingham area, the area code is 205. The area code for Mobile and the Gulf Coast is 251, and south Alabama (Montgomery area) is 334.

Roads: For road conditions, visit the Alabama Department of Transportation website at http://alitsweb.dot.state.al.us/RoadConditions, and for road closings and advisories, go to http://alitsweb2.dot.state.al.us/RoadConditions.

By air: Birmingham-Shuttlesworth International Airport (BHM) is Alabama's main point of entry (www.flybirmingham.com). Your travel agent can best advise you on the least expensive and/or most direct way to connect from wherever you're departing. Mobile Regional Airport (MOB) serves greater Mobile and the Gulf Coast (www.mobairport.com). Shared-ride vans and taxis serve each airport and surrounding areas.

To book reservations online, visit your favorite airline's website or search one of the following travel sites for the best price: cheaptickets.com, expedia.com, priceline.com, travel.yahoo.com, or travelocity.com, to name a few.

By bus: Greyhound serves all major towns and cities in Alabama. Schedules and fares are available online at www.greyhound.com or by phone at (800) 231-2222.

By train: Amtrak makes stops in Anniston, Birmingham, and Tuscaloosa. Schedules and fees are available online at www.amtrak.com.

Visitor information: For visitor information or a travel brochure, call the Alabama Bureau of Tourism and Travel at (800) 252-2262 (ALABAMA) or visit its website at www.alabama.travel.

HOW TO USE THIS GUIDE

This little guide contains just about everything you'll ever need to choose, plan for, enjoy, and survive a hike in Alabama. To assist in your hiking choices, the state has been divided into four regions all based on the current Alabama Department of Tourism and Travel regions: the Gulf Coast, South, Central, and North.

To aid in quick decision making, we start each hike chapter with a short summary to give you a taste of the hiking adventure to follow. You'll learn about the trail terrain and what surprises the route has to offer. If your interest is piqued, read on; if it isn't, skip to the next hike.

The hike specifications that follow are fairly self-explanatory. Here you'll find the quick, nitty-gritty details of the hike: where the trailhead is located, hike distance,

One of many cascades in the "Land of a Thousand Waterfalls," the Sipsey Wilderness (Hike 50).

hiking time, difficulty rating, type of trail terrain, best seasons to hike, what other trail users you may encounter, canine compatibility, land status, nearest town, whether fees or permits are required, trail schedule, available maps, and trail contact (for updates on trail conditions). "Finding the trailhead" provides dependable directions from a nearby city right down to where you'll want to park and includes GPS coordinates.

"The Hike" is the meat of the chapter. Detailed and honest, it's the author's carefully researched impression of the trail. While it's impossible to cover everything, you can rest assured that we won't miss what's important. "Miles and Directions" provide mileage cues to identify turns and trail name changes, as well as points of interest. The "Hiking Information" section at the end of each hike is a hodgepodge of information. Here we'll tell you where to stay, where to eat, and what else to see while you're hiking in the area.

The Honorable Mentions are hikes that didn't make the cut. In many cases it's not because they aren't great hikes, but they may be overcrowded or environmentally sensitive to heavy traffic. Be sure to read through these. A jewel might be lurking among them.

How to Use the Maps

Overview Map
This map shows the location of all hikes described in this book, so you can choose a hike based on geography or see which hikes are nearby. You can find your way to the start of the hike from the nearest sizable town or city. Coupled with the detailed directions provided in the "Finding the trailhead" entries, these maps should visually lead you to where you need to be for each hike.

Route Map
This is your primary guide to each hike. It shows all the accessible roads and trails, points of interest, water, towns, landmarks, and geographical features. It also distinguishes trails from roads. The selected route is highlighted, and directional arrows point the way.

TRAIL FINDER

Best Hikes for Backpacking
7. Perdido River Trail
17. Five Runs Loop
18. Nellie Pond Loop
25. Nubbin Creek Trail
26. Chinnabee Silent Trail

Best Hikes for Beach Lovers
2. Pine Beach Trail
7. Perdido River Trail

Best Hikes for Birding
1. Weeks Bay Nature Trail
4. Gator Lake Trail
7. Perdido River Trail
17. Five Runs Loop
18. Nellie Pond Loop
39. Beaver Pond Loop

Best Hikes to Caves and Rock Shelters
40. Cave Mountain Loop
49. Cane Creek Canyon Nature Preserve
50. Borden Creek (Trail 200)

Best Hikes for Families with Children
1. Weeks Bay Nature Trail
4. Gator Lake Trail
16. Fort Toulouse / Fort Jackson Loop
32. Tunnel Falls Loop
39. Beaver Pond Loop
45. North Plateau Loop
50. Borden Creek (Trail 200)

Best Hikes for Geology Lovers
32. Tunnel Falls Loop
43. Monte Sano Nature Preserve Loop
49. Cane Creek Canyon Nature Preserve
50. Borden Creek (Trail 200)

The Nubbin Creek Trail features two waterfalls. In the fall and winter when the leaves are down you will see several cascades (Hike 25).

Best Hikes for History Buffs

8. Village Point Park Preserve
9. Historic Blakeley State Park
15. Old St. Stephens Historical Park
16. Fort Toulouse / Fort Jackson Loop
24. Horseshoe Bend Nature Trail
31. Ike Maston–BMRR Loop
35. Tannehill Ironworks Historic Trail

Best Hikes for Swimming Spots

7. Perdido River Trail
14. Bell/CCC Trail
17. Five Runs Loop
26. Chinnabee Silent Trail

Best Hikes for Views

19. Perry Lake Loop
23. Smith Mountain Loop
26. Chinnabee Silent Trail
27. Pulpit Rock Trail
45. North Plateau Loop
49. Cane Creek Canyon Nature Preserve

Best Hikes for Waterfalls

25. Nubbin Creek Trail
26. Chinnabee Silent Trail
30. Peavine Falls Loop
32. Tunnel Falls Loop
37. DeSoto Scout Trail
38. Falls Loop
42. Walls of Jericho
49. Cane Creek Canyon Nature Preserve
50. Borden Creek (Trail 200)

Best Hikes for Wildflowers

4. Gator Lake Trail
6. Blue Trail
12. Splinter Hill Bog
19. Perry Lake Loop
43. Monte Sano Nature Preserve Loop
49. Cane Creek Canyon Nature Preserve

Map Legend

═══(65)═══	Interstate Highway	≍	Bridge
═══(98)═══	US Highway	■	Building/Point of Interest
───(42)───	State Highway	▲	Campground
═[CR60]≠[FR336]═	County/Forest Road	▲	Campsite
─────────	Local Road	⊛	Capital
═══════	Unpaved Road	—	Dam
├─┼─┼─┼─┤	Railroad	❢	Gate
•─•─•─•─•	Utility/Power Line	🅿	Parking
▬▬▬▬▬	Featured Trail	▲	Peak/Summit
─ ─ ─ ─ ─	Trail	▣	Picnic Area
|||||||||||	Boardwalk/Stairs	▣	Lodging
─ ─ · ─ ─ ·	State Line	((A))	Radio Tower
∼∼∼	Small River/Creek	🏠	Ranger Station/Headquarters
∼ ∼ ∼	Intermittent Stream	🚻	Restrooms
∼∼∼	Canal	🔲	Scenic View/Viewpoint
≚ ⊥	Marsh/Swamp/Bog	▦	Shelter
⬭	Body of Water	⚲	Spring
⋰⋱	Sand	🗼	Tower
▭	National/State Forest/Park	○	Town/City
▯	Wilderness Area	①	Trailhead
▭	State/County Park	├──┤	Tunnel
▭	Miscellaneous Park	🅿	Visitor/Information Center
▯	Miscellaneous Area	≋	Waterfall
▭	Bench		
⬟	Boat Ramp		

Gulf Coast Region

The Gulf Coast region of Alabama supports not only a wide variety of endangered wildlife, but also countless perches from which to view them. Traveling by foot in this region is rarely strenuous. Elevations range from sea level to around 100 feet. It's in this region that the Mobile and Tensaw Rivers converge to form the Tensaw River Delta and ultimately empty into the Gulf of Mexico. The Tensaw River Delta has the distinction of being the second-largest river delta in the country—second only to the Mississippi Delta. The American alligator calls this area home, as does the largest population of black bear in the state and the once-endangered brown pelican.

This region is also home to the white sand beaches of Gulf Shores and Orange Beach. The Pine Beach Trail in Bon Secour National Wildlife Refuge takes hikers directly to the beach. The refuge protects such endangered species as the beach mouse and the loggerhead sea turtle.

History abounds in this region as well. The Battle of Mobile Bay was fought here during the Civil War. It was in this battle that Union admiral David Farragut reportedly uttered the immortal words, "Damn the torpedoes, full speed ahead!" The battle occurred at Fort Morgan just west of the Bon Secour National Wildlife Refuge. Just north along the Mobile River in Spanish Fort is Historic Blakeley State Park, the site of the Battle of Blakeley, which is recognized as the last major battle of the Civil War.

The weather in the region is subtropical. Late summer heat is accentuated by high humidity that often hits 100 percent, making outdoor activity a bit uncomfortable and sometimes dangerous. The warm air and Mobile's location on the Gulf of Mexico mean that sudden and very heavy rainfall can be expected without warning. The storms are short, but the rain is plentiful. In fact, Mobile has held the National Weather Service title of "wettest city in America" a number of times.

The Gulf Coast has seen its share of disasters over the past ten years. Nature has made her presence felt with several major hurricanes making landfall in or near the area, including Ivan, Dennis, and Katrina. And, of course, there was the Deepwater Horizon oil spill that nearly took out the beaches. With all of this, the fragile coastal wildlife habitats were obviously threatened, but the Gulf is resilient, and so are its

The intersection of the Gator Lake and Pine Beach Trails on Alabama's Gulf Coast

people. The habitats are returning to normal, and the beaches are their beautiful white once again.

Fall and winter along the Gulf Coast are wonderful, to say the least. Most of the time, moderate temperatures, averaging in the low to mid-70s, last well into fall. During this time the humidity is quite low, making hiking a real pleasure. Temperatures in January average around 52°F. Now don't get me wrong, it does get cold in the Deep South. Temperatures have dropped to single digits on several occasions, but those days are few and usually short-lived.

1 Weeks Bay Nature Trail

This trail is a short and very easy walk around the Weeks Bay National Estuary. The estuary, home to a wide variety of birds and other plant and animal life, offers an interesting, enjoyable, and educational experience for all members of the family.

Start: Trailhead on US 98
Distance: 1.4 miles out and back
Hiking time: About 1 hour
Difficulty: Easy over flat paths and boardwalks
Trail surface: Dirt footpath, some boardwalk
Best seasons: Fall-spring
Other trail users: None
Canine compatibility: Leashed dogs permitted
Land status: National estuarine research reserve
Nearest town: Fairhope

Fees and permits: None
Schedule: Trail open year-round dawn to dusk; interpretive center open Mon–Sat 9 a.m.–5 p.m.
Maps: USGS Magnolia Springs, AL; *DeLorme: Alabama Atlas & Gazetteer,* page 63 G6; brochures available at trailhead kiosk
Trail contact: Weeks Bay National Estuarine Research Reserve, 11300 US 98, Fairhope, AL 36532; (251) 928-9792; www.outdoor alabama.com/public-lands/statelands/ weeksbay

Finding the trailhead: From Fairhope at the intersection of US 98 and Fairhope Avenue, take US 98 east 10.2 miles. The trailhead will be on the right. GPS: N30 25.214' / W87 50.080'

The Hike

This is not a high-tech, high-altitude, three-day backpacking trip. This short and simple nature path is included here for the purposes of spotlighting a beautiful reserve and an endangered habitat. If you have children, especially younger ones, this is a perfect opportunity to introduce them to hiking and exploring the great outdoors, and who knows, they just might learn something in the process.

The Weeks Bay National Estuarine Research Reserve is one of twenty-six such estuaries administered by the National Oceanic and Atmospheric Administration. By definition an estuary is a semi-enclosed body of water where freshwater from rivers mixes with saltwater from the ocean creating a brackish mix, a prime ingredient for supporting a wide variety of plant and animal life.

The Weeks Bay reserve was established in 1986 to protect land that was once at high risk of development. In fact, the county where the estuary is located, Baldwin, is one of the fastest-growing counties, if not the fastest-growing county, in the state. The reserve maintains for posterity 3,000 acres of marshland along Weeks and Mobile Bays and is fed by the Magnolia and Fish Rivers.

The reserve's nature trail utilizes a combination of vegetation-friendly dirt paths to lead you through the forested swamps, along the banks of salt- and freshwater marshes, and through the tidal flats. Signs along the way identify animals and rare plants you may encounter (some of the information is provided in a brochure available at the

A beautiful live oak at the beginning of the Weeks Bay Nature Trail

trailhead kiosk or reserve office). Some of the trees you will see here include Japanese climbing fern, lots of loblolly pine, sweet gum, eastern red cedar, sweet pepperbush, and a variety of *Myrica cerifera*, a plant you know better as wax myrtle.

Among the animals that live here are blue crabs, red-bellied turtles, and American alligators. More than 350 species of birds are found at Weeks Bay, either permanently or during migration periods. Among them are the black needlerush, great blue heron, red-winged blackbird, and the once-endangered brown pelican. Plus there is a good contingency of bats here as well, including the brown bat and silver-haired bat.

The trail we describe here begins at a large trailhead on US 98. It is a grass parking area with ample room for twenty-plus cars. For the most part the trail is a wide dirt footpath and is dry except after it rains, when it can be very muddy and boggy. If you plan on hiking the trail in the summer months, be sure to bring along a good dose of insect repellent. You are walking through marshes and bogs, after all. Some of the trail does have short "gangplanks" for you to navigate over when the trail is muddy. These are three 2-by-6 inch, 16-foot boards nailed together and placed in strategic locations for stepping on. The trail is marked with white wooden diamond-shaped markers with the letters WB on them in black.

About 400 feet from the trailhead, the path comes to a Y at a beautiful large live oak tree climbed by a resurrection fern. There is also a very nice wildflower patch with yellow colicroot, milkwort, and threadleaf sundew next to the tree and behind a fence. The blooms are exceptional in the spring. Take the right fork first and head

JUST THE FACTS ... ABOUT ALABAMA

Nickname: Heart of Dixie

Motto: *Audemus Jura Nostra Defendere* **(We Dare Maintain Our Rights)**

Entered the Union: December 14, 1819, as the twenty-second state

Capital: Montgomery

Population: 4,779,745

Area: 51,718 square miles (twenty-ninth in the United States), including 956 square miles of water surface

Highest elevation: Cheaha Mountain (2,407 feet)

Lowest elevation: Sea level along the Gulf of Mexico

Temperature-extreme averages:

Huntsville—January: High 51°, Low 32°; July: High 91°, Low 71°

Mobile—January: High 61°, Low 40°; July: High 91°, Low 73°

Annual rainfall averages:

Huntsville—57.51 inches

Mobile—66.29 inches

The sun sparkles on the waters of Weeks Bay.

south to Weeks Bay. There is a 200-foot boardwalk there with excellent views of the bay and marsh. At the end of the boardwalk, it looks like the trail continues but it doesn't. It quickly dead-ends and you could find yourself standing in the marsh itself. Instead, turn around at the end of the boardwalk and head back to the Y.

Once at the Y, take the right fork and head east to the Weeks Bay Interpretive Center. Here you'll find displays that describe the estuary and its plants and animals. At the back of the building there is a mini-zoo the kids will love (and you, too) with fish, blue crabs, and an alligator.

The Interpretive Center is the turnaround for this trip, where you will begin your walk back to the trailhead. **Option:** You can extend the trip an additional 0.3 mile along a nice boardwalk that takes you to another view of the bay and a dense wetland. The boardwalk begins on the left (east) side of the building. It was closed when I revisited the estuary, but from previous visits I can tell you it's worth the trip.

While you're in the neighborhood, be sure to head down to the Weeks Bay Pitcher Plant Bog. To get there from the estuary trailhead, take US 98 East over the Weeks Bay Bridge 1 mile, turn left onto CR 17, and follow the signs. The curious pitcher plant is a wily carnivore that feasts on insects. The Wintermeyer Nature Trail

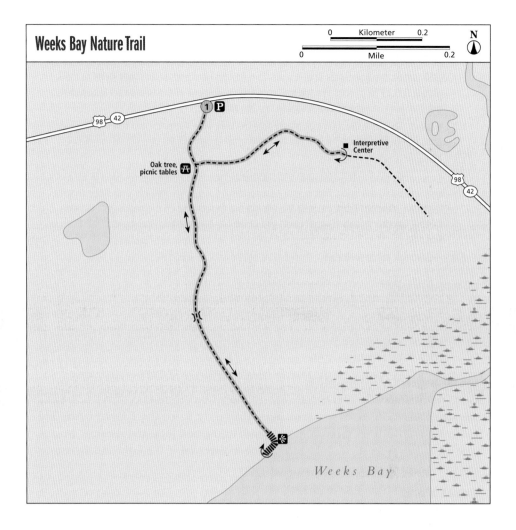

Weeks Bay Nature Trail

guides visitors easily through the bog, which, contrary to what you might think, is a relatively dry environment. The best time to visit the bog is in March and April when the plants are in full bloom.

Miles and Directions

0.0 Start from the trailhead on the south side of the parking lot. The path is a wide grass bed at this point with a wooden fence to your right (west). In 400 feet come to a large oak tree with resurrection fern. There are four picnic tables here and a garbage can. A nice wild-flower patch is on the opposite side of the wooden fence to the west. Cross the dirt road to the east and come to a Y. A sign here shows the direction to the bay and interpretive center. Follow the sign by turning right (south) onto a narrow dirt footpath.

0.2 Pass a large area of standing water (depending on rainfall) to your left (east).

0.3 Cross a creek over a 15-foot bridge. After crossing, turn left (south) onto a dirt road (the turn to the right is blocked by a bench).

0.5 Come to the boardwalk along the bay with a beautiful view and bench. You can walk about 200 feet on the boardwalk until it ends. Turn around here and retrace your steps to the Y at mile 0.0. (*FYI:* It looks like the trail continues at the end of the boardwalk to the west, but it doesn't. It becomes impassable in a few feet.)

1.0 Back at the Y, take the right fork (east) onto the very wide dirt path. In a few feet you will pass an obvious geocache. You will be walking parallel to US 98 through the hardwoods.

1.1 The path is now a grass bed.

1.2 Cross a dirt road to the east and come up behind the Interpretive Center. Stop in for a visit when they are open. This is your second turnaround point. Retrace your steps to the trailhead. (*Option:* Continue past the Interpretive Center and on the building's east side there is another boardwalk that takes you to the bay and wetland and increases the trip by 0.3 mile.)

1.4 Arrive back at the trailhead.

Hiking Information

Local Information
Eastern Shore Chamber of Commerce, 327 Fairhope Ave., Fairhope, AL 36526; (251) 621-8001; www.eschamber.com

Local Events/Attractions
Fairhope Arts and Crafts Festival, 367 Fairhope Ave., Fairhope; (251) 621-8222; www.eschamber.com/artscrafts. For more than sixty years, the Fairhope Arts and Crafts Festival has been showcasing the work of the best local and national artisans. The event, held annually in mid-March, now boasts over 250 booths and, of course, lots of local food and music. There is no admission fee.

Restaurants
Pelican Patio / Church Street Chill Grill, 14 N. Church St., Fairhope; (251) 928-1714. Local seafood, burgers, and live music.

Other Resources
Weeks Bay Foundation, 11401 US 98, Fairhope, AL 36532; (251) 990-5004; www .weeksbay.org

2 Pine Beach Trail

The Pine Beach Trail at the Bon Secour National Wildlife Refuge will lead you to all that makes the refuge spectacular. Along the trail you will experience beautiful ancient oak trees draped in Spanish moss, maritime wetlands and forests, many species of birds and wildlife, and the pristine, and secluded, white beaches of the Gulf of Mexico, a prime habitat for nesting loggerhead sea turtles.

Start: Pine Beach Trailhead located on south end of parking lot
Distance: 3.4 miles out and back
Hiking time: About 2.5 hours
Difficulty: Moderate because of extended powdery sand dune walking
Trail surface: Dirt and gravel road; fine, deep sand
Best seasons: Sept–May
Other trail users: None
Canine compatibility: Dogs prohibited

Land status: National wildlife refuge
Nearest town: Gulf Shores
Fees and permits: None
Schedule: Year-round, dawn to dusk
Maps: USGS Pine Beach, AL; *DeLorme: Alabama Atlas & Gazetteer,* page 64 F1; brochures available at trailhead kiosk
Trail contact: US Fish and Wildlife Service, AL 180, Gulf Shores, AL 36542; (251) 540-7720; www.fws.gov/bonsecour

Finding the trailhead: From the intersection of AL 59 and AL 180, take AL 180 west 9 miles. Trailhead parking will be on the left and is well marked with a sign. GPS: N30 14.872'/W87 49.761'

The Hike

Along Alabama's Gulf Coast, smack dab in the middle of a narrow strip of land known as the Fort Morgan peninsula, there is an area over 7,000 acres in size called the Bon Secour National Wildlife Refuge. The refuge was established by Congress on June 9, 1980, and is one of the last undisturbed areas of coastal barrier remaining in the state.

The refuge is aptly named. *Bon secour* is a French term that means "safe harbor" and it is just that, a safe harbor for a wide range of wildlife. Within the confines of the refuge you will see hundreds of species of water fowl and migratory birds like ospreys, great blue herons, brown pelicans, cattle egrets, and peregrines. Wildlife includes your everyday variety like squirrels, rabbits, and raccoons, but you'll also find armadillos, American alligators, and bobcats.

Bon Secour also plays host to a few endangered species of wildlife including the Alabama beach mouse, which lives in the dunes; the piping plover, a shorebird that nests on beaches; and the loggerhead sea turtle. Bon Secour has a unique program where the public can help the sea turtle by monitoring their nesting grounds during nesting season (May through September). Contact the refuge at (866) SEA-TURTLE to learn more.

Hikers make their way over the dunes on the Pine Beach Trail.

The best way to experience all of the wildlife and beautiful landscapes of Bon Secour is on the Pine Beach Trail. This 3.4-mile out-and-back trail takes you through all that the refuge has to offer, beginning in a maritime forest with wetlands and ending at the pristine white beaches of the Gulf of Mexico.

Starting at the trailhead you will see huge Spanish moss–laden live oak trees. From there the wide dirt footpath meanders through a maritime forest of magnolia, red cedar, wild olive trees, and saw palmetto. You will also pass blueberry and huckleberry bushes, but don't pick them. They are protected in the refuge because they are food sources for the wildlife. Be sure to pick up the "Pine Beach Trail Guide" brochure at the kiosk before you head out to help you identify the many trees you'll see. The trail is not blazed but is easy to follow over an old dirt and gravel road bed.

Just over halfway through the hike, you'll pass the junction with the Centennial Trail, and soon after you will arrive at an impressive elevated wildlife-viewing platform that is a perfect place to stop and have a snack or lunch and take in the view of Gator Lake and Little Lagoon.

After you pass the platform, the trail begins to change. The path follows the wide sand and gravel road between Little Lagoon, a saltwater lagoon, to your left (east) and Gator Lake.

Once you pass these two bodies of water, you begin walking among the white sand dunes of the Alabama Gulf Coast. Sea oats wave in the breeze as you make your way to the Gulf. The trail through here is plainly marked with metal hiker signs mounted on T-posts. Please stay on the trail! The dunes are sensitive habitats for plants and wildlife and as such are federally protected. Some areas are actually roped off, a "subtle" reminder of the rules.

Along this section of the trail you will pass the foundations of two houses. These were beach houses that unfortunately met their match, Hurricane Frederick, in 1979. Hurricanes are a key player along the Alabama Gulf Coast. In 2004 Hurricane Ivan made a direct hit here, with winds over 130 miles per hour, a 16-foot storm surge, and a total of $3.9 million in damages. The US Fish and Wildlife Service did a remarkable job with cleanup and actually recycled over 30 percent of the debris that washed up onshore.

Finally, the trail heads over the last large frontal dune and you are treated to an amazing expansive view of the Gulf of Mexico. This is one of the most secluded areas of Gulf beach you will find anywhere, with not a soul to be seen for miles. Many people ask about the Deepwater Horizon oil spill of 2006 (also known as the BP oil spill). Well, I can tell you the recovery effort was very successful, and the beach and this valuable habitat is as beautiful as ever.

Miles and Directions

0.0 Start at the Pine Beach Trailhead located at the south end of the parking area.

0.3 Pass through a beautiful wetland. The water is dotted with water lily.

0.5 Pass a sign on the left describing how the US Fish and Wildlife Service perform prescribed burns to enhance the habitat for wildlife. Behind the sign you will see the results of the burns.

0.7 Come to a very spacious and clean portable toilet. The facility has a solar-powered fan for ventilation. In about 100 feet you will come to the intersection of the Jeff Friend / Centennial Trail to the left (east). Continue straight (south).

0.8 Arrive at the wildlife-viewing platform. When you're ready, continue straight south on the trail, crossing a single-lane wooden bridge over a small bayou. The trail now travels between the two bodies of water and gradually becomes a sand path.

1.2 The Gator Lake Trail enters from the right (west) and is marked with a sign. The sign also indicates the direction to the beach and back to the trailhead. Continue straight (south).

1.3 Come to a Y in the trail. Take the right fork (south). A sign here points the direction. The left fork is private property. You now begin walking on beautiful, fine white sand dunes. The walking becomes tougher from here to the Gulf in the deep sand. The trail is now marked with 4-by-5-inch hiker signs mounted on 4-by-4-inch posts. (**FYI:** Make sure you stay on the path! The dunes are federally protected habitats.)

1.4 Pass the foundation of a house to the right (west) destroyed by Hurricane Frederick.

1.5 Come to another Y in the trail. Take the right fork to the south. The left fork is closed to hikers. In a few yards you will come to another house foundation.

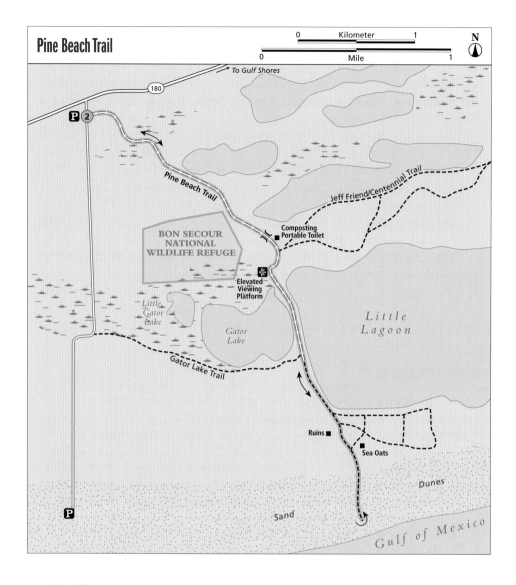

0   Kilometer   1

0   Mile   1

N

To Gulf Shores

180

P 2

Pine Beach Trail

Jeff Friend/Centennial Trail

BON SECOUR
NATIONAL
WILDLIFE REFUGE

Composting
Portable Toilet

Elevated
Viewing
Platform

Little
Gator
Lake

Gator
Lake

Little
Lagoon

Gator Lake Trail

Ruins ■

Sea Oats ■

Dunes

P

Sand

Gulf of Mexico

1.6 Climb over sand dunes to get your first glimpse of the Gulf of Mexico. The trail is lined with ropes to keep hikers off the dunes.

1.7 Arrive at the Gulf of Mexico. Feel free to walk the beach, explore, collect some shells, and enjoy the serenity that the Pine Beach Trail offers. When you're ready, turn around and retrace your steps to the trailhead.

3.4 Arrive back at the trailhead.

A couple enjoys the solitude on the pristine white beach at the southern end of the Pine Beach Trail.

Hiking Information

Local Information

Gulf Shores and Orange Beach Tourism, 3150 Gulf Shores Pkwy., Gulf Shores, AL 36542; (800) 745-7263; www.gulfshores.com

Local Events/Attractions

Interstate Mullet Toss, Flora-Bama Lounge, 17401 Perdido Key Dr., Pensacola; (251) 980-5118; www.florabama.com. This annual event is held the last weekend of April and, as the name implies, is an interstate event where contestants vie for prizes as they toss mullet across the state line. Proceeds benefit various charities.

Lodging

Gulf State Park, 22050 Campground Rd., Gulf Shores; (251) 948-7275; camping reservations (800) 252-7275; 496 sites available

Restaurants

Original Oyster House, 701 AL 59, Gulf Shores; (251) 948-2445; www.theoyster house.com

Hike Tours

Ranger-led tours available throughout the year. Contact refuge headquarters at (251) 540-7720 for current schedule.

Organizations

Friends of Bon Secour, 12295 AL 180, Gulf Shores, AL 36542; www.fws.gov/bonsecour/friends.htm

3 Jeff Friend / Centennial Trail

A beautiful hike of exploration through the transitional maritime forests and wetlands of Alabama's Gulf Coast. If you have younger children, the Jeff Friend Trail alone makes a great trip to the banks of Little Lagoon. The longer trip includes the Centennial Trail that gives you a chance to visit beautiful wetlands with wildflowers and waterfowl.

Start: Jeff Friend Trailhead parking lot
Distance: 5.0-mile lollipop
Hiking time: 2.5-3 hours
Difficulty: Moderate due to length and some sand walking
Trail surface: Gravel, dirt, sand
Best seasons: Late Feb-mid-May
Other trail users: None
Canine compatibility: Dogs prohibited
Land status: National wildlife refuge
Nearest town: Gulf Shores

Fees and permits: None
Schedule: Year-round; electronic gate at parking lot open 6 a.m.-8 p.m. Apr-Oct, 7 a.m.-6 p.m. Nov-Mar
Maps: USGS Pine Beach, AL; *DeLorme: Alabama Atlas & Gazetteer,* page 64 F2; brochures available at trailhead kiosk
Trail contact: US Fish and Wildlife Service, AL 180, Gulf Shores, AL 36542; (251) 540-7720; www.fws.gov/bonsecour

Finding the trailhead: From the intersection of AL 59 and AL 180, take AL 180 west 5.6 miles. Trailhead parking will be on the left and is well marked with a sign. GPS: N30 14.668' / W87 47.235'

The Hike

The Bon Secour National Wildlife Refuge near Gulf Shores is filled with amazing landscapes, birds, and wildlife. From maritime wetlands and forests to dune ecosystems, Bon Secour is a real gem on the Gulf Coast. The Jeff Friend and Centennial Trails allow you to explore the transitional area between the maritime forest and the dunes of the Gulf.

The combination of these two trails makes for a nice 5-mile lollipop hike. The walk begins at the Jeff Friend Trailhead. The Jeff Friend Trail is a 1-mile loop that takes you to a beautiful wetland and a boardwalk along the banks of the saltwater Little Lagoon. The trail is a wide gravel path held in place by a plastic underlayment that allows for drainage. Jeff Friend by itself makes a great hike to take your children on. It's a short, easy walk with enough interesting features to keep them occupied and entertained.

For those looking for something more, continue west on the Centennial Trail. The trail intersects the Jeff Friend Trail about 0.3 mile from the trailhead. The width of the trail varies from nice, enclosed 4-foot-wide dirt paths to 10-foot-plus-wide sand trails. Several times on this trek you will cross small streams and wetlands over wooden boardwalks, the largest being at mile 2.1 where it crosses a wide wetland

A couple takes a morning walk along the boardwalk around Little Lagoon on the Jeff Friend Trail.

filled with blooming water lilies, wildflowers, and waterfowl. Be sure to have your camera ready. The boardwalk is just above the surface of the wetland, so after one of south Alabama's notorious wet summers, it may actually be underwater. In that case you may have to turn around, or there is a small strip of higher ground to the south that parallels the boardwalk that you may be able to use to walk around the water.

Wildlife is abundant along the trail, and signs along the path tell the stories of armadillos, coach whip snakes, pine woods tree frogs, gopher tortoises, and many more animals. One of the interesting sights as you walk this trail is evidence of the power of hurricanes. As you near the boardwalk at mile 2.1, you will see trees simply snapped off like broken matchsticks.

Keep in mind that you are walking through wetlands here, and in the hot summer months mosquitoes are everywhere. Be sure to douse down with insect spray before heading out.

When you arrive at the intersection with the Pine Beach Trail (the turnaround), if you have to heed the call of Nature, a few yards to your right is a very nice composting portable toilet. Also, a short 0.3-mile walk to the south on the Pine Beach Trail takes you to the elevated viewing platform overlooking Gator Lake and Little

Lagoon, a great place to stop for a rest, have lunch, and watch for birds and wildlife, especially in the early morning hours.

From the Pine Beach intersection, you will turn around and retrace your steps back to the Jeff Friend Trail, but at the intersection take the right fork to the south onto Jeff Friend for that walk around Little Lagoon.

The trails are not heavily marked but are easy enough to follow, and where needed, small metallic brown hiker signs with arrows pointing the way will be found. Several times along the trail you will pass dirt access roads coming in from different areas. Heed the signs and don't go exploring down them. They are closed to the public.

Miles and Directions

0.0 Start from the east side of the parking lot. Head east 70 feet to the trailhead (the kiosk is very obvious from the parking lot). A sign here reads "Loop Trail 1 Mile, No Pets." Head to the right (east). The trail is a wide gravel path with thick rows of saw palmetto and oaks laden with Spanish moss lining the way.

0.2 Pass an informative sign explaining maritime wetlands on the left and a bench on the right.

0.3 Come to a Y in the trail. The left fork (south) will be used for our return trip; continue on the right fork and head east on the Centennial Trail. A sign here points the way and identifies the trail. The trail from here on out alternates from dirt to sand base and back again.

0.4 Cross a series of three boardwalks over wetlands, each separated by a 30- to 40-foot dirt path. Bamboo grows alongside the walkways.

0.6 The boardwalks end. Continue to the east. Some of the trail in this area is low-lying and can be muddy, if not covered with water, after a heavy rain.

0.7 Cross a short, 30-foot boardwalk to the east.

0.8 Cross another boardwalk, about 100 feet long, to the east. At the end is a bench.

1.1 A dirt road enters from the right (north). There is an AREA CLOSED sign here telling you not to take the road, and a Centennial Trail sign with an arrow points the direction (east). In about 0.5 mile pass another bench. The canopy thins out here, a disadvantage on hot summer days.

1.4 Pass another bench.

1.5 A dirt road enters from the right (north). An AREA CLOSED sign indicates the road is closed to the public. Follow the arrow on the Centennial Trail sign and continue straight (east). All around you is evidence of damage from hurricanes of the not-too-distant past.

1.6 Cross a 30-foot boardwalk to the east.

1.8 Pass another bench on the right (north). Also to the north you will see the western end of a large wetland.

2.1 Cross the largest boardwalk of the trip over a beautiful wetland. Halfway across is a nice bench and a wide platform for you to view the plants and wildlife. (**FYI:** After a heavy rain the walkway could be underwater. If that's the case, you may be able to walk around the crossing on the uphill side of the wetland.)

2.2 Come to the end of the boardwalk. The canopy again provides good shade. Look for deer moss along the trail. The trail from here to the intersection with the Pine Beach Trail is mostly a dirt path. Little Lagoon can be seen through the trees to the southeast.

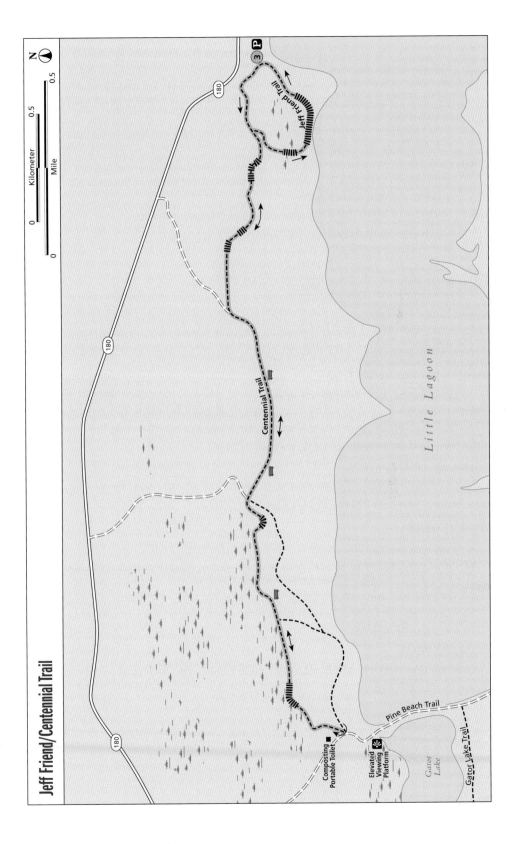

Jeff Friend/Centennial Trail

N

Kilometer
0   0.5

Mile
0   0.5

180

180

P
3

Jeff Friend Trail

Centennial Trail

Little Lagoon

Composting Portable Toilet

Elevated Viewing Platform

Pine Beach Trail

Gator Lake

Gator Lake Trail

2.3 Come to the intersection of the Centennial Trail and the Pine Beach Trail. Turn around here and retrace your steps to the Jeff Friend Trail intersection. (**FYI:** About 250 feet to the right [north] on the Pine Beach Trail is a nice composting toilet. If you turn left onto the Pine Beach Trail and travel about 0.3 mile, you will come to a large elevated wildlife-viewing platform.)

4.4 Arrive back at the Y intersection of the Centennial Trail and Jeff Friend Trail. Take the right fork to the south. Once again the trail is gravel.

4.6 Come to a bench on the right and a short boardwalk over a small slough next to a very pretty wetland on your left. In 200 feet you will come to a long boardwalk that takes you past beautiful views of Little Lagoon.

4.7 Still on the boardwalk, come to a small deck on your right with a bench.

4.8 The boardwalk ends and the trail is once again gravel.

5.0 Arrive back at the trailhead.

Hiking Information

Local Information
Gulf Shores and Orange Beach Tourism, 3150 Gulf Shores Pkwy., Gulf Shores, AL 36542; (800) 745-7263; www.gulfshores.com

Local Events/Attractions
Frank Brown International Songwriters' Festival. Held at various venues in Gulf Shores; (850) 492-7664; www.fbisf.com. This annual event is held in November and is a music lover's dream come true, featuring hit songwriters performing their music and newcomers introducing their style of songwriting.

Lodging
Gulf State Park, 22050 Campground Rd., Gulf Shores; (251) 948-7275; camping reservations (800) 252-7275; 496 sites available

Restaurants
Gulf Shores Steamer, 27267 Perdido Beach Blvd., Ste. 115, Gulf Shores; (251) 948-6344; www.gulfshoressteamer.com. Specializes in steamed seafood, no fried.

Hike Tours
Ranger-led tours available throughout the year. Contact refuge headquarters at (251) 540-7720 for current schedule.

Organizations
Friends of Bon Secour, 12295 AL 180, Gulf Shores, AL 36542; www.fws.gov/bonsecour/friends.htm

4 Gator Lake Trail

A beautiful, and easy, out-and-back hike that allows hikers of all ages to experience some of the wonders of the Bon Secour National Wildlife Refuge. This 1.5-mile path takes you past the freshwater Gator Lake over rolling sand dunes dotted with beautiful black-eyed Susans, wild rosemary, blazing star, and, of course, wildlife including dozens of species of migratory birds, monarch butterflies, and maybe an alligator or two.

Start: Trailhead at parking lot
Distance: 1.5 miles out and back
Hiking time: About 1 hour
Difficulty: Easy to moderate due to deep-sand trail bed
Trail surface: Fine sand
Best seasons: Early March–late May, early Sept–early Nov
Other trail users: None
Canine compatibility: Dogs prohibited

Land status: National wildlife refuge
Nearest town: Gulf Shores
Fees and permits: None
Schedule: Year-round, dawn to dusk
Maps: USGS Pine Beach, AL; *DeLorme: Alabama Atlas & Gazetteer,* page 64 F1; brochures available at trailhead kiosk
Trail contact: US Fish and Wildlife Service, AL 180, Gulf Shores, AL 36542; (251) 540-7720; www.fws.gov/bonsecour

Finding the trailhead: From the intersection of AL 59 and AL 180, take AL 180 west 9 miles. Turn left onto Mobile Street (the turn is just a few feet past the sign for the Pine Beach Trailhead). Travel 0.8 mile. Parking and the trailhead are on the left at a sharp bend to the right. GPS: N30 14.187'/W87 49.816'

The Hike

Alabama's Gulf Coast is known nationally for its pristine white beaches and family-friendly atmosphere. During the summer months, families flock to the towns of Orange Beach and Gulf Shores to enjoy the sun, surf, and attractions, then in the winter retirees, better known to the locals as "snowbirds," migrate to the South to beat the harsh northern winters.

No matter what your reason is for coming to the Gulf Coast, chances are sooner or later you will be looking for something a little different to do besides catching up on your tan. An excellent option is to take a hike on the Gator Lake Trail in the Bon Secour National Wildlife Refuge.

The Gator Lake Trail is an easy to moderate 1.5-mile out-and-back. The only reason for the moderate rating is because the trail follows rolling sand dunes, and sand walking can be a bit tiring even for the best hikers.

▶ What's in a name? Alabama was named after a Native American tribe that lived in what is now central Alabama, the Alabamu or Alibamo, depending on what country tried to spell it. Europeans named a major river in the region after the tribe and then later the state.

Rounding a bend you get your first view of Gator Lake.

As you travel down Mobile Street heading to the trailhead, you get a taste of what lies in store for you on the trail: beautiful expansive wetlands teeming with migratory birds and, depending on the season, a rainbow of wildflowers. You will also pass a number of signs warning you about alligators. Yes, there are alligators in these wetlands and in the trail's namesake, the freshwater Gator Lake. Of course, alligators are dangerous, but they are naturally afraid of humans. Problems occur when people start to feed them. That's when the rules change. If you see an alligator, keep your distance and don't feed it—just enjoy the experience.

The Gator Lake Trail takes you through a much different habitat than the other two trails in the refuge, the Pine Beach and Jeff Friend / Centennial Trails. This is what is known as a transitional habitat, a demarcation line between maritime wetlands and the coastal sand dunes. Depending on the time of year you hike the trail, you will be treated to an amazing variety of wildflowers and plants, including beautiful black-eyed Susans, wild rosemary, blazing star, red basil, and, of course, magnolias, to name just a few.

The 40-acre lake and surrounding wetland plays host to 370 different species of migrating birds. A complete list can be found on the refuge's website. The refuge is also a favorite stop for the monarch butterfly as they wing northward.

The trailhead is at a sharp bend in Mobile Street on the left. There is enough parking for about twenty cars here. The trail is not blazed but is very obvious to follow. From the trailhead the path meanders eastward along the ridge of a sand dune lined with scrub pine, saw palmetto, and wildflowers. Keep your eyes peeled for gopher tortoises.

At mile 0.4 you will get your first glimpse of Gator Lake. An early morning hike will reward you with a Kodak moment—a placid, glassy lake reflecting a blue Alabama sky, the water only disturbed by the occasional landing of waterfowl. As the trail bends around the lake, you will walk over a small wetland area on a short boardwalk and soon

A monarch butterfly makes itself at home along the Gator Lake Trail.

climb a short sand dune and be greeted by a view of the saltwater Little Lagoon and the intersection of the Gator Lake Trail with the Pine Beach Trail. A sign here shows the direction to the Pine Beach Trailhead, the Gulf of Mexico, and the return direction for the Gator Lake Trail. This is where you turn around and return to the trailhead.

Miles and Directions

0.0 Start at the gravel parking lot on Mobile Street. The trailhead is well marked with a Gator Lake Trail sign. Head east and in about 10 yards pass an information kiosk to your left (north).

0.4 Come to a boardwalk over a wetland and your first good view of Gator Lake.

0.8 Walk over a sand dune and get a good view of Little Lagoon, and arrive at the intersection with the Pine Beach Trail. This is the turnaround. Retrace your steps to the trailhead. (***Options***: See below for options to add to your trip at the turnaround.)

1.5 Arrive back at the trailhead.

Options

This hike concludes at the end of the Gator Lake Trail, but if you have the time, I highly recommend you make a left turn here onto the Pine Beach Trail. Follow the trail north between Gator Lake and Little Lagoon for 0.4 mile to visit the huge elevated birding platform located on the north side of Gator Lake. The view is wonderful, especially for birders, and it's a great place to eat lunch.

Another option is to turn right at the Pine Beach Trail (at 0.8 mile) and head south to the Gulf. This adds another mile to this out-and-back hike. At mile 0.9 arrive at a Y in the trail. Take the right fork (south). A sign here points the direction.

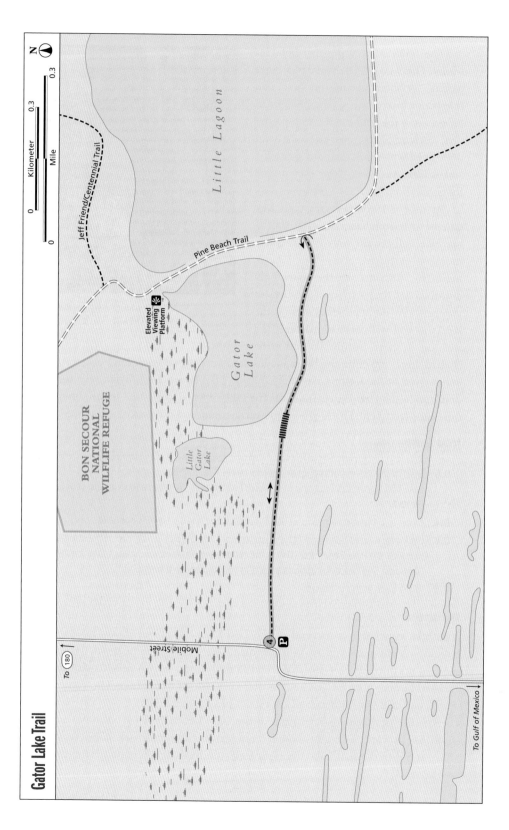

Gator Lake Trail

N

Kilometer
0   0.3

Mile
0   0.3

BON SECOUR
NATIONAL
WILDLIFE REFUGE

Jeff Friend/Centennial Trail

Little Lagoon

Pine Beach Trail

Elevated
Viewing
Platform

Gator
Lake

Little
Gator
Lake

Mobile Street

To 180

4   P

To Gulf of Mexico

The left fork is private property. You now begin walking on beautiful, fine white sand dunes. The walking becomes tougher from here to the Gulf in the deep sand. The trail is now marked with 4-by-5-inch hiker signs mounted on 4-by-4-inch posts. (**FYI:** Make sure you stay on the path! The dunes are federally protected habitats.) At mile 1.0 pass the foundation of a house to the right (west) destroyed by Hurricane Frederick. In 0.1 mile come to another Y in the trail. Take the right fork to the south. The left fork is closed to hikers. In a few yards you will come to another house foundation. At mile 1.2 climb over sand dunes to get your first glimpse of the Gulf of Mexico. The trail is lined with ropes to keep hikers off the dunes. In 0.1 mile arrive at the Gulf of Mexico. Feel free to walk the beach, explore, collect some shells, and enjoy the serenity that the Pine Beach Trail offers. When you're ready, turn around and retrace your steps to the trailhead.

Hiking Information

Local Information
Gulf Shores and Orange Beach Tourism, 3150 Gulf Shores Pkwy., Gulf Shores, AL 36542; (800) 745-7263; www.gulfshores.com

Local Events/Attractions
National Shrimp Festival, 3150 Gulf Shores Pkwy., Gulf Shores; (251) 968-4237. Held annually in March on the white beaches of the Gulf of Mexico, the festival features a variety of entertainment, arts and crafts, and lots of fresh Gulf shrimp.

Lodging
Gulf State Park, 22050 Campground Rd., Gulf Shores; (251) 948-7275; camping reservations (800) 252-7275; 496 sites available

Restaurants
Lulu's, 200 E. 25th Ave., Gulf Shores; (251) 967-5858; www.lulubuffett.com. An eclectic mix of live entertainment and a great selection of local food served up by the restaurant's owner and sister of Jimmy Buffett, Lulu.

Hike Tours
Ranger-led tours available throughout the year. Contact refuge headquarters for current schedule at (251) 540-7720.

Organizations
Friends of Bon Secour, 12295 AL 180, Gulf Shores, AL 36542; www.fws.gov/bonsecour/friends.htm

5 Cotton Bayou Trail

Part of a multiuse trail system through the backcountry of Gulf State Park, this 2.8-mile out-and-back is the lesser used of the system's trails but still has its share of beauty as it takes you past a maritime wetland and leads you to a hummingbird garden, nature pavilion, and the hub of the trail system so you can build even more adventures.

Start: Trailhead parking lot on AL 161
Distance: 2.8 miles out and back
Hiking time: About 1 hour
Difficulty: Easy on flat trail
Trail surface: Gravel service road, short paved path
Best seasons: Year-round
Other trail users: Joggers, cyclists
Canine compatibility: Leashed dogs permitted
Land status: State and city park

Nearest town: Orange Beach
Fees and permits: None
Schedule: Year-round, sunrise to sunset
Maps: USGS Foley, AL; *DeLorme: Alabama Atlas & Gazetteer*, page 64 E4; brochures available at nature center pavilion
Trail contact: Hugh S. Branyon Backcountry Trail, PO Box 458, Orange Beach, AL 36561; (251) 981-1180; www.backcountrytrail.com

Finding the trailhead: From Gulf Shores at the intersection of AL 59 and AL 182, turn left onto AL 182 and travel east 6.4 miles. Turn left onto AL 161 and travel 0.2 mile. The trailhead and parking is on the left next to the big blue Orange Beach water tower. There is a sign here indicating the trailhead. GPS: N30 16.376' / W87 35.122'

The Hike

In the backcountry of Gulf State Park along Alabama's Gulf Coast lies a relatively new series of trails, the Hugh S. Branyon Backcountry Trail. This multiuse National Recreational Trail system is, for the most part, paved and enjoyed by hundreds of walkers, joggers, and cyclists throughout the year, and at times it can actually get pretty crowded, a good sign that this is a popular destination. One trail, the Cotton Bayou Trail, is often overlooked by the summer tourists and snowbirds (retired northerners who come down to escape the cold) because it isn't paved. Because of this, the trail is quiet and provides good opportunities to view the wildlife and plant life of this maritime wetland area.

The Hugh S. Branyon Backcountry Trail system began in 2003 with a partnership between the City of Orange Beach and Gulf State Park to create multiuse recreational trails for walkers, joggers, and cyclists through the "backcountry" of the state park. The project began with the 1.7-mile-long Catman Road Trail and since that time has expanded to over 7.5 miles of trail. Other trails in the system include the Rosemary Dunes, Twin Bridges, Gulf Oak Ridge, and Rattlesnake Ridge. The trail system was named in honor of a former Gulf State Park superintendent.

As I mentioned, Cotton Bayou is different because it isn't paved. It is a wide gravel service road that follows alongside a couple of wetlands. The traffic along this

The nature center on the Hugh S. Branyon Backcountry Trail is the site of many nature- and outdoor-oriented presentations.

section is much less than on the paved section you will be joining up with near the turnaround of this trip.

The highlights of hiking the Cotton Bayou Trail include a wetland at mile 0.3 to the south. During the summer months the wetland could be dried up, but fall through early spring there is ample water to draw in the wildlife. White-tailed deer are not uncommon, as are great blue herons searching the muddy waters for dinner. And keep your eye to the sky for hawks soaring above.

At mile 1.4 the Cotton Bayou Trail ends at the paved Catman Road Trail. Here you will turn left (west) and follow the paved trail for 0.1 mile to the intersection with the Rosemary Dunes Trail. Local folklore says that a half-man/half-cat creature once roamed this area. I don't know if you will see the Catman when you walk this section, but you will find some interesting things here.

At this intersection, or "hub," there is a nature pavilion. Many times throughout the year experts in plants and wildlife hold programs here to educate the public about the environment around them (visit the Backcountry Trail website for times and programs). Also here directly next to the pavilion is a magnificent butterfly garden.

This blue heron is taking advantage of the quietness of the Cotton Bayou Trail.

During spring and early summer, these plants are teeming with an amazing array of butterflies, including the monarch with its deep orange-and-black wings.

And one more thing—a bouldering field! The City of Orange Beach and Friends of the Backcountry Trail are building a bouldering field here, so you can try a little rock hopping and rock wall climbing as well.

If you need to use the restroom, there are very nice men's and women's facilities; turn left at the pavilion and head a few hundred feet down the Rosemary Dunes Trail. There is also a water fountain.

Although this is the turnaround point, you have the option of extending your hike down one of several other trails from this point. And by the way, there is a donation box at this intersection. Please consider donating a dollar or two to help maintain these beautiful, and popular, trails.

Be sure to visit the trail's official website, www.backcountrytrail.com, for information on nature presentations, guided hikes, and a free downloadable app with additional useful information.

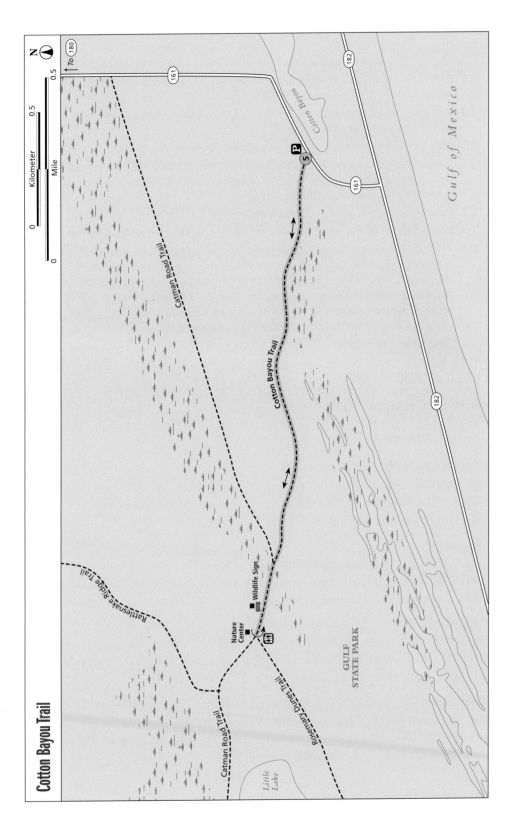

Cotton Bayou Trail

N

| 0 | 0.5 | Kilometer |
| 0 | 0.5 | Mile |

To 180

161

182

161

182

Cotton Bayou

Gulf of Mexico

Catman Road Trail

Cotton Bayou Trail

5

P

Rattlesnake Ridge Trail

Catman Road Trail

Rosemary Dunes Trail

Nature Center

Wildlife Sign

Little Lake

GULF STATE PARK

Miles and Directions

0.0 Start at the Cotton Bayou Trailhead on AL 161, heading west. The trail is a wide gravel service road.

0.2 Pass a wooden rail fence on the left (south). For a short distance you will be traveling behind a Publix shopping center.

0.3 Pass a wetland on the left. This is a great spot to view some wildlife.

1.1 Arrive at the junction of the Cotton Bayou Trail and Catman Road Trail. Turn left and head west on the paved multiuse trail. The trail is dotted with benches dedicated to loved ones or displaying appropriate quotations for the area.

1.2 Pass another wetland and a place to view wildlife to the right (north).

1.3 Pass a series of three benches and an informative sign describing the wildlife in the park.

1.4 Arrive at the intersection of the Catman Road and Rosemary Dunes Trails. Here you will find the nature pavilion, butterfly garden, and coming soon, a bouldering field. A short 0.1 mile down the Rosemary Dunes Trail is a restroom with water fountain. There is also a donation box here. Turn around and retrace your steps to the trailhead. (***Options:*** Several extended walks are available from here either down the Rosemary Dunes Trail or farther along the Catman Road Trail, which intersects with even more trails and wetland habitat.)

2.8 Arrive back at the trailhead.

Hiking Information

Local Information

Alabama Gulf Coast Convention and Visitors Bureau, PO Drawer 457, Gulf Shores, AL 36547; (800) 745-SAND (7263); www.gulfshores.com

Local Events/Attractions

The Hangout Music Festival, PO Drawer 457, Gulf Shores, AL 36547; (800) 745-SAND (7263); www.hangoutmusicfest.com. Held each May on the beach at Gulf Shores, the event brings in top touring music artists.

Lodging

Gulf State Park, 22050 Campground Rd., Gulf Shores; (251) 948-7275; www.alapark .com/gulfstate. One of the crown jewels of the Alabama state park system, Gulf State Park offers resort-style camping for tents and RVs as well as newly renovated cabins.

Restaurants

Doc's Seafood Shack and Oyster Bar, 26029 Canal Rd., Orange Beach; (251) 981-6999. Described as "laid back with local stuff," it is all that. Great seafood with reasonable prices in a laid-back atmosphere.

Hike Tours

City of Orange Beach, 4099 Orange Beach Blvd., Orange Beach, AL 36561; (251) 981-1063. Two-hour guided tours are available (for a fee) that spotlight the flora and fauna along the Hugh S. Branyon Backcountry Trail.

6 Blue Trail

An amazing array of wildlife and native plants await you along the Blue Trail at the Graham Creek Nature Preserve. On this easy walking trail you may encounter bobcats, coyotes, gopher tortoises, and hundreds of migratory birds, plus swaying pine savannah grasses, flowering magnolias, and acres of beautiful white-topped pitcher plants.

Start: Trailhead across from parking area
Distance: 3.2-mile figure eight
Hiking time: About 2 hours
Difficulty: Easy over firm, level ground
Trail surface: Sand, dirt, grass
Best seasons: Early Mar–mid-May, mid-Sept–mid-Nov
Other trail users: Cyclists, disc golfers
Canine compatibility: Leashed dogs permitted

Land status: City nature preserve
Nearest town: Foley
Fees and permits: None
Schedule: Year-round, dawn to dusk
Maps: USGS Gulf Shores, AL; *DeLorme: Alabama Atlas & Gazetteer*, page 63 H8
Trail contact: City of Foley, 407 E. Laurel Ave., PO Box 1750, Foley, AL 36536; (251) 952-4041; www.visitfoley.org

Finding the trailhead: From the intersection of US 98 and AL 59 in Foley, take AL 59 south 3.5 miles and turn left onto CR 12. Travel 1 mile and turn right onto Wolf Bay Drive. Drive 1 mile on Wolf Bay Drive. The road will make a sharp left curve just before the park entrance. Turn right into the preserve (a large Graham Creek Nature Preserve sign marks the turn). Follow the dirt road 0.2 mile. The parking area is to the left at a kiosk. The trailhead is across the road from the parking area and is marked with a round orange disk with an arrow on it attached to a 4-by-4-inch post. GPS: N30 20.734' / W87 37.471'

The Hike

The newest nature preserve on Alabama's Gulf Coast, Graham Creek Nature Preserve, is a testament to the City of Foley, local utility company Riviera Utilities, and the hard work of city environmental manager Leslie Gahagan to protect an environmentally significant piece of land, 484 acres to be exact, that could have otherwise been engulfed by the growth of one of the fastest-growing counties in the state.

Graham Creek Nature Preserve is named after a creek that flows through the property and feeds Wolf Bay, a brackish body of water that borders Florida and Alabama and creates a unique and diverse environment. Wildlife abounds in and around the bay. It's not unusual to see bald eagles, ospreys, Florida manatees, red-cockaded woodpeckers, gopher tortoises, coyotes, and American alligators.

The preserve boasts two walking trails: the main Blue Trail, which is described here, and a smaller 2-mile subset of the Blue Trail called the Red Trail. Both trails are marked with round metal medallions mounted on 4-by-4-inch poles. The Blue Trail

A big sign welcomes you to the Graham Creek Nature Preserve.

uses blue medallions; the red trail uses red medallions. Major mile markers such as 1.0, 2.0, and 2.5 miles are indicated along the path as well.

Parking is located about 0.2 mile south of the main entrance next to an informative kiosk that describes the preserve's habitat and also has brochures to help guide you through your visit. Just remember to practice Leave No Trace and pack the brochures out with you.

The trailhead is located across the road from the parking lot and is marked with a round orange medallion. The orange marker indicates the path of the preserve's 7.5-mile-long bike path. Follow the orange marker about 100 feet to begin walking the Blue Trail. Don't let the brochure at the kiosk throw you. As of this writing, the trail is labeled on the map in the brochure as being marked in green but it's actually blue.

The trail is a nice, easy walk over flat dirt roads. One striking feature of this hike is the large fields that you will skirt along the route. The first, coming almost immediately after starting the hike, is part of the preserve's nine-hole disc golf course. Watch for flying Frisbees!

At 0.3 mile you will cross Graham Creek itself as it cuts through the path. The stream isn't deep (unless you hike the trail after one of south Alabama's infamous heavy afternoon downpours), but the rocks can be slippery. All around you are towering pines, and depending on the season you are hiking, you will see over 700 plant

Lily pads bloom on one of the preserve's ponds.

species including lilies, arums, sunflowers, and several different species of rare orchids such as the rosebud orchid.

At the 0.9-mile mark you can make the trek shorter by taking the Red Trail back to the trailhead, but there is plenty more to see. At 1.97 miles, as the trail crosses a boggy area, you will get your first glimpse of white-topped pitcher plants. These are rare carnivorous plants much like a Venus flytrap that grow in the bogs surrounding pine savannahs. But wait, there's more! At 2.0 miles you will make a turn to the north and be surrounded by hundreds of these beautiful cupped plants.

Besides hiking, Graham Creek Nature Preserve provides plenty of additional recreational activities like biking and disc golf, as mentioned earlier. There is also a wonderful canoe launch on the creek just a few yards south of the parking area that gives you access to explore the bayou and the wonders of the bay itself by canoe or kayak. A large picnic pavilion is also available, along with nice restrooms near the entrance of the preserve.

The preserve hosts many tours and special events throughout the year. Visit their website at www.visitfoley.org for a listing.

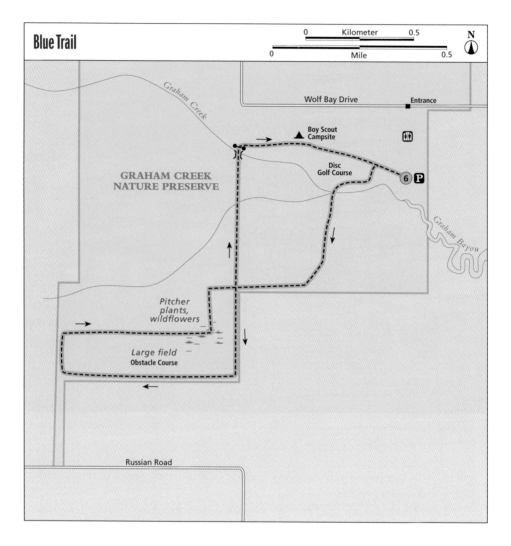

Miles and Directions

0.0 Start at the trailhead across from the parking lot and head west. The trail runs along the south side of a large field that is also a disc golf course.

0.1 The trail bends to the left (south). It is now marked with color-coded medallions for all three trails: blue for this 3-mile trail, red for the 2-mile walking trail, and orange for the 7.5-mile bike trail.

0.3 Cross Graham Creek. The crossing isn't deep under normal conditions but can be after a good afternoon thunderstorm. Be careful of slippery rocks.

0.4 A spur of the Orange Bike Trail enters from the right (west).

0.5 The Orange Bike Trail leaves the walking trails to the left (east).

0.6 The Orange Bike Trail rejoins the walking trails as they all head to the west.

0.7 Reach a major four-way intersection where all three trails loop around each other. Turn left here and head south.

0.9 The Red Trail exits to right (west) at the northeast corner of a large field; continue straight ahead (south). The Orange Bike Trail continues to follow the path you're on.

1.0 Turn right (west). Travel along the south side of the large field. This part of the trail runs along the southernmost property line.

1.2 Pass a small obstacle course with a climbing wall and tubes on the right (north).

1.5 Come to a closed gate on the left. The path goes straight to a dead end. Turn right here and head north.

1.6 Turn right (east). You are now traveling on the north side of the field.

1.7 Come to a boggy area where a small creek crosses the trail. Keep your eyes peeled for the first signs of white-topped pitcher plants.

2.0 Turn left (north) and rejoin the Red Trail. The Orange Bike Trail continues straight. Hundreds of pitcher plants and different varieties of wildflowers will be seen in this pine savannah in the spring.

2.3 Return to the intersection with the Red Trail at mile 0.9 and turn left (north). The Orange Bike Trail rejoins here.

2.6 Pass through an open gate and cross a short bridge over Graham Creek.

2.7 The trail bends to the right (east).

2.8 You are now walking on the north side of the first field where you started the hike. The disc golf course will be on your right (south).

3.2 Arrive back at the trailhead.

Hiking Information

Local Information
South Baldwin Chamber of Commerce, 112 W. Laurel Ave., PO Box 1117, Foley, AL 36536; (877) 461-3712; www.southbaldwinchamber.com

Local Events/Attractions
Earth Day Extravaganza at Graham Creek Nature Preserve; (251) 952-4041; www .visitfoley.org. Held annually on the second Saturday in April, this environmentally centered event is hosted by the City of Foley and is a day of hands-on learning and fun for the entire family.

Restaurants
Foley Coffee Shop, 213 N. McKenzie St., Foley; (251) 943-7433

7 Perdido River Trail

A beautiful little wilderness hike in the midst of one of the fastest-growing counties in Alabama. Along the Perdido River Trail you get a good mix of the natural beauty of the Gulf Coast, including Atlantic white cedar bogs, a beautiful black-water river (that's also great for swimming), and white sandbars. You'll also have excellent wildlife-spotting opportunities. Keep your eyes peeled for bald eagles, ospreys, and maybe an alligator.

Start: Parking area / trailhead alongside the river
Distance: 2.8 miles out and back
Hiking time: About 1.5 hours
Difficulty: Easy over level terrain
Trail surface: Dirt forest roads, sand and dirt footpaths
Best seasons: Year-round
Other trail users: None
Canine compatibility: Dogs permitted
Land status: State wildlife management area
Nearest town: Robertsdale
Fees and permits: None

Schedule: Year-round
Maps: USGS Barrineau Park, FL; *DeLorme: Alabama Atlas & Gazetteer,* page 63 D10
Trail contact: Alabama Hiking Trail Society, PO Box 231164, Montgomery, AL 36123; www.hikealabama.org
Special considerations: This trail is located in a state wildlife management area. In the fall and winter, check hunting seasons and times before heading out at www.outdooralabama.com/hunting and wear hunter orange during these times.

Finding the trailhead: From Robertsdale at I-65 exit 53 (Wilcox Road), head north on CR 64 for 7.1 miles. Turn right onto AL 112 (Old Pensacola Road). Travel 9.4 miles and turn left at Duck Place Road (Barrineau Park Road). Immediately after you turn onto the paved Duck Place Road, turn right onto the dirt River Road. Follow River Road for approximately 1.7 miles, then turn left onto Nims Fork Road. Travel 0.3 mile and turn right onto an unnamed road. Travel approximately 0.5 mile around a curve to the left, then turn right onto another unnamed road. Follow this road approximately 0.4 mile and cross railroad tracks, then take a right at the fork. Travel approximately 0.7 mile and turn left onto yet another unnamed road. Travel 1 mile. The road makes a sharp curve to the right. After the curve, continue another 1.7 miles to a triangle clearing where you can park. The trail begins on the north side of this parking area. GPS: N30 39.477' / W87 24.244'

The Hike

A few years ago no one would have ever dreamed that you could take a walk in a wilderness environment in one of the fastest-growing counties in Alabama, Baldwin, along the Gulf Coast, but today you can on the Perdido River Trail.

The trail is located on the banks of its namesake river that borders Florida and Alabama. The hike described here is a 2.8-mile out-and-back over a nice mix of dirt and sand footpaths and old logging roads that take you through amazing Atlantic white cedar bogs and past beautiful white sandbars. All in all it makes a wonderful

Relaxing on the banks of the Perdido River

outing for families and individuals looking for a day hike in the woods with plenty to do and see along the way, and it's only a stone's throw from the white beaches of the Gulf of Mexico.

The reason that there is a trail here at all is because of the efforts of the Conservation Fund and Nature Conservancy (two national land conservation organizations) and the Alabama Forever Wild program. The land was originally owned by International Paper (IP), but in 2006 the company decided to sell. Fearing that this unique environment and important watershed would be divvied up into subdivisions, the Conservation Fund and Nature Conservancy moved quickly to make IP an offer, which the company accepted. Forever Wild then purchased the property from the other organizations.

In addition to protecting the area and its natural beauty, the state began work to open it up for public recreation. The result is an amazing area for birding, wildlife viewing, swimming, canoeing, hiking, hunting, fishing, horseback riding . . . well, you get the idea.

There are two trails on the Perdido River: One is a new 20-mile paddling trail; the other will be the first backpacking trail on Alabama's Gulf Coast and part of a new long trail, the Alabama Trail, that will stretch from the Gulf to Tennessee. When completed, this section of the Alabama Trail along the river will be over 20 miles in length, with camping allowed along the many sandbars it passes (see trail contact for where to get more information). I will throw in a plug and a tip of the hat to a group that I am proud to be a part of, the Gulf Coast Chapter of the Alabama Hiking Trail Society. It is our volunteers that are getting out there and building this remarkable trail year–round, including during some incredibly hot weather.

The first 4 miles of the trail are completed, but the section I am describing here is a nice 2.8-mile out-and-back that ends at a gigantic white sandbar, the perfect place to spend some time catching rays, picnicking, and swimming in the deep, cool water. (Remember, there are no lifeguards. Swimming is at your own risk, and children need to be under adult supervision.)

A picturesque view of the black–water river awaits you at the trailhead. From here you will get your first glimpse of the many white sandbars that line the river. Directly

ALABAMA'S LONG TRAILS

Alabama is truly becoming a destination for hikers and backpackers, and for good reason: Deep canyons, beautiful mountains, cascading waterfalls, meandering black-water rivers, pristine white Gulf beaches—the state has something for everyone, and the best way, and many times the *only* way, to see them is on a hiking trail.

Alabama has some great day-hiking adventures that can be combined to form extended overnight backpacking trips, but do you want something longer and more adventurous? In the not too distant future, the state will have some world-class long paths for you to try out.

One trail is already up and running, the famous Pinhoti Trail. Started as a small trail project just south of Cheaha State Park in 1973 by the US Forest Service and a group of young volunteers called the Youth Conservation Corps, the Pinhoti is now a footpath that stretches over 130 miles from near the town of Sylacagua to the Georgia state line and is maintained by several nonprofit trail groups. Across the state line, a group known as the Georgia Pinhoti Trail Association picked up where Alabama left off and built their own Pinhoti Trail that connects to the Benton MacKaye Trail, and eventually to the Appalachian Trail.

The Pinhoti is a linchpin for two new long trails in the state, the Eastern Continental Trail (ECT) and the Great Eastern Trail (GET). Both trails will use the Pinhoti as part of their route. The GET is being touted as an alternative to the Appalachian Trail. As of this writing, the trail will begin on the Alabama/Florida state line in Conecuh National Forest and take users north to the Pinhoti Trail and then veer more northerly, eventually ending in upstate New York.

across the river is Florida. Take a look to the sky; I have seen numerous bald eagles soaring overhead here.

The trailhead is located in a dirt and gravel cul-de-sac that is also the parking area. The area has enough room for maybe ten cars, but there is plenty of extra parking along the old logging road that leads to the trailhead. This area is also used by paddlers as a takeout for the 20-mile-long Perdido River Canoe Trail, so it could get crowded from spring to fall.

The trail is blazed yellow, and where the path makes a sharp turn, it uses what is affectionately known as the "dit-dot" method of blazing—two dollar–bill-size blazes, one on top of the other. The top blaze indicates the direction of the turn: If it's offset to the left, the trail turns left; to the right, the trail turns right.

The first part of the hike is along an old logging road that runs parallel to the river on your right (east). Every now and then you will get a glimpse of the river until mile 0.7, when you will come to a short and very obvious 30-foot side trail to a nice bluff

The ECT begins in Key West and uses the Florida Trail to arrive in Alabama at Conecuh National Forest. It then takes virtually the same route to Georgia, where it veers to the northeast taking the Appalachian Trail to Maine and then the International Appalachian Trail to Quebec, Canada—a trip of 5,500 miles. Many hikers are already walking the ECT. Currently about 200 miles of both the GET and ECT from the Alabama/Florida state line to Weogufka, Alabama, is a road walk, but the nonprofit Alabama Hiking Trail Society (AHTS) is working hard to change that and move the trail off into the woods.

A brand-new trail is being planned on the west side of the state called the Alabama Trail (ALT). The ALT will begin at historic Fort Morgan on Alabama's Gulf Coast and wind its way 550 miles to the Tennessee state line just east of Huntsville. The trail will take hikers to all of the beautiful landscapes the state has to offer and then some.

Currently the trail from Little River State Forest (Hikes 13 and 14) to Tennessee is in the planning stages. South of that to the Gulf of Mexico, the Gulf Coast chapter of AHTS is working hard to complete their 120-mile-long section of the trail. At one time many hikers believed that there would never be wilderness trails in this area since it's located in one of the fastest-growing population areas in the state, but with the help of the Alabama Forever Wild program and many local municipalities and federal agencies, this section is becoming a reality. Although it's still a work in progress, that progress is moving along fast!

Some of the hikes in this book that are part of the Alabama Trail include Pine Beach Trail (Hike 2), Jeff Friend / Centennial Trail (Hike 3), Blue Trail (Hike 6), Splinter Hill Bog (Hike 12), Gazebo Trail (Hike 13), and Bell/CCC Trail (Hike 14).

A small boat cruises the black-water Perdido River.

giving you excellent views of the river and maybe a paddler or two sailing past. From here the path ducks into the woods and takes you through some magnificent stands of Atlantic white cedar in picturesque bogs. This is a good place to see some wildlife, including white-tailed deer, quail, armadillo, and coyote.

Keep in mind that you are hiking through some substantial bogs here. If you plan on hiking in the summer, be sure to slather on plenty of insect repellent.

The trail finally arrives at the large sandbar. Believe me, you won't miss it! Bring along a lunch and something to swim in, and enjoy the water and beach. This is a favorite spot for locals in the summer, so it could get crowded on hot days. You will notice that the blazes continue to the north. That is the remaining 2.6 miles of the completed trail that takes you through a pine savannah. Unless you plan to continue on a longer trip, this is your turnaround to head back to the trailhead.

By the way, camping is permitted along any of the sandbars alongside the trail. This would make a great little overnight trek. But keep in mind the river is in a low-lying area, so flash flooding is possible. Keep your eyes and ears open for severe weather, and leave if the weather is threatening.

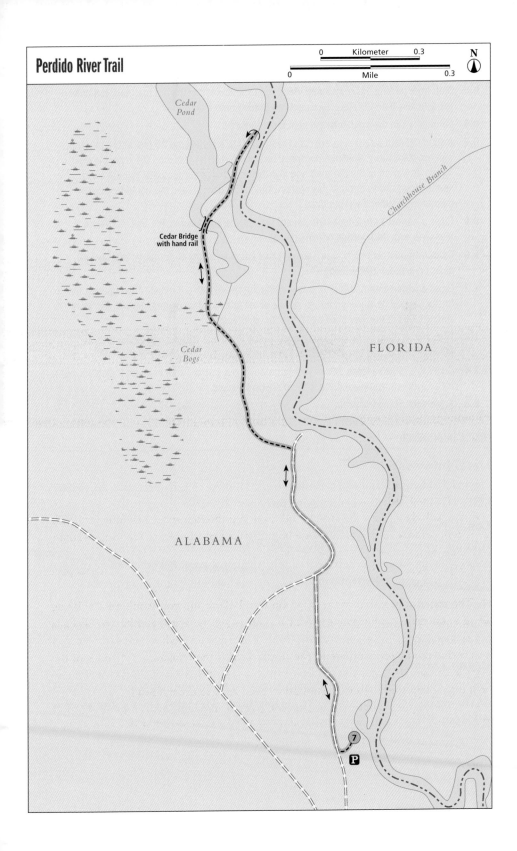

Perdido River Trail

Cedar Pond

Churchhouse Branch

Cedar Bridge
with hand rail

Cedar
Bogs

FLORIDA

ALABAMA

7

P

0   Kilometer   0.3

0   Mile   0.3

N

Miles and Directions

0.0 Start from parking area / trailhead. Head to the southwest on the dirt road that you drove in on. In less than 200 feet, turn right (northwest) onto a dirt road.

0.4 Come to a Y in the road. Take the right fork (northeast).

0.7 A short, 30-foot side trail to the right (east) leads to a bluff some 20 feet above the river, with excellent views. Continue northwest on the dirt road. In less than 0.1 mile, the trail makes its way off of the dirt road and into the woods on a dirt footpath. You will cross several boggy areas through this section. After a few days of rain, this could be thick in mud or even rather deep puddles.

0.9 Cross a narrow, 1- to 2-foot-wide stream (it's easy to hop across). The trail narrows to 2 feet wide, with thick foliage on either side.

1.0 Cross over another boggy area. One part has a narrow, 3-foot-wide stream that you will cross on a cedar log footbridge.

1.2 Cross another stream, this time over a cedar log bridge with a handrail. After crossing the bridge, you will be walking through stands of tall Atlantic white cedars. You will also start getting views of the river once again to your right (east).

1.3 Pass a nice, deep cedar pond on the left (west). The pond is seasonal, depending on rainfall. The trail bed turns sandy here and follows the top of a 20-foot bluff along the river.

1.4 Come to a large sandbar. This is your turnaround, but you will want to linger. It also makes for an excellent campsite if you want to spend the night.

2.8 Arrive back at the trailhead.

Hiking Information

Local Information

Central Baldwin Chamber of Commerce, 23150 AL 59, Robertsdale, AL 36567; (251) 947-4809; www.centralbaldwin.com

Local Events/Attractions

Baldwin County Strawberry Festival, 4999 S. Magnolia St., Loxley; (251) 947-4809; www.baldwincountystrawberryfestival.org. An annual event held the middle of April with arts and crafts, entertainment, and plenty of Baldwin County strawberries.

Restaurants

Mama Lou's Restaurant, 22288 Pine St., Robertsdale; (251) 947-1988; www.mama lousbuffet.com

Organizations

Alabama Forever Wild, Alabama Department of Conservation and Natural Resources, 64 N. Union St., Montgomery, AL 36130; (334) 242-3484; www.alabamaforever wild.com

8 Village Point Park Preserve

Rich history, fascinating wildlife, and beautiful native plants make one of the latest National Recreational Trails a great hike for you and your family. The Village Point Park Preserve Trail winds along the banks of Mobile Bay, where you can view alligators in the wetlands, take a walk on a sand island in the bay, and experience over 300 years of history at the massive Jackson Oak and the D'Olive Cemetery.

Start: Village Point Preserve trailhead at Bayfront Park
Distance: 1.8-mile lollipop
Hiking time: About 1.5 hours
Difficulty: Easy over level terrain
Trail surface: Gravel and dirt roads, boardwalks
Best seasons: Late Feb–mid-May, mid-Sept–early Nov
Other trail users: Cyclists
Canine compatibility: Leashed dogs permitted

Land status: City nature preserve
Nearest town: Daphne
Fees and permits: None
Schedule: Year-round, dawn to dusk
Maps: USGS Bridgehead, AL; *DeLorme: Alabama Atlas & Gazetteer*, page 63 D6; brochures available online (see trail contact)
Trail contact: City of Daphne Parks & Recreation Department, 2605 US 98, PO Box 400, Daphne, AL 36526; (251) 621-3703; www.daphneal.com/residents/parks-recreation

Finding the trailhead: From the intersection of I-10 and US 98, take US 98 south 1.7 miles. Turn right onto Main Street (a Publix shopping center is on the right at the turn). In 200 feet turn right onto Bay Front Drive. Travel 0.4 mile to the parking area. The trailhead is well marked on the west side of the parking lot next to Mobile Bay. GPS: N33 37.793' / W87 55.117'

The Hike

It's rare that you get so much history and natural beauty in a single trail within the heart of a city, but that's what you'll find on the Village Point Park Preserve Trail in Daphne.

Located on the eastern shore of Mobile Bay, the city of Daphne is situated on the southern end of the second-largest river delta in the country, the Mobile-Tensaw Delta, a fertile land teeming with wildlife, fish, and reptiles, making it a perfect location for civilization to take root. Native Americans, including Choctaws, Tensaw, Creeks, and Seminoles, called this land home thousands of years ago.

The region, however, has had an identity crisis. It was first settled by Europeans, Spain to be exact, in 1557. The Spaniards named the land La Aleda, or "the village." France came in to claim the territory in the early 1700s only to lose the land to Great Britain after the French and Indian War in 1763. The area then became part of the United States following the defeat of the British in the War of 1812.

The park was created in 2004 by the City of Daphne to protect its history and environment, and the trail here was named a National Recreational Trail in 2011. The trail at Village Point will take you back in time to explore a little of that history as it

A view of Mobile Bay and a bayou along the Village Point Park Preserve Trail

makes its way over a boardwalk around the mighty Jackson Oak, a giant, sprawling, Spanish moss–laden oak tree where some historians believe General Andrew Jackson made an address to his troops before the famous Battle of New Orleans.

The trail also winds its way around D'Olive Cemetery. In the early 1800s Village Point was the site of the D'Olive Plantation, home of the oldest family in Daphne and Baldwin County. The cemetery is all that remains of the plantation, with many of the tombstones engraved in French. You will learn more about the D'Olive family and Jackson Oak at audio kiosks located at each site.

Besides history, Village Point Park Preserve is a favorite for nature lovers. Just after leaving the trailhead, the path takes you over a beautiful wetland with floating lilies, a wonderful view of Mobile Bay to the west, and a good chance for you to see American alligators in their natural habitat. I can't stress it enough, alligators are naturally afraid of humans, but feeding them changes the rules. Do *not* feed the alligators!

From there the trail takes a short side trip to Mobile Bay itself. A small boardwalk takes you over a slough to a nice sand island, where you can take in a gorgeous sunset over the bay.

Most of the trail from here on out uses wide gravel and dirt service roads. You won't find much motorized traffic here, only the occasional city truck doing trail maintenance. The tall pines and magnolias along this section provide a nice, shady canopy. Depending on the time of year you hike the trail, you will see a wide variety of wildflowers and trees, many of which are identified with signage.

The walk around Jackson Oak is over a composite boardwalk and deck, allowing you good access to the tree but keeping you far enough away. Several ancient live oaks in south Alabama have been killed intentionally by vandals, and the City of Daphne wants to keep this one safe.

The only exception to the service road and boardwalks the trail uses comes at the west end of the trail's loop. Here the path takes you into the woods on a more traditional 2-foot-wide dirt footpath on the D'Olive Plantation Nature Trail. Along this section, many of the trees are identified with signs and there are several benches for you to rest on as you make your way to the cemetery and Jackson Oak.

Miles and Directions

0.0 Start from the Village Point Park Preserve trailhead located about 250 feet west of the parking lot on Mobile Bay. The trailhead is well marked. The hike begins on a boardwalk over a wetland.

0.2 Come to the end of the boardwalk. The trail becomes a wide dirt and gravel road and heads off in two directions, to the left (east) and straight ahead. For now, continue straight ahead to the south.

0.3 The trail turns to the right (west), crosses a bridge over a slough, and comes out on a small sand island. There is a fishing pier at the end of the bridge. When you're ready, turn around and retrace your steps to the end of the first boardwalk at mile 0.2.

JUBILEE!

It's a phenomenon that occurs only once or twice a year between June and September, if at all, and only in a few rare places on earth. It's a time after the sun sets when the breeze is still, the water of Mobile Bay is calm, and the residents of the Eastern Shore of Mobile Bay in the city of Daphne wait for the call.

What happens is hundreds of thousands of fish, crabs, and other marine life swim right up to the shores of the bay and end up on the sandy beaches. The cry goes out around town, *Jubilee!*—which is what this phenomenon is known as—and residents rush out to pick up buckets full of fresh seafood for their tables. But just as quickly as it starts, the Jubilee is over.

No one is exactly sure what causes the Jubilee, but it's believed that a seasonal drop in the water's oxygen level draws both prey and predator to the surface, looking for food and air.

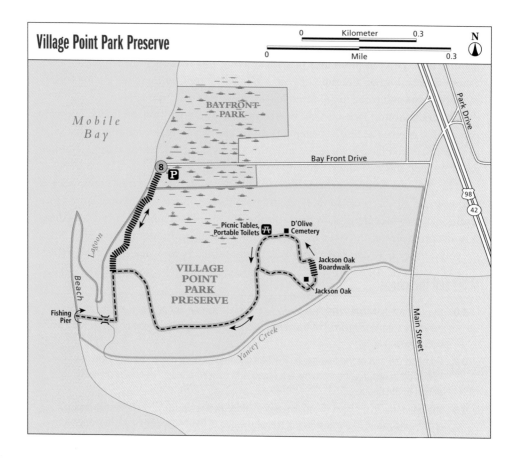

Village Point Park Preserve

0   Kilometer   0.3

0   Mile   0.3

N

Mobile Bay

BAYFRONT PARK

Park Drive

Bay Front Drive

98

42

Picnic Tables, Portable Toilets

D'Olive Cemetery

Lagoon

Jackson Oak Boardwalk

VILLAGE POINT PARK PRESERVE

Beach

Jackson Oak

Fishing Pier

Main Street

Yancey Creek

0.5   Return to the south end of the boardwalk and turn right (east).

0.6   Come to a T intersection with another dirt road. Turn left here and head east. A right turn dead-ends at a locked fence and gate.

0.8   Pass a side trail with a bridge over Yancey Creek to your right (south). This is an access trail to the Harbor Place condominiums and is private property. Don't go there. Continue straight (east). In about 400 feet come to a fork in the trail. This is the southwest end of the trail's east loop. Take the right fork. In just a few feet, turn right (south) onto the D'Olive Plantation Nature Trail. There is a small sign indicating the trail entrance, but it can be hard to see when the area is overgrown. The trail is a narrow, 2-foot-wide dirt footpath through a thick forest with a good, shady canopy.

1.0   Come to a boardwalk that encircles the massive Jackson Oak. The boardwalk is made of a composite material to alleviate problems with rotting. There is an audio kiosk here that tells the history of the oak tree, along with picnic tables off to the side. After the board-walk, continue on the dirt footpath to the north and in 200 feet cross a dirt service road. A sign points the way to D'Olive Cemetery.

1.1   Arrive at D'Olive Cemetery. Another audio kiosk is located here that tells the history of the D'Olive family and their plantation. After exploring the cemetery, continue west on the trail.

In just a few hundred feet there are portable toilets and picnic tables. Shortly after that arrive at the south end of the loop.

1.6 Return to the boardwalk. Turn right (north).

1.8 Arrive back at the trailhead.

Hiking Information

Local Information

Eastern Shore Chamber of Commerce, 29750 Larry Dee Cawyer Dr., Daphne, AL 36526; (251) 621-8222; www.eschamber.com

Local Events/Attractions

Jubilee Festival, Main Street, Daphne; (251) 621-8222; www.eschamber.com/area _jubilee.php. Held September of each year, the Jubilee Festival is a celebration of living on the Alabama Gulf Coast with plenty of entertainment, arts and crafts, and food.

5 Rivers Delta Safaris, Bartram Landing, 30841 Five Rivers Blvd., Spanish Fort; (251) 259-8531; www.5rds.com. The Mobile-Tensaw Delta is the second-largest river delta in the country, and 5 Rivers Delta Safaris can take you right into the bayous with American alligators, black bears, and more with ecotours, canoe and kayak trips, and camping trips.

Restaurants

Market by the Bay Takeout Restaurant, 29145 US 98, Daphne; (251) 621-9994; www.marketbythebay.com. Serves up great local seafood at affordable prices.

Organizations

Village Point Foundation, PO Box 1374, Daphne, AL 36526; www.villagepoint park.org

9 Historic Blakeley State Park

Historic Blakeley State Park looks like a postcard of the archetypal South: long, flowing Spanish moss hanging from the trees, shady walkways along the riverbank, and let us not forget Civil War history. While General Lee was surrendering to Grant in Virginia, the last major battle of the war was being waged here. Today the park is a Civil War National Historic Site and a great hike along the banks of the second-largest river delta in the country.

Start: Parking lot along Mobile Bay
Distance: 4.1-mile multiloop
Hiking time: About 2.5 hours
Difficulty: Moderate due to length, easy if you break the hike down into one of the shorter sections
Trail surface: Dirt path, gravel road, boardwalk
Best seasons: Sept–May
Other trail users: Cyclists, motorists (on road sections), equestrians
Canine compatibility: Leashed dogs permitted

Land status: Historic state park
Nearest town: Spanish Fort
Fees and permits: Day-use fee (under 6 free)
Schedule: Year-round, 9 a.m.–dusk (gate often opens at 8 a.m.)
Maps: USGS Bridgehead, AL; *DeLorme: Atlas & Gazetteer*, page 62 C5; brochure with map available at office
Trail contact: Historic Blakeley State Park, 34745 AL 225, Spanish Fort, AL 36527; (251) 626-0798; www.blakeleypark.com

Finding the trailhead: From the intersection of US 98 and AL 225 in Spanish Fort, take AL 225 north 5 miles. The park entrance is on your left. Once you pay the attendant, travel 2 miles, continuing straight on Old Blakeley Road to its end at the boat ramp. This is the trailhead for the hike. GPS: N30 44.851' / W87 55.400'

The Hike

The Paleo Indians were the first to live in the area now occupied by Historic Blakeley State Park some 4,000 years ago. The land changed hands numerous times over the years and would fall under the rule of several countries during its history, including Spain in the late 1500s and France in the early 1700s, followed by Britain, and then the United States in 1813. Soon after becoming a US territory, Josiah Blakeley stepped into the picture and bought this land and established the town of Blakeley.

The town, long since vanished, was chartered in 1814 and became a bustling port city that rose to rival neighboring Mobile. By 1828 a series of yellow fever epidemics, coupled with the greed of land speculators, forced the city of 4,000 into a spiral of decay, and by the mid-1800s it was abandoned. Today all that remains of the old port town are the 400-year-old live oaks that once lined the city streets and a recently unearthed foundation—the original brick and wood base of the town's courthouse.

The town's greatest claim to fame came on April 8, 1865. It was on that date that 55,000 Union and Confederate soldiers converged in the fields surrounding the old

The trails at Historic Blakeley State Park lead you to some of the best-preserved breastworks and redoubts in the region.

town. The Union army intended to seize Fort Blakeley and then attack and capture the city of Mobile from its eastern shore.

The fighting was fierce—216 killed, 955 wounded, and 3,054 captured (3,050 of them Confederates). It was a decisive Union victory, but what made the battle significant had little to do with the casualties. On the second day of this two-day campaign, Confederate general Robert E. Lee surrendered to Union general Ulysses S. Grant at Appomattox Courthouse in central Virginia, thus making the battle at Blakeley the last major battle of the Civil War.

More than a hundred years later, in 1974, the Alabama Historic Commission placed the site on the National Register of Historic Places and the effort to preserve the battle site began. Trails were built, breastworks were located, and in 1993 Congress designated the site a Class A Civil War Site. Three years later it was added to the

National Civil War Trail list. Be sure to pick up a brochure at the entrance gate that describes the battle through numbered signs along the trail.

Within Historic Blakeley State Park's 3,800 acres are a total of 15 miles of nature and historic trails. The trails cross one another so that you can form shorter or longer loops to suit your schedule or what you want to see.

Since we last visited Blakeley, there has been a new addition: the original brick and wood foundation of the town's courthouse. It's an impressive structure to view, and you will pass it along this hike.

Not only is Blakeley steeped with history, but it is filled with natural beauty as well. This hike will take you past the Wehle Nature Center, which is used for conferences and special presentations (visit the park's website for schedules). There is also a display behind the building of some of the wildlife that calls the Mobile-Tensaw River Delta home.

The trail will also take you down a boardwalk along the banks of the second-largest river delta in the country and one of the largest intact wetland systems left in America, with over 300,000 acres of swampland, river bottom, and marshes. The delta plays host to 300 species of birds, 70 percent of all of Alabama's reptiles, and 40 different species of mammals. It is one of the largest drainage basins in the world, with runoffs from four states feeding into it and into the Gulf of Mexico. Blakeley is at the very southern end of the delta but has exceptional views of some marshland and views across the river of the city of Mobile.

The hike begins at the park's boat ramp at the very end of the main road into the park. There is room for about fifteen cars here and a nice portable toilet. Your trip begins along the Jaque Pate Nature Trail. Along this section you will be walking through some bottomland. Many of the trees in this area have signs indicating what you will see. Some species include live oak, saw palmetto, and yellow poplar.

The Cockleshell Mound Trail then takes you past the Wehle Nature Center and a dirt road that takes you to the battlefield where some of the best-preserved breastworks and redoubts from the Civil War can be seen. You will also head over to the Union side to see the "Zig Zag," an approach trench that took the Union soldiers right up to the Confederates doorstep at the redoubts.

The path returns the way you came, taking a turn on the nature trail farther down Old Blakeley Road to the site of the old courthouse, the Mary G. Grice Pavilion, and then the walk along Mobile Bay on the boardwalk.

Options: There are several intersections along the way, so you can make the hike as long or as short as you like. The hike described here can easily be divided into three separate routes. The first is the loop from the trailhead to the courthouse foundation, then back to the trailhead on the boardwalk along the delta. The second would be a nature loop from the trailhead to the Wehle Nature Center and back. Finally, you can do a simple battlefield walk from the Wehle Nature Center and loop around the battlefield for a 2-mile hike.

Miles and Directions

0.0 Start at the parking lot along Mobile Bay. In a few yards turn left onto the Jaque Pate Nature Trail, a narrow dirt and sand path through thick forest. Many tree species are identified with signage. The trail is not blazed but easy enough to follow. In 100 feet come to the Cockleshell Mound Trail boardwalk and walk across to the other side of a wetland.

0.2 On the other side, make a left turn to the north onto an unnamed trail. In 20 feet cross another boardwalk. As of this writing, the boardwalk was in disrepair with loose boards and tipped to an angle; be cautious crossing.

0.3 Climb down a steep set of stairs. The treads are far apart, so be very careful climbing down. Many people walk next to the stairs, which is causing an erosion issue.

0.4 Come to the intersection with Green Street Extension, a wide dirt and gravel road. Turn left (east) onto the road. From here on to the battlefield, the trail is open with little shade.

0.5 Pass the Wehle Nature Center.

0.6 Green Street Extension dead-ends at Battlefield Road. Turn left (north) onto the road and head to the battlefield.

0.8 Cross Baptizing Branch, with a wetland on the right.

1.0 Pass Marker #3. Turn right (south) on a dirt road and head to the redoubt.

1.1 Arrive at Redoubt #2. Walk around on the right side.

1.3 Pass Marker #16. Turn right (southeast) and head across the grassy battlefield. In less than 0.1 mile, arrive at another dirt road. Turn right (south) onto the dirt road.

1.4 Pass Marker #15. In a few yards pass a dirt road on the right and Marker #5, then in a few feet Marker #6. Union trenches can be seen along this stretch.

1.5 Arrive back at Battlefield Road at Marker #14 and turn right (east) onto it.

1.6 Pass Marker #7 on the left (this will be the return route for the loop end of this section). Continue straight (east) on the dirt road and in a few feet pass Marker #9. One hundred feet later, cross the Union breastworks.

1.7 Arrive at the Union redoubt. Walk to the far end and turn left (west). Follow the clear-cut in the thick grass to the left (southwest), following the "Zig Zag" on the left.

1.9 Come to Marker #8. Turn right and head back to the main park road. In 200 feet return to Battlefield Road. Turn right (west) onto the road and head back to Green Street Extension at mile 0.4.

2.5 Turn right onto Green Street Extension and head back the way you came.

3.2 At the intersection with the Cockleshell Mound Trail, continue straight on Green Street Extension until you come to a cul-de-sac in the dirt road. A sign with a blue arrow about 10 feet off the ground is hung on a tree indicating the route to take. Follow the arrow onto a sandy footpath to the right (southwest). Once again the trail travels through a thick forest with a good canopy.

3.4 Return to the Cockleshell Mound Boardwalk and cross it to the northwest. In less than 0.1 mile, come to the end of the boardwalk at the Jaque Pate Nature Trail. A sign here reads "Parking Area 0.1 Mile" (arrow pointing to right) / "Trail Fork 0.2 Mile" (arrow pointing to left). If you take the right turn to the north, you will return to the parking lot. Instead, turn left (south) onto the nature trail. The vegetation is very thick here.

Historic Blakeley State Park

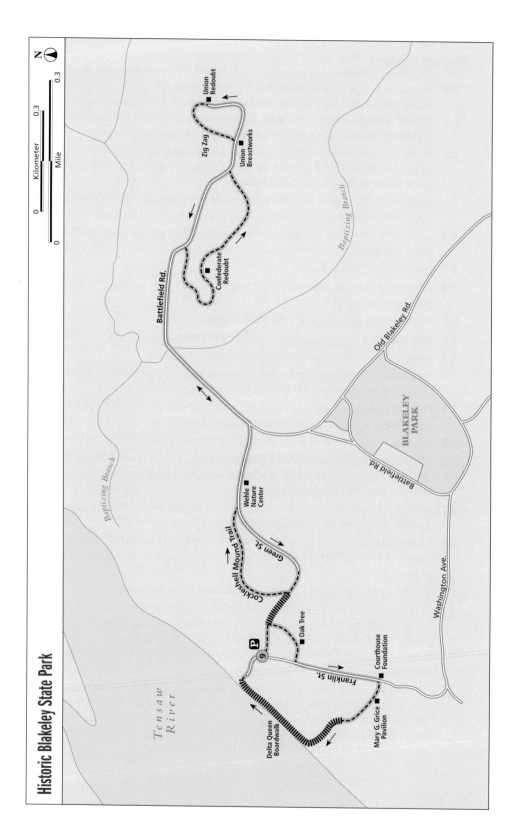

3.6 Come to a Y at a large live oak tree (the tree is indicated by an informational sign). Take right fork (west) onto a short spur trail. In less than 0.1 mile, you will be back at Old Blakeley Road. If you want to return to your vehicle, turn right (north); otherwise, turn left onto the road and head south.

3.7 Pass the foundation of the old courthouse. Turn left (west) here, cross the road through a wood fence, and head toward the Mary G. Grice Pavilion. In a few yards arrive at the pavilion. There are picnic tables and grills here. Behind and to the right of the pavilion is a sign describing big-leaf magnolia trees and a large cement barbecue grill. The Nature Trail begins here, with descriptive signs for Florida anise, live oak, saw palmetto, yellow poplar, American beech, and pignut hickory. In less than 0.1 mile, arrive at the delta boardwalk. Follow it to the north.

4.0 Come to the end of the boardwalk (the *Delta Queen* tour boat is docked here). Turn right onto the dirt road.

4.1 Arrive back at the trailhead.

Hiking Information

Local Information
Eastern Shore Chamber of Commerce, 29750 Larry Cawyer Dr., Daphne, AL 36526; (251) 621-8222; www.eschamber.com

Local Events/Attractions
Annual Battle of Blakeley Reenactment, 34745 AL 225, Spanish Fort; (251) 626-6798; www.blakeleypark.com. The event occurs around the weekend of the actual battle date of April 9.

Blakeley Bluegrass Festival, 34745 AL 225, Spanish Fort; (251) 626-6798; www.blakeleypark.com. Held annually in mid-October.

Lodging
Blakeley Historic State Park Campgrounds, 34745 AL 225, Spanish Fort, AL 36527; (251) 626-0798; www.blakeleypark.com. Two separate campgrounds, one for RV use the other for tent and pop-ups only.

Restaurants
Blue Gill, 3775 Battleship Pkwy., Spanish Fort; (251) 625-1998; www.bluegill restaurant.com

Original Oyster House, 3733A Battleship Pkwy., Spanish Fort; (251) 626-2188; www.theoysterhouse.com

10 Muddy Creek Interpretive Trail

A beautiful family-friendly hike featuring many boardwalks that lead you through and educate you about the amazing wetlands and longleaf pine ecosystems found on Alabama's Gulf Coast and how industry can take a lead in preserving the environment.

Start: Parking lot on Industrial Road
Distance: 2.2-mile lollipop
Hiking time: About 1.5 hours
Difficulty: Easy over flat, level ground
Trail surface: Dirt and clay footpaths, boardwalk
Best seasons: Late Feb–mid-May
Other trail users: None
Canine compatibility: Leashed dogs permitted

Land status: State wetland preserve
Nearest town: Theodore
Fees and permits: None
Schedule: Year-round, dawn to dusk
Maps: USGS Theodore, AL; *DeLorme: Alabama Atlas & Gazetteer,* page 62 F3
Trail contact: Alabama State Port Authority, 250 N. Water St., Mobile, AL 36602; (251) 441-7001; www.asdd.com

Finding the trailhead: From the intersection of US 90 and Bellingrath Gardens Road in Theodore, take Bellingrath Gardens Road south 2.2 miles. Turn left onto Industrial Road and travel 1 mile. The paved parking lot is on the left. GPS: N30 31.029' / W88 09.158'

The Hike

So, I live on Alabama's Gulf Coast and thought I had hiked all there is to hike down here. Then I saw online a posting for someone leading a hike on the Muddy Creek Interpretive Trail in the town of Theodore. Curious, I shot them an e-mail and asked where Muddy Creek was and what it was like. They replied that they didn't know. They had only heard a vague mention of it themselves from a friend and thought they would check it out. And so did I.

You wouldn't think that there would be much to the hike when you consider the trail's location. You are in the bustling town of Theodore on the west side of one of the state's biggest counties, Mobile, heading to the trailhead down a road called Industrial Road through an area known for its chemical plants. But there it was, and what a great little hike.

The Muddy Creek Interpretive Trail is a 2.2-mile lollipop loop through wetland areas on the western bank of Mobile Bay. The property itself is owned by the Alabama State Port Authority, the folks who handle shipping in and out of the bay. The trail project began in 1998,

New Orleans might have made it famous, but Mardi Gras in the United States began in Mobile. The first celebration was at Twenty-Seven Mile Bluff, the first Mobile settlement, in 1703. The first float was a papier-mâché bull's head pulled on a cart for the Boeuf Gras (Fatted Ox) Society in 1711.

Much of the Muddy Creek Interpretive Trail is over long boardwalks through wetlands.

when it was decided that the best use of the property was to preserve and enhance the wetland as part of a wetland mitigation measure. Five long, hard years later, the trail was completed.

Some of the goals of the Muddy Creek project included the removal and control of invasive exotic plant species, restoration of native wetland and upland plant ecosystems, installation of nesting boxes, replanting of 66 acres of upland agricultural fields with native longleaf pines, and the development of an interpretive trail and boardwalk system. The first goal, the removal of invasive plants, proved challenging. The process was all done by hand—everything from pulling bushes to hand-cutting trees to treating stumps with herbicide then replanting native species. By the time the project was completed, it had become the largest invasive plant removal ever in the state.

The resulting interpretive trail is a fascinating educational experience and nice walk in the woods, one that is suitable for families with children of all ages, over wide, packed dirt paths and long boardwalks. If you have younger children, you may want to cut the trip short due to the length.

The path is well marked with metal directional signs, and at key turns in the trail, a large map of the route shows you where you are. Throughout the trek there are informational signs that identify the many species of native trees you will pass, such as tupelo gum, sweet bay, red maple, wax myrtle, and bald cypress. Signs also describe the wetland ecosystem and the Muddy Creek project itself.

The hike begins along a 0.2-mile paved section of trail, but after that it is a wide, hard-packed dirt and clay path. Several long boardwalks are encountered on the trip over beautiful wetlands and streams, including the trail's namesake. Remember, water in streams and wetlands can be seasonal in Alabama. The best time to visit is late February to mid-May, when the spring rains are plentiful along the Gulf and the creek is wide and flowing, and the wildflowers and trees are blooming. The boardwalks are wide, with tall handrails and an occasional viewing platform or bench.

One of the more interesting boardwalks at the northern end of the loop takes you through a beaver pond management area. As the sign will tell you, beavers were once considered nuisances but it was found that the careful management of beaver ponds results in a healthier wetland system.

As you head back, you will be treated to a few sections of trail where the footing is thick green moss. The cushion of the moss is quite the transition from the hard-packed dirt, and on sunny days the moss has a beautiful green glow to it.

Miles and Directions

0.0 Start at the parking lot trailhead on Industrial Road. A Muddy Creek Interpretive Trail sign is here that shows the route of the trail. Head north on a paved path a few yards and come to a Y. The right fork is a dirt road. Turn left (west) and continue following the paved path. You will soon see the first of many signs describing the habitat you will be walking through.

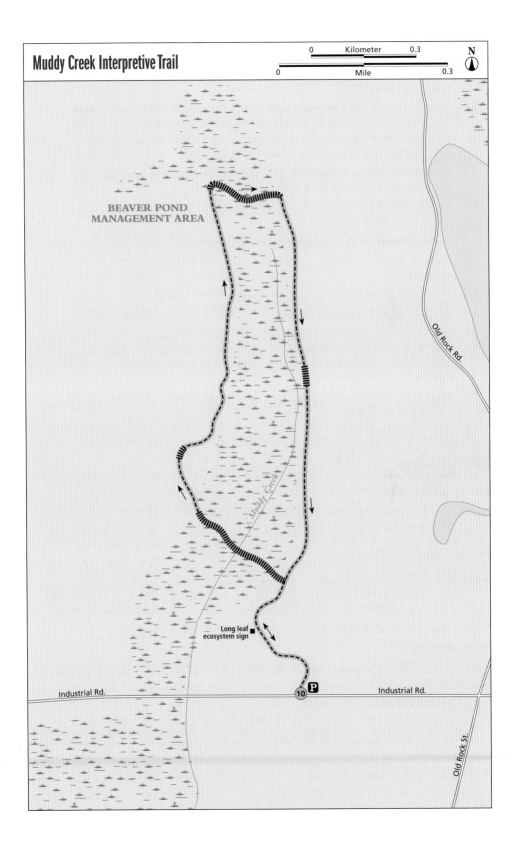

Muddy Creek Interpretive Trail

0 Kilometer 0.3

0 Mile 0.3

N

BEAVER POND
MANAGEMENT AREA

Muddy Creek

Long leaf
ecosystem sign

Old Rock Rd.

Industrial Rd.

Industrial Rd.

10 P

Old Rock St.

0.2 The paved path comes to a T intersection with another paved road. Cross the road to the north and enter the woods on a narrow footpath. Through this section you will be surrounded by longleaf pines.

0.3 Come to a Y in the trail. A map here shows you where you are. The right fork is the route you will be returning on. Take the left fork (northwest). A long boardwalk begins in about 30 feet. The boardwalks are very nice, with high railings. Through here you'll see tupelo gum, sweet bay, elderberry, red maple, and bald cypress trees.

0.4 The boardwalk crosses Muddy Creek. (*FYI:* The streams and wetlands are seasonal and may be dry at certain times of the year.)

0.5 The boardwalk ends at another trail map sign and turns to the right (north).

0.6 Cross a short, 30-foot boardwalk.

0.7 The trail gets very dense with longleaf pines and wax myrtles.

1.1 Pass another trail map sign and in a few yards cross another boardwalk. This is the north end of the loop.

1.2 Pass a series of signs with information on beavers and their importance to the wetland.

1.3 The boardwalk ends at another trail map sign and the trail turns to the right (south).

1.6 Pass another trail map sign and cross another short boardwalk.

1.7 For a few hundred feet the trail bed is soft, green moss. Along this section you'll see a steel cable with yellow metal posts through the trees to your left (east). This is a barrier for a dirt road that parallels the trail.

1.9 Return to the Y at the southern end of the loop. Take the left fork to the south and retrace your steps to the trailhead.

2.2 Arrive back at the trailhead.

Hiking Information

Local Information
Mobile Bay Visitors and Convention Bureau, PO Box 204, Mobile, AL 36601; (800) 566-2453; www.mobile.org

Local Events/Attractions
Bellingrath Gardens and Homes, 12401 Bellingrath Gardens Rd., Theodore; (800) 247-8420; www.bellingrath.org. An array of color, fragrances, and scenic views are in store for you year-round at this world-renowned garden. Don't miss the Magic Christmas in Lights display from Thanksgiving to New Year's Day.

Restaurants
Time to Eat, 7351 Theodore Dawes Rd., Theodore; (251) 654-0228; www.time toeatmobile.com. Offers mountains of some of the best Southern down-home cooking for dine in or take out.

11 Cemetery Loop Trail

An interesting trail used by both hikers and cyclists within Chickasabogue Park, a park operated by the Mobile County Parks and Recreation Department. The trail is easy enough for younger members of the family and will lead you to a historic cemetery from the 1800s and views of the wide Chickasaw Creek. After hiking, there are plenty of other activities you can do in the park, like disc golf.

Start: Parking lot / trailhead at the sports field
Distance: 2.4-mile loop
Hiking time: About 1.5 hours
Difficulty: Easy on level and well-maintained dirt paths
Trail surface: Dirt
Best seasons: Sept–May
Other trail users: Cyclists
Canine compatibility: Leashed dogs permitted
Land status: County park

Nearest town: Chickasaw
Fees and permits: Day-use fee
Schedule: Year-round, 7 a.m.–5 p.m.
Maps: USGS Chickasaw, AL; *DeLorme: Alabama Atlas & Gazetteer,* page 62 B3; trail maps available at entrance gate
Trail contact: Chickasabogue Park, 60 Aldock Rd., Eight Mile, AL 36613; (251) 574-2267; www.mobilecountyal.gov/living/parks_chick asabogue.html

Finding the trailhead: From the intersection of I-65 and Whistler Street in Prichard, take Whistler Street west 2 miles. Turn right onto Aldock Road and travel 1 mile. The park entrance is straight ahead. After paying the attendant, the trailhead is ahead on the right in about 0.1 mile. GPS: N30 46.868' / W88 06.288'

The Hike

Owned and operated by Mobile County, Chickasabogue Park encompasses more than 1,100 acres of forest, wetlands, and creeks. In addition to preserving the natural environment, the county has made it their mission to provide a quality family getaway within the second-biggest county in the state—and they have succeeded.

Chickasabogue features easy walking trails over lightly rolling hills, just right for children, with plenty of intersections with dirt and paved roads in case you need to bug out early. The trails are mostly sandy and cross several creeks and wetlands. The decking on the boardwalks you will cross throughout the hike is covered with farm fence to give you traction.

The path is generally narrow throughout the trek, about 3 feet wide, with a hard dirt bed, and is surrounded by thick stands of pine trees. The wildlife, including white-tailed deer, gives parents plenty to talk about with their children as they spend an afternoon together.

In addition to superb hiking and cycling trails, the park offers ball fields, playgrounds, picnic areas, and a swimming beach along Chickasaw Creek, as well as access for paddling. The park is also home to an eighteen-hole disc golf course that

The Cemetery Loop Trail comes out to the banks of Chickasaw Creek.

is sanctioned by the Professional Disc Golf Association. Keep in mind that since the park is located in one of the state's biggest counties population-wise and with all of the recreational opportunity the park affords, Chickasabogue can get quite crowded on weekends in the summer months.

You will also get a little bit of a history lesson at the park. At the entrance to the park next to the information center you will find the former Eight Mile A.M.E. Church. This small structure, built in 1879 in the neighboring town of Eight Mile, was moved to the park to serve as a museum. The museum features artifacts of Native American culture from as far back as 1500 BC and photos and items from the city's past. Admission is free. If the building is locked, just ask the attendant at the office to let you in.

The area around the park has had quite a history. Explorer Hernando DeSoto first visited the area around 1540. Pirates also ventured through this region, using Chickasaw Creek as their primary point of entry from the Mobile River and Bay. And the outlaw Cooper Gang, who roamed the Southeast robbing stagecoaches and businesses, lived here in the late 1800s. This rugged gang helped runaway slaves flee the area, only to sell them to plantations in other states.

As I said, Chickasabogue Park offers several different hiking opportunities, but my favorite is the Cemetery Loop Trail. The trail is used by both hikers and cyclists and for this trek incorporates a short portion of the Beach Loop Trail. The trail is marked with red paint blazes. Some are faded and hard to see, but you should be able to follow the route without much trouble. I will tell you that a sign near the trailhead says that hikers should use the yellow-blazed trail and cyclists the red-blazed trail, but you'll be hard-pressed to find the yellow along most of the route, so we opted for the red-blazed trail. Just keep an eye out for cyclists.

The Cemetery Loop Trailhead is well marked.

The Cemetery Trail begins at the parking area next to the park's sports field. As the trail meanders away from the parking area and through several wetlands, it runs parallel to I-65 for a while before coming to Myers Cemetery, which was established in the 1800s. The interstate proves to be the only drawback to hiking this trail. Throughout your walk you will hear the drone of cars in the distance, and then just before coming to the cemetery, the trail is right next to the highway with a short spacing of trees in between. The noise never proved that distracting, however, and you will quickly tune it out.

Continuing on, the trail circles around and comes to the intersection of the Cemetery Loop and Beach Loop trails. Here you'll take the right fork and head down to the banks of Chickasaw Creek for a look at this wide black-water river. From there it is a short road walk back to the trailhead and your vehicle. Along the way you'll pass the nature center on your right that has informative posters describing the wildlife and plant life found in the park.

Miles and Directions

0.0 Start at the parking lot next to the sports field. A red-and-yellow Cemetery Loop Start sign leads the way to the northeast from the parking lot. This first section parallels the sports field to the right (west). The trail has red blazes, some faded but still visible. Soon you'll cross a narrow boardwalk.

0.1 A short trail comes in from the right (west) that leads to the sports field, followed by another short boardwalk.

0.2 Cross a dirt road to the south.

0.3 Cross another dirt road to the south. A picnic area is down the road to the left (east), with the sports field to the right.

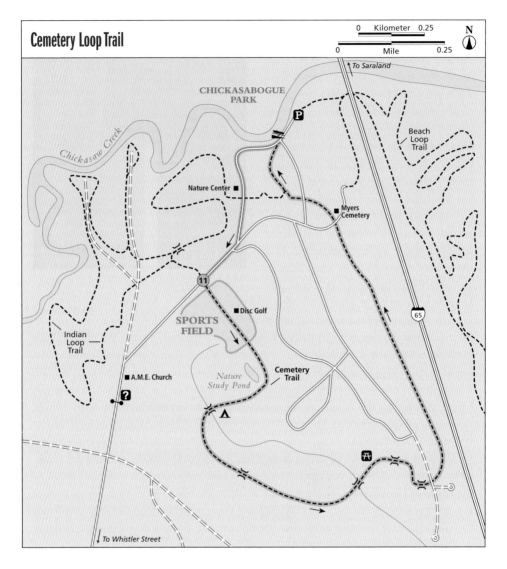

0   Kilometer   0.25   **N**

0   Mile   0.25

To Saraland

CHICKASABOGUE PARK

Chickasaw Creek

Beach Loop Trail

Nature Center ■

■ Myers Cemetery

11

■ Disc Golf

SPORTS FIELD

Indian Loop Trail

65

■ A.M.E. Church

Nature Study Pond

Cemetery Trail

To Whistler Street

0.4   Cross another dirt road to the south away from the sports field. The trail widens to 4 to 5 feet. In less than 0.1 mile, the wide trail continues straight to the park's campground (you will see the campground through the trees in front of you to the southeast). Turn right (southwest). The trail narrows once again and in a few yards you will come to a Y. A sign here reads CEMETERY TRAIL with arrows pointing back the way you just came and toward the left fork. Take the left fork (southwest). Just after the sign there is a picnic table on a hill to the right.

0.5   Cross another boardwalk over a creek. This one is a bit rickety.

0.7   Come to a Y. Take the left fork (southeast). You'll soon cross another boardwalk.

0.8   Come to another Y. Take the right fork (east) and soon cross another boardwalk.

0.9   Come to another Y. Take the right fork (northeast).

1.0 Come to another Y. Take the right fork (southwest).

1.1 Come to another Y. Take the right fork (east).

1.2 Cross a small footbridge and come to a paved road. Cross the road off to an angle to your left (northeast) to reenter the woods. (*FYI:* A bathhouse is a few yards up that paved road on your left.) You are now walking parallel to the interstate.

1.3 Cross a long boardwalk.

1.6 Come to another Y. Take the left fork.

1.7 The trail comes out to an open area with some nice live oak trees. Walk along the brush line on your right (east) and arrive at Myers Cemetery. After visiting, the trail continues along the left side of the chain-link fence that encircles the cemetery to the north.

1.8 Make a left at the T intersection to the north. In less than 0.1 mile, come to a paved road. Go straight across the road. A sign on the other side reads CEMETERY LOOP / BEACH LOOP. Reenter the woods here.

1.9 Come to a Y. Take the right fork down a steep hill to the northwest. This is part of the Beach Loop Trail. The trail is now marked with yellow blazes.

2.0 The trail crosses a wetland over two very narrow, 2-foot-wide footbridges. The water is only about 6 inches below the bridges, so this could be underwater after a heavy rain. In less than 0.1 mile, you will come to a paved road and arrive at Chickasaw Creek. There are benches and picnic tables here for you to sit and take in the river. Turn to the left (west) and follow the road around back to the trailhead.

2.3 Pass the park's nature center.

2.4 Arrive back at the trailhead.

Hiking Information

Local Information

Mobile Bay Visitors and Convention Bureau, PO Box 204, Mobile, AL 36601; (800) 566-2453; www.mobile.org

Local Events/Attractions

Chickasaw Founders Day, Paul Divine Park, Chickasaw; (251) 452-8623; www .cityofchickasaw.org; A fun biannual weekend of arts, crafts, and music.

Lodging

Chickasabogue Park Campground, 60 Aldock Rd., Eight Mile; (251) 574-2267; www.mobilecountyal.gov/living/parks_chickasabogue.html. The park has excellent secluded camping for car campers and RVs alike.

Restaurants

Burger Master Restaurant, 4616 St. Stephens Rd., Eight Mile; (251) 457-1472. Great burgers and more (like fried seafood).

12 Splinter Hill Bog

Located at the headwaters of the Perdido River in a nondescript pine seepage bog is Splinter Hill Bog. The trail here is an easy hike to what is described as the "most visually impressive pitcher plant bog in the world." In early spring you will find yourself surrounded by literally thousands of the beautiful white-tubed plants. Oh, and there's plenty of wildlife to view as well.

Start: East trailhead on Splinter Hill Road
Distance: 4.0 miles out and back
Hiking time: About 2 hours
Difficulty: Easy
Trail surface: Dirt and sand footpaths, gravel service road
Best seasons: Mar–May
Other trail users: Mountain bikes, equestrians
Canine compatibility: Leashed dogs permitted
Land status: State wildlife management area
Nearest town: Perdido
Fees and permits: None
Schedule: Year-round, sunrise to sunset

Maps: USGS Perdido, AL; *DeLorme: Alabama Atlas & Gazetteer,* page 56 G4; map available online at www.alabamaforeverwild.com
Trail contact: Alabama State Lands ADCNR, 64 N. Union St., Montgomery, AL 36130; (334) 242-3484; www.alabamaforeverwild.com
Special considerations: This trail is located in a state wildlife management area. In the fall and winter, check hunting seasons and times before heading out at www.outdooralabama.com/hunting and wear hunter orange during these times.

Finding the trailhead: From I-65 exit 45 in Perdido, take CR 47 west 0.1 mile. Turn right onto Splinter Hill Road and travel 0.7 mile. The trailhead will be on the left. GPS: N31 01.607'/W87 39.237'

The Hike

Several of the trails I have written about in this edition make mention of pitcher plants. By now some of you are asking, "What exactly is a pitcher plant?" In a nutshell, a pitcher plant is a carnivorous plant, like a Venus flytrap, eating any insects that come its way. An unsuspecting insect is lulled into a false sense of security by fragrant nectar and enters the plant's long, hollow stem. The plant doesn't actually "eat" the insect; rather, the nectar works to dissolve its prey.

There are several different species of pitcher plants around the world, like the marsh variety that lives in the forests of Latin America. The extreme southern region of the American South, including the Alabama Gulf Coast, plays host to its own variety, the white-topped pitcher plant.

The white-top is a long, beautiful, white-and-green tapered tubular plant. The very top part of the stem is white with red or maroon vein-like patterns. The tube is topped with a single large leaf. This variety is found in pine forest seepage bogs, such as those found in south Alabama, and are currently classified as rare and endangered.

Splinter Hill is located in one such bog, a 627-acre tract at the headwaters of the

The Splinter Hill Bog Trailhead is well marked and informative.

Perdido River at Dyas Creek. The Perdido eventually flows south, forming the border between Florida and Alabama as it empties into the Gulf of Mexico. The land is managed by the Alabama Forever Wild program and Department of Conservation and Natural Resources as a nature preserve to help protect the plants. During peak season, usually March through early May, you will literally be surrounded by thousands of these plants in a display that the Nature Conservancy describes as "one of the most visually impressive pitcher plant bogs in the world."

But pitcher plants aren't the only draw to Splinter Hill Bog. The property is also home to many animals that you may cross paths with, including deer and wild turkey. If you don't see one of them in person, you will definitely see their presence in the tracks they leave along the trail.

The trail itself is an old dirt road repurposed to allow public access to the property. It's wide with either a sand or gravel base. You will notice a distinct lack of trees throughout most of the hike. Some of the tract is pine savannah with long waving grasses. The clear-cut areas are part of the state's efforts to bring the native long-leaf pine back to the property. You may see some plots staked out with orange surveyor flags. These are areas where biologists are monitoring the growth of the longleaf.

The trail is easy to follow, but just to make sure you stay on-route, it is marked with bright yellow diamond markers with black arrows pointing directions. At key intersections or turns, large wooden green signs point the way.

When you arrive at the trailhead, you will notice that the path is actually a loop trail, so why did I make this a 4-mile out-and-back? Two reasons: water and more water.

The trail actually has two trailheads, one on the east side of the property and one on the west. The massive amounts of rain this area receives in the spring makes access to the trail from the western trailhead difficult, with water knee to waist deep at times as it crosses a bog area. Forever Wild tells me that funding is available for them to build bridges along this

The highlight of hiking the Splinter Hill Bog Trail: pitcher plants, thousands of them!

side of the trail, so hopefully by the time you read this, the 4-mile loop will be walkable all year and you can simply continue on where I indicate the turnaround. In the mean-time, enjoy the beautiful display of pitcher plants along this out-and-back hike.

Miles and Directions

0.0 Start from the east trailhead kiosk by walking around the yellow steel gate to the northwest on a wide gravel service road.

0.2 Come to a T intersection with another dirt road. Turn right (northwest).

0.4 Travel through a very small stand of pines. Pass several plots marked with orange surveyor flags.

0.7 Come to a Y. (**FYI:** This would be the end of the loop if you could make it through the bog on the west side.) A green sign with white lettering reads "Pitcher Plant Loop" and points to the north. Take the right fork and head north.

0.9 A side road comes in from the left (west). Continue straight to the north.

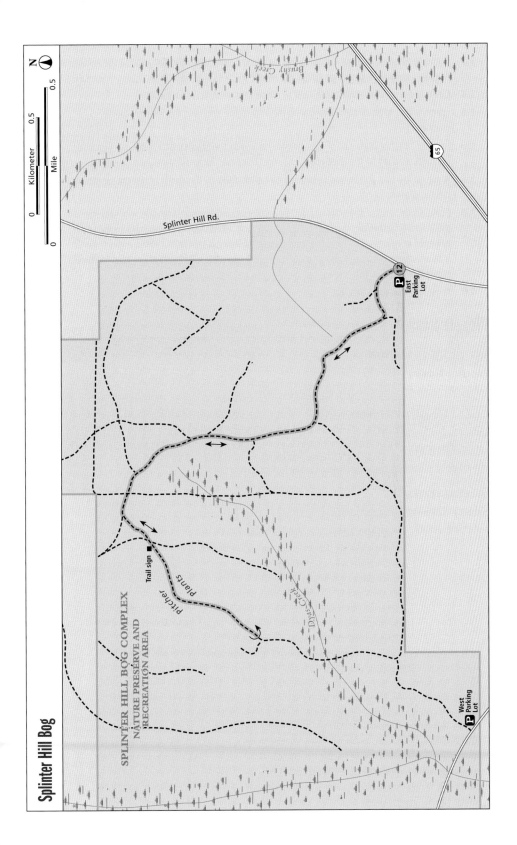

Splinter Hill Bog

SPLINTER HILL BOG COMPLEX
NATURE PRESERVE AND
RECREATION AREA

Trail sign

Pitcher
Plants

Brushy Creek

Splinter Hill Rd.

Dyas Creek

East
Parking
Lot

West
Parking
Lot

65

N

Kilometer   0.5

0

Mile

0

0.5

1.3 Come to another T with a dirt road. Turn left and continue on the dirt road to the northwest. Another Pitcher Plant Loop sign points the way.

1.4 Cross a dirt service road to the west. A small savannah is on your right.

1.5 Come to a Y. Another sign here points the way to the left. Take the left fork to the southwest.

1.6 Another "Pitcher Plant Loop" sign points the way to the southwest. Follow the sign and continue straight to the southwest. The road becomes more hard-packed clay at this point.

1.8 Arrive at the bog. In the spring you will be surrounded by hundreds, if not thousands, of pitcher plants.

2.0 Come to the end of the pitcher plant bog. Turn around here and retrace your steps to the trailhead. (**Option:** You can continue the loop, which will take you back to mile 0.7; however, in another 0.4 mile the road becomes very boggy. When I hiked it the water was anywhere between knee and waist deep. If you wish to complete the loop, continue straight and follow the arrows, but be ready to get wet, and watch for snakes.)

4.0 Arrive back at the trailhead.

Hiking Information

Local Information
North Baldwin Chamber of Commerce, 301 McMeans Ave., Bay Minette, AL 35607; (251) 937-5665; www.northbaldwinchamber.com

Local Events/Attractions
Old Time Country Festival, 51233 AL 225, Stockton; (251) 580-1897. Held the third weekend of April, this is a good old-fashioned festival with lots of food and entertainment plus plowing demonstrations and classic tractors.

Restaurants
Street's Seafood Restaurant, 251 S. US 31, Bay Minette; (251) 937-2664. Great seafood, especially the crab claws!

Gulf Coast Region Honorable Mentions

There are plenty of great hikes throughout the Gulf Coast region of Alabama that didn't make the A-list. Although many are shorter in length, they offer fantastic scenery and interesting wildlife. Pay a visit and let us know what you think. Maybe the hike should be upgraded, or maybe you know of a little-known hike that would make a good honorable mention.

A Alligator Alley

A unique trail if ever there was one, Alligator Alley lets tourists view American alligators in their natural habitat while within walking distance of shopping and restaurants.

The City of Daphne put its proximity to Mobile Bay and its marshes to good use by creating this well-traveled boardwalk. The hike is a 1-mile out-and-back that takes you over the back bays of Mobile Bay via boardwalks for a good view of the gators and waterfowl, including brown pelicans. The trail is open year-round from dawn to dusk.

For more information contact the City of Daphne at (251) 621-3703 or visit the city's website at www.daphneal.com/residents/parks-recreation. *DeLorme: Alabama Atlas & Gazetteer:* Page 62 D5.

B Trails of Gulf State Park

Two and a half miles of sugar-white beaches, a 500-acre freshwater lake, bicycling trails, and 4.2 miles of nature trails are in store for visitors to Gulf State Park. Located on the Gulf of Mexico, Gulf State Park is one of Alabama's premier resort parks, with many amenities that make spending a week, or more, there a real pleasure.

All of the nature trails within the park center around the park's campground. Trails like Hurricane Ridge, Bobcat Branch, Bear Creek, and Alligator Marsh take you to see the effects of hurricanes on the coast firsthand, gulf marshes, and a wide range of foliage including live oak, palmetto, sawgrass, and muscadine, which is commonly used to make wine in the region and is a food source for birds, gray fox, and black bear.

For information contact Gulf State Park at (251) 948-7275 or visit www.alapark .com/gulfstate. *DeLorme: Alabama Atlas & Gazetteer:* Page 64 E3/F3.

C Hugh Branyon Backcountry Trail

The Hugh Branyon Backcountry Trail in Orange Beach is a National Recreational Trail consisting of six multiuse trails totaling 11 miles in length that will take you through six different ecosystems (we feature one of the trails, Cotton Bayou, in Hike 5).

Hikers taking to the Backcountry Trail in the city of Orange Beach

Located in the city of Orange Beach and the northern side of Gulf State Park, the trail allows hikers, joggers, and cyclists to experience a beautiful butterfly garden, freshwater marshes, hardwood swamps, and maybe bobcats, white-tailed deer, or an American alligator.

For more information about the Hugh Branyon Backcountry Trail, the location of the trailheads, and a trail app for your phone, visit www.backcountrytrail.com or contact the City of Orange Beach at (251) 981-1180. *DeLorme: Alabama Atlas & Gazetteer:* Page 64 E3/E4.

South Region

Geographically speaking, the South region of Alabama does not differ greatly from the Gulf Coast region. The hills are a bit higher, at times around 300 feet above sea level, but overall the region is flat coastal plain. The main distinguishing features of this region are the rivers, *lots* of rivers! Take a look at the state seal and you will see what I mean. It is here where hundreds of rivers, creeks, and brooks all converge as they head to the Gulf of Mexico, making this a rich and fertile land.

Hikers take time to enjoy the view along the spillway at Little River State Forest.

One of the highlights of the region is Conecuh National Forest, renowned for its towering longleaf pines, crystal-blue spring lakes, and cypress ponds. It is also known for the 20-mile-long Conecuh Trail (see Honorable Mentions), an easy weekend hike along ponds and lakes and through dogwood, holly, magnolia, cypress, and, of course, longleaf forests. Here you will find three excellent day hikes that will take you to see these features without hiking the entire 20 miles.

As with the Gulf Coast region, the weather in the South is subtropical, and late summer heat and humidity can make outdoor activities impossible at times. If you're hiking the region during this time, carry plenty of water and, of course, insect repellent. Much of the hiking in this region is around swamps and marshes, so expect mosquitoes. Also like the Gulf Coast region, close proximity to the Gulf of Mexico means that the warm, moist Gulf air can produce brief but very heavy rainfall unexpectedly.

As mentioned in the Gulf Coast introduction, 2004–5 was one of the worst hurricane seasons on record for south Alabama. Several trails in the region were severely damaged but have been cleared and are safe once again for public use. Remember to keep track of the tropics during hurricane season (generally June through November) before heading out.

In the spring the temperature moderates from the mid-60s to low 70s. The hot, humid summer gives way to great hiking weather from fall through winter. It does get a bit colder in this region than in the Gulf Coast, with temperatures averaging in the 40s in January. Cold snaps of below 30 degrees are more frequent here than in the Gulf Coast region.

13 Gazebo Trail

The first sign of any elevation gain in south Alabama occurs in Little River State Forest (formerly Claude D. Kelley State Park). Here the Gazebo Trail travels up the shallow inclines of 300-foot ridges, past slash and longleaf pines towering over pine-needle floors, as it makes its way to its namesake gazebo built by the Civilian Conservation Corps (CCC). The trail crosses a nice little creek that feeds the lake. Along the way, look for small fern forests, beautiful white dogwoods in the spring, and eastern wild turkeys, white-tailed deer, and red-tailed hawks.

Start: At the park office and bathhouse
Distance: 2.8 miles out and back
Hiking time: About 1.5 hours
Difficulty: Easy to moderate due to a few small hill climbs
Trail surface: Dirt footpath, short dirt road
Best seasons: Year-round
Other trail users: None
Canine compatibility: Dogs permitted but must be on leash in recreation areas
Land status: Alabama state forest
Nearest town: Atmore

Fees and permits: Day-use fee; paddleboat rental and lake zip line fees
Schedule: Year-round, 9 a.m.–5 p.m.; zip line open weekends Memorial Day–Labor Day
Maps: USGS Uriah East, Uriah West, Huxford, and McCullough, AL; *DeLorme: Alabama Atlas & Gazetteer*, page 57 D6
Trail contact: Little River State Forest, 580 H. Kyle Rd., Atmore, AL 36502; (251) 862-2511; www.forestry.state.al.us/little_river_state _forest.aspx?bv=6&s=2

Finding the trailhead: From I-65 exit 57, take AL 21 north 11 miles. Turn right onto H. Kyle Road and travel 0.4 mile to the pay station. The office and the start of the trail are straight ahead in another 0.2 mile. GPS: N31 15.436'/W87 29.129'

The Hike

Hidden away like a little secret off AL 21 is Little River State Forest, yet another gift of the Depression era's CCC program. The park is a gem for families, offering plenty to do. There are playgrounds; swimming, canoeing, paddleboating, and fishing in the park's centerpiece 25-acre lake; and, of course, hiking.

One of my favorites at Little River is the Gazebo Trail. Now, I am a bit partial to this trail, which was originally built in 1935 by the CCC to take visitors to its namesake gazebo. I only discovered the path in 2000 while doing research for the first edition of this book. Soon after, a series of devastating hurricanes virtually wiped the trail off the map, but with the help of the Alabama Forestry Commission and the local chapter of the Alabama Hiking Trail Society, we painstakingly found the original trail bed under mounds of downed trees, and today the trail is almost exactly back to where it was in 1935.

The view from the Gazebo Trail's namesake

There are two trails in the park: The first (and the longer of the two) is this trail, the Gazebo Trail; the second is the Bell/CCC Trail. Both trails start at the park office and bathhouse (you can find drink and snack machines inside). The Bell/CCC Trail heads west then south, skirting the lake and forming a lollipop loop. The Gazebo Trail heads northeast from the office, away from the lake along rolling ridges.

The trail is marked with yellow paint blazes. This is the official color for the new Alabama Trail that begins (or ends) on the Fort Morgan peninsula on the Gulf of Mexico and ends (or begins) at the Tennessee state line some 550 miles away. The two trails here at Little River State Forest are an important piece of the Alabama Trail.

As you meander down the Gazebo Trail, you'll encounter a variety of plant life. Sweet gums and live oaks provide shade in the hot, humid summer; in the fall you get your first taste of the season this far south as they blaze in red, yellow, and gold. As in most of the Gulf Coast region, there is an abundance of slash and longleaf pines along the trail, and in the spring it is white with hundreds of blooming dogwoods.

While walking the trail, keep your eyes to the skies to see if you can spot red-tailed hawks and turkey vultures flying high overhead. Also watch for woodpeckers in the trees, including the red-headed and downy species. And look for the tracks and burrows of armadillos and gopher tortoises. In the right season you'll see many varieties of wildflowers lining the way: black-eyed Susans, yellow-flowered winter honeysuckle, and the lavender flowers of morning glory.

The trail crosses a nice but seasonal stream over a wooden footbridge at mile 0.6. This is a good place to see white-tailed deer and eastern wild turkeys. The bridge was being rebuilt as of this writing but should be in operation by the time you read this. If not, you will have to do a little log-hopping to get across.

The Gazebo Trail reaches its farthest point at the top of a ridge where you'll find a log gazebo with a stone fireplace built by the CCC. You can reserve the gazebo for picnics, but reserve it early, as it gets a lot of use in summer. A short section of the hike uses a portion of the dirt Gazebo Road. Be aware that picnickers use the road to ferry their supplies and guests to the gazebo, so watch for vehicles. Once you reach the gazebo, have lunch and take in the view before you turn around and retrace your steps to the trailhead.

Before I move on, I need to commend the Alabama Forestry Commission and a nonprofit church organization, Iron Men Ministries, for keeping the park open. Financial constraints nearly forced Little River to close not too long ago, but a partnership between these two organizations kept the gates open and now hundreds of families can continue to enjoy this little gem.

And one more thing: You can view an interesting film produced by the US Department of the Interior about the Mobile area and the construction of Little River State Forest from 1935 at www.youtube.com/watch?v=N23Vpy6VTmw.

Miles and Directions

0.0   Start at park office and bathhouse. Head away from the lake to the northeast toward the picnic pavilion and picnic area. The trail here is neatly mowed grass.

0.2   Cross the dirt Campground Road to the north. The trail now follows a 3- to 4-foot dirt and grass path through some beautiful pines. Watch for deer in this area.

0.6   Come to a 78-foot-long bridge across a stream that feeds the lake. The stream is seasonal. Once on the other side of the bridge, turn to the left (northeast).

0.8   Cross a dirt road to the east.

0.9   The trail merges with a dirt logging road that comes in from the left. Keep going straight (north), following the blazes. In about 100 feet come to a double yellow blaze indicating a turn. Turn left (north) and leave the dirt road, continuing on a narrow grass and dirt footpath.

1.0   The trail intersects with the dirt Gazebo Road. Turn right here (southeast) onto the road and follow it uphill.

1.3   Pass a stone CCC culvert that funnels water from a stream under the road. This area is beautiful in the spring, with hundreds of white blooming dogwoods. In 200 feet you will come to a double blaze indicating a right turn. Turn right (southwest) onto a narrow dirt footpath back into the woods.

1.4   Cross the dirt Gazebo Road to the southeast and scramble up a short hill. In a few hundred feet, you will reach the gazebo and some nice views of the surrounding hills. Turn around here and retrace your steps to the trailhead.

2.8   Arrive back at the trailhead.

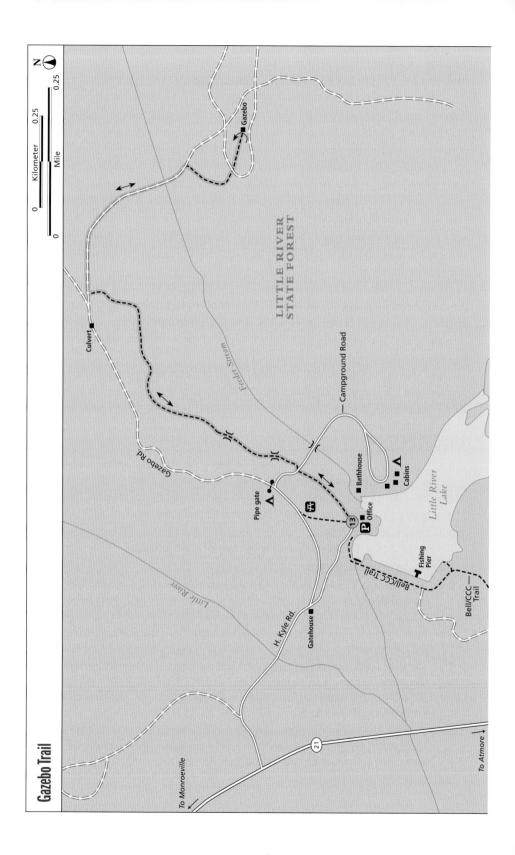

Gazebo Trail

Gazebo

Culvert

Gazebo Rd.

Feeder Stream

Pipe gate

LITTLE RIVER
STATE FOREST

Campground Road

Bathhouse

Cabins

Office

Little River
Lake

Fishing
Pier

Bell/CCC Trail

Bell/CCC
Trail

H. Kyle Rd.

Gatehouse

Little River

21

To Monroeville

To Atmore

N

0   Kilometer   0.25

0   Mile   0.25

Hiking Information

Local Information

Atmore Chamber of Commerce, 501 S. Pensacola Ave., Atmore, AL 36502; (251) 368-3305; www.atmorechamber.com

Local Events/Attractions

William Station Day, 501 S. Pensacola Ave., Atmore; (251) 368-3305; www.atmore chamber.com. "A simpler way of life" is how the residents of Atmore describe the William Station Day celebration commemorating the town's founding in 1866, when it was a supply stop called William Station. There are plenty of arts and crafts booths, music, and stories of the trains that once ruled the area and the legends of the Poarch Creek Indians.

Lodging

Little River State Forest Campground, 580 H. Kyle Rd., Atmore; (251) 862-2511; www.forestry.state.al.us/little_river_state_forest.aspx?bv=6&s=2. Primitive camping and improved sites (water and power).

Restaurants

Creek Family Restaurant, 6141 AL 21, Atmore; (251) 368-4422

Organizations

Alabama Hiking Trail Society, PO Box 231164, Montgomery, AL 36123; www .hikealabama.org

TRAIL TERIYAKI CHICKEN

Don't throw away those soy sauce packets from that Chinese dinner you had the other night! Save them for this delicious and easy trail dinner.

- 1 cup instant rice
- ½ teaspoon garlic powder
- ½ teaspoon ginger powder
- 1½ cups water
- 1 (5-ounce) can or package chicken
- 1 packet honey
- 2 packets soy sauce

At home, mix the dry ingredients and place in a ziplock bag. On the trail, boil the water and then add the dry ingredients. When the rice is ready, stir in the chicken, honey, and soy sauce. Makes 1 serving.

14 Bell/CCC Trail

A wake-up call for those who have hiked the flatter trails of the Gulf Coast region, the Bell/CCC Trail leaves the sea-level hiking behind and starts to take on some hills. Granted, these are not massive mountains, but some of the inclines can get you breathing hard if you're not in reasonably good shape. The trail crosses the beautiful spillway that flows from the dam that forms Little River Lake, then rounds the lake before ducking into a thick forest where some nice views of the surrounding hills will be had at the top of the ridge.

Start: At the park office and bathhouse
Distance: 2.0-mile lollipop
Hiking time: About 1.5 hours
Difficulty: Easy to moderate due to hill climb
Trail surface: Dirt footpath, dirt road
Best seasons: Year-round
Other trail users: None
Canine compatibility: Dogs permitted but must be on leash in recreation area
Land status: Alabama state forest
Nearest town: Atmore

Fees and permits: Day-use fee; paddleboat rental and lake zip line fees
Schedule: Year-round, 9 a.m.–5 p.m.; zip line open weekends Memorial Day–Labor Day
Maps: USGS Uriah East, Uriah West, Huxford, and McCullough, AL; *DeLorme: Alabama Atlas & Gazetteer,* page 57 D6
Trail contact: Little River State Forest, 580 H. Kyle Rd., Atmore, AL 36502; (251) 862-2511; www.forestry.state.al.us/little_river _state_forest.aspx?bv=6&s=2

Finding the trailhead: From I-65 exit 57, take US 21 north 11 miles. Turn right onto H. Kyle Road and travel 0.4 mile to the pay station. The park office and the start of the trail are straight ahead in another 0.2 mile. GPS: N31 15.436' / W87 29.129'

The Hike

The folks who drive past Little River State Forest (formerly Claude D. Kelley State Park) and never stop to visit don't know what they're missing. The forest, hidden in the woods about 11 miles north of Atmore, features nearly 2,000 forested acres and the 25-acre Little River Lake. This man-made lake provides swimming and fishing year-round. The Bell/CCC Trail affords wonderful views of the lake, plus a bit more of a hiking challenge than many other south Alabama hikes.

The Civilian Conservation Corps (CCC) built the park in 1935 (you can view an actual film of the construction of the park online at www.youtube.com/watch?v=N23Vpy6VTmw). This trail utilizes an old dirt road that was once used by CCC workers and a newer trail built by former Alabama forestry ranger Paul Bell, hence the name Bell Trail. The combination of the two trails gives you a nice walk in the woods with exceptional views of the lake and of the surrounding hills at the intersection of the two.

Hikers take a look at the lake at Little River State Forest on a T fishing pier.

The park is located in Monroe County, which was immortalized in Harper Lee's *To Kill a Mockingbird*, the best-selling novel about racial tensions in a small Southern town. The story was set in Maycomb, a fictional alias for the nearby town of Monroeville.

This region is home to the Poarch band of Creek Indians. Following the 1814 Battle of Horseshoe Bend, which pitted the Creek's Red Stick band against US soldiers and the Lower Creek tribe, the federal government relocated most of the local tribes to Oklahoma. In appreciation for fighting alongside General Andrew Jackson's troops, the Poarch Creeks were allowed to establish a reservation here. Each Thanksgiving the tribe invites the public to its annual Thanksgiving Pow Wow that features native foods, rituals, costumes, and dances. The pow wow is held on the Poarch Creek Reservation on Jack Springs Road in Atmore (see "Local Events" below).

The Bell/CCC Trail begins by tracing the banks of Little River Lake. Early on, you cross the lake's overflow stream. The crossing makes for a scenic spot to sit and just watch the rushing waters.

After following the banks of the lake over a man-made earthen dam, the trail turns and heads southeast into the woods, where it follows a nice, narrow 3- to 4-foot-wide dirt bed. Here loblolly and longleaf pine, sweet gum, and hickory fill

The beautiful spillway at Little River State Forest looks almost exactly as it did some eighty years ago.

the forest. In the fall live oaks provide a sparkling display of color that reflects from the surface of the lake. In early spring the dogwood blooms are particularly beautiful. While hiking, be sure to watch for the many varieties of woodpeckers that live here, including downy, hairy, red-headed, and pileated.

Eventually the trail moves away from the lake and begins to head up the side of a ridge that has a grade that is much steeper than most other south Alabama hikes covered in this guidebook, but the average hiker shouldn't find it too difficult. As the trail nears the top of the ridge, it becomes an old dirt road. For the most part it is maintained, but sometimes after heavy rains you may find a few washouts, though nothing insurmountable.

At the top of a ridge, the trail comes to the very edge of the soft clay banks of a large pit. Be careful here: There's a drop-off of 50 to 75 feet. Turn around and you will have a nice view of the rolling hills surrounding the forest, something you don't normally see this far south. From the dirt pit you will turn to the right (northwest) and follow the old CCC Road downhill to complete the loop. This is a dirt road and

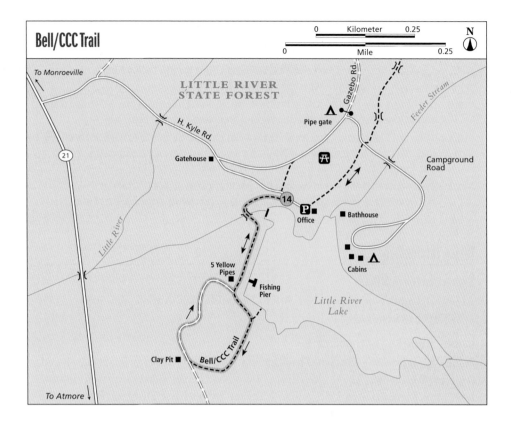

Bell/CCC Trail

a really nice walk in the woods. Be sure to keep your eyes peeled for the stone crafts-manship of the CCC. Along the sides of the road they constructed, by hand, stone culverts to keep water from washing the road away.

Miles and Directions

0.0 Start at the park office and bathhouse. The trail is blazed with the yellow markings of the Alabama Trail. Head southwest along the banks of the lake toward the park's pay station and entrance.

0.1 The trail comes to a 50-foot-long footbridge that spans the lake's spillway. Cross the bridge heading to the south; once across, turn to the east and head back toward the lake. At the lake, turn right and follow the dirt road atop the earthen dam.

0.3 Pass a T fishing pier that extends out into the lake on the left (east).

0.4 Come to a T intersection. To the right you will see a dirt road. This is the CCC Trail and will be where you will return. Turn left (southeast) into the woods. The trail is now a dirt footpath.

0.5 Cross a short, 20-foot metal grate bridge over a small stream.

0.6 Come to a Y. Take the right fork to the southwest. (**FYI:** The left fork is a side trail that takes you to a nice walk along the banks of the lake. It will eventually meet back up with the main trail at mile 0.7.)

0.7 The side trail to the lake rejoins the main trail from the northeast. Continue about another 20 feet and come to a Y. Take the right fork to the southeast. (**FYI:** The left fork is the forest's property line and is marked with yellow-and-white rings around the trees and has a grass-covered service road along the perimeter.) Soon the trail begins a pretty decent climb up the hill until the intersection with the CCC Trail.

1.0 Come to a Y. Take the right fork up the hill to the southwest. The trail is now a dirt road that is usually well maintained but can sometimes have deep ruts after heavy rain.

1.1 Come to a T intersection. Straight ahead is a clay pit. (**FYI.** Be sure to turn around and catch the views of the surrounding hills to the southeast.) Turn right (northwest) at the pit onto the dirt CCC Road. This is the un-blazed CCC Trail.

1.7 The trail comes to the end of the loop that you first started at mile 0.4. Turn left (northeast) and retrace your steps over the earthen dam and spillway back to the trailhead.

2.0 Arrive back at the trailhead.

Hiking Information

Local Information
Atmore Chamber of Commerce, 501 S. Pensacola Ave., Atmore, AL 36502; (251) 368-3305; www.atmorechamber.com

Local Events/Attractions
Annual Poarch Creek Indian Thanksgiving Pow Wow, 5811 Jack Springs Road, Atmore, AL 36502; (251) 368-9136; www.poarchcreekindians.org/westminster/pow_wow.html. Each year the public is invited to celebrate Thanksgiving with the Poarch Creek Indians. The event brings tribal members together and features brilliant displays of authentic dress and exhibition dancing by a variety of tribes. In addition, there are arts and crafts, barbecue, fried chicken, and more.

Lodging
Little River State Forest Campground, 580 H. Kyle Rd., Atmore; (251) 862-2511; www.forestry.state.al.us/little_river_state_forest.aspx?bv=6&s=2. Primitive camping and improved sites (water and power).

Restaurants
Creek Family Restaurant, 6141 AL 21, Atmore; (251) 368-4422

Organizations
Alabama Hiking Trail Society, PO Box 231164, Montgomery, AL 36123; www.hikealabama.org

15 Old St. Stephens Historical Park

A little bit nature and a whole lot of history along the Old St. Stephens Historical Park Trail. This loop trail takes you along the banks of a quarry with water reflecting deep blue skies and white limestone bluffs, plus the history of the first capital of Alabama at a live archeological site.

Start: Trailhead adjacent to parking lot
Distance: 1.9-mile multiloop
Hiking time: About 2 hours
Difficulty: Easy to moderate due to some hills
Trail surface: Dirt
Best seasons: Late Feb–May, Sept–Nov
Other trail users: Equestrians
Canine compatibility: Leashed dogs permitted
Land status: City historic park

Nearest town: St. Stephens
Fees and permits: Day-use fee
Schedule: Year-round, 7 a.m.–3 p.m.
Maps: USGS Saint Stephens, AL; *DeLorme: Alabama Atlas & Gazetteer,* page 48 H5
Trail contact: Old St. Stephens Historical Commission, PO Box 78, St. Stephens, AL 36569; (251) 246-6790

Finding the trailhead: From Jackson and the intersection of AL 69 and US 43, take US 43 south 8.4 miles. Turn right onto Mobile Cutoff Road and travel 1.9 miles. Turn right onto Gib Bailey Road / Cement Plant Road. Travel 0.8 mile and come to a fork in the road. Take the right fork onto an unnamed street (Cement Plant Road continues on the left fork). The park entrance gate is ahead on the right in 0.2 mile. After paying the attendant, continue another 1 mile to the parking lot and trailhead. The trail begins at the information shelter that has details about the park and its history. GPS: N31 33.315' / W88 02.220'

The Hike

The Old St. Stephens Historical Park Trail is unique. Not only does it take you through some beautiful scenery, including great views of limestone bluffs (more on that in a moment), but it is also an active archeological site. Volunteers from around the country come to the park each year to help uncover a piece of the state's history, the site of the first territorial capital of Alabama. As with many historic sites, Old St. Stephens is facing a financial crisis and is seeing its budget cut drastically, but dedicated volunteers do a remarkable job at keeping the gates open.

The trail that meanders through the site gives you a unique perspective of this 220-plus-year-old city. The town of Old St. Stephens has an eclectic history, beginning as the site of a fort in 1789 that was built by the Spanish governor of Mobile, Juan Vicente Folk. The location was perfect for the economy of the area. Built on a sharp bend in the Tombigbee River and high atop a limestone bluff, ships would have to dock here because after the bend the river shallows.

The fort was eventually turned over to the United States, and in 1799 the town began growing exponentially. At the height of its success, Old St. Stephens sported

The limestone walls of the quarry can be seen as you hike along the trail at Old St. Stephens Historical Park.

high-class boardinghouses, hotels, theaters, and the state's first chartered school, Washington Academy.

The Alabama Territory was formed in 1817, and Old St. Stephens became the state's first capital, thus giving the park its motto, "Where Alabama began." But success was short-lived. In one year the capital was moved to Cahawba, and as it moved, so did the population, which relocated a few miles away to New St. Stephens.

The town fell into ruin and was reclaimed by nature until, through the efforts of the University of South Alabama Archeological Department, it was rediscovered, and now you can walk the streets of the long-forgotten town on this trail.

The trail begins by weaving its way through dogwood and redbud trees along the ancient streets. Signs along the route tell the story of life in the town at its zenith, when it boasted a population of over 7,000 people. The old streets are marked with signs such as "High Street," and individual properties where houses once stood are identified by signs bearing their street address. One of the historical highlights of the hike is the site where archeologists are unearthing the grand Globe Hotel, once the main stopping point for travelers and businessmen in the region.

The trail deviates a bit from the archeological site as it treks along the banks of a large, deep quarry. The quarry is now full of water and makes an impressive picture

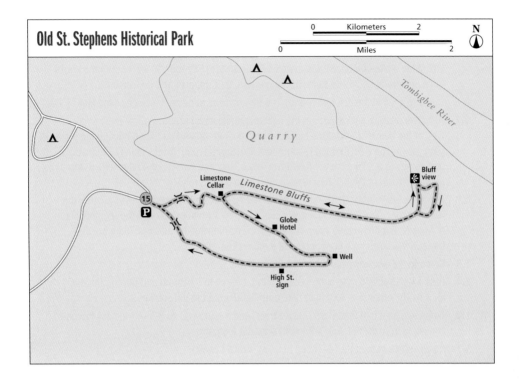

Old St. Stephens Historical Park

Quarry

Tombigbee River

Limestone
Cellar

Limestone Bluffs

Bluff
view

15

P

Globe
Hotel

Well

High St.
sign

when it reflects a deep blue sky. As you hike along the eastern bank of the quarry, be sure to turn around for a good view of the limestone bluffs that line the banks.

The trail is not blazed and can become a bit confusing to follow. There are several dirt service roads that run through the tract that can get you turned around. Also, be aware that equestrians use the trail, too. Keep eyes peeled for them as they round the bends.

If you'd like to do a little car camping while here, the park has two nice campgrounds. Lakeview is situated atop a limestone bluff high above the lake, with a wonderful view of the quarry. The second campground is a primitive area called Cedar Ridge, with easy access to the quarry for swimming. Keep in mind that this is a deep lake and there are no lifeguards on duty, so be safe.

Miles and Directions

0.0 Start at the trailhead a few yards to the southeast of the parking lot. A small building housing informative panels describing the town's history and the site's archaeology is there. The trail begins to the right of the building. In a few short yards, come to a Y. The right fork is the return route; take the left fork (east) and a few yards later cross a short bridge over a creek. Another short walk takes you to a sign that reads "You are now crossing Chambers Street" and describes where you are, but the rest of the sign is hard to read. Follow the path up the hill to a dirt road and turn to the right (east) onto the road. To the left you will see the archeological building.

0.2 Pass the remnants of a limestone cellar labeled 142 HIGH STREET and a marble marker. Just past this the trail comes to a Y (a sign reading "High Street" is in the center of the Y). Take the left fork (northeast). Along this wide dirt road section, you will be walking atop the limestone bluffs of a quarry with beautiful blue water. *(FYI:* You can walk out to the bluff's edge on several short side trails, but be warned, they are high and dangerous!)

0.6 Come to a Y. Take the left fork (north). The trail narrows and has a nice enclosed feel.

0.7 Just after passing a wide path to the right, continue straight (north) a few yards to get a look at the beautiful limestone bluffs behind you. Turn around and head back to the wide path you just passed. Turn left (east) and follow the dirt road. In less than 0.1 mile, the trail comes to a Y. Take the left fork down into a gully and back up the other side to the dirt road at the top of the hill. Turn right (south) onto the dirt road.

0.8 Return to the Y from mile 0.2 (the High Street Y). Take the left fork and head west on the wide dirt road. To your right along this section, 4-by-4 white posts mark the property lines of houses that once stood here; some have signs marking the address. There are also signs with articles from newspapers of the day (late 1800s).

1.3 Come to the archeological dig of the Globe Hotel.

1.4 Pass a well house on the right. Circle around the well to the south and pick up the dirt road on the other side. Turn right here onto the dirt road to the southeast.

1.6 Come to a sign that reads "132 High Street" and a narrow, 2- to 3-foot-wide dirt footpath coming in from the left. Turn left (west) onto the footpath.

1.7 A trail comes in from the left. Keep heading straight (west).

1.8 Come to a creek crossing. There are two bridges here; use the smaller one on the left.

1.9 Arrive back at the trailhead.

Hiking Information

Local Information

Washington County Economic Development, PO Box 854, Chatom, AL 36518; (251) 847-2810; www.washingtoncountyal.com

Accommodations

Old St. Stephens Historical Park Campground, Cement Plant Road, St. Stephens, AL 36569; (251) 246-6790. RV, primitive, and improved tent camping is available.

16 Fort Toulouse / Fort Jackson Loop

A beautiful blend of history and Southern landscapes will be found on the Fort Toulouse / Fort Jackson Loop trail as you walk among beautiful oak trees adorned with thick blankets of Spanish moss; visit the wide Tallapoosa River; retrace the steps of William Bartram, Botanist to the Queen; and visit the site of the historic fort itself.

Start: Parking lot in front of visitor center
Distance: 2.0-mile multiloop
Hiking time: About 1.5 hours
Difficulty: Easy over rolling hills
Trail surface: Dirt and crushed gravel trail, some dirt road and boardwalks
Best seasons: Sept–May
Other trail users: Cyclists on dirt roads
Canine compatibility: Leashed dogs permitted
Land status: Alabama historic state park
Nearest town: Wetumpka

Fees and permits: Day-use fee
Schedule: Year-round, dawn to dusk; visitor center open 8 a.m.–5 p.m.; closed Thanksgiving, Christmas Day, and New Year's Day
Maps: USGS Wetumpka, AL; *DeLorme: Alabama Atlas & Gazetteer,* page 45 C8
Trail contact: Fort Toulouse / Fort Jackson National Historic Park, 2521 W. Fort Toulouse Rd., Wetumpka, AL 36093; (344) 567-3002; www.forttoulouse.com

Finding the trailhead: From Wetumpka at the intersection of AL 112 (W. Bridge Street) and AL 111, take AL 111 south 0.2 mile and turn right onto S. Main Street. Travel 0.8 mile and turn right onto AL 9 South. Travel 0.3 mile and turn left onto Old Montgomery Highway. In 0.8 mile turn right onto Fort Toulouse Road. In 3.4 miles you will arrive at the park entrance. Pay your day-use fee at the entrance kiosk or to the guard on duty and continue straight another 0.2 mile. The visitor center parking and trailhead is on the left. GPS: N32 30.335' / W86 15.170'

The Hike

Of all the historic hikes I have included in this and the previous three editions, Fort Toulouse / Fort Jackson has to be the one with the most diverse modern history crammed into one park.

The history of this plot of land begins around 5,000 BC, when bands of nomadic hunters roamed the region. Native Americans settled the area permanently during what is known as the Mississippian period (AD 1100–1400). Here on this fertile land rich in wildlife at the confluence of three rivers they built a society. Several mounds were constructed from mud, sticks, and branches that were used for ceremonies and as temples. One of those mounds, which this trail will lead you to, still exists and is dated as being built during this time.

The first European to arrive in the area was Hernando DeSoto in 1540. By the 1700s the French and British were making moves to control this new world. The French, wanting to halt the advance of Britain, decided to build a fort on the eastern side of the Louisiana Colony and, by invitation of their trading partners in good

A single log cabin is all that remains of the original Fort Toulouse from the mid-1700s.

standing, the Creek Indians, built the first fort, Fort Toulouse (named after the son of King Louis XIV), on this spot.

In 1763 when the French and Indian War came to an end, with the French ending up on the losing side, France was forced to turn much of its territory over to Britain, including the fort. Britain was forced to abandon the fort soon after because the Creek Indians, loyal to the French, wouldn't let them man it. Eventually the fort fell into disrepair and was reclaimed by nature.

In 1776 Botanist to the Queen William Bartram explored this area. After finding the ruins of the fort and seeing rich land and its proximity to the rivers, he wrote in his journals that the area was the "most eligible situation in the world for a city."

During the War of 1812 after the battle of Horseshoe Bend, General Andrew Jackson came to this same location and established an earthen fort. He later began a campaign here against the British and Spanish armies, which culminated in the Battle of New Orleans in 1815.

Whew, that's *a lot* of history! To learn more, stop by the visitor center at the fort to take a look at the exhibits and pick up a book or two on the long, rich history of this land.

The trail begins on the south side of the visitor center on a wide crushed gravel footpath but soon turns into a 2- to 3-foot-wide dirt footpath. This is the nature trail portion of the hike, and for the first 0.8 mile you will find yourself wandering through a beautiful floodplain forest. A floodplain forest occurs in the drainages of black-water rivers like you find here where the Tallapoosa and Coosa Rivers join to make the Alabama River.

The floodplain creates a rich, fertile environment for plants and wildlife. Some of the many species of trees you will come across include southern red, water, and laurel oaks; flowering dogwoods; yaupon holly; sweet gum; and Atlantic white cedar. Catch the trail in early to late spring for wildflowers like black-eyed Susans. Wildlife that may cross your path on this hike include mallard ducks, red fox, and white-tailed deer. Plus, Fort Toulouse / Fort Jackson is a stopover for the monarch butterfly.

Now, keep in mind what "floodplain" means. The trail gets a little muddy after a good rain, especially at mile 0.5 when you come to your first view of the river. The trail winds its way around many bogs, so be prepared for mosquitoes if you hike it in the warmer months. The loop eventually opens on a bluff to beautiful views of the confluence of the Tallapoosa and Coosa Rivers.

On the leg back to the trailhead, you will come to the site of the original fort itself. You can quite clearly make out where the diamond-shaped corners of the fort once stood, see the earthworks of a later reincarnation of the fort, and in the center visit a rustic building of the period.

Miles and Directions

0.0 Start at the trailhead from the south side of the parking lot. In 50 feet pass a monument to Jean-Louis Fonteneau, a sergeant in the French Colonial Marines who died at the fort in 1755.

0.1 A short side trail to the left (east) takes you to two tombstones. Continue straight ahead to the south and cross a creek over a wooden footbridge. After crossing, come to a Y; take the left fork to the southeast.

0.2 Come to a wide deck with informational signs and benches. In less than 0.1 mile, cross a seasonal creek over a 60-foot wood bridge with steel railings. In 200 feet come to a T intersection; turn left (west).

0.3 Come to another deck with informational signs and benches. Head down a flight of stairs to the south. You will leave the crushed gravel path at the bottom as the trail becomes a dirt footpath. It's very green and lush through here in late spring and early summer. In less than 0.1 mile come to another T intersection. Turn left (south). In 100 feet cross another seasonal stream over a footbridge.

0.4 Come to a Y. A boat launch is to the left (east). Take the right fork to the south (a sign here points the way to the waterfront).

0.5 Head down a series of railroad tie stairs and cross a boggy area (could be fairly deep after a good rain). Continue straight to the southwest. In 100 feet arrive at your first look at the Tallapoosa River. When ready, turn around and head back to mile 0.4.

0.6 Arrive back at the Y at mile 0.4. Take the left fork.

0.7 Take a series of wooden stairs up to a large deck.

0.8 Arrive at the top of the stairs, with a large deck with signage describing the William Bartram Arboretum. Turn left (north) onto a short crushed gravel path. In 175 feet the trail

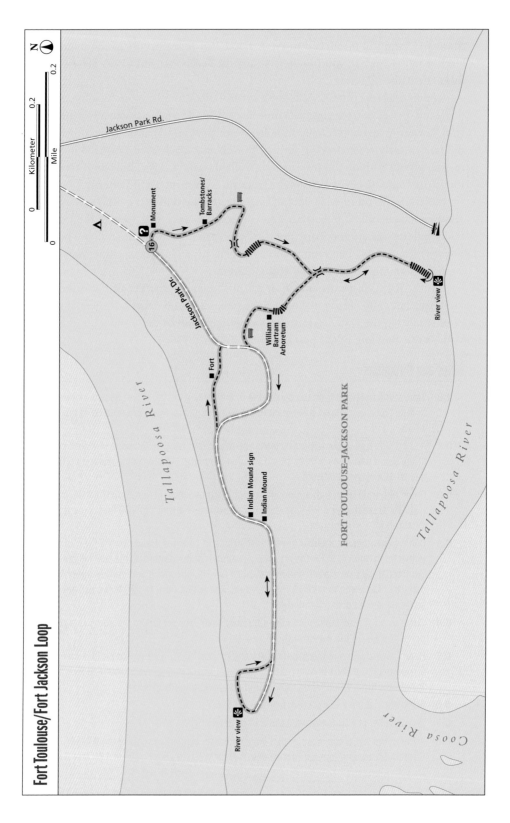

Fort Toulouse/Fort Jackson Loop

Jackson Park Rd.

Jackson Park Dr.

16

Monument

Tombstones/ Barracks

William Bartram Arboretum

River view

Fort

Indian Mound sign

Indian Mound

River view

FORT TOULOUSE–JACKSON PARK

Tallapoosa River

Tallapoosa River

Coosa River

N

Kilometer
0   0.2

Mile
0   0.2

ends at a gravel area with benches. You will see the fort to the right (northwest). Head west until you come to a dirt road. In 100 feet turn left (southwest) onto the dirt road and follow it around to the north. There are excellent views of the fort and the diamond shape of the structure along the route to your right. Beautiful Spanish moss–laden trees line the route on your left.

1.0 The road bends to the left (west). A large sign points the direction to the Indian mounds. Follow the dirt road to the west.

1.1 Come to an Indian mound on the right marked by a large sign reading "Mississippian Phase Mound Circa 1100-1400 AD." You can move off-trail and explore the area, then continue on the dirt road. The road turns into mostly grass as you follow the edge of a large field.

1.2 The path ducks back into the thick forest.

1.3 Cross a dirt road to the northwest.

1.4 Come out on an open bluff overlooking the river. There is a bench here. Turn right (northeast) and follow the grassy path around, making a small loop back to mile 1.3.

1.5 Return to the dirt road and turn left (east) to head back to the fort.

1.8 At the Indian mound sign you passed at mile 1.1, get off the road and head straight (northeast) toward the fort on an unmarked grassy path. In just over 200 feet, arrive at the log cabin that was once part of the fort. After exploring, head straight from the fort to the east and return to the dirt road.

1.9 Arrive at the dirt road. Turn left (northeast) onto the road and head back to the trailhead.

2.0 Arrive back at the trailhead.

Hiking Information

Local Information
City of Wetumpka, 408 S. Main St., Wetumpka, AL 36092; (334) 567-5147; www
.cityofwetumpka.com

Local Events/Attractions
French and Indian War Encampment, 2521 W. Fort Toulouse Rd., Wetumpka; (334) 567-3002; www.forttoulouse.com. Held annually the third weekend of April, reenactors portray French marines, English soldiers, and Creek warriors from the war (also known as the Seven Years War) for control of the eastern United States.

Accommodations
Fort Toulouse / Fort Jackson Campground, 2521 W. Fort Toulouse Rd., Wetumpka; (344) 567-3002; www.forttoulouse.com. Improved tent camping is available.

Restaurants
Must Stop Cafe, 60 Village Loop, Wetumpka; (334) 567-9955; www.muststopcafe.com. Southern food and homemade desserts.

17 Five Runs Loop

This is a beautiful section of the Conecuh Trail that will take you to Five Runs Creek. The creek is a wide, swift stream that flows through the forest into the Yellow River. The trail also leads to Blue Spring, a beautiful, aqua-blue natural spring pond great for swimming on hot summer days.

Start: Parking lot at south bathhouse next to Open Pond
Distance: 5.8-mile loop
Hiking time: About 3 hours
Difficulty: Easy to moderate (due to distance) over flat to mildly rolling hills
Trail surface: Dirt footpath, some sandy service road
Best seasons: Fall–late spring
Other trail users: Cyclists
Canine compatibility: Leashed dogs permitted
Land status: National forest
Nearest town: Andalusia

Fees and permits: Day-use fee per car
Schedule: Year-round, sunrise to sunset
Maps: USGS Wing, AL; *DeLorme: Alabama Atlas & Gazetteer,* page 58 F5
Trail contact: Conecuh National Forest, 24481 AL 55, Andalusia, AL 36420; (334) 222-2555; www.fs.usda.gov/recarea/alabama/recreation/picnickinginfo/recarea/?recid=30107&actid=71
Special considerations: Hunting is permitted in all of Alabama's national forests and may restrict access to trails. Please visit the Forest Service website for dates and restrictions.

Finding the trailhead: From Andalusia at the intersection of US 84 (River Falls Street) and US 29, take US 29 south 11.2 miles and turn left onto AL 137 South. Travel 5.4 miles and turn left onto Open Pond Road. Travel 0.3 mile and turn right onto CR 28 (Tower Road). Travel 1.1 miles and come to a Y. There is a self-pay kiosk here. Pay your day-use fee and put the tag in your window. Take the left fork and park in the lot behind the bathhouse. The trailhead is on the south side of the parking lot. Three 6-inch-round creosote poles blocking an old, short dirt road mark the beginning of the hike. GPS: N31 05.408' / W86 32.675'

The Hike

There are two distinct sides to Conecuh National Forest. To the north are some amazing cypress ponds that you can visit on the Nellie Pond Loop. To the south is the wide and fast-flowing Five Runs Creek and a big, beautiful, crystal-clear blue spring cleverly called Blue Spring. You will experience the latter along the Five Runs Loop Trail.

The trail takes you far from the Open Pond Recreation Area, a campground that can be very crowded most any time of the year. Because you're removed from the

▶ Since 1947 the small town of Evergreen in south Alabama has been making Conecuh Sausage, with a unique blend of spices making it a favorite of Southern backpackers. It's an easy keeper and can be added to almost anything or is great on its own.

Your first glimpse of the Five Runs Loop Trail's namesake

madding crowd, you'll have a better chance of seeing some of the wildlife that calls the forest home. Many endangered species live here, including the flattened musk turtle and red-cockaded woodpecker, which was placed on the Endangered Species List in the 1970s due to timber cutting that resulted in the rapid disappearance of the bird's habitat. The good news is that cooperation among timber companies, government agencies, and private organizations seems to be resulting in survival of both the red-cockaded woodpecker and the timber industry.

This species differs from other woodpeckers in that it is only about 6 inches long, does not sport a red head, and resides in live trees instead of dead or dying ones. These woodpeckers prefer to burrow into live pines, taking advantage of the tree sap, which serves as a deterrent to predators and protects the trees from fire. The woodpecker got its name during the Civil War. The Confederate army distinguished the rank of its officers with a red feather, known as a cockade, on the side of their hats. The male woodpecker of the species has a small red cockade on the side of its head.

There is also a good chance you will encounter white-tailed deer, bobwhite quail, and wild turkeys, plus a variety of waterfowl including wood ducks, pied-billed grebes, and belted kingfishers.

As you walk the trail, keep an eye out for white-topped pitcher plants in the small bogs along the route. During the right season you'll see plenty of wildflowers, including pink orchids and black-eyed Susans. And in the warmer months, you'll definitely cross paths with snakes like corn snakes, black racers, and black pine snakes.

The highlight of the trip is the water features. You will pass both Buck's and Ditch Ponds, then come to Five Runs Creek. This is a wide and fast-flowing black-water stream that feeds the Yellow River and eventually flows into the Gulf of Mexico. The creek is dotted with small drops and shoals.

Finally you will come to Blue Spring. This is a beautiful crystal-clear, icy blue natural spring. It is so clear, you can see the rock formations far below the surface. The spring is plenty deep and makes a great place to swim in the hot summer months. There is a dirt bank on one side, while a retaining wall holds the bank up on the opposite side.

The final pond you'll come to is Alligator Hole. Alligators are sometimes sighted here. Heed the posted warnings. It is a federal crime punishable by jail time and a $5,000 fine for an individual, or $10,000 for a group, to injure or molest an alligator. I'm sure you're thinking the same thing: Who in their right mind would molest an alligator? Just don't tangle with them!

There are only two issues with this hike. First, if you do decide to hike this in the summer, be ready for mosquitoes, lots of them along the creek. The second is that all the trails in Conecuh National Forest, including the Five Runs Loop, are marked with the same white diamond blazes. There are a few times at the beginning of the loop that you will see white blazes on side trails that are not part of the hike. Review the "Miles and Directions" section carefully for tips on not taking the wrong path.

Miles and Directions

0.0 Start from the parking area next to the south bathhouse at Open Pond. The entrance to the trail is about 100 yards northwest of the bathhouse. Three 6-inch-round creosote poles mark the entrance (they are actually used to keep people from driving in on the abandoned dirt road at this point). In 300 feet pass a white-diamond-blazed trail on the right (south). You will see Buck's Pond straight ahead to the east. Continue straight toward the lake. In another 200 feet turn right (south) onto a second white-diamond-blazed trail. The trail is now a 2-foot-wide dirt path. Nice views of the pond are to your left (northeast).

0.5 Ditch Pond is to your left (west).

0.6 A trail comes in from the north. A sign here points the direction to Blue Spring to the east and the Blue Lake Recreation Area to the north. Turn right onto the side trail and head north. The trail is still blazed with white diamond markers.

1.0 Cross an abandoned service road. You will see an established campsite to the left (east). In about 400 feet cross another abandoned service road.

1.3 Pass a bench.

1.4 Cross a creek and wetland over a 25-foot-long bridge.

1.5 Pass a bench.

1.9 Cross FR 348A to the east.

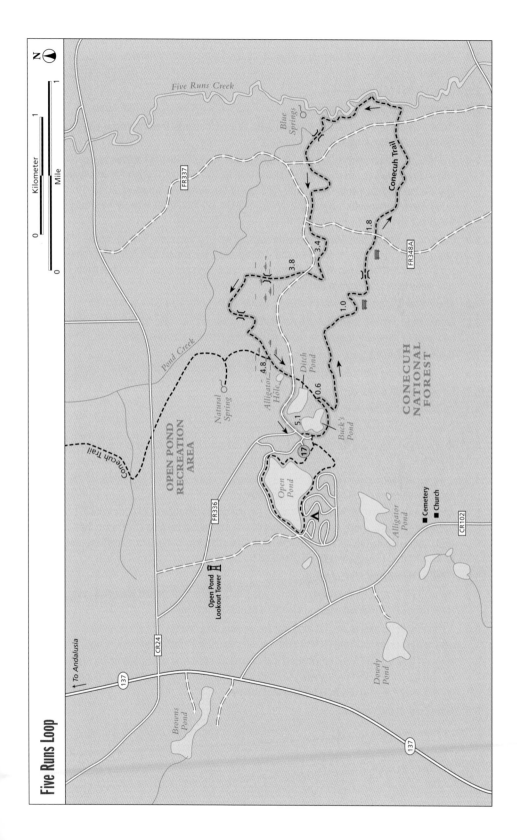

Five Runs Loop

N

Kilometer
0   1

Mile
0   1

Five Runs Creek

FR337

Blue Springs

Conecuh Trail

3.4

3.8

1.8

FR348A

1.0

OPEN POND RECREATION AREA

Pond Creek

4.8

Natural Spring

Alligator Hole

Ditch Pond

0.6

5.1

17

Buck's Pond

CONECUH NATIONAL FOREST

Conecuh Trail

FR336

Open Pond

Open Pond Lookout Tower

CR24

137

Alligator Pond

CR102

■ Cemetery
■ Church

To Andalusia

137

Browns Pond

Dowdy Pond

2.2 The path is more grassy here for a short distance. Look for pitcher plants alongside the trail.

2.5 Cross FR 337 to the northwest.

2.6 Cross a narrow creek. After the crossing, Five Runs Creek will be on your right (east).

2.7 Cross a runoff on a makeshift bridge: two 2-by-12-by-10 boards. There is a pond on your left (west) and Five Runs Creek on your right.

2.8 The trail is a bit washed out, about a 3-foot section. You will need to hop this one carefully. A steep bank to the creek is next to the trail. In 100 feet you'll see a line of shoals in the creek and then come to a Y. The right fork to the northeast is a short, 20-foot trail to the creek with a better view of the rapids. Take the left fork. You will be walking away from the creek.

2.9 Come to a T intersection. Turn right (northeast) and walk across a long wooden bridge. After crossing the bridge, come to another T with a dirt service road. Turn right (east) onto the road. In 200 feet arrive at Blue Spring. After visiting the spring, turn around and retrace your steps back to the bridge and cross it to the southwest.

3.0 After crossing the bridge, continue straight (west) on the wide hard-packed clay path.

3.1 Come out to a small, open, grassy area. In 200 feet come to a Y. Take the left fork to the northeast (a large brown sign that reads TRAIL is here, pointing the way).

3.2 Cross FR 337 to the west.

3.5 Pass a small bog with a few pitcher plants.

3.7 Cross FR 348A to the west.

4.1 Cross FR 348 to the north.

4.5 Cross a wetland over a 120-foot-long bridge.

4.7 Pass a wildlife food plot on the right. In 200 feet cross an abandoned service road to the west.

4.9 Cross an abandoned service road. In 500 feet cross a creek over a 20-foot bridge. In the right season there are wildflowers blooming here.

5.1 A trail comes in from the southeast. A sign here points the direction to the Open Pond Recreation Area (0.7 mile to the south) and Blue Pond Recreation Area (3 miles to the west). Turn left onto the dirt footpath (the blazes are still white diamond markers). You will be walking next to Alligator Hole on your right (west).

5.2 Cross a creek over a 15-foot bridge.

5.3 Come to FR 348. Turn right (west) onto the road. In 200 feet take the left fork of a Y onto a small sandy road that will take you along the banks of Ditch Pond.

5.6 A paved road T-bones at the dirt road you are walking on. Continue straight on the dirt road to the southwest. A sign here points the direction to both Ditch and Buck's Ponds.

5.7 The road crosses over a culvert (there is a short split-rail fence on either side of the road). You are back at Buck's Pond, where you started the loop. Turn right (northwest) and follow the dirt road the short distance back to your vehicle.

5.8 Arrive back at the trailhead.

The highlight of the Five Runs Loop Trail is a visit to the beautiful clear blue waters of Blue Spring, a favorite swimming hole for locals and hikers.

Hiking Information

Local Information

City of Andalusia, PO Box 429, Andalusia, AL 36420; (334) 222-3312; www.cityof andalusia.com

Local Events/Attractions

Sweetgum Bottom Antiques, 27388 Straughn School Rd., Andalusia; (334) 222-6647; www.sweetgumbottomantiques.com. Located in a restored 1875/1905 home, Sweetgum is a unique antiques store located in a country setting of wildflowers and wildlife and, of course, antiques. Open Thursday–Saturday 10 a.m.–4 p.m.

Lodging

Open Pond Recreation Area, Conecuh National Forest, Open Pond Road, Andalusia; (334) 222-2555; www.fs.fed.us/r8/alabama; 65 improved sites with water and electricity and 10 primitive sites

Restaurants

Hideaway Pizza, 922 River Falls St., Andalusia; (334) 222-5350

18 Nellie Pond Loop

This trail uses a section of the Conecuh Trail that is known as the North Loop. It is an easy walking path that takes you to two of the trail's highlight cypress ponds, Gum and Nellie. The path winds through dense, shady tree cover, and you're likely to see plenty of wildlife. Eastern wild turkeys and quail dart from the brush, hawks sail overhead, and frogs serenade.

Start: Parking lot at north Conecuh Trail trail-head on AL 137

Distance: 3.8-mile lollipop

Hiking time: About 2 hours

Difficulty: Easy over flat to mildly rolling hills

Trail surface: Dirt footpath, sandy service road

Best seasons: Late fall–late spring

Other trail users: Cyclists

Canine compatibility: Leashed dogs permitted

Land status: National forest

Nearest town: Andalusia

Fees and permits: None

Schedule: Year-round, sunrise to sunset

Maps: USGS Wing, AL; *DeLorme: Alabama Atlas & Gazetteer,* page 58 F4

Trail contact: Conecuh National Forest, 24481 AL 55, Andalusia, AL 36420; (334) 222-2555; www.fs.usda.gov/recarea/alabama/recreation/picnickinginfo/recarea/?recid=30107&actid=71

Special considerations: Hunting is permitted in all of Alabama's national forests and may restrict access to trails. Please visit the Forest Service website for dates and restrictions.

Finding the trailhead: From Andalusia at the intersection of US 84 (River Falls Street) and US 29, take US 29 south 11.2 miles and turn left onto AL 137 South. Travel 1.7 miles and turn left onto Hogfoot Road. Immediately after turning, turn right onto a short dirt road. The trailhead is only a few yards ahead. GPS: N31 09.225' / W86 34.413'

The Hike

Conecuh National Forest not only provides backpackers with a rare opportunity to do an overnight trek in south Alabama on the 20-mile-long Conecuh Trail, but also gives day hikers some interesting opportunities to explore the longleaf pine forest and its wonders. One of those day trips is the Nellie Pond Loop.

The Nellie Pond Loop is an easy 3.8-mile lollipop hike. The trail is a small section of the 13-mile North Loop of the Conecuh Trail. The trip to Nellie Pond described here is the perfect day hike that will take you to two of the standout features of the longer trail, Gum and Nellie Ponds.

The trail leads you through a thick longleaf pine forest. Dogwoods and magnolias can be seen blooming here in the spring. At the right time of the year, a little extra color is added to the scene with white-topped pitcher plants blooming in the bogs, white water lilies blanketing the surface of Gum and Nellie Ponds, and black-eyed Susans, honeysuckle, and blackberry bushes dotting the landscape.

Nellie Pond is teeming with wildflowers, frogs, and waterbirds and makes a great camping area for an overnight backpacking trip.

The area in which the trail travels, with all of its water features, makes it another one of those great wildlife-viewing trails. At the ponds and bogs you will see great blue herons, yellow-throated warblers, yellowthroats, and quail, plus hear many different varieties of songbirds.

Several species of frogs can be seen, and heard, along the trail around the ponds. These include the dusky gopher frog and the pine barren tree frog. Not long ago the dusky gopher frog came close to being named the official state amphibian, but lost out to the red hill salamander. While you will hear frog song most any time of the day, the best time to hear it is in the early evening when the chorus crescendos and echoes through the forest.

You are also likely to come across salamanders, box turtles, and snakes like corn snakes, black racers, and timber rattlers. Remember that most of the time if you stand still (at a safe distance, of course) and wait, a snake will move off on its own. And, as always, when there is a freshwater pond, there is always a chance that you might catch a glimpse of an alligator. With the trail being far removed from campgrounds and picnic areas, you may also see red or gray foxes, white-tailed deer, armadillos, and turkeys.

For the most part the trail is a 3- to 4-foot-wide dirt footpath, with the exception of the loop itself around Nellie Pond, which uses a sandy forest service road for three-quarters of the loop. There are a few benches along the way where you can take a break. You will also pass through two old abandoned cattle gates. Years ago cows grazed this land, providing income to farmers and the forest itself from leasing of the land to cattle farmers.

I know several hikers who like to use this short route for a quick overnight getaway. They'll throw a few things in their car after work on a Friday afternoon, hike in, and spend the night under the stars at Nellie Pond. There are some really nice areas to pitch a camp just off the trail to the east of the pond. Remember, campfires are not permitted. Use a backpacking stove.

Mosquitoes can be a problem along the bogs during the summer months, so hose down with insect repellent. Also keep in mind that hunting is allowed in the forest in the fall and winter. Visit the Conecuh National Forest website or contact the ranger station for dates and recommendations on hiking the trail at this time of year.

Miles and Directions

0.0 Start from the north trailhead on AL 137 to the east. A sign here tells you that Nellie Pond is straight ahead. The trail is blazed with white diamond reflector markers.

0.1 Gum Pond is on the right (east).

0.3 Best view of Gum Pond to the right (west) at a bench.

0.4 Pass through an old cattle gate. In about 100 feet cross a dirt forest service road to the east.

0.6 Pass a bench.

0.7 Pass through another cattle gate. In 100 feet the trail narrows as it heads through a tunnel of thick shrubs and hardwoods.

0.9 Cross a 30-foot footbridge over a seasonal creek.

1.2 Cross a 100-foot footbridge over a seasonal wetland. Be looking for pitcher plants.

1.3 Pass between two small ponds on each side of the trail.

1.4 Pass a bench.

1.5 Come to the beginning of the loop. Cross a forest service road to the northeast. An orange alligator warning sign is posted here.

1.6 Arrive at Nellie Pond. (*FYI:* If you would like a nice, short overnight trip just to get out for a night under the stars, this is an excellent place to pitch camp. Be sure to follow USFS guidelines, especially the one about not building fires.)

1.9 Turn left onto a sandy forest service road to the north. Some nice views of the pond will be had on your left along this section (southwest). (*FYI:* The Conecuh Trail and North Loop Trail continues to the east here.)

2.1 Pass a side trail to the left (southwest) that leads to the pond. Continue straight (northwest) on the forest service road.

2.4 Arrive at the end of the loop at mile 1.5. Turn right here into the woods (the turn is clearly marked) onto the white-diamond-blazed trail and retrace your steps to the trailhead.

3.8 Arrive back at the trailhead.

Nellie Pond Loop

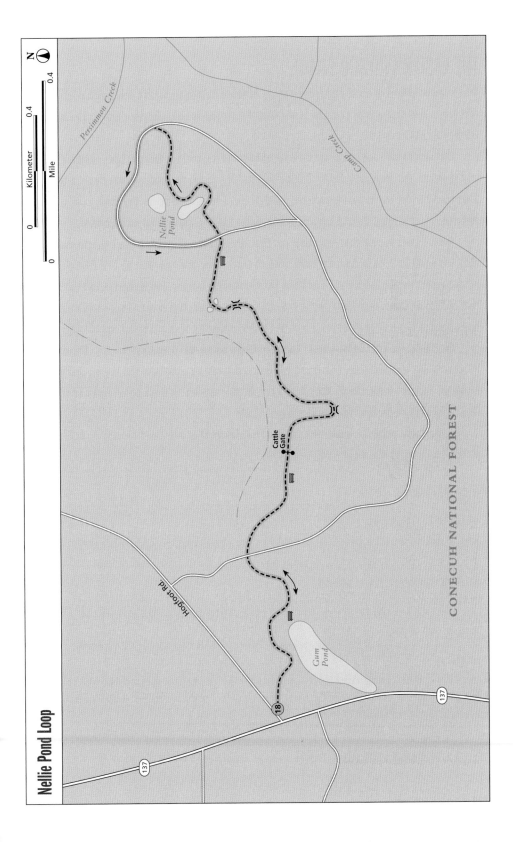

THE EASTERN INDIGO SNAKE

When you're hiking on state and federal lands in south Alabama, you will see a sign posted on kiosks, a wanted poster of sorts, that reads "Protected Species: Eastern Indigo Snake— DO NOT HARM!"

The eastern indigo is one of the rarest snakes in the region. They thrive in open, sandy, dry environments like those provided by longleaf forests. Due to the decimation of longleafs in the South and the decline in gopher tortoise populations (a favorite home for the snake is in the tortoise's burrow, often sharing the space), the indigo has become a threatened species.

The indigo is so rare that scientists say that the chances of spotting one are extremely slim. The snake is thick in diameter, with a bluish-black color, and can grow up to 8 feet long. Many people mistake black racers or black pine snakes for indigos. The biggest difference is that indigos are smooth-skinned, while the others have scales. It is nonvenomous and rarely bites, but it has a unique defense—it imitates a rattlesnake by shaking its tail and hissing.

The USDA Forest Service and Alabama Department of Conservation and Natural Resources are working hard to reestablish longleaf forests throughout the region and to bring the eastern indigo back. They have brought the species in from other areas of the Southeast in the hope they will breed and repopulate.

If you come across a snake that meets this description and can't identify it, take a picture and contact ADCNR at (251) 626-5474.

Hiking Information

Local Information
City of Andalusia, PO Box 429, Andalusia, AL 36420; (334) 222-3312; www.city ofandalusia.com

Local Events/Attractions
World Championship Domino Tournament, 200 Kiwanis Dr., Andalusia; (334) 222-2030. More than 300 competitors from around the world compete for the world title and over $20,000 in cash prizes.

Lodging
Open Pond Recreation Area, Conecuh National Forest, Open Pond Road, Andalusia; (334) 222-2555; www.fs.fed.us/r8/alabama; 65 improved sites with water and electricity and 10 primitive sites

Restaurants
Larry's Bar B Que, 1309 MLK Expressway, Andalusia; (334) 427-0140

19 Perry Lake Loop

Perry Lakes Park is a beautiful 600-acre tract of land along the Cahaba River. The park is filled with wonderful day-hiking trails, including this easy 1.5-mile loop that will treat you to a walk through an impressive hardwood forest, views of beautiful bald cypress and tupelo swamps with majestically flowing Spanish moss, and a bird's-eye view above the canopy from a 100-foot observation tower.

Start: Parking area
Distance: 1.5-mile loop
Hiking time: 1–1.5 hours
Difficulty: Easy unless you climb the observation tower
Trail surface: Dirt
Best seasons: Fall–spring
Other trail users: None
Canine compatibility: Leashed dogs permitted

Land status: County recreational area, Nature Conservancy preserve
Nearest town: Marion
Fees and permits: None; contributions requested for park upkeep
Schedule: Year-round, sunrise to sunset
Maps: USGS Summerfield, AL; *DeLorme: Alabama Atlas & Gazetteer*, page 36 H3; brochures available in box at park entrance
Trail contact: www.perrylakes.org

Finding the trailhead: From Marion at the intersection of AL 14 East / Green Street and AL 175 North, take AL 14 East / Green Street east 0.2 mile and turn left onto AL 14 East / Martin Luther King Parkway. Travel 2.2 miles and turn left onto AL 14 East / AL 183 North. In 2.4 miles make a sharp right onto AL 175 North. Travel 2.2 miles and turn right at the Alabama Aquatic Biodiversity Laboratory. Follow the dirt road 1.3 miles to the parking area on the right. GPS: N32 41.883' / W87 15.639'

The Hike

For years Alabama's Perry County had a little secret. It was a secret that was mainly known to birders and the students of nearby Judson College, but more and more hikers are learning of it. It's a gem of a park called Perry Lakes Park.

Located on the banks of the Cahaba River between the Alabama Aquatic Biodiversity Laboratory and the Nature Conservancy's Barton Beach Preserve, the park was originally a project of the Civilian Conservation Corps (CCC) and was opened in the mid-1930s as the Perry Lakes Recreation Area. At one time during its history, it was a US Fish and Wildlife refuge. The park remained open until 1974, when thefts at the adjacent fish hatchery forced its closing. The closing of the Southeastern Fish Cultural Laboratory in 1994 paved the way for probate judge Donald Cook, Judson College professor of biology Thomas Wilson, and a group of dedicated volunteers, environmental groups, and educators to begin the task of reopening it, and in 2002 Perry Lakes Park was reopened.

Perry Lakes Park is fantastic blend of hardwood forest and water features. In fact, this is one of the best mature hardwood floodplain forests in the country. A prime

The first stop along the Perry Lake Loop is a beautiful bald cypress swamp.

time to visit is in the fall when the beech trees blaze with vibrant yellow colors. The park also boasts four Champion Trees.

The many water features within the boundaries of this 600-acre tract include four oxbow lakes that were formed when the Cahaba changed its channel over 150 years ago, leaving behind not only the lakes but also picturesque Spanish moss–laden tupelo trees in the swamps. And Perry is a birder's paradise, with over 200 species of birds having been identified here (a complete list is available in the free brochure that you can pick up at the park's entrance).

There are three man-made features of interest. Near the parking lot are several unused buildings with a unique architectural design, built by students of the Auburn University Rural Studio. There is also a covered bridge over a swift stream and a 100-foot observation tower that you can climb to get a bird's-eye view of the park and river from above the canopy.

You will find several trails here that lead you to all of this beauty. But before I go on, I need to commend the work of the many volunteers, including those from the Judson College "Earth Team," for doing such a great job of creating and maintaining the trails.

The Perry Lake Loop is a nice, easy 1.5-mile loop that uses portions of the Ridge, Secret, Bird, and Perry Lake Trails to give you a good overview of the park. For the most part this route is a traditional dirt footpath with the occasional dirt fire lane. Travel is easy over flat terrain. The trail is marked with plastic green-and-red direction indicators tacked to trees or on red 4-by-4-inch posts. Major intersections have very nice wood-burned signs showing the way.

Like I said, this trail is a good overview walk of the park. Right at the beginning you'll cross the tin-roof covered bridge and soon after that come to the 100-foot observation tower, a decent little climb for those who care to make it (and can) but well worth the view. As the trail wanders through the forest, you'll have the chance to experience many of those picture-postcard views, especially as you walk the banks of Round Lake. As you near the end of this hike, there is an optional side trip on the Barton's Beach Trail that will take you to the beach.

Admission to the park is free; however, just after the observation tower there is a lockbox where they ask that

If you're up to the climb, head to the top of the 100-foot observation tower on the Perry Lake Loop for an impressive view of the swamps and the Cahaba River.

you leave a donation for park upkeep. Also keep in mind that after a good rain, some of the trail could be deep in water. When I visited, the Barton's Beach Trail was impassible. Needless to say, in the summer all this water means mosquitoes, so be prepared with insect repellent.

Miles and Directions

0.0 Start from the parking lot and head north on the dirt road that you entered the park on. The road parallels a nice, swift-flowing stream and Perry Lake. In less than 0.1 mile, cross the covered bridge over a wide stream to the northeast. The trail then follows a long board-walk. At the end of the boardwalk is the Alabama Red Hickory Champion Tree. There is also a lockbox to the right for donations for the park's upkeep.

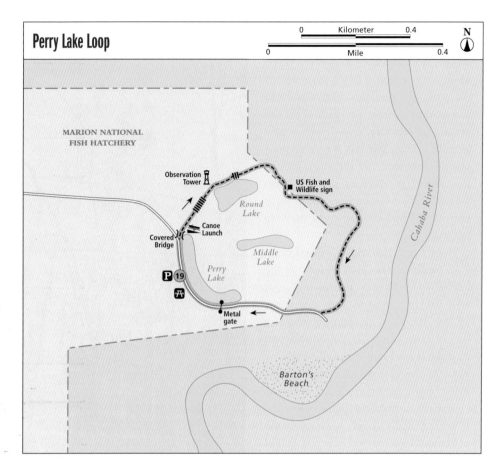

Perry Lake Loop

0   Kilometer   0.4

0   Mile   0.4

N

MARION NATIONAL
FISH HATCHERY

Observation
Tower

US Fish and
Wildlife sign

Round
Lake

Canoe
Launch

Covered
Bridge

Middle
Lake

Perry
Lake

P (19)

Metal
gate

Barton's
Beach

Cahaba River

0.1 Pass a canoe launch to the right (east). There are great views of the lake and tupelo and cypress swamps along this section.

0.2 Walk along another boardwalk.

0.3 Come to the observation tower. Feel free to make the climb, but take your time. It is a steep climb. Continuing on, the trail leaves the boardwalk and becomes a narrow dirt footpath. In less than 0.1 mile, cross a 30-foot bridge over a creek to the north. A wood-burned sign here shows the direction to Secret Lake. You will begin seeing the red-and-green trail directional signs on the trees and posts here. There are also several benches from here on. After the boardwalk the trail becomes a narrow dirt path. Watch for atamasco lilies in the spring along with silverbells.

0.4 The trail follows the banks of another cypress pond to your left (northeast), then narrows as it travels between two ponds. A rusty barbwire fence is between you and the pond to the right.

0.5 Pass an old US Fish and Wildlife boundary sign. In 50 feet cross a wooden footbridge over a creek. In less than 0.1 mile, pass through an area of smooth-leaf palmettos with a pond to your left (east). This section is low-lying and can be muddy, if not underwater, after a good rain.

0.7 The trail crosses through a boggy area and across a runoff stream for about 100 feet (be ready to get your feet wet after a rain), then turns into an old fire lane.

0.8 The trail dips down into a gully and after a heavy rain can be impassable. Your best bet is to take a route around the gully on the left (east).

1.0 Come up behind a sign that reads "Barton's Beach" (arrow pointing to left) / "Secret Lake Trail" (arrow pointing to right). Take a right (west). (*Option:* The Barton's Beach Trail (to the south) is a short, 0.1-mile trail to the only sand and gravel beach on the Cahaba River.)

▶ **The Cahaba lily can only be found in three states: Alabama, Georgia, and South Carolina. This beautiful white flower with a delicate fragrance requires swift-running water to grow. It blooms from late May to late June, but each flower blooms for only one day. The Cahaba River Society schedules float tours to see the flowers (see appendix A, "Clubs and Trail Groups").**

1.1 Come up behind a sign that reads "Welcome to Barton's Beach Preserve, the Nature Conservancy of Alabama." Just after the sign the trail crosses over a stream.

1.3 Come to a locked metal gate with a sign that says "Barton's Beach Cahaba River Preserve." There is a hiker entrance on the left to walk through.

1.4 Arrive at the dirt road that led you into the park. A picnic pavilion with restrooms is in front of you (east). Follow the dirt road back to the parking lot.

1.5 Arrive back at the parking lot.

Hiking Information

Local Information

Perry County Chamber of Commerce, 1200 Washington St., Marion, AL 36756; (334) 683-9622; www.perrycountyalabamachamber.com

Local Events/Attractions

Alabama Women's Hall of Fame, Judson College, 302 Bibb St., Marion; (334) 683-5156; www.awhf.org. Located on the campus of Judson College, the Alabama Women's Hall of Fame pays homage to the lives of outstanding women of the state, including Helen Keller, Tallulah Bankhead, and Julia Strudwick Tutwiler, to name a few.

Restaurants

Kalico Kitchen, 12310 AL 5, Marion; (334) 683-6739

20 Chewacla State Park Loop

Set within the rustic confines of this small state park just outside a bustling college town, the trails at Chewacla State Park offer a chance to get away from college crowds and provide excellent opportunities for bird watching and a view of the beautiful 25-acre lake and the falls at the CCC dam.

Start: Parking lot at CCC pavilion
Distance: 1.8-mile loop
Hiking time: About 1 hour
Difficulty: Easy along lake bank and ridge, moderate climb down to falls
Trail surface: Dirt and rock
Best seasons: Late Feb–May
Other trail users: None
Canine compatibility: Leashed dogs permitted
Land status: State park
Nearest town: Auburn
Fees and permits: Day-use fee

Schedule: Year-round, 7 a.m.–sunset
Maps: USGS Auburn, AL; *DeLorme: Alabama Atlas & Gazetteer,* page 37 B6; trail map available at entrance
Trail contact: Chewacla State Park, 124 Shell Toomer Pkwy., Auburn, AL 36830; (334) 887-5621; www.alapark.com/chewacla
Special considerations: This is a major SEC college football town. Check dates for Auburn University home games before traveling. The park is usually packed those weekends.

Finding the trailhead: From Auburn at I-85 exit 51, take US 29 south 0.2 mile and turn left onto Shell Toomer Parkway. Drive 1.5 miles to the park entrance to pay your fee or reserve a campsite. Continue through the gate on Murphy Drive 1.7 miles. The road comes to a loop with parking. The trailhead will be on your right side (north) as you pull in. It is a short series of cement stairs. GPS: N32 32.982' / W85 28.561'

The Hike

Located outside the town of Auburn just off of I-85 is Chewacla State Park. The park is 696 acres of hardwood and pine forest with a rich history, much of which is still visible throughout the park and along this hike.

The site has always been a popular swimming area. Chewacla Creek was a well-known swimming hole in these parts throughout the 1800s. In the mid-1800s a small sawmill was built here that was eventually purchased by W. W. Wright in 1873. The sawmill was highly successful until it closed in the early 1900s.

In 1935, as with many such areas in the state, the Civilian Conservation Corps (CCC) came in and began constructing a state park. The first order of business was to create a lake for fishing and swimming by building a dam which still stands, and which you will visit on this hike.

Other CCC amenities that you will see at the park include impressive stacked stone cabins, picnic pavilions, a bathhouse, an arched stone bridge, and 2 miles of

Water from Chewacla Lake cascades over the CCC spillway.

hiking trails. Today there are over 11 miles of hiking and biking trails in the park as well as a campground with forty-six improved sites and ten primitive tent sites.

The Chewacla State Park Loop is made up of three separate trails: the Mountain Laurel, Womelsdorf, and Fox Trails. Part of the hike tracks along the banks of Chewacla Lake and Moore's Mill Creek. If you plan on hiking this loop in the summer, bring plenty of bug spray.

The hike begins at the upper picnic pavilion. The pavilion is well used, so odds are when you arrive there will be a party going on. Your best bet to begin the hike is to park in the large paved lot in front of the pavilion and look for a short set of cement stairs heading down into the woods. Climb down the stairs and follow a short, 50-foot dirt path to the restrooms and then turn left (north). The trail is a well-worn path through here and easy to follow. It will take you behind the pavilion and then down to the falls on the Mountain Laurel Trail.

You will quickly see why this was rated a moderate hike. From the pavilion to the falls it is a pretty good downhill scamper, but one the average hiker shouldn't have too much trouble with. At the bottom you will come to the 35-foot-tall waterfall created by the CCC dam that built the park's centerpiece lake. The dam makes for a picturesque scene. Access to the falls is limited, with a chain-link fence surrounding parts of the pool.

From here on the trail is not blazed but for the most part is easy to follow. The path is a mix of dirt and rock bed that runs along the shoreline of the lake. This is the quiet side of the lake, away from the playground and swimming area. Most anytime you will be serenaded by frog song along this section. In the spring and early summer, the trail is thick with mountain laurel. In the summertime the overgrowth of brush may be a little overwhelming, so much so that you may think you are bushwhacking.

The trail continues until it reaches the stream that feeds the lake near Murphy Drive. Here the path turns uphill and uses the short Womelsdorf Trail to connect to the Fox Trail. The Fox Trail is a nice, wide dirt footpath enclosed with a good tree canopy. This is the best trail in the park to hike for bird watching. Also along the Fox Trail you may stir up white-tailed deer, red fox, wild turkey, and quail.

Keep in mind that being so close to the interstate and near a major Southeastern Conference football college, Auburn University, the park can be very crowded. During the weeks when there is a home game at the university, the crowds increase considerably.

And by the way, take a moment to view an interesting film produced by the US Department of the Interior in 1935 about the Auburn area and the development of the park at www.alapark.com/chewacla.

Miles and Directions

0.0 Start at the short set of cement stairs on the right (north) side of the parking lot. Head north 50 feet and just before the restrooms, turn left (southwest) onto a dirt footpath. Walk about 500 feet and you will cross over a CCC culvert just behind the pavilion. The trail turns right (northwest) and heads steeply downhill to the waterfall.

0.2 Go around a split-rail fence and in 50 feet the trail will turn to the right (northeast). A short side trail continues straight to the north to the base of the falls. From here the trail follows the banks of the lake. In less than 0.1 mile, the trail narrows to about 1 foot wide with a washout or two.

0.4 Pass a trail on the right that heads uphill back to the parking area. Continue straight to the northeast.

0.5 Come to the end of the lake, where Chewacla Creek flows in. This is a nice wetland with plenty of frog song. The path is a bit more thick and overgrown here but is well worn and easy to follow. In 100 feet pass through a short tunnel of mountain laurel.

0.6 Cross a short, 10-foot bridge over a runoff.

0.9 After thick overgrowth the trail opens up and you will see the park road on the left (north). In 150 feet come to a Y. Take the right fork (southeast) uphill on the Womelsdorf Trail.

1.0 Come to a T intersection with a wide dirt path. Turn to the right (south) onto the path.

1.2 Come to another T intersection. Turn right (northeast) onto the Fox Trail (you will see the park road on the left). The trail is a little bit rockier through here.

1.7 Pass a side trail to the creek on the right (north).

1.8 Come to the restrooms at the parking lot. Turn left (south) and head up the stairs to arrive back at the trailhead.

Chewacla State Park Loop

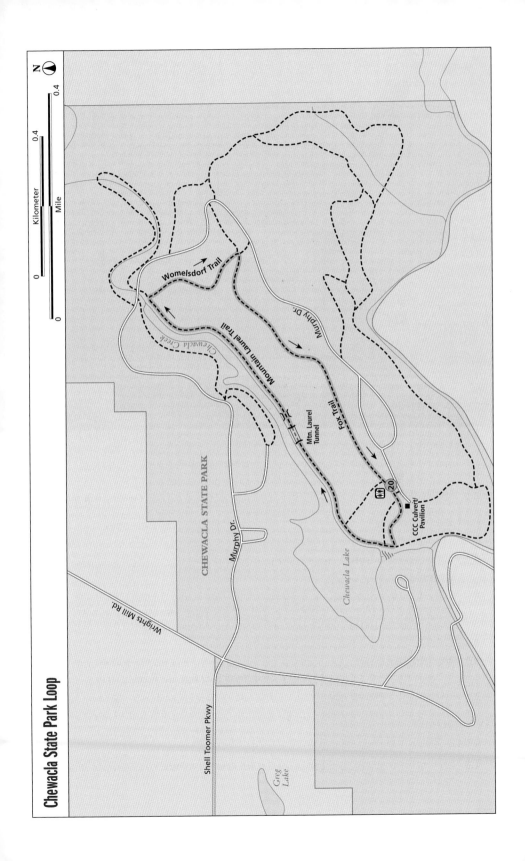

Colorful mountain laurel graces the trail that bears its name at Chewacla State Park.

Hiking Information

Local Information

Auburn/Opelika Tourism Bureau, 714 E. Glenn Ave., Auburn, AL 36830; (866) 880-8747; www.aotourism.com

Local Events/Attractions

Museum of East Alabama, 121 S. Ninth St., Opelika; (334) 749-2751; www.east alabama.org. This regional museum has over 4,000 artifacts providing a glimpse of east Alabama's past.

Accommodations

Chewacla State Park Campground, 124 Shell Toomer Pkwy., Auburn; (334) 887-5621; www.alapark.com/chewacla

Restaurants

Toomer's Drugs, 100 N. College, Auburn; (334) 887-3488

21 Wood Duck Trail

The Wood Duck Trail at Forever Wild's Coon Creek Tract will take you on a beautiful hike along a slough and banks of Coon Creek. Along the trail you will be treated to scenic views of the slough and creek, wild turkeys, turkey vultures and hawks soaring overhead, belted kingfishers, and the beautiful wood duck. Oh, and maybe, just maybe, you might see an alligator . . . maybe.

Start: Kiosk on west side of boat ramp
Distance: 4.4-mile lollipop
Hiking time: About 2 hours
Difficulty: Easy to moderate with some climbs up and down ravines on the north side
Trail surface: Dirt and rock
Best seasons: Year-round
Other trail users: None
Canine compatibility: Leashed dogs permitted
Land status: State wildlife management area

Nearest town: Tallassee
Fees and permits: None
Schedule: Year-round, sunrise to sunset
Maps: USGS McCalla, AL; *DeLorme: Alabama Atlas & Gazetteer,* page 46 A2; online at www .alabamaforeverwild.com
Trail contact: Alabama State Lands ADCNR, 64 N. Union St., Montgomery, AL 36130; (334) 242-3484; www.alabamaforeverwild.com

Finding the trailhead: From Tallassee at the intersection of AL 14 / E. Barnett Avenue and AL 229 / Jordan Avenue, take AL 14 east 2.3 miles. Turn left onto Macedonia Road and travel 3.1 miles. Turn left onto Hicks Store Road and travel 1 mile. Turn right onto Gravel Pit Road and in 400 feet turn right onto Coon Creek Landing Road. Follow the road to the boat ramp / parking area. The kiosk and trailhead is on the left (west) side of the parking lot. GPS: N32 35.838' / W85 52.831'

The Hike

Coon Creek is a feeder of the Tallapoosa River and Yates Reservoir near the town of Tallassee (the reservoir is created by the nearby Yates Dam). Much of the land around the creek is owned and managed by the state's Forever Wild program as the 320-acre Coon Creek Tract. Once again the program wanted to create recreational opportunities for the area such as hiking, paddling, hunting, and fishing, while at the same time protecting the natural habitat formed by the creek.

In 2009 the state built two new hiking trails on the property: the Overlook Loop and this hike, the Wood Duck Trail. The Wood Duck Trail is a 4-mile out-and-back hike (with a small loop at the turnaround) that hugs the banks of Coon Creek and the slough that feeds the wider creek. For the most part the trail is a narrow, 2-foot-wide dirt footpath with a leaf and pine straw bed, but it does use some old dirt roads to make its way around the creek. It's an easy-to-follow trail with excellent red paint blazes leading the way.

It is an interesting, and beautiful, environment that you will be walking through. For much of the trip you will be only a few feet from, if not directly on, the banks of the creek itself, with excellent views and a chance to hear frog song, do a little bird

Beautiful views of Coon Creek from the Wood Duck Trail

watching, or maybe see some wildlife like white-tailed deer or turkey vultures soaring overhead, or the telltale signs that a beaver was hard at work.

As you make your way to the east, you will walk the banks of the slough that feeds the larger creek. The slough is thick with lily pads, reeds, and hyacinth beds. In spring and early summer, it is a beautiful and colorful scene. Now, as my wife and I made our way around the slough, we were greeted by a *very* large splash. Was it an alligator? Chris Smith with Forever Wild and the Department of Conservation and Natural Resources, who lives in the area, says that he's never seen one here, but there are gators in the Tallapoosa River so it is possible.

The forest around the creek consists of mixed hardwoods and conifers. Walking around to the north side of the creek, you will cross a really pretty, wide, swift-flowing stream over a stout wooden bridge with a steel reinforced frame. As you walk through here, be on the lookout for wood ducks and wood duck houses.

Wood ducks are unique to the duck family. They have broad wings and crested heads and are more buoyant than any other duck, so they sit higher in the water and more of their large, rectangular tail can be seen. Wood ducks are slower flyers than other ducks, but they are nimble. Their broad wings give them the ability to thread their way quickly through tree branches.

Wood Duck Trail

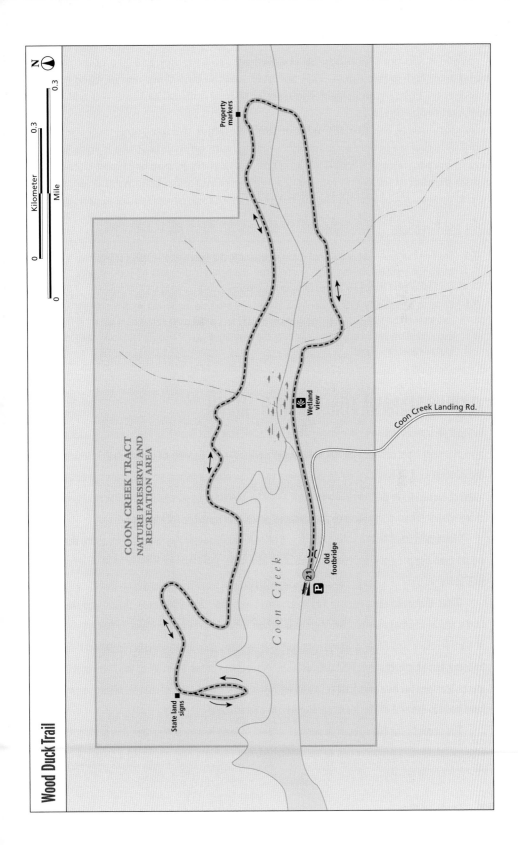

Property markers

COON CREEK TRACT
NATURE PRESERVE AND
RECREATION AREA

Wetland
view

Coon Creek Landing Rd.

Coon Creek

Old
footbridge

P
21

State land
signs

Kilometer
0   0.3

Mile
0   0.3

N

Wood ducks are found near creeks, wetlands, and swamps, and like other birds found here (such as kingfishers), they are cavity-nesting birds. They nest in abandoned woodpecker holes, natural cavities in trees, or special houses, like those you will see here, that people erect.

Unfortunately, the first 0.1 mile of this hike tends to have some trash strewn about. Whether it's people accidentally dropping items off their boat and it washes up here or because of easy access to a hiking trail with a water feature like Coon Creek, it is disheartening to see. If you can, bring along a trash bag and take some of it out, and help keep this area as beautiful as the rest of the trail. Your efforts will be appreciated!

Miles and Directions

0.0 Start on the east side of the boat ramp across from the information kiosk. For this first section you will be walking just a few feet from the banks of the creek on your left, with numerous side trails (10 feet or less) to the creek.

0.1 Come to a footbridge that is supposed to help you across a runoff, but as of this writing was washed off to the side by heavy rains. In 100 feet a dirt road enters from the right. The trail is right on the creek's bank. Just after the road there is a 50- to 75-foot rocky section with some quartz rocks.

KEEPING ALABAMA FOREVER WILD—AGAIN

In 1992 Alabama's House of Representatives had a brilliant idea. The state was receiving a large sum of money from offshore oil and natural gas wells. What to do with all of that cash? Besides the general fund, it was decided to put before voters an idea to take a small percentage of the interest earned from the revenue and set it aside for the state to purchase land that is of environmental or historic significance that without protection would be lost forever.

The public went to the voting booth and almost unanimously approved the measure that would fund the program for twenty years. And with that, the Alabama Forever Wild program was born.

Since that vote the program has purchased more than 200,000 acres of land and wetlands, and the acreage keeps growing. The program, administered by the Alabama Department of Conservation and Natural Resources, not only secures sensitive habitats for generations to come, but also turns that land into useable recreational areas. Most all of the Forever Wild tracts are open for hunting, fishing, paddling, horseback riding, and, of course, hiking, as you have seen in several of the hikes spotlighted in this edition.

The process for the agency to acquire a tract of land is very simple and has been quite successful. First, a property has to be nominated. Any resident may nominate a property for

0.2 The trail runs parallel to Coon Creek Landing Road on your right for a short distance and around the east end of the slough and wetland.

0.3 Come to a T intersection with a dirt service road. Turn left (northeast) onto the dirt road. In 200 feet you will have great views of the slough and wetland.

0.5 Cross a 4-foot-wide stream with a nice cascade down smooth rocks on your right.

0.6 Cross a 6-foot-wide streambed. In less than 0.1 mile, you will be walking directly alongside the wetland. The brush is a little thicker here, with plenty of smooth palmetto.

0.8 The trail turns right (east) onto an old dirt road. In just under 0.1 mile, cross a nice wooden bridge over a pretty, wide stream.

0.9 Yellow property boundary markers are painted on trees to your right.

1.2 You will be heading up and down ravines as you cross a few runoffs. This one is a deep gully. From the top of the hills, you will have nice views of the wetlands late fall through winter.

1.3 Nice view of wetland below.

1.6 Cross a runoff, then 50 feet later cross a wide bog. This could be deep in water after heavy rain.

1.7 You will be directly across the creek from the trailhead and can see it on the other side. In less than 0.1 mile, the trail is right alongside the creek with good views.

purchase, but it must be of historical or environmental significance. Once the property is nominated, the Forever Wild board of directors must approve the purchase. If they do, they will then approach the owner with an offer. Many times the owner isn't a willing seller. If that's the case, the process ends there.

Sometimes there is a property that comes up for sale but Forever Wild cannot purchase it at that moment. That's when other organizations such as the Nature Conservancy and the Conservation Fund come in to secure the property, with Forever Wild purchasing it from them at a later time.

But the last twenty years haven't been as easy as it sounds. In April 2005 state senators proposed diverting 30 percent of Forever Wild's funding to other agencies. When the bill was announced, voters were so outraged that they flooded the phone lines at the state capital. The bill died before the ink had dried. Then in 2012 the program was up for funding renewal. A bitter battle was waged between proponents of Forever Wild and those who wanted funding diverted, if not suspended. Once again it was brought before the voters, and again the public voted overwhelmingly to continue funding through 2032.

To learn more about Forever Wild, visit its new website at www.alabamaforeverwild.com. You can also learn about the work of the Nature Conservancy in Alabama at www.nature.org and the Conservation Fund at www.conservationfund.org.

Walking past the slough and wetland at the east end of Coon Creek

2.1 The path heads uphill on what looks like an old logging road but is now more of a runoff. In less than 0.1 mile, pass a sign on the left that reads "No Off Road Vehicles Allowed, State Lands" then come to a T intersection with a dirt road. Turn left (west) onto the road.

2.2 Come to a Y and take the left fork. In less than 0.1 mile, come to a T intersection with a dirt road. The left fork takes you to the creek. Turn right.

2.3 Come to a T intersection with another dirt road. The left fork takes you to the creek. Turn right. In less than 0.1 mile, arrive back at the Y at mile 2.2. Retrace your steps to the trailhead.

2.4 Keep your head up and watch for a right turn (it's easy to keep walking straight past it). You will see the sign from mile 2.1 on the right.

4.4 Arrive back at the trailhead.

Hiking Information

Local Information

Elmore County Economic Development, PO Box 117, Wetumpka, AL 36092; (334) 514-5843; www.visitelmoreco.com

Local Events/Attractions

Down by the River: An Evening of Storytelling, 300 S. Main St., Wetumpka; (334) 567-4811; www.facebook.com/events/177075282454851/?ref=22; Experience the character and history of this region during this annual storytelling event that is held mid-June.

22 Overlook Loop

The Overlook Loop on the Forever Wild Coon Creek Tract is best experienced in the early fall when the leaves of the hardwoods are at their peak and in winter when the leaves drop, leaving you with a beautiful view of Coon Creek below. The climb up is a rather steep one, but with a series of switchbacks and its short distance (only 1 mile), the hike is made much easier.

Start: Kiosk on west side of boat ramp
Distance: 1.0-mile loop
Hiking time: 1–1.5 hours
Difficulty: Moderate due to short elevation gain
Trail surface: Dirt and rock
Best seasons: Year-round
Other trail users: None
Canine compatibility: Leashed dogs permitted
Land status: State wildlife management area

Nearest town: Tallassee
Fees and permits: None
Schedule: Year-round, sunrise to sunset
Maps: USGS McCalla, AL; *DeLorme: Alabama Atlas & Gazetteer,* page 46 A2; online at www.alabamaforeverwild.com
Trail contact: Alabama State Lands ADCNR, 64 N. Union St., Montgomery, AL 36130; (334) 242-3484; www.alabamaforeverwild.com

Finding the trailhead: From Tallassee at the intersection of AL 14 / E. Barnett Avenue and AL 229 / Jordan Avenue, take AL 14 east 2.3 miles. Turn left onto Macedonia Road and travel 3.1 miles. Turn left onto Hicks Store Road and travel 1 mile. Turn right onto Gravel Pit Road and in 400 feet turn right onto Coon Creek Landing Road. Follow the road to the boat ramp / parking area. The kiosk and trailhead is on the left (west) side of the parking lot. GPS: N32 35.838' / W85 52.831'

The Hike

The Tallapoosa River flows from the Appalachian Mountains in Georgia some 265 miles until it merges with the Coosa River. Several sections along its route have been dammed, creating a number of lakes and reservoirs. Near the town of Tallassee the Yates Dam was constructed to provide power to the region. A side benefit to the dam was the creation of recreational opportunities in the area, in particular boating and fishing on Yates Reservoir.

In February 1995 the Alabama Forever Wild program purchased a 320-acre tract of land along the banks of a feeder creek to the river, Coon Creek, to provide environmental education as well as recreational opportunities such as fishing, hunting, boating, and paddling. In 2009 the agency added to those recreational possibilities by opening two hiking trails here: the Wood Duck Trail and this trail, the Overlook Loop.

Colorful mushrooms grow all along the Overlook Loop.

The north shore of Coon Creek is reflected in its placid early morning waters.

This aptly named 1-mile loop takes you high above the creek for some impressive views. Late spring through summer the foliage is thick so the view is obscured, but in late fall and winter it's really nice. In the spring the white flowering dogwoods brighten the way. All along the route you will see a wide variety of mushrooms and fungi like turkey tail, plus wildflowers including trillium, silver bells, and hypatia.

The path is a dirt bed that is well groomed no matter what time of year it is. Late spring through summer the thick foliage gives the route a nice enclosed feel (and the shade is welcome in the dog days). The trail is marked with a single red paint blaze, making this an easy trail to follow.

The Overlook Loop trail starts at the kiosk on the west side of the well-used boat ramp. There is a large topo map of the tract's two hiking trails in the kiosk. Now, don't be scared: Looking at the map of the Overlook Loop, it looks like this is going to be one long and steep climb to the top. Actually, the trail builders put in a good amount of switchbacks, and the climb is much easier than you would expect.

Your hike actually begins along the southern banks of Coon Creek. Throughout the first 0.2 mile you will be right next to the creek. If you like to fish, you might want to bring a pole so that after your hike you can wet a line for some spotted bass. As for wildlife, you are most likely to see white-tailed deer and wild turkeys, and along the creek, wood ducks.

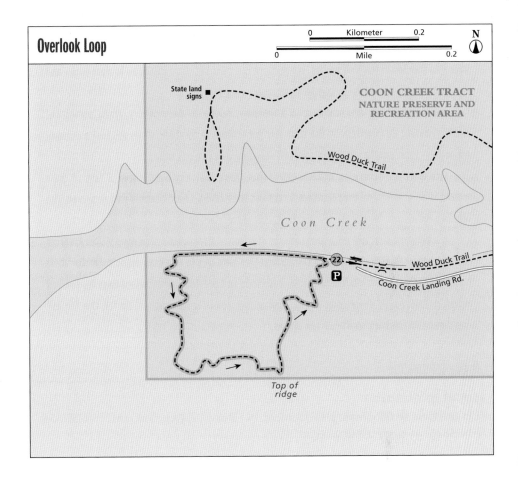

Overlook Loop

COON CREEK TRACT
NATURE PRESERVE AND
RECREATION AREA

State land signs

Wood Duck Trail

Coon Creek

Wood Duck Trail

Coon Creek Landing Rd.

Top of ridge

Miles and Directions

0.0 Start on the left side of the informational kiosk and head west. The trail is marked with single red paint blazes. In just a few feet, cross a 20-foot bridge over a stream that feeds the creek. You may see some termite mounds here. You will be walking only a few feet from the banks of the creek. In 300 feet come to a Y. The left fork is the return path. Go straight to the west. There are two nice, short side trails to the banks of the creek just after the Y.

0.2 The trail turns uphill and uses a series of switchbacks to make the trek easier. You will have nice views of the creek in late fall and winter and will see boat sheds and boats plying the waters. There are lots of mushrooms and wildflowers through here.

0.7 Arrive at the top of the hill. Once again there are very nice views from late fall through winter.

1.0 Arrive back at the Y that completes the loop. Turn right (east). In 300 feet arrive back at the trailhead.

WATCH YOUR STEP

Hiking in the South isn't all smiles. We do have our own set of annoyances to deal with—and one that affects many hikers may be right under your feet.

Picture this: You are standing in a meadow, taking in the scenery, when something starts crawling up your leg. By the time you get around to swatting at it, you feel a burning sensation—then another. You find yourself standing in a fire ant hill.

Fire ants are ferocious little boogers that think that anything within 2 feet of their mound is an enemy, and they'll attack to defend their home. Their name is well deserved. The bite is painful and, for people allergic to it, can sometimes be fatal.

It's believed that fire ants first came to the United States on a ship from South America that docked in Mobile, Alabama, in the 1920s. Fire ants like to use man-made roads for their travels. Road construction loosens soils, and loose soil provides an excellent base for fire ant travel. In the rapidly developing South, finding new roads is no problem. So far, the fire ant has spread to thirteen southeastern states.

Hiking Information

Local Information

Elmore County Economic Development, PO Box 117, Wetumpka, AL 36093; (334) 514-5843; www.visitelmoreco.co

Local Events/Attractions

Wetumpka River and Blues Festival; (334) 567-5147; www.riverandblues.net. Held annually in mid-June along the Coosa River walk in downtown Wetumpka, the event features the hottest blues and jazz bands in the region.

South Region Honorable Mentions

Cypress ponds and crystal-blue springs await the hiker in these lesser-traveled hikes through South Alabama that didn't make our top list. As with other honorable mention hikes in this book, these treks are typically shorter, but there is plenty of fantastic scenery and interesting wildlife to be seen. Pay a visit and let us know what you think. Maybe a particular hike should be upgraded, or maybe you know of some hidden trip that would make a great honorable mention.

D Frank Jackson State Park

The 2,050-acre Frank Jackson State Park is located in Opp, Alabama, 30 miles north of Conecuh National Forest and only 10 miles east of Andalusia. In the center of the park is a 1,000-acre stream-fed lake. While there is the standard fare of fishing and swimming here, several very nice nature trails provide excellent hiking, with one that takes you out onto a small island in the center of the lake.

An interesting time to visit is in the fall when the park hosts "Scarecrows in the Park." Over 300 unique scarecrows are displayed along the park's trails and bike paths.

For more information call the park at (334) 493-6988 or visit www.alapark.com/frankjackson. *DeLorme: Alabama Atlas & Gazetteer:* Page 59 C8.

E Eufaula Wildlife Refuge Nature Trail

The Eufaula Wildlife Refuge along the banks of the Chattahoochee River that borders Alabama and Georgia is a wonderful spot to view the widest variety of wildlife anywhere in the region. You can walk along the miles of dirt roads and berms that border wetlands or take in the Nature Trail, an out-and-back hike totaling about 1.5 miles.

This hike begins at the southwest end of the parking lot at the ranger station and is clearly marked with a wooden sign. The trail is a dirt road for its entire length. To the left are open fields used to produce hay for livestock. To the right, slash and loblolly pines tower above the trail, with magnolias and oaks intermingled. Along the trail many varieties of birds will be seen darting through the trees. In the fields be sure to watch for white ospreys looking for dinner as they follow the tractors cutting the hay.

For more information contact the Eufaula National Wildlife Refuge at (334) 687-4065 or visit www.fws.gov/eufaula. *DeLorme: Alabama Atlas & Gazetteer:* Page 54 B5.

F Geneva State Forest

Located just east of Conecuh National Forest in Geneva County is the 7,120-acre Geneva State Forest. It is described as the perfect example of a multiple-use forest, with wildlife management, forestry experimental work, and enhancement of environmental quality working hand in hand. Centered in the forest is a 100-acre lake and recreation area. New hiking trails are currently being built in the forest to enhance

133

your visit, including the Lake Loop which is now open and, as the name implies, circles the lake.

If you love bird watching, you're in good company. Groups such as the South Alabama Birding Association frequent the forest to watch for birds that call these woods home, including the rare red-cockaded woodpecker.

For information call (334) 898-7013 or visit www.forestry.state.al.us/geneva _state_forest.aspx?bv=2. *DeLorme: Alabama Atlas & Gazetteer:* Page 59 E9.

Ⓖ Conecuh Trail

The Conecuh Trail provides the best opportunity for a backpacking trip near the Gulf Coast region. The trail is a 20-mile point-to-point hike requiring a shuttle vehicle, but several connector trails allow for loop trips. The trail passes cypress ponds, bogs, and blue springs as it meanders through this amazing longleaf forest.

The trail actually is a dogleg using the 13-mile north loop (part of which is used in Hike 18, Nellie Pond Loop) and the Five Runs Loop (Hike 17) with a connector in between. If you are learning about backpacking, this is a great trail to do it on, with level to lightly rolling hills, plenty to see, and lots of routes out in case you have to bail. Camping is allowed anywhere along the trail using the dispersal method but remember, hunting is allowed and could restrict your access to the trail. Contact the USDA Forest Service at (334) 222-2555 or visit www.fs.usda.gov/recarea/alabama/recreation/ picnickinginfo/recarea/?recid=30107&actid=71 for additional information. *DeLorme Alabama Atlas & Gazetteer:* Page 39 G7.

Wildflowers blooming along the Conecuh Trail

Central Region

Alabama's Central region encompasses the area from just north of Birmingham to just north of Montgomery. Geologically, central Alabama forms what is known as the Piedmont Plateau, an area where the Appalachian mountain range terminates. The Central region provides the most challenging and some say the most scenic treks you'll find in the state. It's in this region that you'll find the state's highest mountain, Cheaha Mountain, which stands 2,407 feet above sea level. From high atop the mountain within the confines of Cheaha State Park, you get a spectacular view from Pulpit Rock, an outcropping hanging out into space.

The park is within the boundaries of Talladega National Forest. Here you will find many great backpacking adventures and, of course, day hikes. One of the more famous trails here is the Chinnabee Silent Trail, which will lead you past several cascading waterfalls, including Cheaha Falls, and to breathtaking views from atop a narrow wood and stone footbridge that clings to the face of rock bluffs high above the rushing water of Devil's Den.

One of the more famous trails in the state, the Pinhoti Trail, travels the mountain ridges of Talladega National Forest for more than 130 miles. A National Millennium Trail, the Pinhoti is a perfect training hike for Appalachian Trail hikers, and, in fact, the trail now connects to the AT, so you can walk the entire Appalachians from Alabama to Maine and beyond.

At Oak Mountain State Park, just south of Birmingham in the town of Pelham, hikers are treated to a beautiful waterfall along the Peavine Falls Trail, the tranquil serenity of Maggie's Glen, and an educational hike along the Treetop Trail to the Alabama Wildlife Rehabilitation Center.

For history buffs, just northeast of Montgomery is Horseshoe Bend National Park. One of only two National Park Service areas in the state, Horseshoe Bend was the setting for the decisive 1814 battle between General Andrew Jackson and the local Native Americans that resulted in the forced removal of the tribes from the region.

One of several historic mines at Red Mountain Park in Birmingham

Another historic trail in the region of note is the fascinating Tannehill Ironworks Historic State Park, where you will visit the old iron forge that once made munitions for the Confederate army and has since been rebuilt.

23 Smith Mountain Loop

The Smith Mountain Loop trail is short in length but oh so satisfying as you scamper up and around rock bluffs to the top of the mountain. There you are rewarded with spectacular views of Lake Martin not only from the summit, but also from atop a 80-foot restored fire tower—that is, if you have the energy to climb it.

Start: Smith Mountain trailhead on north side of parking lot
Distance: 0.9-mile loop
Hiking time: About 1.5 hours
Difficulty: Moderate up rocky hillsides and bluffs
Trail surface: Dirt and rock
Best seasons: Sept–May
Other trail users: None
Canine compatibility: Leashed dogs permitted

Land status: Deeded Alabama Power land
Nearest town: Dadeville
Fees and permits: None
Schedule: Year-round
Maps: USGS Dadeville, AL; *DeLorme: Alabama Atlas & Gazetteer,* page 39 G7
Trail contact: Cherokee Ridge Alpine Trail Association, PO Box 240503, Eclectic, AL 36024; www.cherokeeridgealpinetrail.org

Finding the trailhead: From Dadeville at the intersection of AL 49 / S. Broadnax Street and W. Lafayette Street, take W. Lafayette Street west 1.3 miles and turn left onto Young's Ferry Road. Travel 3.3 miles and turn left onto Smith Mountain Drive. The parking area and trailhead is ahead in 0.5 mile at the end of the road. GPS: N32 48.692' / W85 50.119'

The Hike

The summit isn't the highest in the state, only 780 feet, but the view from atop Smith Mountain along the banks of Lake Martin is spectacular, especially from the cab of the 80-foot-tall fire tower that graces the peak. More on the tower in a moment.

The Smith Mountain Loop is only one of several trails built by the Cherokee Ridge Alpine Trail Association (CRATA). Since incorporating in 2004, its members and volunteers have been busy building trails such as this all along the southern shores of the lake. Other trails in their inventory include the 3-mile Chimney Rock Loop and the Deadening Trail.

The trail itself is located on 10 acres of land that was once an Alabama Forestry Commission fire lookout from 1939 to 1980. The property was purchased by Alabama Power and eventually deeded to CRATA so that they could build this beautiful trail.

The trail is a steady but fairly easy climb to the top over a rock and dirt footpath. Along the route you will walk alongside and through some massive gneiss bluffs and boulders. Wildflowers such as mountain laurel and rhododendron brighten the path from spring through early summer.

Then there are the views. You are in for some really spectacular vistas as you walk toward the summit. Heading up from the trailhead on the north side of the mountain,

Stunning views are your reward atop Smith Mountain.

you will have a panoramic view of the surrounding hills. Then things get rockier as you make your way up and over the rocks past those bluffs and come to views of Lake Martin far below.

The trail then heads straight up one of those bluffs using a set of wood and stone stairs until you reach the top of the mountain for even better views—but it doesn't end there. An 80-foot fire tower stood here at the top of the mountain for many years, giving forest rangers a bird's-eye view of the surrounding forests for spotting fires. Along with acquiring the property, CRATA was granted permission to rebuild the tower, and under the supervision of a structural engineer, the organization set about refurbishing the structure, making it better than new. The tower was completed and installed in late 2011 and is now the centerpiece of the hike, where you can climb the ninety-seven steps and twelve landings to check out such lake scenery as Chimney Rock, Hog Mountain, Pleasure Point, and Sandy Creek, and the many boaters plying the lake's waters.

There is an excellent gravel parking area waiting for you at the trailhead that can easily accommodate twenty cars. The surrounding property is owned by Alabama Power. You will see roads heading up toward the top here. Heed the signs that ask you to not use those roads. It is private property.

The trail begins on the northeast side of the parking lot. A large white sign reading "To Tower" points the way. The path is well blazed with white paint markings. CRATA uses standard double blazes ("dit-dots") to indicate turns in the trail.

A couple of warnings are in order. While the climb is fairly easy, you do have some drop-offs around the rocky bluffs. Use caution. And being the tallest structure in the

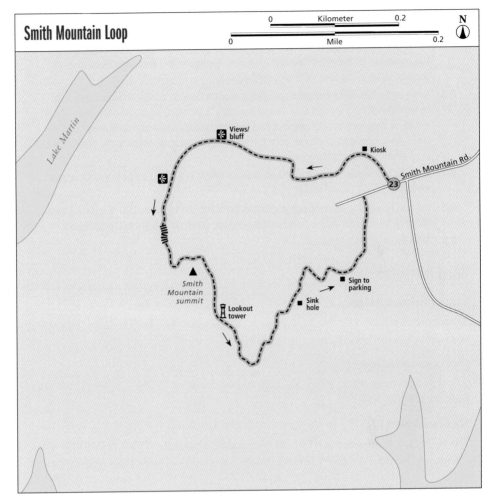

area on top of an open mountain top means that the tower is not the safest place to be in a thunderstorm. If bad weather starts moving in, move down off the mountain.

There is one other thing of interest at the summit. Once you get to the top, you will see the foundation of an old building. This building was once the ranger station for the fire tower. CRATA has plans to rebuild the structure in the future and set up a museum.

Miles and Directions

0.0 Start at the trailhead on the north side of the parking lot. The entrance to the trail is clearly marked with a white-and-red sign reading "To Tower." In 400 feet come to a kiosk with basic rules for hiking the trail. A large wood sign reads "To Tower / To Little Smith Mountain Trail."

0.1 Cross the dirt road to the south.

0.3 The trees begin to thin out and you start seeing views of the surrounding hills to the north along a nice rock bluff and outcropping. There is an Alabama Power No Trespassing sign here. The path is a 2-foot-wide rocky bed and lined with mountain laurel.

0.4 Come to a Y at a sign that points the direction to the tower and the Smith Mountain / Lakeshore Trail. Take the left fork to the south (to tower). In less than 0.1 mile, come to another Y at a sign that points the direction to the boat landing / Island Hop Trail / Little Smith Mountain Trail (to the right). Take the left fork to the south. In a few yards climb a set of wooden stairs to the east, up a rock outcropping.

0.5 Arrive at the top of the mountain, passing a foundation with a brick chimney. There is a cement bench on the north side. Follow the ridge to the southwest to the fire tower. There is a kiosk here with a list of climbers and summit toppers and a register (please sign in). Great views here and, of course, atop the tower. After exploring, return to the trail (it continues under the tower to the south).

0.7 Come to a sinkhole in the trail. A short wooden bridge crosses it. It's best to walk around the hole.

0.8 The trail leaves the outcroppings and ducks back into the forest. In 100 feet pass a sign showing the direction to the tower and parking lot. Continue straight to the northeast.

0.9 Arrive back at the trailhead.

Hiking Information

Local Information

Tallapoosa County, 125 N. Broadnax St., Dadeville, AL 36853; (256) 825-9242; www.tallapoosa.infomedia.net

Accommodations

Wind Creek State Park, 4325 AL 128, Alexander City; (256) 329-0845; www.ala park.com/windcreek

Restaurants

Uncle Nick's Smokehouse, 7051 AL 49 South, Dadeville; (256) 307-1405; www .nicksmokehouse.com. Great barbecue with a beautiful view of Lake Martin.

CREAMY CHICKEN AND RICE

A really delicious, easy to make, and easy packing meal for those overnight hikes.

  1 cup instant rice

  ½ package mushroom soup mix

  ½ package onion soup mix

  1 teaspoon dry milk

  1½ cups water

  1 (5-ounce) can or package chicken

At home, mix the dry ingredients together and place in a ziplock bag. On the trail, boil the water and add the dry ingredients. When the rice is done, stir in the chicken. Makes 1 serving.

24 Horseshoe Bend Nature Trail

This is an easy, 2.5-mile trek that takes the hiker along dirt and gravel paths through beautiful white oak, hickory, chestnut, and dogwood trees; over gently rolling, grassy hillsides; and along the banks of the Tallapoosa River. The trail visits several interpretive exhibits that trace the history of the Battle of Horseshoe Bend that ended the Creek Indian War in 1814.

Start: North side of Overlook parking lot
Distance: 2.5-mile loop
Hiking time: About 1.5 hours
Difficulty: Easy over rolling hills
Trail surface: Dirt footpath, very little paved trail
Best seasons: Year-round
Other trail users: None
Canine compatibility: Leashed dogs permitted
Land status: National military park
Nearest town: Alexander City

Fees and permits: None; donation requested
Schedule: Trails open year-round 8 a.m.–5 p.m.; visitor center open 9 a.m.–4:30 p.m.; closed Thanksgiving, Christmas, and New Year's Day
Maps: USGS Buttston, AL; *DeLorme: Alabama Atlas & Gazetteer*, page 39 D8; trail map and brochure available at visitor center.
Trail contact: Horseshoe Bend NMP, 11288 Horseshoe Bend Rd., Daviston, AL 36256; (256) 234-7111; www.nps.gov/hobe

Finding the trailhead: From Alexander City at the intersection of AL 22 and Madison Street, take AL 22 east 12.8 miles. Turn right onto Hamlet Mill Road and travel 4.7 miles. The park entrance will be on your left. Turn left into the park and stop by the visitor center before you start. Continue past the visitor center 0.1 mile to the Overlook parking area. The trail begins here on the north side of the parking lot. GPS: N32 58.832' / W85 44.093'

The Hike

Horseshoe Bend National Military Park, located just east of Alexander City, is a quiet and serene park operated by the National Park Service. The park is off the beaten path, so for the most part you won't be encountering big crowds (the only exception is when the park hosts its living history days), which gives you plenty of opportunity to take your time and enjoy, and experience, the history and beauty of the park.

The park itself is located at the elbow, or "horseshoe," of the Tallapoosa River. The spit of land within the horseshoe would ultimately be the site of a major battle that brought an end to the Creek Indian War that ran from 1813 to 1814. Sadly, it would also see the removal of many of the Creeks to the plains and the acquisition of their land by the United States.

Before we hit the trail, a little history lesson. When Europeans arrived in North America, they bartered heavily with the Creek Indians and began a long and trusting partnership. The partnership was strengthened following the American Revolution, as the Creeks signed an agreement with the fledgling country guaranteeing their right to their land.

A monument to the Battle of Horseshoe Bend

Through the years leading up to the Creek War, many of the tribes in the South followed US Indian Agent Benjamin Hawkins and his programs for improving their way of life, especially in agriculture. By 1810, however, a split erupted between Creek tribes, separating them into two factions. One tribe, the Red Sticks, believed in Indian nationalism and feared the growing expansion of white settlements into the South. In 1813 a group of Red Sticks were told erroneously that war had broken out between the United States and the Creek Nation. Upon hearing this, the Red Sticks attacked and murdered several frontier families.

A Creek tribal council captured, convicted, and executed those who were involved in the murders, but Red Stick Chief Menawa vowed to eliminate everyone connected with the executions and remove white influences on the region. And with that, the Creek War began.

Battles were fought throughout the region. General Andrew Jackson was in charge of US forces, but despite outnumbering the Creeks in every battle, Jackson could not bring a decisive end to the war. The situation became worse in July 1813 when a group of Creeks ambushed a Red Stick ammunition train. In retaliation, the Red Sticks attacked and massacred 250 settlers in Fort Mims, located just outside of present-day Bay Minette.

The war raged for two years, until it moved to this location, which was called *Cholocco Litabixee* (horses flat foot) by the Creeks, Horseshoe Bend by the United States. Most of the battle was fought by 2,000 men of a Tennessee militia and 600 allied Cherokee and Creek Indians. By the end of the battle, 1,000 Red Sticks were dead, and soon after, this land was ceded to the United States.

The park trail takes you through some interesting scenery and key sites of the battle. Be sure to pick up a free brochure at the visitor center before starting, which describes the exhibits and the battle in more detail. Also ask the park ranger to see the fifteen-minute video that gives an overview of the battle and the park. The trail passes most of the exhibits in the park that describe the battle. The exhibits contain text panels describing what to look for and benches, and each has a roof over it for a little shade.

The hike is a very easy 2.5-mile loop over gravel and dirt footpaths about 3 to 4 feet wide through white oak, hickory, chestnut, and dogwood trees, and along the banks of the Tallapoosa River. Families of white-tailed deer share the path with hikers.

Admission to the park is free, but a donation is requested to help maintain the facility.

Miles and Directions

0.0 Start at the Overlook parking area. The trail begins as a paved path on the north side of the parking lot.

0.1 A short, 50-foot walkway takes you to the overlook above the battlefield. An informational kiosk is here. When done viewing, head back to the main trail and turn right (southeast). Here the path is crushed gravel as it heads into the woods.

0.4 Walk alongside a nice seasonal stream on your right. In 100 feet cross the stream over a 20-foot wooden bridge and again in another 100 feet.

0.5 Cross the stream twice more over wooden bridges.

0.6 Pass a bench. Start seeing the Tallapoosa River to the left (east).

0.7 Pass another bench and a better view of the river to the left (east). Young bamboo plants grow here.

0.9 Cross an old dirt service road to the southwest (a brown post with a very small black arrow points the direction in front of you). In 200 feet pass a bog on your left.

1.0 Come to a large open field on your left (east) side. The trail skirts the edge of the field to the southwest before heading back into the woods.

1.3 Pass another bench just before crossing the paved tour road to the northwest. In 300 feet come to a parking lot and walk along the north side of the lot. The trail continues on the west and is once again paved for a short distance.

1.4 Arrive at the Village Overlook. After viewing and reading, turn left and continue on the dirt and gravel path to the north.

1.6 Cross a footbridge over a ditch, then cross the paved tour road to the north. You will hear the rushing waters of a long set of shoals in the distance.

1.8 Pass a bench.

1.9 Cross the paved tour road to the southwest. Here in the field across the road white poles mark "The Barricade." After crossing, follow the south side of the parking lot and rejoin the trail (now a paved path again) to the north.

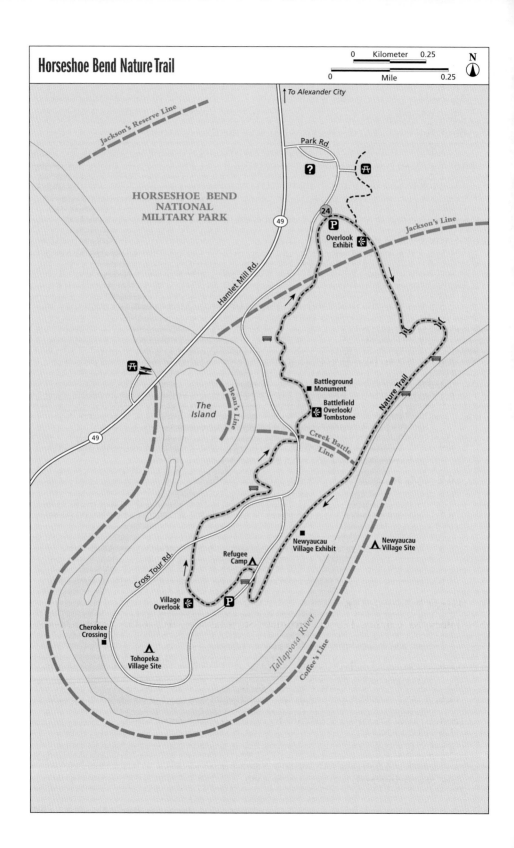

Horseshoe Bend Nature Trail

0 Kilometer 0.25

0 Mile 0.25

N

To Alexander City

Park Rd.

Jackson's Reserve Line

HORSESHOE BEND
NATIONAL
MILITARY PARK

Hamlet Mill Rd.

49

24

P

Overlook
Exhibit

Jackson's Line

Bean's Line

The
Island

Battleground
Monument

Battlefield
Overlook/
Tombstone

Nature Trail

Creek Battle
Line

49

Cross Tour Rd.

Newyaucau
Village Exhibit

Newyaucau
Village Site

Refugee
Camp

Village
Overlook

P

Cherokee
Crossing

Tohopeka
Village Site

Tallapoosa River

Coffee's Line

Your first view of the wide and swift Tallapoosa River

2.0 Arrive at an exhibit overlooking the battlefield. In 100 feet to the northeast, view the grave of Lemuel Purnell Montgomery. The trail turns left here at the exhibit (north).

2.1 Come to the battle monument. Continue on the dirt and gravel footpath to the southwest.

2.3 Pass a bench.

2.5 Arrive back at the trailhead.

Hiking Information

Local Information

Tallapoosa County, 125 N. Broadnax St., Dadeville, AL 36853; (256) 825-9242; www.tallapoosa.infomedia.net

Local Events/Attractions

Battle of Horseshoe Bend Reenactment, 11288 Horseshoe Bend Rd., Daviston; (256) 234-7111; www.nps.gov/hobe. Held the last weekend of March, the reenactment is an educational experience featuring living history exhibits.

Accommodations

Wind Creek State Park, 4325 AL 128, Alexander City; (256) 329-0845; www.ala park.com/windcreek

25 Nubbin Creek Trail

Although the full Nubbin Creek Trail is 4 miles long (one way), the first 2 miles are the most enjoyable and are described here. The trail meanders gradually up the side of a mountain, passing two waterfalls and ending with panoramic views and a great campsite. The trail is lined with a variety of wildflowers in spring.

Start: Nubbin Creek Trailhead on Nubbin Creek Road

Distance: 4.1 miles out and back

Hiking time: About 2.5 hours

Difficulty: Moderate with a long but steady climb

Trail surface: Dirt footpath, rock near falls

Best seasons: Fall–spring

Other trail users: None

Canine compatibility: Dogs permitted, although it could be tough on older dogs making the steady climb; ample water available

Land status: National forest

Nearest town: Lineville

Fees and permits: None

Schedule: Year-round

Maps: USGS Cheaha, AL; *DeLorme: Alabama Atlas & Gazetteer,* page 32 F5; US Forest Service Pinhoti Trail Map #4 featuring Cheaha Mountain available at Cheaha State Park camp store or online at www.nationalforeststore.com

Trail contact: US Forest Service Talladega Ranger District, 1001 North St., Talladega, AL 35160; (256) 362-2909; www.fs.usda.gov/alabama

Finding the trailhead: From Lineville at the intersection of AL 9 and AL 49, take AL 49 north 10.7 miles and turn left onto Nubbin Creek Road (there is a brown USFS sign pointing the way at the turn). In 0.8 mile the pavement ends. Continue another 2.3 miles. The parking lot is on the right and well marked. The trailhead is on the east side of the parking lot. Don't use the wide dirt road on the left (west). GPS: N33 24.946' / W85 48.356'

The Hike

Waterfalls abound in Talladega National Forest, and the Nubbin Creek Trail highlights a couple of them. The trek described here is a 4.1-mile out-and-back. The actual full trail is 4 miles long and ends at its intersection with the Cave Creek Trail, but my favorite section is the first 2 miles, and for good reason: There is a water-filled gorge, two waterfalls, nice mountain views, and a terrific campsite if you want to take an easy overnight backpacking trip.

Overall, the trail is not too difficult, but you will find that it is a steady, moderate climb up and around rocky waterfalls and streams to the turnaround. The most picturesque time to hike the trail is in early to mid-spring, when rains fill the creeks and the waterfalls run full. Late September through October is another great time—the foliage is fantastic!

From its beginning at the Nubbin Creek Trailhead, the route is narrow, with longleaf pines, white oak, and thick brush giving the path an enclosed feeling. When hiking in spring you will find yourself walking through a few "tunnels" of beautiful white mountain laurel.

One of several stream crossings along the Nubbin Creek Trail

Details on trail conditions and national forest rules are posted on an information board near the start of the trail. Sometimes there is a register here. If it's there, it is a good idea to fill it out before starting your trip in the Cheaha Wilderness. You never know when you might want searchers to be able to find you in an emergency.

The trail winds gradually uphill, and before long you will hear the sounds of Mill Shoals Creek. The first of two short side trails toward the creek comes in from the right. This first side trail goes about 100 yards to the banks of the fast-flowing creek. But the real scenery is on the second side trail, which takes off about another 100 feet farther along. This short path takes you to the edge of a bluff that rises above the creek, which tumbles here over a series of falls. This is definitely the highlight view of the trip.

Back on the trail, you'll hike through an area where white bloodroot and tooth-wort dot the sides of the path in spring. In places where the trees thin, the surrounding mountains and ridges come into view; look for white dogwoods on the hillsides.

You will cross two streams with very nice waterfalls along the route. The first comes at mile 1.2, with several cascades tumbling down the rocky slope. At the 1.6-mile mark—about the time you can hear and spot the next waterfall ahead—the trail makes its way along the side of a ravine and becomes little more than a ledge about a foot wide. Pay attention to your footing. At one point a feeder creek to the stream far below cuts across the trail. The path is a bit washed out here, so be careful as you make your way around this spot.

Shortly after the washout you'll reach the second falls, another beautiful tiered cascade. The trail crosses the creek at the base of the falls. From here the trail makes

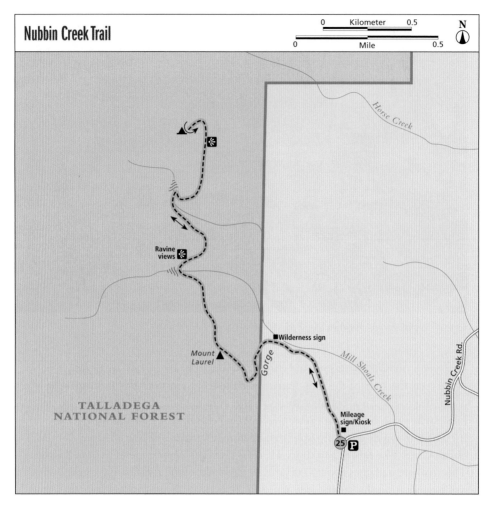

its way just below a ridge for nice mountain views, especially in late fall and winter when the leaves are down.

The turnaround for this trip is a great campsite right on the trail. It is a large, flat area with ample room for several tents. A very large fire ring was built here, and the area is groomed (raked) to help prevent fires. If you're looking to get away for a night, I highly recommend this spot.

Miles and Directions

0.0 Start from the Nubbin Creek Trailhead on Nubbin Creek Road. Don't make the mistake of heading down the trail on the left (west)! The actual trail is on the right (east) side. In a few yards come to a sign showing Cave Creek Trail ahead in 2 miles, Odum Trail 4 miles, and in a few more feet pass a kiosk on the left.

0.5 Mill Shoals Creek flows swiftly on your right (north). Just after passing a sign indicating you are now in the Cheaha Wilderness, pass a side trail to the creek and in 100 feet pass a short side trail leading to an overlook into a gorge (the trail may be overgrown and difficult to find). In another 100 feet cross a small creek.

0.6 Walking alongside a small creek on the left.

0.8 Pass through a thick section of mountain laurel. In less than 0.1 mile, cross a seasonal stream.

0.9 Cross an intermittent stream.

1.0 Cross an intermittent stream.

1.1 The trail narrows to less than 1 foot, with a sharp drop-off to the right (northeast). You will start hearing the sounds of the first falls.

1.2 Just before coming to the first falls, a small runoff stream flows down. The stream is washing away a portion of the trail. Cross cautiously. In just a few yards, come to the first waterfall. Cross the stream to the northeast.

1.3 Nice views of the ravine to the right (southeast) in the winter.

1.5 Walk through a tunnel of mountain laurel. A nice creek flows on your right, which you will cross in 100 feet.

1.6 Come to the second waterfall. Cross the stream to the southeast.

1.7 Nice wintertime views of the surrounding mountains and valley to the east.

1.9 The trail becomes thick with small hardwoods for about 200 yards, then opens up and levels out.

2.0 Come to a really nice campground. This is the turnaround for this trip. Head back to the trailhead. (*Option:* Extend the trip by continuing straight to the intersection with the Cave Creek Trail. You can make this into an excellent weekend backpacking trip by using the Nubbin, Cave Creek, Odum Scout, and Pinhoti Trails. See the US Forest Service Pinhoti Trail Map #4 for information.)

4.1 Arrive back at the trailhead.

Hiking Information

Local Information

Clay County Chamber of Commerce, 88855 AL 9, Lineville, AL 36266; (256) 396-2828; www.alabamaclaycounty.com

Local Events/Attractions

Clay County Blueberry Festival, 37993 AL 77, Ashland; (256) 354-7778; www.ccca.us. Held annually the middle of June, the festival features blueberries—what else?—and lots of them, with a blueberry bake-off, pie-eating contest, music, and more.

Lodging

Cheaha State Park Campground, 19644 AL 281, Delta; (256) 488-5111; www.alapark.com/cheaharesort. The park has 4 campgrounds with 73 improved (water and electricity) sites and 55 primitive sites.

Restaurants

Court Square Cafe, 20 Court Square, Ashland; (256) 354-5000. Great down-home cooking.

26 Chinnabee Silent Trail

The Chinnabee Silent Trail, meandering up a hillside from Lake Chinnabee, show-cases the beauty of Talladega National Forest. Along the way, the wonders of the forest are revealed again and again. Just when you think it can't get any better, it does. You will pass a great swimming hole with beautiful waterfalls, find yourself climbing high above a gorge along an elevated wooden platform clinging to a rock wall, and visit a gorgeous three-level waterfall.

Start: Lake Chinnabee Recreation Area
Distance: 5.4 miles out and back
Hiking time: About 2.5 hours
Difficulty: Moderate climbs and some stairs
Trail surface: Dirt and rock
Best seasons: Fall–early summer
Other trail users: None
Canine compatibility: Dogs permitted, although it could be tough on older dogs making the climbs; ample water available
Land status: National forest
Nearest town: Lineville
Fees and permits: Day-use fee per car

Schedule: Year-round; however, road to trail-head closed Dec–Feb due to freezing potential. Trail periodically closed due to hunting; visit USFS website for details and schedule.
Maps: USGS Cheaha, AL; *DeLorme: Alabama Atlas & Gazetteer,* page 32 F5; US Forest Service Pinhoti Trail Map #4 featuring Cheaha Mountain available at Cheaha State Park camp store or online at www.nationalforeststore.com
Trail contact: US Forest Service Talladega Ranger District, 1001 North St., Talladega, AL 35160; (256) 362-2909; www.fs.usda.gov/alabama

Finding the trailhead: From Lineville at the intersection of AL 9 and AL 49, take AL 49 north 14.2 miles. Turn left onto AL 281 South. Travel 4.9 miles (passing Cheaha State Park on the way) and turn right onto Cheaha Road. Travel 3.6 miles and turn left onto Lake Chinnabee Road. In 1.3 miles arrive at the Lake Chinnabee Recreation Area. The trailhead and parking is on your left. GPS: N33 27.624' / W85 52.464'

The Hike

Everyone who visits Cheaha State Park, Cheaha Mountain, and Talladega National Forest seems to return with endless stories about how gorgeous it all is: the overlooks, the waterfalls, the mountain landscapes. Sometimes it seems they exaggerate a bit, but seeing is believing. Cheaha Mountain—the highest point in the state, coming in at an elevation of 2,407 feet—and the surrounding Cheaha Wilderness is truly a sight to behold, with massive quartzite rock outcroppings, raging streams, and impressive waterfalls. The Chinnabee Silent Trail is rightfully one of the most popular hiking routes in Alabama because you will see all of that along its route.

The trail is named for Creek Indian Chief Chinnabee, an ally of Andrew Jackson during the Creek Indian War. The designation "Silent Trail" comes from the trail's builders. Between 1973 and 1976, Boy Scout Troop 29 from the Alabama Institute for the Deaf and Blind created the trail with the help of the USDA Forest Service.

Contemplating Cheaha Falls

The full Chinnabee Silent Trail is actually 6 miles long (one way) from the recreation area to its terminus with the Pinhoti Trail near the Turnipseed parking area on the Skyway Motorway. The easiest, and many say the best, way to experience the trail is to do it as a 5.4-mile out-and-back day hike which starts from the lake and heads south to the Cheaha Falls Shelter and the shelter's namesake waterfall before returning to the trailhead. And that's the trip described here.

The trail begins at the southern end of Lake Chinnabee and heads south following the banks of Chinnabee Creek. Here you will find beautiful cascades several tiers tall tumbling into a deep, cool pool. In the hot summer months, and with its close proximity to a major recreation area, this location is teeming with people swimming in the cold mountain stream.

The crowds thin out as you move away from the recreation area, where you find yourself climbing up the side of a rock bluff on a series of wood and stone steps and soon arrive high above an area called the Devil's Den. Far below, the waters of Chinnabee Creek tumble white through the canyon over the rocks, a beautiful sight from the platform.

At this point the trail moves away from the stream and begins a moderate ascent up the side of a hill to the top of the ridge. Depending on the season, you may see wildflowers like spring beauty and downy rattlesnake plantain along the way.

At the top of the ridge, you will come to the Cheaha Falls Shelter. This is a spacious and popular shelter that is first-come, first-served for overnight backpackers. It's

ALABAMA'S FIRST LONG PATH: THE PINHOTI TRAIL

The ultimate backpacking excursion in the state of Alabama is the Pinhoti Trail, located within the confines of Talladega National Forest and Cheaha State Park.

Pinhoti is a Native American word, loosely translated meaning "turkey home." Since the first section was built by the USDA Forest Service and volunteers with the Youth Conservation Corps in 1976, the trail has grown in size to over 130 miles in length, was named a National Millennium Legacy Trail in 1999, and in 2010 was connected to the Appalachian Trail, so now it is possible to walk the entire Appalachian mountain range from Alabama to Maine and beyond.

Along the route you'll find some nice Appalachian-style trail shelters, breathtaking panoramas, and beautiful waterfalls. If you're looking for something a bit shorter—say, a weekend backpacking trip—combine the Pinhoti with one of the many intersecting trails to create several different loops of varying lengths. Maps of the Pinhoti Trail (seven in all) are available from the Forest Service at the Talladega ranger station or at the Cheaha State Park camp store. Also visit the Pinhoti Trail Alliance website at www.pinhotitrailalliance.org.

usually occupied, and when you pass through, take the time to chat with them. Most love to talk about their backpacking adventures.

After passing the shelter you will come to Cheaha Falls, which is formed by the churning waters of Cheaha Creek. The falls is a series of cascades with a nice pool at the bottom. There used to be a bridge across the top of the falls, but Hurricane Opal took care of that years ago, so if you cross the stream, use extreme caution. The rocks are slippery, the falls high, and the water can be swift flowing. After visiting the falls, it's time to turn around and head back to the trailhead.

There are three other options you can consider when hiking the Chinnabee Silent Trail. The first is extending the trip all the way to the Turnipseed parking area. This would require either a shuttle vehicle if you weren't planning on spending the night or hiking back the way you came (that would be a 12-mile out-and-back).

A second option, and one I have done many times, is a single overnight backpacking trip from Lake Chinnabee to the Cheaha Falls Shelter.

The third option is a weekend backpacking trip using the Chinnabee Trail, the Pinhoti Trail, and the Skyway Loop Trail to make one incredible loop. Take the Chinnabee all the way to the Turnipseed parking area, where it intersects with the Pinhoti Trail, then take the Pinhoti to the Skyway Loop Trail, and Skyway back to Lake Chinnabee, a hike of about 17 miles with some good views along the Skyway Loop Trail.

Miles and Directions

0.0 Start from the southeast end of the Lake Chinnabee Recreation Area at the information kiosk. The trail is a narrow dirt and rock footpath through here as it follows Chinnabee Creek.

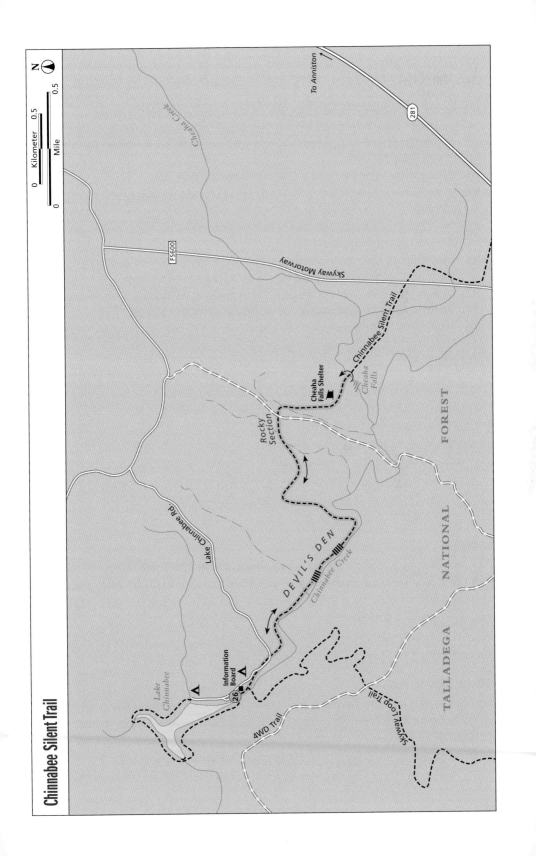

Chinnabee Silent Trail

0.2 Pass a sign pointing to the right that marks the turn for the Lakeshore Loop Trail. Continue straight and in 10 feet pass a stone marker recognizing Boy Scout Troop 29 for building the trail.

0.3 Pass a sign on the right showing the turn for the Skyway Loop Trail. Continue straight (southeast) and in 50 feet pass a sign giving mileages to Devil's Den (0.5 mile), Cheaha Falls Shelter (3.0 miles), Turnipseed (4.0 miles), and the Pinhoti Trail (6.0 miles). Continue straight to the southeast.

0.5 Begin climbing higher and higher on a series of wood and stone steps.

0.6 At the top of the climb, arrive at a 75- to 100-foot wooden walkway clinging onto the rock wall.

0.7 Devil's Den gorge is to your right down below. Spectacular views. The trail returns to a dirt and rock bed and levels out here.

2.6 After climbing a moderate hillside, arrive at the Cheaha Falls Shelter. Nice views of the mountains here, especially early morning. Continue straight to the southeast.

2.7 Arrive at Cheaha Falls. Feel free to explore, but be careful on the rocky bluffs and crossing the stream. When ready, turn around and retrace your steps to the trailhead.

5.4 Arrive back at the trailhead.

Hiking Information

Local Information

Clay County Chamber of Commerce, 88855 AL 9, Lineville, AL 36266; (256) 396-2828; www.alabamaclaycounty.com

Local Events/Attractions

Walter Farr Indian Artifacts Museum, 19644 AL 281, Delta; (256) 488-5111. An interesting museum of Native American artifacts donated by Walter Farr. The museum is located at Cheaha State Park directly across from the country store. Hours vary and tours are available. Call ahead for information.

Lodging

Cheaha State Park Lodge, 2141 Bunker Loop, Delta; (256) 488-5115; www.ala park.com/cheaharesort. A beautiful little hotel perched on top of the state's highest mountain.

Restaurants

Cheaha State Park Restaurant, 2141 Bunker Loop, Delta; (256) 488-5115. A great setting for dining with a panoramic view from the top of the state.

Other Resources

Trail Talk (www.hikealabama.org/trailtalk) and AlaTrails (www.alatrails.org) are two excellent nonprofit forums designed to keep hikers and backpackers up to date on the latest trail conditions, with detailed information about hiking in the state from the people with "boots on the ground." Membership is free.

27 Pulpit Rock Trail

What would a trip to the state's highest mountain be without some spectacular views? One of the best can be found at the end of the Pulpit Rock Trail. The rock is one of the most popular destinations in the park for hikers and rock climbers. It juts far out into space from a height just below the summit of the state's highest mountain, with breathtaking panoramic views.

Start: Trailhead near cabins 1–4 just off Bunker Loop
Distance: 0.7 mile out and back
Hiking time: About 1 hour
Difficulty: Moderate with a steep climb down and back up from the trailhead
Trail surface: Dirt, rock, rocky outcrop
Best seasons: Fall–spring
Other trail users: None
Canine compatibility: Leashed dogs permitted
Land status: State park

Nearest town: Lineville
Fees and permits: Day-use fee
Schedule: Year-round, sunrise to sunset
Maps: USGS Cheaha, AL; *DeLorme: Alabama Atlas & Gazetteer,* page 32 E5; USDA Forest Service Pinhoti Trail Map #4 featuring Cheaha Mountain available at Cheaha State Park camp store or online at www.nationalforeststore.com
Trail contact: Cheaha State Park, 19644 AL 281, Delta, AL 36258; (256) 488-5111; www.alapark.com/cheaharesort

Finding the trailhead: From Lineville at the intersection of AL 9 and AL 49, take AL 49 north 14.2 miles. Turn left onto AL 281 South. Travel 3.4 miles and come to the entrance of Cheaha State Park on the right. Turn right onto Bunker Loop. You can either pay your day-use fee at the camp store here at the entrance or at the entrance station only a few yards straight ahead. Continue straight on Bunker Loop, circling around the top of Cheaha Mountain for 1.5 miles. The trailhead and parking will be on the right. GPS: N33 29.042' / W85 48.891'

The Hike

If you're looking for a hike with a little view, check out Pulpit Rock at Cheaha State Park.

Cheaha, as you know by now, is the state's highest mountain, coming in at 2,407 feet. The mountain is part of the southern Appalachian Mountains, a range that was created eons ago, some say 500 to 600 million years ago, by the heating of the earth's crust. The crust was then compressed and thrust upwards, creating these peaks. Over the centuries the soft upper layers of dirt and rock eroded, leaving numerous quartzite outcroppings, such as Pulpit Rock. No matter how old they are or how they were formed, they make for one outstanding view.

There are two easily accessible overlooks in the park. The first is located at the end of the Doug Ghee Boardwalk Trail that follows the ridge of the mountain to Bald Rock, a bluff that towers above the surrounding valley. The second is right here at Pulpit Rock. The rock is so-named because it stands out—literally—like a pulpit high

The well-marked Pulpit Rock Trailhead

above the valley. The rock juts far out into space, allowing for an amazing panoramic view. From here, on a clear day, you can see up to 6 miles away.

The Pulpit Rock Trail is short, only 0.7 mile round-trip, but packs in a lot over that distance. For starters there are bursts of color throughout the year. From September through early November, the oaks line the path with brilliant fall colors. Then from early spring through summer, you will be treated to beautiful flame azalea and oak leaf hydrangea. And in the winter, there is always the chance of a white blanket of snow.

Of course, being at over 2,100 feet you can expect to see raptors soaring, including red-tailed and broad-winged hawks and peregrine falcons. You will also hear the song of evening grossbeaks and a wide variety of warblers.

The trail itself is very rocky and moderate in difficulty. That is because of the initial climb down the side of the mountain, an elevation gain (or loss) of over 100 feet in the first 0.1 mile. The average hiker will not have any problem with it, but someone new to hiking or out of shape will probably be winded by the time it's over.

Then there is the Pulpit itself. This is a favorite spot for rock climbers, but if you are a climber, you must register with the park at the country store before attempting it.

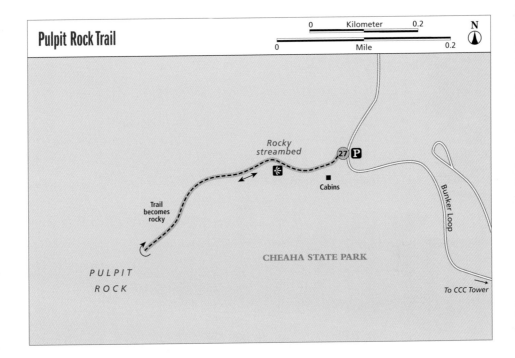

Pulpit Rock Trail

Kilometer 0 — 0.2

Mile 0 — 0.2

N

Rocky streambed

27 P

Cabins

Bunker Loop

Trail becomes rocky

CHEAHA STATE PARK

PULPIT ROCK

To CCC Tower

For the rest of us, while the view is spectacular from here, it can also be dangerous. Many people try to climb out onto the Pulpit. If you are not sure-footed, do *not* attempt climbing out there! And be extra cautious on the high bluff and boulders that surround the Pulpit. It's a long way down.

Miles and Directions

0.0 Start from the trailhead near cabins 1–4 just off Bunker Loop to the north, then to the southwest. The trail immediately heads steeply downhill.

0.1 Cross a rocky seasonal streambed. The path is thick with mountain laurel bushes and plenty of reindeer moss. In the winter when the leaves are down, shortly after this you begin seeing views of the surrounding mountains to the right (northwest).

0.2 Come to a Y. Take the left fork to the southwest.

0.3 The trail becomes very rocky as you walk over and around small outcroppings. In 250 feet arrive at Pulpit Rock. Explore the high bluffs and enjoy the view, but be careful! It is extremely dangerous. When finished, turn around and head back to the trailhead.

0.7 Arrive back at the trailhead.

Hiking Information

Local Information

Clay County Chamber of Commerce, 88855 AL 9, Lineville, AL 36266; (256) 396-2828; www.alabamaclaycounty.com

The best seat in the house

Local Events/Attractions

Alabama Outdoor Expo, 88855 AL 9, Lineville; (256) 396-2828; alabamaclaycounty
.com/alabama-outdoor-expo. Held the last weekend of August, the expo features
products and activities geared toward the many recreational opportunities in the area.

Lodging

Cheaha State Park Lodge, 2141 Bunker Loop, Delta; (256) 488-5115; www.alapark
.com/cheaharesort. A beautiful little hotel perched on top of the state's highest mountain.

Restaurants

Cheaha State Park Restaurant, 2141 Bunker Loop, Delta; (256) 488-5115. A great
setting for dining, with a panoramic view from the top of the state.

28 Maggie's Glen Loop

The Maggie's Glen Loop at Oak Mountain State Park is an easy 2.2-mile trek that takes you alongside a nice, sparkling—but seasonal—stream to the glen that is located in a hollow. The glen is a perfect spot for picnicking, especially in the spring with the stream cascading next to the trail and white beeches and dogwoods flowering around you.

Start: North Trailhead on Oak Mountain Park Road
Distance: 2.3-mile lollipop
Hiking time: 1.5 to 2 hours
Difficulty: Easy on the White Trail, moderate climbs on the Yellow Trail
Trail surface: Dirt and rock
Best seasons: Winter–late spring
Other trail users: Cyclists
Canine compatibility: Leashed dogs permitted

Land status: State park
Nearest town: Pelham
Fees and permits: Day-use fee
Schedule: Year-round, sunrise to sunset
Maps: USGS Chelsea, AL; *DeLorme: Alabama Atlas & Gazetteer*, page 31 G7; trail maps available at entrance gate or camp store
Trail contact: Oak Mountain State Park, 200 Terrace Dr., Pelham, AL 35124; (205) 620-2524; www.alapark.com/oakmountain

Finding the trailhead: From Pelham on I-65 at exit 248, take AL 119 South / Cahaba Valley Road 0.2 mile and turn left onto Oak Mountain Road. Travel 1.9 miles and turn left onto John Findley III Drive. In 0.3 mile you will arrive at the entrance gate, where you pay your day-use fee. Continue straight (northeast) 5.8 miles on John Findley III Road. Watch for the many cyclists on the road. The trailhead is on the right side of the road and well marked. Parking is on the left. GPS: N33 21.453' / W86 42.285'

The Hike

If you are looking for a fun and relaxing walk in the woods or if you would like to introduce your family to hiking, take a hike on the Maggie's Glen Loop at Oak Mountain State Park near Birmingham.

This beautiful little 2-mile loop follows alongside a nice stream that flows down from a hollow and Maggie's Glen. The stream tumbles down a rocky bed, making small cascades. There are several short (10- to 20-foot) side trails that take you to its banks, so you can take a look and maybe dip your feet in.

The trail's namesake Maggie's Glen is at the halfway point of the trip. There are several benches here thanks to local Eagle Scouts and access to the stream. This is a great place to just sit and take in the soothing sounds of the rushing water. It's also a good place to bring along a picnic lunch and let the kids run around and enjoy the forest. There is an informational kiosk here that provides plenty of information about the local wildlife.

Speaking of which, along the trail you are very likely to meet up with eastern gray and fox squirrels darting from tree to tree, white-tailed deer, or wild turkeys. Listen carefully and you may hear the sounds of the yellow-billed cuckoo or pine warbler.

Maggie's Glen is a great place to picnic and take in the sounds of the babbling stream.

The forest itself is a mix of hardwoods like oak and hickory trees, as well as your usual southern pine trees including longleaf and loblolly. Maggie's Glen is especially beautiful in early spring when the flowering dogwoods and white beeches bloom.

The trail begins at the park's North Trailhead. The trailhead will be on your right as you drive up the main park road, with a very large gravel parking lot on the left. There is plenty of parking for thirty or so cars, and it's a good thing since this is the main trailhead for several trails used not only by hikers, but by cyclists and runners as well. The parking area has a nice portable toilet and a little something extra: a his-and-hers changing room.

The trailhead is the starting, or ending, point for several of the park's trails. When you first set out, you will be walking on a combination of the Red (bike), White, and Yellow Trails. The trails are so-named because of their blazing. Shortly after setting out, you will turn off the Yellow/Red Trail and onto the White Trail. A sign here clearly marks the turn.

The trails are very well blazed, and it's virtually impossible to get lost. The blazes are reflective markers the same color as the trail you are on—white, yellow, etc. Along the route you will pass 4-by-4 posts painted the same color as the trail you are on that have numbers on them. The numbers correspond to mileages on the trail, sort of like mile markers along the highway. If you get lost or in trouble, you can call the park ranger and tell them you are on, for example, the "White Trail at [or near] marker 59" and they can easily come to your rescue.

This loop actually uses two different trails—the White Trail and the Yellow Trail—to complete the loop. The White Trail from the North Trailhead to Maggie's Glen is 1 mile long, level, and easy walking, so if you have younger children, you can take the easy route back by skipping the loop and simply retracing your steps to the trailhead.

The Yellow Trail includes some moderate climbs which you will immediately encounter as you leave Maggie's Glen. It is a short but steep climb up to a ridgeline. In the winter when the leaves are down, you will be able to catch a view of the ridge across the valley.

Several trails intersect at Maggie's Glen, and it can be a little confusing. There are directions and mileages posted on the kiosk to help out. If that doesn't help, keep this in mind: As you face southwest toward the different trail signs, you will see the Yellow Trail sign and blazes on your left. That's the way to go.

Miles and Directions

0.0 Start from the parking lot and cross the street to the North Trailhead (there are obvious signs here). One sign shows the distances to Peavine Falls (6.2), Peavine Trail (5.3), and South Trailhead (6.5). Go straight to the south. The trail starts as a 10-foot-wide gravel path and is actually three trails: the Red, the White, and the Yellow. In 400 feet the Red Trail (a 16-mile bike loop) splits off to the right.

0.1 Take the right fork at a Y (a sign shows that this is the way to Maggie's Glen), crossing a runoff ditch on a short footbridge. The trail is now a narrow dirt footpath.

0.2 Come to a Y. The left fork is our return trip on the Yellow Trail. Take the right fork to the west on the White Trail.

0.4 Pass white mile marker 27, then cross a stream over a 15-foot bridge.

0.5 You will be walking next to a creek on the right and will cross it over a footbridge in a few feet.

0.6 Pass white marker 28.

0.8 Pass white marker 29.

0.9 Come to a Y. A sign here points the way to cabins to the north (back the way you came) and Maggie's Glen to the left. Take the left fork.

1.0 The trail begins to parallel a wide stream on the right with nice cascades.

BAMA FIRSTS

- Alabama was the first state to declare Christmas a legal holiday in 1836.
- Mobile held the first Mardi Gras celebration in the United States in 1830 and is now known as the "Mother of Mystics."
- The world's first electric trolley system was introduced in Montgomery in 1886.
- Orville and Wilbur Wright opened the nation's first aviation school near Montgomery (later to become Maxwell Air Force Base).

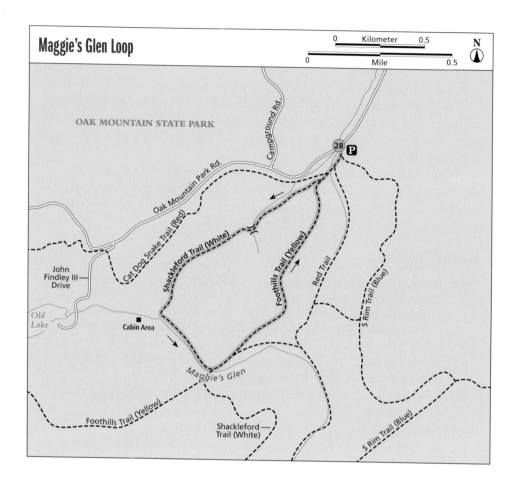

Maggie's Glen Loop

Kilometer 0 — 0.5

Mile 0 — 0.5

N

OAK MOUNTAIN STATE PARK

Campground Rd.

28 **P**

Oak Mountain Park Rd.

Cat Dog Snake Trail (Red)

Shackleford Trail (White)

Foothills Trail (Yellow)

Red Trail

S Rim Trail (Blue)

John Findley III Drive

Old Lake

Cabin Area

Maggie's Glen

Foothills Trail (Yellow)

Shackleford — Trail (White)

S Rim Trail (Blue)

1.1 Pass a short side trail to the stream on the right (nice cascades here). Pass white marker 30 and in 50 feet pass another side trail to the stream.

1.2 Come to a sign pointing the direction of the White Trail. There is a rock jumble with the stream and cascades to the right. The trail narrows to 1½ to 2 feet wide, with a short drop to the stream on the right and an uphill slope on the left. In 200 feet you will arrive at Maggie's Glen. There is an informational kiosk and four benches here, along with a three-prong fork in the trail: the Red-Yellow Connector (center), the Yellow Trail (left), and the White/Yellow Trail (right, to the south, with a bridge crossing the stream). Take the left fork uphill on the Yellow Trail. The blazes are now yellow.

1.3 Pass yellow marker 81. This is a climb to the top of a ridge on the uphill side of the Maggie's Glen stream (which is now on your left). Nice views along this ridge in the winter.

1.6 Pass yellow marker 82.

1.8 Pass yellow marker 83.

2.1 Pass yellow marker 84. In 100 feet you will be back at the intersection with the White Trail at mile 0.2. Turn right onto the White/Yellow Trail and retrace your steps to the trailhead.

2.3 Arrive back at the trailhead.

Cyclists and hikers share the first section of the Maggie's Glen Loop.

Hiking Information

Local Information

Greater Birmingham Convention and Visitors Bureau, 2200 Ninth Ave. North, Birmingham, AL 35203; (800) 458-8085; www.birminghamal.org

Local Events/Attractions

Vulcan Park and Museum, 1701 Valley View Dr., Birmingham; (205) 933-1409; www.visitvulcan.com. The statue of Vulcan, the Roman god of the forge, is the world's largest cast-iron statue and a fitting tribute to this iron and steel city. You can climb the 100-plus-year-old statue for a beautiful view of the city and also visit the interactive museum that tells the statue's story and the history of the Magic City's iron industry.

Lodging

Oak Mountain State Park Campground, 200 Terrace Dr., Pelham; (205) 620-2527; www.alapark.com/oakmountain/camping. Primitive and improved campsites.

Restaurants

Purple Onion Deli and Grill, 2296 Pelham Pkwy., Pelham; (205) 403-8600

29 Treetop Trail

If you're looking for a trail to keep the kids' attention, this would be the one. The Treetop Trail is a short, easy walk along a dirt footpath with a cascading brook running next to it. Along the route you'll see birds and raptors that cannot be returned to the wild because of their injuries and pay a visit to the Alabama Wildlife Rehabilitation Center (AWRC), where sick and injured birds and animals are rehabbed so they can be released.

Start: Day-use parking lot on Terrace Drive
Distance: 1.1-mile lollipop
Hiking time: About 1 hour, longer depending on your stay at AWRC
Difficulty: Easy
Trail surface: Dirt footpath, boardwalk
Best seasons: Year-round
Other trail users: None
Canine compatibility: Leashed dogs permitted on the trail, not permitted in AWRC
Land Status: State park

Nearest town: Pelham
Fees and permits: Day-use fee
Schedule: Year-round, sunrise to 1 hour before dark
Maps: USGS Chelsea, Helena, AL; *DeLorme: Alabama Atlas & Gazetteer,* page 31 G6; trail maps available at gate or camp store
Trail contact: Oak Mountain State Park, 200 Terrace Dr., Pelham, AL 35124; (205) 620-2524; www.alapark.com/oakmountain

Finding the trailhead: From Pelham on I-65 at exit 248, take AL 119 South/Cahaba Valley Road 0.2 mile and turn left onto Oak Mountain Road. Travel 1.9 miles and turn left onto John Findley III Drive. Travel 2.6 miles and make a right turn onto Terrace Drive. Travel 1 mile and park in the day-use parking lot on the left. The trailhead is across the street from the parking area to the southwest. GPS: N33 19.501'/W86 45.447'

The Hike

Sometimes trying to get your kids outside more and to appreciate nature is a battle. It's hard to fight those video games. But hiking in Alabama presents some truly remarkable adventures that can make your battle easier, and probably one of the best trails is at Oak Mountain State Park—the Treetop Trail.

The Treetop Trail combines two things kids love: animals and water. For most of the hike, you will be walking next to a beautiful little cascading brook. This is a seasonal stream, so it may not be flowing in the heat of summer.

Then there are the animals. Oak Mountain is the home of the Alabama Wildlife Rehabilitation Center (AWRC), a nonprofit organization with a simple mission: "To provide medical and rehabilitative care for Alabama's injured and orphaned native birds in order to permit their return to the wild and to educate people in order to heighten awareness and appreciation of Alabama's native wildlife." The center is the state's oldest and largest such facility. On average it receives over 1,800 birds representing 100-plus species to rehabilitate per year.

The boardwalk on the Treetop Trail takes you to view different species of birds that cannot be released into the wild because of injury.

Of course, some of the birds cannot be rehabilitated and would not survive on their own. AWRC provides a special home for them along the Treetop Trail. At the very beginning of the hike, you will make an immediate right turn to the southwest to pay them a visit. The trail here is an elevated boardwalk with large cages housing the birds. Informative signs next to the cages tell you about the birds, which include several owls such as barred, screech, and great horned, as well as turkey vultures and red-tailed hawks. Many times a volunteer from the center will be on hand to answer questions.

The trail before the boardwalk begins as a wide dirt path, almost a dirt road. After the boardwalk it becomes a narrower dirt footpath as it meanders up the hillside until it reaches the top of the ridge and the AWRC building itself. The facility is open year-round from 9 a.m. to 5 p.m. Inside is an amazing display of educational exhibits as well as live birds. You may see hummingbirds and butterflies in the garden or watch as the volunteers feed orphaned babies. Outside behind the building is the Freedom Flight Cage, where red-tailed hawks in for rehabilitation can literally stretch their wings and freely fly about.

In 2011 the center began holding monthly educational programs on a wide variety of bird-related topics, everything from how to attract hummingbirds to raptor demonstrations. Be sure to visit their website for event schedules. And by the way, AWRC is always looking for volunteers to help out.

Miles and Directions

0.0 Start from the trailhead across the street to the south from the day-use parking area on Terrace Drive. A large wooden sign and a short footbridge over a ditch marks the way. Just after the bridge there is a Y; a kiosk here tells about the trail. Take the right fork and head up the stairs and boardwalk to view birds that cannot be released into the wild because of their condition.

0.2 Come off the boardwalk at a wide dirt footpath that heads to the left and right (northwest/southeast). This is the un-blazed Treetop Trail. Turn to the right (southeast) onto the Treetop Trail. A nice little creek flows alongside the trail. In less than 0.1 mile, you will cross the creek twice over short footbridges. Shortly after, you will be walking alongside a split-rail fence to your right between you and the creek.

0.3 Cross the creek again over a footbridge and make a short climb uphill over some rock stairs. In 100 feet cross the creek again over a footbridge.

0.4 The Yellow Trail enters from the left (north). Continue straight (southeast). In 100 feet come to a sign that shows the Yellow and Treetop Trails turning right (southwest). Do not turn here but continue straight to the south. The trail turns into a hard-packed dirt bed. You will be walking between several buildings on each side of the trail on top of hills.

0.6 Arrive at the Alabama Wildlife Rehabilitation Center. Take your time to visit the exhibits, talk to the volunteers, and visit the birds. When done, retrace your steps back to the boardwalk at mile 0.2.

1.1 Back at the boardwalk, instead of heading back over the boardwalk (although you can if you want to), continue straight on the wide dirt footpath to the trailhead. In 100 yards arrive back at the trailhead.

Option

To make a longer trip of it, you have the option of turning this into a lollipop loop, but be warned, it's a rugged hike with several steep climbs. To make the loop, follow the Treetop Trail to just before making the turn to the rehabilitation center. Turn right on the Yellow Trail to the southwest. You'll cross the Green Trail once and the Red Trail twice before coming to the Green-Yellow Connector Trail, which will take you back to the Green Trail. Turn south on the Green Trail and continue until you return to the Yellow Trail. Turn left (northeast) and head back to the Treetop Trail and the trailhead.

Hiking Information

Local Information

Greater Birmingham Convention and Visitors Bureau, 2200 Ninth Ave. North, Birmingham, AL 35203; (800) 458-8085; www.birminghamal.org

Local Events/Attractions

Birmingham Zoo, 2630 Cahaba Rd., Birmingham; (205) 879-0409; www .birminghamzoo.com. Fun and education for the entire family await you at the Birmingham Zoo. Some of the wildlife at the zoo include rhinos, giraffes, wildebeests, and zebras. Open daily 9 a.m.–5 p.m.

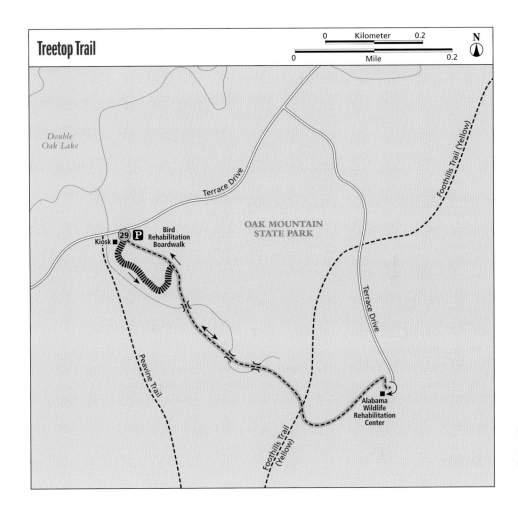

Lodging

Oak Mountain State Park Campground, 200 Terrace Dr., Pelham; (205) 620-2527; www.alapark.com/oakmountain/camping. Primitive and improved campsites.

Restaurants

Cafe Tretuno, 3018 Pelham Pkwy., Pelham; (205) 664-7887; www.cafetrentuno.com. Pizza, pasta, and more.

Hike Tours

Oak Mountain State Park, 200 Terrace Dr., Pelham; (205) 620-2520; www.alapark. com/oakmountain/Nature%20Programs%20&%20Events. Oak Mountain State Park has naturalists that love to talk about nature within the park. Contact them for information about setting up a tour, or visit the website for a list of special tours and events.

30 Peavine Falls Loop

The Peavine Falls Loop Trail uses sections of three of Oak Mountain State Park's popular hiking trails to take you to its centerpiece, Peavine Falls, a 65-foot tumbling cascade into a beautiful stony gorge. While the trail has steep climbs downhill, it is still a popular route most any time of the year, with its lush forest and, of course, the waterfall itself.

Start: Northwest side of parking area at Peavine Falls trailhead
Distance: 1.6-mile loop
Hiking time: 2 to 2.5 hours
Difficulty: Moderate with a steep downhill
Trail surface: Dirt and rock path, gravel road
Best seasons: Winter–early summer
Other trail users: None
Canine compatibility: Leashed dogs permitted
Land status: State park

Nearest town: Pelham
Fees and permits: Day-use fee
Schedule: Year-round, sunrise to 1 hour before dark
Maps: USGS Chelsea, Helena, AL; *DeLorme: Alabama Atlas & Gazetteer,* page 31 G6; trail maps available at entrance gate or camp store
Trail contact: Oak Mountain State Park, 200 Terrace Dr., Pelham, AL 35124; (205) 620-2524; www.alapark.com/oakmountain

Finding the trailhead: From Pelham on I-65 at exit 248, take AL 119 South / Cahaba Valley Road 0.2 mile and turn left onto Oak Mountain Road. Travel 2.7 miles and turn right onto Peavine Falls Road. Follow the winding road 3 miles to the parking lot. Be careful on the winding turns and watch out for bicycles. The Green Trail trailhead is on the northwest side of the parking lot. GPS: N33 18.155' / W86 45.735'

The Hike

Hundreds of people flock to Peavine Falls each weekend to view this 65-foot beauty that cascades down a sheer rock wall into a clear pool. It's not quite true that all trails at Oak Mountain State Park lead to Peavine Falls, but many do. First there is the Green Trail, a rugged 1.9-mile climb up a ridge that starts at the park office along Terrace Drive. You can also follow the White or Blue Trails from the north trailhead on John Findley III Drive to reach the falls. Both of these trails are long hikes, each over 6 miles one way, that require either a shuttle or a long walk back to your vehicle.

An alternative is this little gem, the Peavine Falls Loop. The loop uses a section of all three trails for some ridgetop views, wildflower viewing, creek-side cascades, and, of course, the falls themselves.

The loop begins at the Peavine Falls trailhead. This is a large gravel lot capable of holding a good hundred cars (which shows you the popularity of the falls). There are two information kiosks here—one on the east side where the loop will return, the other on the northwest side where we begin the hike—along with a nice, clean portable toilet.

The drive up to the trailhead is on Peavine Falls Road, a long and winding dirt road that you will be sharing with cyclists. They cross the road several times on the

A portion of the Peavine Falls Loop follows just below the ridgeline of a hill.

Red Trail and other connector trails or use the road to ride up to the parking area. Just be watchful of the cyclists as you make your way around the sharp bends.

The trail itself is a combination dirt and rock footpath for most of its length, with the exception of the last 0.4 mile to the parking area where it is a wide dirt and gravel road. Your hike begins with a steady climb to the top of a ridge where dogwoods bloom in the spring and the live oaks and silver maples paint a brilliant picture in the fall. In the winter with the leaves down, you will catch a few views of the surrounding hills. Also along the ridge you might hear the sounds of yellow-billed cuckoos and pine warblers. In the summer thrushes and wrens dart through the brush, and throughout the year broad-winged and red-shouldered hawks soar overhead.

At mile 0.6 you will take the Green-White Connector Trail to the White Trail. This is a very steep and rocky descent to the banks of a good-size creek, Peavine Creek, where you'll turn to the southwest and follow alongside the creek on the White Trail. The creek is fast flowing, with some nice cascades from fall through spring with seasonal rains. In the summer the flow tapers off, but it's still a nice companion along this section. It won't be long before you hear the sounds of the falls in the distance.

Soon you make a left turn to the east and take the Blue Trail to the falls themselves. The trail is very rocky and narrow here. You have two options at this point: You can go to the right and head to the bottom of the falls and a nice, clear, cool pool or go to the left and take in the tumbling waters and the gorge from high above. The trek I describe here takes the upper route, but either way is well marked and well worth the effort. If you go to the upper falls, your best views will come winter to early spring when the leaves are down.

Be warned, however, that the cliffs and bluffs around the falls are slick and the drop is precipitous. Use extreme caution in this area. Not doing so could result in severe injury or death.

All of the trails used have plenty of blazes to help keep you on track. Each blaze is a rectangular reflective marker in the color of the trail (even the Green-White Connector). You will also pass several 4-by-4 posts along the trail. These are painted the same color as the trail name and are numbered. The numbers correspond to mileages on the trail, sort of like mile markers along the highway. If you get lost or in trouble, you can call the park ranger and tell them you are, for example, on the "Green Trail at [or near] marker 59" and they can easily come to your rescue.

While overnight backcountry camping is permitted along several trails in the park, it is not allowed in the areas just above and below the falls. Also, rappelling and climbing are not allowed on the rock walls of the gorge.

Miles and Directions

0.0   Start from the Peavine Falls trailhead on the northwest side of the Peavine Falls parking lot. There is a kiosk here with general trail information and a park trail map. The trail is marked with green reflective markers. In a few yards you will pass your first numbered trail

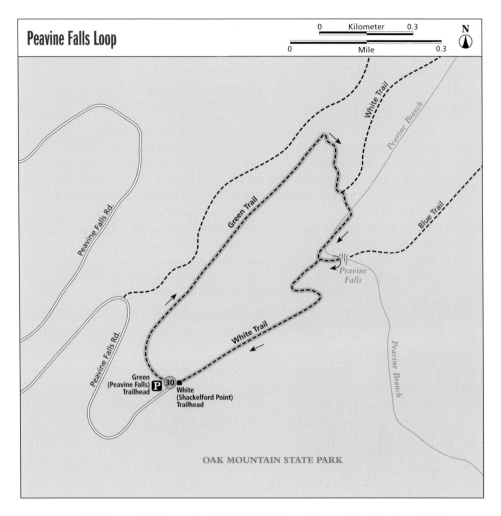

0   Kilometer   0.3

N

0   Mile   0.3

Peavine Falls Rd.

White Trail

Peavine Branch

Green Trail

Blue Trail

Peavine Falls

Peavine Falls Rd.

White Trail

Green (Peavine Falls) Trailhead

P 30 White (Shackelford Point) Trailhead

Peavine Branch

OAK MOUNTAIN STATE PARK

post; it is green with the number 60. The trail starts uphill on a wide, 4-foot gravel bed through a thick pine forest. Not far in, the trail narrows to a 2-foot-wide dirt path. After a short climb, the trail levels out and follows the level ridgeline.

0.1 Pass the Green-Red Connector Trail on your left (northwest). Continue straight (northeast) on the Green Trail. Lots of grass lines the sides of the trail, and the bed is a bit rockier at this point. (**FYI:** Excellent wooden signs indicate all trail intersections.)

0.2 Pass another green marker, 59. There are some views through the trees as you walk the ridgeline. In the spring this section is lined with cardinal flower.

0.4   A short, 15-foot trail to right (southeast) leads to the top of the ridge for a view of the valley.

0.5 Pass trail post #58.

0.6 Come to an intersection. Turn right (north) here onto the Green-White Connector Trail. The trail is blazed with green and white reflectors, and it is very steep and rocky. Mostly hardwood trees line this section.

0.8 Come to a T intersection. The White Trail heads to your left and right (northeast/southwest). Turn right (southwest) onto the White Trail. The trail is now marked with white paint blazes or reflective markers. A fast-flowing stream (depending on rainfall) will be on your left (southeast) through this section. The path is level with rocks, dirt, and tree roots.

0.9 Pass white marker 50. In less than 0.1 mile, come to an intersection with the Blue Trail; a sign here says "Falls/Blue Trail" with an arrow pointing left (east) and "Parking Lot" with an arrow point straight ahead (southwest). Turn left onto the Blue Trail, crossing the creek over a footbridge. In 100 feet come to a sign that reads "Top of Falls" with an arrow pointing left (east) and "Bottom of Falls" with an arrow pointing right (southeast). For this hike I chose the top of the falls to the left, but feel free to explore either direction. Either way the path is very rocky and narrow, coming right up to the edge of the cliff. Use extreme caution! (A sign here reads "Peavine Falls Area. Caution—Rocky, Steep, Dangerous. Enter at Your Own Risk.")

1.0 Arrive at the top of the falls. Again, use caution! It's dangerously close to the edge of the cliff. When you're ready, turn around here and head back the way you came.

1.1 Return to the intersection with the White Trail at mile 0.9. Turn left (southwest) onto the White Trail. The trail soon changes from a dirt path into a wide gravel road that winds its way steeply uphill. Benches are available for resting at each bend.

1.6 Arrive at the Peavine Falls parking lot. You will be on the east side of the lot across from the Green Trail where you originally started.

Hiking Information

Local Information
Greater Birmingham Convention and Visitors Bureau, 2200 Ninth Ave. North, Birmingham, AL 35203; (800) 458-8085; www.birminghamal.org

Local Events/Attractions
Birmingham Barons Baseball, 1401 First Ave. South, Birmingham; (205) 988-3200; www.milb.com/index.jsp?sid=t247. The Birmingham Barons minor league (Southern League) baseball team has been around since 1885 and has produced many stars over the years, including Reggie Jackson and Rollie Fingers.

Lodging
Oak Mountain State Park Campground, 200 Terrace Dr., Pelham; (205) 620-2527; www.alapark.com/oakmountain/camping. Primitive and improved campsites.

Restaurants
Johnny Ray's, 2252 Pelham Pkwy., Pelham; (205) 989-7211. Great local barbecue.

Hike Tours
Oak Mountain State Park, 200 Terrace Dr., Pelham; (205) 620-2520; www.alapark .com/oakmountain/Nature%20Programs%20&%20Events. Oak Mountain State Park has naturalists that love to talk about nature within the park. Contact them for information about setting up a tour, or visit the website for a list of special tours and events.

31 Ike Maston–BMRR Loop

Red Mountain was once a major iron-ore mining area. Today the mountain has been reclaimed and is now a beautiful and popular park with a touch of history and lots of fun for visitors of all ages, including zip lines and rope bridges. The Ike Maston–BMRR Loop Trail is short but a bit challenging with moderate to difficult climbs. The trail leads you away from the crowds that usually pack the park and takes you to an impressive piece of mining history, the Redding Shaft Mine and Hoist House.

Start: Trailhead on Frankfurt Drive
Distance: 3.2-mile lollipop
Hiking time: About 2 hours
Difficulty: Moderate to difficult due to steep inclines
Trail surface: Dirt footpath, gravel road
Best seasons: Year-round
Other trail users: Cyclists, joggers on the BMRR Trail
Canine compatibility: Leashed dogs permitted
Land status: City park
Nearest town: Birmingham

Fees and permits: None; fee for Iron Ore Zip Line (reservations required)
Schedule: Year-round, sunrise to sunset
Maps: USGS Bessemer, Bessemer Iron District, Birmingham South, AL; *DeLorme: Alabama Atlas & Gazetteer,* page 30 F5; trail maps available at information kiosk (free but donation requested)
Trail contact: Red Mountain Park, 277 Lyon Ln., Birmingham, AL 35211; (205) 202-6043; www.redmountainpark.org

Finding the trailhead: From I-65 in Birmingham, take exit 255 and head west on W. Lakeshore Parkway. Travel 3.2 miles and turn right onto Frankfurt Drive. The trailhead is at the bend as Frankfurt Drive becomes Lyon Lane. Park anywhere along Frankfurt Drive. GPS: N33 26.712' / W86 51.753'

The Hike

Many people know that the city of Birmingham was once the center of iron production in the South. Parks such as Tannehill Ironworks Historic State Park allow you to hike that piece of the city's history. But what many people do not realize is that to become the industrial powerhouse it was in the 1800s and the bustling city it is today, it took a little red dust—iron ore. Red Mountain Park gives hikers a chance to visit that part of the history and learn about the sweat and backbreaking work it took to bring the ore to market, plus there's a little something extra. More on that in a moment.

The abridged story of iron ore in central Alabama goes back centuries to the Native Americans who lived in the region and used the dust for dyeing clothes and pottery. It wasn't until the 1840s that a local farmer, Baylis Earle Grace, identified the

▶ Alabama is the only state that has all of the natural resources to make iron and steel. And when it comes to production, the state is the largest supplier of cast iron and steel pipe in the country.

The Ike Maston Trail portion of this loop is rated "most difficult" by park officials.

dust as hematite (iron ore) and began scraping the land and shipping it to a foundry in a neighboring county. As the Civil War approached, speculators began buying up large tracts of land on and near Red Mountain, the goal being to capitalize on the now-burgeoning iron-mining industry. The area's first commercial mine, known as Eureka 1, was opened in 1863 (the mine is located on the eastern side of the park). And with that the mining boom was on, the population increased, and in 1871 the city of Birmingham was founded.

The iron-mining boom continued for a century, until it was finally shut down for a variety of reasons, including an increase in foreign imports. The last active mine on the mountain was closed by its owner at the time, US Steel, in 1962. After that, Red Mountain stood virtually untouched until 2007 when—through the efforts of a neighbor of the mountain, Ervin Battain; the work of many volunteers; and an amazingly generous donation by US Steel of its 1,200 acres of land on the mountain—the vision to create a historic park was born.

Today Red Mountain Park is not only a testament to an industry that built a city, but also a beautiful nature preserve. The park boasts over 10 miles of hiking trails, most being dirt and rock footpaths with the remainder being old mining roads. The trails interconnect, allowing you to create your own loop adventures. The paths take you to two beautiful overlooks, three historic iron-mining structures and mines (which are sealed off), and some unique fun for you and your family. Red Mountain is the home of the Red Ore Zip Line, a fun and fast ride through the mountain's canopy, and the SkyHy Treehouse, a platform high up in the trees that can be reached by rope bridges.

The trailhead is located on a bend in the road where Frankfurt Drive becomes Lyon Lane. You can park anywhere along the side of Frankfurt Drive. (By the way, the park's office is located less than a half mile away on Lyon Lane on the right.) The trail described here is a 3.2-mile lollipop loop that uses three trails: the Ike Maston Trail, a short section of the Songo Trail, and the BMRR South Trail.

The Ike Maston Trail is a dirt and rock path that is labeled as being "most difficult." There are some pretty steep and long grades to tackle. The good thing about these climbs is that they take you away from the crowds that use the more level mining roads. The trail was named for one of the last miners to work on the mountain when it closed. (You can hear Mr. Maston tell his story in an oral history on the Red Mountain website, www.redmountain.org/park-overview/oral-history-project.) The BMRR South Trail is a nice, level path that was once a mining road that will lead you back to the trailhead.

The highlight of the hike is the Redding Shaft Mine and Hoist House that you'll find near the intersection of the Songo and Ike Maston Trails. The mine, which has been sealed off, was a 400-foot-deep shaft mine that was in operation from 1917 to 1927. The electric-powered hoist house helped haul the ore from the mine and is a beautiful mission-style structure.

As I said, this is only one of many possible loop hikes in the park, but be forewarned: Be ready for some crowds on the weekend! This is one popular park. The facility regularly holds runs and walks for fun and charity, and it's well used by the locals. On the day I visited, I had to park a good 0.75 mile from the trailhead on Frankfurt Drive.

Miles and Directions

0.0 Start at trailhead at the bend in the road where Lyon Lane and Frankfurt Drive meet. The trail heads up a short hill to the northeast and then turns north. The path is a dirt and gravel road.

0.2 Come to the welcome kiosk with information about the park and its trails. Maps are available here. Please drop a dollar or two into the lockbox for the map, and remember to pack it out with you. Two very nice portable toilets are located to the right. Turn left (west) here. The path is still a dirt and gravel road at this point and unmarked.

0.4 Come to the intersection with the BMRR South Trail. Turn left (southwest) onto the BMRR. The trail continues to be a dirt and gravel road. In less than 0.1 mile, come to a sign indicating that the Ike Maston Trail is to the northwest and the BMRR continues to the southwest. Turn right (northwest) onto the unmarked gravel connector trail.

0.5 A chain blocks the road to the north. Turn left (southwest) onto the Ike Maston Trail. Shortly after the turn, a small sign warns that the trail is "most difficult." The trail is now a dirt footpath and begins a steady and steep climb.

0.7 Cross an intermittent creek. The dirt has a red iron hue here.

0.8 In a hollow to the left (southwest), you will see a clearing for a petroleum pipeline.

0.9 Come to a sign indicating that the Smythe Trail connects from the left (south). In less than 0.1 mile, cross the petroleum pipeline clearing (the pipe is underground).

1.1 There is a view of the valley to your left (east).

1.2 Cross an intermittent stream with a stone water bar. After crossing, climb a hill to the west on some old wooden stairs made from railroad ties.

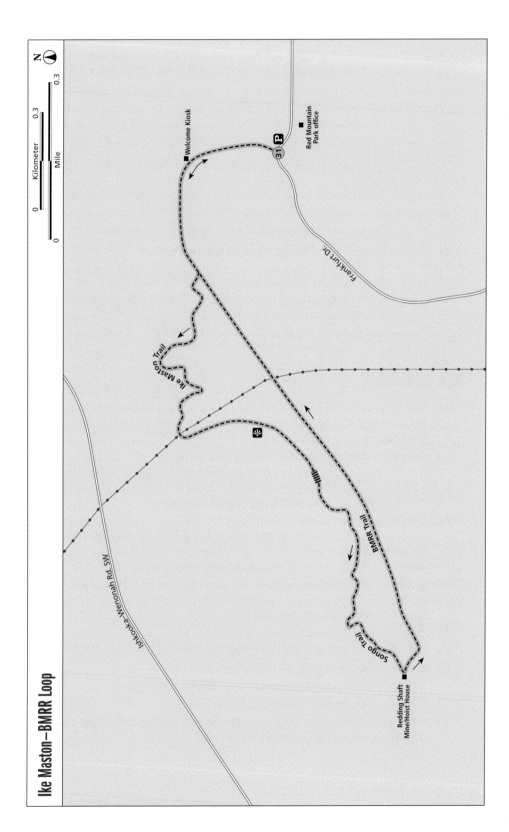

Ike Maston–BMRR Loop

Welcome Kiosk

Ike Maston Trail

Songo Trail

BMRR Trail

Redding Shaft
Mine/Hoist House

Iskhookok-Wenonah Rd. SW

Frankfurt Dr.

Red Mountain
Park office

N

Kilometer
0   0.3

Mile
0   0.3

1.6 The Songo Trail joins the Ike Maston Trail from the left (south). Continue straight to the northwest on the Ike Maston Trail. In a few hundred feet, cross a stream over a nice wooden bridge.

1.7 Pass an old 4-by-4-inch cement post on the right.

1.9 Arrive at the Redding Shaft Mine and Hoist House. There are interesting signs here telling the story of the hoist and the mine. Turn left (southeast) onto the Songo Trail, which is now a gravel and dirt road. In less than 0.1 mile, turn left onto the BMRR South Trail. A frog pond is here at the bend and the frog song is marvelous. (*Option:* At the Hoist House, continue straight on the Ishkooda Trail to visit the SkyHy Treehouse and Ishkooda Overlook, then follow the Smythe Trail back to mile 2.6 of the hike.)

2.5 Cross the petroleum pipeline clearing again.

2.6 Pass the Smythe Trail to the left (north).

2.8 Pass the connector trail to the Ike Maston Trail to the left (north).

3.0 Arrive back at the welcome kiosk. Turn right (south) onto the dirt and gravel entrance road and head back the way you came to the trailhead.

3.2 Arrive back at the trailhead.

Hiking Information

Local Information
Homewood Chamber of Commerce, 1721 Oxmoor Rd., Homewood, AL 35209; (205) 871-5631; www.homewoodchamber.org

Local Events/Attractions
Birmingham Barons Baseball, 2230 Second Ave. South, Birmingham; (205) 988-3200; www.milb.com/index.jsp?sid=t247. A storied baseball franchise, the Barons have been playing Southern League (minor league) baseball since 1885 and are currently an affiliate of the Chicago White Sox.

Restaurants
Hamburger Heaven, 180 Oxmoor Blvd., Homewood; (205) 941-1668

Hike Tours
The Friends of Red Mountain lead hikes for all skill levels the third Sunday of each month.

Organizations
Friends of Red Mountain, 277 Lyon Ln., Birmingham; (205) 202-6043; www.fws.gov/bonsecour/friends.htm

32 Tunnel Falls Loop

Moss Rock Preserve is a beautiful and unique city park located in the town of Hoover. You'll be surprised to find that a drive through a subdivision will lead you to this park that seems a world away from civilization. There are plenty of trails and features to explore here, but the short Tunnel Falls Loop gives you an overview of the lovely forest, amazing rock features, and an unusual waterfall—Tunnel Falls.

Start: Sulphur Springs trailhead
Distance: 1.8-mile lollipop
Hiking time: About 1 hour
Difficulty: Moderate due to some steep inclines
Trail surface: Dirt and rock
Best seasons: Year-round
Other trail users: None
Canine compatibility: Leashed dogs permitted
Land status: City preserve

Nearest town: Hoover
Fees and permits: None
Schedule: Year-round, sunrise to sunset
Maps: USGS Helena, AL; *DeLorme: Alabama Atlas & Gazetteer,* page 30 G5; trail map available online at City of Hoover website
Trail contact: City of Hoover, 100 Municipal Ln., Hoover, AL 35216; (205) 444-7500; www.hooveral.org/index.aspx?NID=219

Finding the trailhead: From I-459 exit 10, head northwest on John Hawkins Parkway. Travel 0.2 mile and turn right onto Grove Boulevard. Travel 0.6 mile and turn left onto Preserve Parkway. Travel 1 mile and turn left onto Sulphur Springs Road. The well-marked trailhead is 0.1 mile ahead on the right. GPS: N33 22.586' / W86 51.204'

The Hike

To say Moss Rock Preserve is an oasis is an understatement. To get to the preserve, you have to drive through a very nice subdivision with smartly manicured lawns and even small shops lining the roadways. But then you come to the trailhead and it all changes. Suddenly you are removed from the people and immersed in a beautiful park that holds even more surprises.

Moss Rock is located in the city of Hoover, which is only a stone's throw from Birmingham. The preserve is owned by the city and is just 250 acres in size, but what it lacks in size it more than makes up for in natural features.

The preserve is situated between Pine and Shades Mountains. Overall there are 12 miles of hiking trails here that you can use to form loops of various lengths and difficulties. Some of the unique features you will find are amazing boulders and outcroppings, including an ancient Native American rock shelter, beautiful creeks, and sparkling cascading waterfalls. The water features are courtesy of the Hurricane Branch, which has its headwaters here.

This is also a plant lover's paradise, with some 66 species of trees and 136 species of wildflowers. Some of the plants you will see include a mix of hardwoods and pines

The trail's namesake falls flows under a natural sandstone bridge.

including longleaf pine, natural bonsai, and a wide variety of wildflowers—lots of them—growing trailside and on rock outcroppings. These are known as sandstone glades, and they are one of only thirty-five such areas in the world. Wildflowers include spiderwort, bird's-foot violets, bellwort, and liverleaf, to name only a few.

The trail I have chosen to include in this edition, which we're calling the Tunnel Falls Loop, is a short 1.8-mile loop that gives you a good sampling of what to expect at Moss Rock. The trail begins at the Sulphur Springs trailhead. From here it heads south on the blue-blazed, and aptly named, Blue Trail to what is called Patriotic Junction. I was a little slow the day I visited, and it took me a second to figure the name out. Duh. This is where the Red, White, and Blue Trails meet. Near this location is a short side trail to a frog pond where on a peaceful evening you will be serenaded by frog song.

From here we take the White Trail to the loop's namesake, Tunnel Falls. This is a beautiful and unusual waterfall. The stream flows under the sandstone rocks that form a flat, natural bridge. Remember that all waterfalls in Alabama are seasonal. The best time to visit to see the falls is in fall or spring.

If you have the time, it is worth your while to continue a little farther down the White Trail just past the loop's turn north to meet up with the Blue Trail. The path continues to follow the stream and is a great place to just sit and relax.

Turning north, the trail meets up with the Blue Trail and comes to a giant outcropping known as the Great Wall. Don't worry about missing it—you won't! From here the trail starts heading south and back to the trailhead.

As I said, there are 12 miles of trail here, with plenty of opportunities to create your own loop and explore. I recommend that you also head to the southern trailhead and take the 0.5-mile walk to the Boulder Field to check out huge rocks with such names as Ship Rock. This is a favorite area for climbers to get in a little face time with the rocks. There are also more waterfalls farther along and a rugged hike affectionately known as the "Cardio Trail."

Before I forget, I can't say enough about the work that area volunteers and organizations do to maintain the trails. They are well groomed and blazed at all times. But, of course, trail maintenance is never done, and if you fall in love with Moss Rock Preserve and want to help maintain this beautiful area, contact the city of Hoover and they'll be glad to get you started.

Miles and Directions

0.0 Start at the Sulphur Springs parking lot and trailhead. The trail begins through a split-rail fence to the east. A sign here indicates the distances to Patriotic Junction, Frog Pond, the Boulder Field, and the Great Wall. The path is initially gravel. Boy Scouts have put up really nice signs identifying trees along the path. In less than 0.1 mile, come to an intersection. Turn right (south) onto the Blue Trail. The trail is now a dirt footpath.

0.1 Arrive at Patriotic Junction. This is where three trails meet: the Red, the White, and the Blue. Turn left (northeast) onto the White Trail (now blazed white).

0.2 Come to a Y; take the left fork to the northeast. The canopy thins a bit through this area.

0.3 Cross a gravel road (one of the connector trails) to the east; you will see a post with a sign on it where the trail continues. The sign here shows the way to the Frog Pond (ahead to the east) and the Boulder Field to the left (north). Turn left and continue on the White Trail to the north. The path is paralleling Preserve Parkway. (***Option:*** A short, 200-foot side trail takes you to the Frog Pond, a small pond just below Preserve Parkway.)

0.5 Start heading away from the parkway through a small rock garden downhill. At the bottom of the hill, cross a small creek.

0.6 Cross a narrow creek.

0.7 Cross a narrow creek.

0.8 Arrive at Tunnel Falls. The trail passes right next to the waterfall on its left side (west). About 40 feet north of the falls, the trail crosses a nice wooden bridge over the creek that forms the falls. The bridge was built by Boy Scout Troop 119 in 2003.

0.9 Come to a Y (a sign shows the directions). Take the left fork to the northeast, leaving the White Trail and joining a blue-blazed connector trail. The connector basically follows a

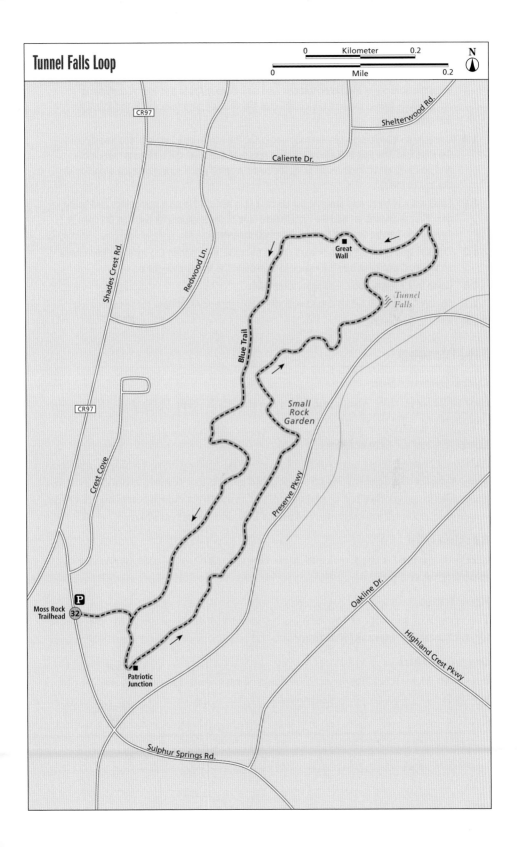

gravel runoff area. (***Option:*** The White Trail continues to the east. It's worth your while to walk another 0.2 mile on the trail as it follows the swift-flowing creek. Take your time and enjoy the serenity of the water. You can also add more miles to this trip by continuing on the White Trail to the next blue connector trail that will also take you to the Blue Trail mentioned below.)

1.0 Come to an intersection (another sign indicates the way to go). Turn left (southwest) onto the Blue Trail. The trail is blazed in blue. In less than 0.1 mile, the trail turns more rocky and narrows, with thicker brush lining the route. A small creek runs alongside a portion of the trail to the left.

1.1 Cross a small creek and arrive at the Great Wall, a series of large outcroppings and boulders. The trail heads around the right (north) side of the boulders for the next 0.1 mile. A subdivision can be seen to your right through the trees.

1.3 The Blue Trail turns right (southwest) onto a dirt road. In less than 0.1 mile, the trail moves off the road and back into the woods to the south. The trail is rocky here.

1.5 Come to a T intersection. Turn right (southwest).

1.7 Come to a Y (a sign here shows directions). Turn right and head back to the parking lot.

1.8 Arrive at the parking lot.

Hiking Information

Local Information

City of Hoover, 100 Municipal Ln., Hoover, AL 35216; (205) 444-7500; www .hooveral.org

Local Events/Attractions

Aldridge Gardens, 3530 Lorna Rd., Hoover; (205) 682-8019; www.aldridgegardens .com. Aldridge Gardens is a 30-acre woodland garden that features beautiful hydrangeas, camellias, and other native Alabama plants and flowers. Admission charged. Open year-round except Thanksgiving, Christmas Day, and New Year's Day.

Restaurants

Creekside Tavern, 4330 Creekside Ave., Hoover; (205) 402-7281; www.creekside tavernhoover.com

Hike Tours

The Friends of Moss Rock Preserve lead guided tours of the preserve by reservation. Contact them for more information.

Organizations

Friends of Moss Rock Preserve, 2253 Rock Creek Trail, Hoover, AL 35226; (205) 823-1641

33 Quarry Trail

Once a major limestone-mining area, Ruffner Mountain is now one of the state's premier nature centers. The Quarry Trail is the backbone of the center's hiking trail system. This out-and-back will take you along the ridgeline of the mountain past interesting trees and flowers, then to great views of the quarry itself.

Start: North side of Ruffner Mountain Nature Center parking lot under wooden trailhead entrance

Distance: 2.7 miles out and back

Hiking time: About 1.5 hours

Difficulty: Easy to moderate with some short climbs

Trail surface: Dirt and rock

Best seasons: Winter–late spring

Other trail users: None

Canine compatibility: Leashed dogs permitted

Land status: Nonprofit, city-funded nature center

Nearest town: Birmingham

Fees and permits: None; donation requested

Schedule: Trails open year-round dawn to dusk; visitor center open Tues–Sat 9 a.m.–5 p.m., Sun 1–5 p.m.; closed Thanksgiving, Christmas Eve, Christmas Day, and New Year's Day

Maps: USGS Irondale, AL; *DeLorme: Alabama Atlas & Gazetteer,* page 31 D7; trail maps available at kiosk at trailhead

Trail contact: Ruffner Mountain Nature Center, 1214 81st St., Birmingham, AL 35206; (205) 833-8264; www.ruffnermountain.org

Finding the trailhead: From Birmingham at the intersection of I-65 and I-59/I-20, take I-59/I-20 east 6.4 miles. Take exit 131 (Oporto Madrid Boulevard) and in 0.2 mile turn right onto 77th Street North / Oporto Madrid Boulevard. In 0.6 mile turn left onto Rugby Avenue and travel 0.7 mile. Turn right onto 81st Street South and in 0.4 mile you will arrive at the nature center. Drive past the visitor center. The road will loop around past parking for special events, and you will come to another parking lot on the uphill side near the gift shop / visitor center. The trailhead is here on the south side of the parking lot. GPS: N33 33.516' / W86 42.429'

The Hike

Since 1977 the Ruffner Mountain Nature Center has been educating students—and yes, parents, too—about nature. The center began with only 28 acres of land along a ridge of Red Mountain called Ruffner Mountain. Today the center encompasses over 1,000 acres of wetlands, hardwood forests, and, of course, hiking trails—12 miles of hiking trails to be exact.

Since the beginning it has been the center's mission to connect people with nature. From impressive educational programs for students and visitors alike to passive recreational programs, Ruffner Mountain fosters an appreciation for nature and living things in the busy metropolitan area. On any given weekend there is a presentation of some sort going on (check the Nature Center's website for times and dates).

Then there is the site's new Tree House and Back Porch Complex. The complex is one of only six LEED (Leadership in Energy and Environmental Design) buildings in

The Quarry Trail, and all trails, at Ruffner Mountain Nature Preserve are well marked, especially at intersections.

the state, meaning that it has met certain high standards for energy efficiency and sustainability. Inside the complex there is an information booth manned by friendly and knowledgeable staff members and volunteers, and a series of exhibits that will teach you about the mining history of the area. Also within the complex is the Woodland Animal Exhibit Hall. Live animals and reptiles of the region are available for viewing in an environment much like their own natural habitat.

Ruffner Mountain is an area approximately 1 mile wide and 3 miles long, and along this narrow ridge is a series of interesting hiking trails that take you through wetlands, hardwood forests, and back in time to the area's mining past. The main trail that connects them all—or the "backbone," as the Nature Center calls it—is the Quarry Trail. This white-blazed trail runs the length of the southern end of Ruffner Mountain, and as you walk along you will see many trails intersecting it, making it a place that you can return to over and over again to get a new experience.

While the actual Quarry Trail is 1.1 miles (one way), I have added the Overlook Trail as an extension, making the trip into a 2.7-mile out-and-back. The hike is easy to moderate in difficulty, with a few climbs. The climbs uphill are made a bit easier in many spots with stone steps. Generally the path is a dirt and rock bed that can be very muddy after a good, hard rain. From spring through early fall, the canopy is very thick, providing excellent shade as it gets warmer outside.

The trails at Ruffner Mountain have excellent blazing, and getting lost is virtually impossible. The Quarry Trail is blazed with white paint blazes, the Overlook Trail with red blazes. All intersections have unique wooden signs pointing the directions to each trail. They resemble the old "hometown signs" you see in movies about World War II or the Korean War—you know, the large wooden signs with one end tapered, pointing the direction to "San Francisco 2,000 miles" or "New York 5,000 miles."

The Quarry Trail has some of the best and most informative signage to help you identify the trees along the route that I have ever seen. They are very descriptive and easy to read. You will learn about shagbark hickory, littlehip hawthorne, tulip poplar, sassafras, red buckeye, white oak, black gum, black locust . . . the list goes on and on.

A highlight of the hike is at the end of the Overlook Trail, where you begin a challenging climb up to the Cambrian Overlook, a deep cut with impressive limestone walls. This is the turnaround for this trip. I had to leave the mountain in a hurry, as a severe thunderstorm was bearing down on me. But I can tell you from past hikes of Ruffner Mountain, it is well worth your while to continue on just a bit farther to get a bird's-eye view of the city of Birmingham from the Hawkeye Overlook.

Miles and Directions

0.0 Start from the north side of the parking lot. The trailhead is a large wooden gateway that you walk under. In 100 feet pass the kiosk with maps to the left. In another 300 feet come to a Y. The Geology Trail goes straight to the east, the Quarry Trail to the right (south). Turn right onto the Quarry Trail.

0.2 Cross a paved service road to the south and pass another kiosk with a trail map and Forever Wild sign. The Trillium Trail branches off to the right. Continue straight to the south. In 100 feet pass the Hollow Tree Trail on the left, going straight up a set of stairs.

0.4 Come to Miner's Junction. The Ridge Valley Trail comes in from the left; continue straight to the south.

0.6 Pass the Mine Ruins / Crusher Trail. There is also a bench here. This section can be very muddy and hold some good-sized puddles after a heavy rain. In 50 feet pass the Jimmie Dell Wright Overlook / Winter Overlook Trail on the right.

0.8 Pass the Silent Journey Trail on your right. The blazes are white and yellow here as the Possum Loop begins. There is also a "Don't Pick the Flowers" sign here.

1.0 Pass an unmarked trail on your right.

1.1 Arrive at Grey Fox Gap. There is an information kiosk here with a map. The Quarry Trail ends at this major trail intersection where the Silent Journey, Possum Loop, and Ridge Valley Trails all converge. Continue straight on the red-blazed Overlook Trail to the southwest. In 50 feet you will pass two signs at a Y; one points to the right (northwest) and the Quarry

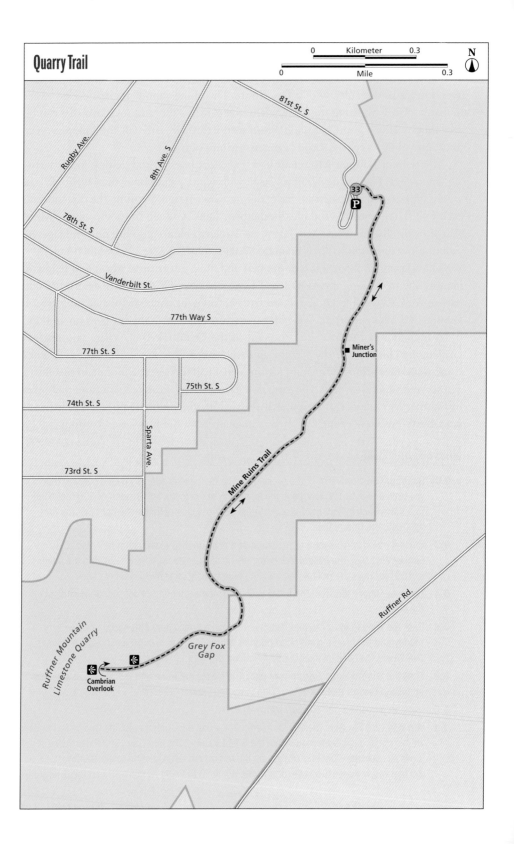

0   Kilometer   0.3

0   Mile   0.3

N

81st St. S

Rugby Ave.

8th Ave. S

78th St. S

33

P

Vanderbilt St.

77th Way S

Miner's
Junction

77th St. S

75th St. S

74th St. S

Sparta Ave.

Mine Ruins Trail

73rd St. S

Ruffner Rd.

Ruffner Mountain
Limestone Quarry

Grey Fox
Gap

Cambrian
Overlook

Entrance Trail, the other points to the left (west) and the Possum Loop. Take the left fork to the west. The trail is now blazed red and yellow.

1.3 Start getting views to your right of the quarry, especially when the leaves are down in late fall and winter. In 150 feet climb down a steep set of rock stairs. At the bottom there is a Y. The left fork is the Possum Loop. Take the right fork to the north and follow the sign to the Cambrian Overlook. In only 50 feet come to a short, rocky side trail on the right. Turn onto that trail to the northwest (a small sign reads "Cambrian Overlook").

1.4 Arrive at the Cambrian Overlook. Enjoy the view but be very careful on the dangerous, steep bluff. Turn around and retrace your steps to the trailhead.

2.7 Arrive back at the trailhead.

Hiking Information

Local Information

Greater Birmingham Convention and Visitors Bureau, 2200 Ninth Ave. North, Birmingham, AL 35203; (800) 458-8085; www.birminghamal.org

Local Events/Attractions

Ruffner Mountain Nature Center Summer Programs, 1214 81st St., Birmingham; (205) 833-8264; www.ruffnermountain.org. The Nature Center offers a wide array of programs on nature and the environment throughout the summer for kids—and adults—of all ages. Visit their website for the latest schedule.

Lodging

Oak Mountain State Park Campground, 200 Terrace Dr., Pelham; (205) 620-2527; www.alapark.com/oakmountain/camping. Primitive and improved campsites.

Restaurants

Green Acres Cafe, 1819 Crestwood Blvd., Irondale; (205) 956-4648; www.green acres-cafe.com

34 Turkey Creek Loop

The Turkey Creek Loop is a nice walk in the woods on this Forever Wild tract to the top of a ridge of a small hill. From the rocky bluff on top, you'll have a view of the surrounding valley. The return trip takes you just above the banks of the fast-flowing waters of Turkey Creek itself and to a rushing waterfall and boulder field.

Start: Trailhead on Narrows Road
Distance: 2.3-mile loop
Hiking time: About 2 hours
Difficulty: Moderate on a few steep inclines
Trail surface: Dirt footpath, paved footpath and road
Best seasons: Year-round
Other trail users: None
Canine compatibility: Leashed dogs permitted

Land status: Alabama Forever Wild tract
Nearest town: Pinson
Fees and permits: None
Schedule: Year-round, sunrise to sunset
Maps: USGS Pinson, AL; *DeLorme: Alabama Atlas & Gazetteer*, page 31 B7
Trail contact: Forever Wild, 64 N. Union St., Montgomery, AL 36130; (334) 242-3484; www.alabamaforeverwild.com

Finding the trailhead: From Birmingham on I-59 exit 128, take AL 79 north 10.4 miles. Turn left onto CR 131/Narrows Road. In 0.2 mile turn right onto Turkey Creek Road and follow it 0.7 mile. The trailhead will be on the left. Remember that this is a one-way loop road. GPS: N33 42.171'/W86 41.781'

The Hike

In Jefferson County, just north of Birmingham in the town of Pinson, you will find the perfect example of conservation at its finest, with a state agency partnering with nonprofits and a college to preserve a property that has been described as one of the most biologically diverse habitats in the region. It's called the Turkey Creek Nature Preserve.

The preserve is 462 acres in size and is owned by Alabama's Forever Wild. The agency entered into a unique partnership with the Southern Environmental Center, Freshwater Land Trust, the City of Pinson, and Birmingham Southern College to protect, maintain, and manage this property. The result is an area with plenty of educational and recreational opportunities such as hiking, photography, and birding, but more importantly, it provides for the protection of this unique habitat and gives scientists a place to study several rare and endangered species of fish that call the creek home.

The preserve's namesake, Turkey Creek, is a tributary of Locust Fork and is a water feature with a lot of character. It is a swift-flowing stream surrounded by impressive boulders and outcroppings and is dotted with many rapids and small waterfalls. The waterway is the home of three endangered species of fish: the watercress darter, rush darter, and vermilion darter. The vermilion darter is only found here in Turkey Creek and nowhere else in the world. They were listed as endangered by US Fish and

A beautiful falls along Turkey Creek

Wildlife because of the fear that development in the upper Turkey Creek watershed could severely impact the fish's habitat.

If you are into birding, you've come to the right place. According to Alabama Birding Trails, the number of birds you can add to your list is tremendous. Some species include eastern phoebe, great blue heron, red-tailed and broad-winged hawks, Acadian flycatcher, and a long list of warblers, to name only a few.

The trail itself takes in two different views of the preserve. One is from high atop a ridge that runs northeast to southwest through the property. The other is the creek itself and some impressive rapids, a waterfall, and a boulder field.

The trail begins at the parking lot trailhead and ascends rather steeply and steadily up to the ridgeline. You have the work of the Vulcan Trail Association to thank for the nicely maintained and blazed footpath. The tread is a mix of dirt with some rock throughout this section. The trail through here is clearly marked with blue paint blazes or yellow diamond signs with the hiker symbol on them. From the top of the ridge, you will have some views of the surrounding valley through the trees (best time for that is in the winter when the foliage is little to none), with the best view coming from a bluff about 0.7 mile into the hike. A short, 20- to 30-foot side trail takes you there.

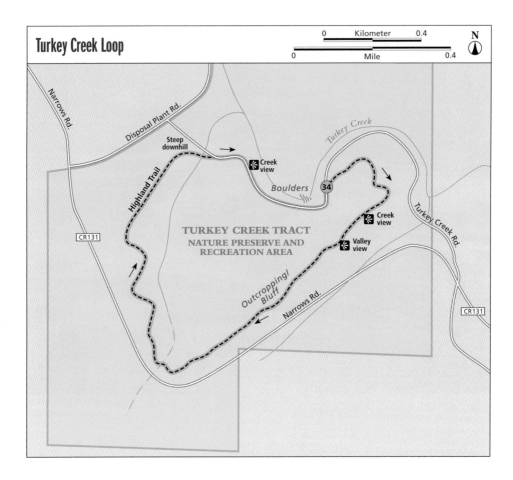

After descending steeply back to Narrows Road, the trail crosses the road and heads up a paved path called the Highland Trail to the top of a smaller ridge before returning to the road where you will be walking just above Turkey Creek, which will be down to your left. The road is one-way and traffic will be heading toward you, so the walk is made easier without you having to look over your shoulder constantly. The road walk is only 0.4 mile in length but has some really nice views of the rapids. The best view of the trip, however, comes just at the end when you get to walk through a boulder field next to a wide scenic set of rapids and falls.

I know it goes without saying and is true for every hike you take, but it needs to be stressed here: Please do not disturb the wildlife or pick the wildflowers, and be sure to pack out what you pack in. This is one special place that needs your help to protect it.

Miles and Directions

0.0 Start at the parking lot trailhead. The trail begins on the northeast side of the parking lot. It is a short scramble up a 10-foot clay bank. The trail is a dirt footpath marked with blue blazes or yellow diamond signs with either a hiker or an arrow. The canopy is rather thin at the start. From the start the path begins a steady, moderate climb to the top of a ridge. The canopy and trees thicken in about 0.1 mile.

0.4 Through the trees you can glimpse the rapids to the northwest.

0.5 Reach the top of the ridge. The path levels out here. A view of the valley can be seen to the southeast.

0.7 Come to a rock outcropping on the left (southeast). A 30-foot side trail takes you to a bluff.

1.0 Begin a steep downhill walk. Narrows Road can be seen on your left (south).

1.1 Reach the bottom of the incline, cross an intermittent creek, and start a climb up the other side.

1.4 Come out of the woods and turn right onto the paved Narrows Road. A picnic area will be on your left (west).

1.5 Cross the road to the northwest. This is the beginning of the Highland Trail (there is a sign here). Cross through four yellow posts (used to keep vehicles off the path) and begin a moderate climb up the hill.

1.7 Begin a very steep downhill walk.

1.8 Arrive once again at Narrows Road. Turn right (northeast) onto the road. Turkey Creek will soon be seen on the left (north).

1.9 You will start getting your first good look at the rapids of Turkey Creek to the left (northeast).

2.1 Pass a beautiful 30- to 50-foot-wide rapid in the creek and a view of an upcoming waterfall.

2.2 Arrive at the waterfall. There are a few impressive large boulders here. Turn left (northwest) off the road and head down toward the boulders and creek (there is a picnic table here). Follow the creek less than 0.1 mile to the northwest then northeast and you will come to a set of stairs that lead back to Narrows Road. At the top of the stairs, cross the road to the northeast.

2.3 Arrive back at the parking lot trailhead.

Hiking Information

Local Information
Clay-Pinson Chamber of Commerce, 4410 Main St., Pinson, AL 35126; (205) 529-7247; www.homewoodchamber.org

Local Events/Attractions
Darter Fest, 1600 First St. South, Birmingham; (205) 521-9933; www.bhamdarter .com. Held annually the first weekend in April at Railroad Park, the event features food and music with all proceeds going to help restore the watercress darter habitat along Turkey Creek.

Alabama Butterbean Festival, 4110 Main St., Pinson; (877) 691-6088; www.alabama butterbeanfestival.com. Held annually the first weekend of October, with parades, food, entertainment, arts and crafts, and kids' entertainment

Organizations
Birmingham Southern College, 900 Arkadelphia Rd., Birmingham, AL 35254; (800) 523-5793; www.bsc.edu/sec/ecoscape/turkeycreek.cfm

35 Tannehill Ironworks Historic Trail

The ironworks at Tannehill produced many iron implements used by the Confederate army during the Civil War. The forge, which was restored in 1976, is today the centerpiece of Tannehill Ironworks Historical State Park. The Tannehill Ironworks Historic Trail travels around the buildings of the ironworks and its furnace. Heading into the woods, the trail takes you to the rolling blue-green waters of Roupes Creek and the cemetery of the slaves who worked at the ironworks.

Start: Behind the Iron and Steel Museum of Alabama

Distance: 4.1-mile lollipop

Hiking time: 2–2.5 hours

Difficulty: Moderate due to some short climbs

Trail surface: Dirt and gravel

Best seasons: Year-round

Other trail users: Cyclists

Canine compatibility: Leashed dogs permitted

Land status: Alabama historic state park

Nearest town: McCalla

Fees and permits: Day-use fee; Iron and Steel Museum fee

Schedule: Year-round; day use sunrise to sunset; visitor center open Mon–Fri 8:30 a.m.–4:30 p.m., Sat 9 a.m.–4:30 p.m.; Iron and Steel Museum open Mon–Fri 8:30 a.m.–4:30 p.m., Sat 9 a.m.–4:30 p.m., Sun 12:30–4:30 p.m.

Maps: USGS McCalla, AL; *DeLorme: Alabama Atlas & Gazetteer,* page 30 H3; trail maps available at country store

Trail contact: Tannehill Ironworks Historical State Park, 12632 Confederate Pkwy., McCalla, AL 35111; (205) 477-9400; www.tannehill.org

Finding the trailhead: From the intersection of I-459 and I-20 West/I-59 South, take I-20 West/I-59 South 5 miles. Take exit 100 (Abernant/Bucksville) and turn left onto AL 216 East. (Shortly after turning onto AL 216, it becomes Bucksville Road.) Follow AL 216/Bucksville Road 0.6 mile and make a slight right onto Tannehill Parkway. Travel 1.9 miles and turn right onto Eastern Valley Road. In less than 0.1 mile, turn left onto Confederate Parkway. The park entrance is ahead in 0.7 mile. GPS: N33 14.970'/W87 04.297'

The Hike

At one time Birmingham and its environs rivaled the steel-production machine of Pittsburgh and helped keep the Confederate army supplied with weapons. In 1830 Daniel Hillman came to Alabama from Pennsylvania and built a forge along Roupes Creek. Two years after setting up the operation and well before he had a chance to see the fortune the forge would make, Hillman died. Local farmer Ninian Tannehill purchased the forge.

Three tall furnaces were constructed on the site with the use of slave laborers who cut the sandstone bricks by hand. By 1862 the ironworks was in full swing, producing pig iron for the Confederacy. On March 31, 1865, the Eighth Iowa Cavalry of the US Army shelled and set fire to the foundry, while a few miles up the road, Union troops torched the slave quarters.

The main furnace at Tannehill fully restored

A businessman bought the ironworks after the Civil War and tried to rebuild it, but times during Reconstruction were bad, and the facility was eventually abandoned and soon overtaken by nature.

This brings us to the 1970s, when the state of Alabama and several colleges resurrected the site. Archeological digs uncovered the old blower house and the main furnace. The furnace was rebuilt to its former glory and is now listed on the National Register of Historic Places.

The historic park encompasses more than 1,500 acres of forest just south of Bessemer. Forty historic structures of the period (1830 to 1870) have been brought in and restored for the public to view. Local craftspeople demonstrate the making of quilts, furniture, and pottery at the site each year between March and November. But, of course, the restored furnace is the park's centerpiece.

The Tannehill Ironworks Historic Trail takes you through the major sites of the park. The trail itself is actually a combination of four separate routes: the Iron Works

Trail, Slave Quarters Trail, Old Bucksville Stage Road, and Iron Haul Road. Along its route the trail passes through thick oak and dogwood forests and alongside several creeks, including Roupes Creek, which once helped power the furnace.

We begin the hike at the Alabama Iron and Steel Museum, a great museum that exhibits many of the artifacts discovered through the years at the site and well worth the small admission. The trail begins directly behind the museum next to Plank Road, which features cabins from the mid to late 1800s.

After crossing a creek you will come to a Y intersection with three trails. The top trail simply loops back into the middle trail. The center trail leads you to the top of the furnace to take a look at the massive stone structure from above. Our walk uses the lower trail on the left, which is called the Iron Works Trail. The trail takes you along beautiful views of the creek, with several boiling rapids churning its blue-green waters, before taking you to the base of the furnace, an impressive sight. Take your time to stroll around the structure and take it all in.

As the trail moves into the woods away from the campgrounds, it joins the Slave Quarters Trail. You'll have to look hard, but you will pass the foundations of several of the slave cabins burned by Union troops during their raid. The trail soon turns onto Old Bucksville Stage Road, which was the main highway into the area during the mid-1800s. At the end of the road, a short side trail leads to the slave cemetery. All that remains are simple, plain rock headstones marking the graves.

The hike is rated moderate due to some good inclines. The trail itself uses well-maintained dirt, gravel, and clay roads. After a good rain, however, some of the route, especially the Iron Road returning to the trailhead, can be deep in mud or have several water runoffs crossing it.

Your park day-use fee covers hiking, admission to the craft houses, and a visit to the furnace. The museum is a separate fee. And remember, artifacts are protected by the State of Alabama and cannot be removed. In other words, don't take home a brick from the furnace.

Miles and Directions

0.0 Start from behind the Alabama Iron and Steel Museum. Head down a set of cement stairs toward the creek to the southeast. Cross the creek on a small wooden bridge (a playground is on the opposite side of the creek on your right; a picnic area is to the left). There is a Y after the bridge. Take the left fork to the east (a sign here reads "Iron Works Trail"). This trail takes you behind the craft buildings and great views of the creek.

0.4 Come to the furnace. Cross the creek to the left (east) over the wood and steel Jim Folsom Bridge. On the other side come to the intersection with the Iron Haul Road Trail. A sign here points to the left (northeast), showing the way to the cemetery and Stagecoach Road. Turn left here onto the Slave Quarters Trail.

0.5 Pass a short pier that juts into a pond to the left (west).

0.9 Cross a stream that flows under the road.

Tannehill Ironworks Historic Trail

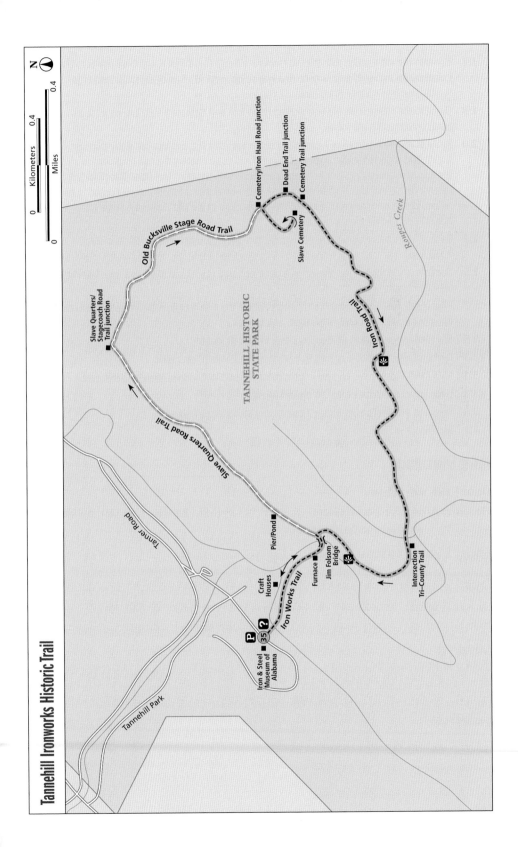

1.2 Come to the intersection with the Old Bucksville Stage Road Trail. A sign here points to the cemetery (to the right) and furnace (the way you just came). Turn right (southeast) onto the Old Bucksville Stage Road Trail.

1.9 Come to the intersection of the Iron Haul Road Trail and Cemetery Trail. Turn right (southwest) onto the Cemetery Trail.

2.0 Arrive at the slave cemetery. A chain-link fence encircles the site. You can enter through a gate that is tied shut with a rope. (***Option:*** From the cemetery the trail continues to the southeast another 0.1 mile, where it connects with the Iron Haul Road Trail [mile 2.3 below]. On my visit this section of trail was underwater with a runoff stream. I opted to turn around at the cemetery and return to the intersection of the Old Bucksville Stage Road and Iron Haul Road Trails.)

2.1 Back at the intersection of the three trails, turn right (southeast) onto the Iron Haul Road Trail.

2.2 Come to a Y. To the left (southeast) is a dead-end trail (and it's marked as such). Take the right fork (south).

2.3 Pass a side trail on the right (north). This is where the side trail from the cemetery joins the Iron Haul Road Trail. Continue straight (southwest).

2.8 Start seeing good views of Roupes Creek to the left (south).

3.3 A nice, grassy, 30-foot-long side trail leads to the banks of the creek.

3.4 Pass the Tri-County Trail coming in from the right (north). Continue straight to the west.

3.6 Good views of Roupes Creek to the left (west).

3.8 Return to the Jim Folsom Bridge. Retrace your steps to the parking lot.

4.1 Arrive back at the parking lot.

Hiking Information

Local Information

Bessemer Area Chamber of Commerce, 321 N. 18th St., Bessemer, AL 35020; (888) 423-7736; www.bessemerchamber.com

Local Events/Attractions

Trade Days at Tannehill, 12632 Confederate Pkwy., McCalla; (205) 477-9400; www.tannehill.org. The third weekend of each month from March through November, Tannehill plays host to one of the largest arts and craft shows around. People come from around the country to purchase handmade items, jewelry, furniture, and more.

Lodging

Tannehill Ironworks Historical State Park, 12632 Confederate Pkwy., McCalla; (205) 477-9400; www.tannehill.org. Tannehill has an excellent campground with both primitive and improved sites. Reservations are not accepted, so get there early to get a good spot.

36 Confederate Memorial Park Nature Trail

Once again we take you on a fascinating little hike that combines a nice interpretive nature walk, which features the second-largest yellow poplar tree in the state, with Civil War history—not history from the war itself but after it, as you walk around the grounds and remnants of a retirement home for Confederate soldiers.

Start: Museum parking lot
Distance: 1.4-mile lollipop
Hiking time: 1–1.5 hours
Difficulty: Easy on wide, flat trail
Trail surface: Dirt and gravel, some pavement near end
Best seasons: Sept–May
Other trail users: None
Canine compatibility: Leashed dogs permitted
Land status: Alabama historic state park
Nearest town: Verbena

Fees and permits: None to hike; admission fee for museum
Schedule: Year-round; park open 6 a.m.–dark; museum open 9 a.m.–5 p.m.
Maps: USGS Marbury, AL; *DeLorme: Alabama Atlas & Gazetteer*, page 38 H1; brochures with trail map available at museum gift shop
Trail contact: Confederate Memorial Park, 437 CR 63, Marbury, AL 36051; (205) 755-1990; www.preserveala.org/confederatepark.aspx

Finding the trailhead: From exit 200 on I-65, take CR 59 south 2.4 miles. Turn right onto US 31 South. Travel 2.3 miles and turn left onto CR 23. Travel 0.7 mile and make a right onto CR 63. The park entrance is straight ahead in 0.5 mile. The museum and parking is on the right, just after the entrance. GPS: N32 43.122' / W86 28.449'

The Hike

Normally when we talk about a hike through a Civil War park, we talk about the battle that occurred there. This time, however, we're talking about a time not too removed from the end of the war, when the veterans of the Confederate military needed help just to survive.

Confederate Memorial Park is the former site of the Alabama Old Soldiers Home. Following the war, several Southern states began an effort to help their veterans who could not support themselves. Hundreds, if not thousands, of former Confederate soldiers found themselves without family, jobs, money, land, or a place to live. Many had physical disabilities and lived in poorhouses. Unlike their Northern counterparts, who received fairly decent pensions from the federal government, Confederate soldiers had to rely on whatever they could to get by on.

▶ Just what is Dixie? Shortly before the Civil War, the State of Louisiana issued a note of currency worth $10 called a dix—French for "ten"—and eventually the South became known as "Dixie." Montgomery, Alabama, was the first capital of the Confederacy, and Alabama is officially known as the Heart of Dixie.

The trail leads to the solitude of Cemetery #2 where many of the veterans who lived here were buried.

In the late 1800s Montgomery attorney and Confederate veteran Jefferson Manly Falkner began a crusade to do something about this situation. Donating 80 acres of his own land, Falkner set out to build the Alabama Old Soldiers Home. Funds to construct and eventually run the facility came in from across the state, until finally the twenty-two-building facility, complete with a twenty-five-bed hospital, began operation in 1901. At its height, the facility housed 104 Confederate veterans and their wives. It ended operation in 1939, when the last remaining residents, five surviving widows, were placed into the care of the state welfare department. The buildings were soon dismantled and the land all but forgotten, except for the two cemeteries where the remains of many former residents are buried.

The land was resurrected by the state in 1964 when the Alabama legislature created Confederate Memorial Park, which, as they said, would be a "shrine to the honor of Alabama's Citizens of the Confederacy." Today the park is a fascinating look back in time at an era almost lost to history. The park boasts a beautiful museum that tells the story of the facility and its residents, and the trail here takes you not only to some interesting natural settings, but back to the time when the home was in full operation. There is no fee to enter the park or hike the trails, but there is a small admission fee to tour the museum.

The trail itself is a myriad of fire lanes, old dirt and gravel roads, and dirt footpaths that wind their way around the grounds. There are several side roads you can take to visit other areas not described here, all following similar wide paths. While for the most part the trails are not marked, it's difficult to lose your way since most loop back around toward the main path described there.

Before starting your hike, stop by the gift shop at the entrance of the museum for a brochure that describes some of the history you will be passing. Many of the features are numbered and correspond to a description in the handout.

The trail begins directly across the street from the museum. A sign reading "Nature Trail" leads the way through a wooden gate. One of the impressive bits of nature you will encounter on the trip is the second-largest yellow poplar tree in Alabama. When last officially measured, the tree had a circumference of 174½ inches and stood 105 feet tall. The canopy of the tree is 70 feet wide. You will also pass a spring that flows at a rate of 10 gallons per minute and was the source of water for the home.

As for the history, the trail will take you past the remains of an old dam built in 1905, the Old Marbury Methodist Church, and the site's reservoir and pumping station. The reservoir is an impressive large white structure that held 85,000 gallons of water that was pumped to a tower and then pumped into the home.

The hike culminates with a visit to Cemetery #2, a beautiful and peaceful resting place atop a hill overlooking the valley. As you enter the gates of the cemetery, the first grave you will pass is that of Jefferson Manly Falkner himself, the man whose vision created this site to honor and care for Alabama's Confederate veterans.

Miles and Directions

0.0 Start at the parking lot in front of the museum. (*FYI:* Be sure to pick up a brochure at the museum that lists the historic sites along the route.) Cross the road to the west. There is a wooden fence here with a sign that reads "Nature Trail". The trail is a wide dirt footpath.

0.1 Come to a sign that reads "Nature Trail" on the left and a trail leading in. Turn left (west) here onto a gravel footpath. Many signs dot the trail through this area identifying the plants you will see. In less than 0.1 mile, come to the second-largest poplar tree in the state on the right. It also happens to be the largest poplar in Lawrence County.

0.2 Come to a Y in the trail. Take the left fork (south). In about 200 feet come to a T intersection. Turn left (south).

0.3 Arrive at the remains of a water-pumping station. The trail veers to the right (northwest).

0.4 Come to the remnants of a reservoir pumping station that was used to supply water to the facility in the early 1900s. Follow the trail around the white building and cross a stream on a wooden bridge. A small trail comes in from the right. Continue straight (southwest).

0.5 Cross a wooden bridge over a spring. The trail parallels the stream to the right a short distance. Come to another T intersection. Take a right and head north.

0.6 Pass the remains of an old dam and pond on the left.

0.7 The trail returns to the dirt path that you started on. Turn left (north) onto the dirt path and pass a cylindrical metal gas tank on the right that was used for cooking and lighting at the home.

0.8 Pass the site of the old hotel as the trail swings around to the north. You will be passing a grassy field on your left (north). The Old Marbury Methodist Church can be seen to your right.

0.9 Turn right (east) onto a short, narrow 4-foot gravel path. In about 100 feet pass a picnic area and an old building used for gatherings on your left. Turn right (southwest) onto a dirt road and in a few yards you will pass the church. Continue straight (south) past the church on the dirt road to the paved park road (you are heading toward the museum).

1.1 Pass by the J. M. Falkner monument and a stand of memorial cedars on the right. Just before the museum, turn left (northeast) onto a paved side road that heads up a hill.

1.3 Arrive at Cemetery #2. After exploring the cemetery and taking in the views, turn around and retrace your steps to the main park road. When you arrive, turn left (south) and return to the museum parking lot.

1.4 Arrive back at the parking lot.

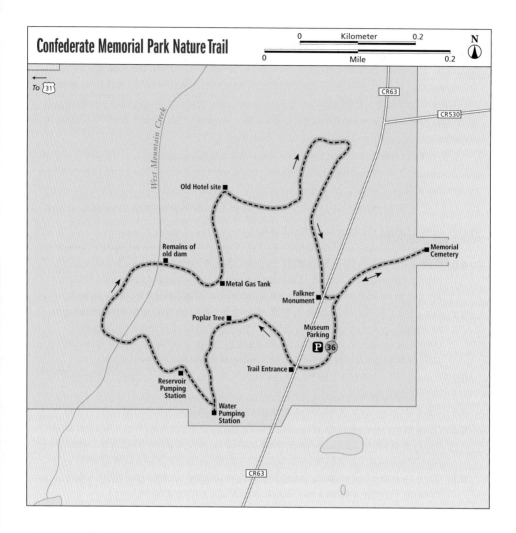

Confederate Memorial Park Nature Trail

0 ___ Kilometer ___ 0.2

0 ___ Mile ___ 0.2

N

To 31

West Mountain Creek

CR63

CR530

Old Hotel site ■

Remains of
old dam ■

■ Metal Gas Tank

Memorial
Cemetery ■

Falkner
Monument ■

Poplar Tree ■

Museum
Parking
P 36

Trail Entrance ■

Reservoir
Pumping
Station ■

Water
Pumping
Station ■

CR63

Hiking Information

Local Information

Chilton County Chamber of Commerce, 500 5th Avenue North, Clanton, AL 35046;
(205) 755-2400; www.chiltonchamberonline.com

Local Events/Attractions

Civil War Military and Civilian Life Living History, Confederate Memorial Park, 437
CR 63, Marbury; (205) 755-1990; www.preserveala.org/confederatepark.aspx. A day
of "up close and personal" living history of the War Between the States. Held annually in late April from 9 a.m. to 3 p.m.

Restaurants

Patsy's Kitchen, 3054 AL 31, Marbury; (205) 755-3768

Central Region Honorable Mentions

As we've seen, the Central region offers the hiker much in the way of scenery, history, and challenging treks. Unfortunately we only have limited space within these pages. There are plenty more trails for you to explore in this region. Here are a few other favorites of mine. Most of these trails are within striking distance of other trails listed in the Central region section of this book, so stop in, pay a visit, and let us know what you think.

H Rock Garden Trail

Ready for a challenge? Then hit the Rock Garden Trail at Cheaha State Park. This is a 1.6-mile out-and-back that climbs straight up the side of the state's highest mountain to just below the summit, and I mean straight up! How many trails can you say that when you get to the turnaround, you can see the trailhead far below?

The trail begins at the Cheaha Lake Recreation Area, then heads uphill; in fact, the trail goes uphill 1,143 feet in only 0.8 mile. As you clamber up the rocks to the top, you will likely pass rock climbers practicing their hobby right next to you.

The trail opens at 7 a.m. and closes at sunset. There is a park day-use fee. (See the Pulpit Rock Trail, Hike 27, for park directions and additional information.) *DeLorme: Alabama Atlas & Gazetteer:* Page 32 E5.

I Bald Rock / Doug Ghee Boardwalk Trail

Located on the very top of the highest mountain in the state, the Bald Rock / Doug Ghee Boardwalk Trail gives you what you would expect from the highest point— spectacular views! There are two ways you can walk this trail, and both are 1 mile in length. You can take the dirt footpath along the ridgeline to Bald Rock (the path parallels the boardwalk) or walk the boardwalk itself.

The boardwalk is perfect for families with small children and persons with disabilities. It runs down the center of the ridge and is elevated, approximately 4 feet off the ground. It's quite wide, at least 6 feet, with 4-foot-high handrails, and it leads directly to the rock. This makes the trip easily accessible for those in wheelchairs, and the railings have cables so that small children are kept in check.

The trail begins at the north end of the parking lot, next to the Cheaha Lodge, a fine example of CCC craftsmanship. A half mile into the trip, you arrive at Bald Rock with an amazing panoramic view of the surrounding mountains and valley.

Another magnificent view from atop Cheaha Mountain from the Bald Rock / Doug Ghee Boardwalk Trail

The trail opens at 7:00 a.m. and closes at sunset. There is a park day-use fee. (See the Pulpit Rock Trail, Hike 27, for park directions and additional information.) *DeLorme: Alabama Atlas & Gazetteer*: Page 32 E5.

J Deadening Trail

Not long ago a small group of hikers gathered together, solicited the help of local officials and the blessing of Alabama Power, and built a series of fantastic day hikes along the banks of beautiful Lake Martin. One of those, the 3.6-mile Deadening Trail, is a very strenuous trek but well worth the effort as you clamber through such rock features as Jasmine Bluff and Needles Eye, all with a backdrop of beautiful mountain laurel and rhododendron.

The Cherokee Ridge Alpine Trail Association, the group credited with building the trail, warns that children under 12 should not attempt this hike and young teens should be closely supervised. Sections of the trail are very narrow, with dangerous drops off the cliff.

Visit www.cherokeeridgealpinetrail.org for more information. *DeLorme: Alabama Atlas & Gazetteer*: Page 39 H6.

North Region

The North region generally stretches from the Tennessee-Alabama border to just north of Birmingham and is known geologically as the Cumberland Plateau. This mountainous region has seen its sandstone heights carved and weathered by the elements and the many waterways that flow through it, creating spectacular gorges, cascading waterfalls, and ancient caverns.

Hikers in the region will find plenty of challenge and beauty. Little River Canyon atop Lookout Mountain is one such stop. Carved over thousands of years, the canyon resonates with the thunder of the river, culminating in a spectacular 60-foot waterfall. The views from the canyon rim are something to behold. This is a popular location for whitewater rafters and rock climbers.

DeSoto State Park is located here, with a multitude of trails to visit the many faces of its landscapes. In addition to panoramic views of the West Fork of Little River and the gorge it creates, you will find several waterfalls here, including Lost Falls, Azalea Cascade, and Indian Falls. You will also walk the trails along the banks of the swift and boiling waters of the river itself.

Spectacular waterfalls, canyons, and rock shelters are found throughout northern Alabama. One of the highlights of hiking this region is the Cane Creek Canyon Preserve in Tuscumbia. The 400-acre preserve has a myriad of trails winding down from a beautiful mountain vista called "The Point" into a canyon carved by the weather and the preserve's namesake creek. No matter what trail you take, you will be treated to towering rock bluffs, deep rock shelters, and amazing tumbling waterfalls. And wildflowers run rampant here.

Then there is the Sipsey Wilderness, 25,000 acres of forest tucked away in Bankhead National Forest. The Borden Creek Trail is one of the best trails to introduce you and your family to hiking in the "Land of a Thousand Waterfalls." Along this 2.8-mile-long point-to-point hike (or 5.6 miles out and back), you will encounter rock shelters, bluffs, waterfalls, and a cave, the "Fat Man's Squeeze," that you have to make your way through.

History will probably remember this region most for the Marshall Space Flight Center. This site, along with the nearby Redstone Arsenal, played a key role in sending Americans to the moon. It was here that Wernher von Braun and NASA engineers

Stairs along the DeSoto Scout Trail

developed the Saturn V rocket that would put Apollo astronauts on the moon. Today the center is used by NASA to test and assemble parts of the new Space Launch System (SLS) that will take us out into deep space. This is also home to one of the nation's space camps for both children and adults. The museum and guided tours at the Space and Rocket Center are a must-see when in the area.

37 DeSoto Scout Trail

The DeSoto Scout Trail (DST) described here is only a short section of the much longer 16-mile hike, but along this route you will be treated to a little of everything that makes the trail special—views, rapids, and waterfalls. The trail begins with a view of a canyon and the rushing waters of the West Fork of Little River before moving down to river level, where you will be right next to the foaming blue-green waters, with a little trip to the 50-foot-tall Indian Falls. The trail is moderate in difficulty, with plenty of ups-and-downs.

Start: DeSoto State Park pool or tennis courts
Distance: 1.9-mile multiloop
Hiking time: About 2 hours
Difficulty: Moderate due to some short climbs
Trail surface: Dirt and rock
Best seasons: Late fall–late spring
Other trail users: None
Canine compatibility: Leashed dogs permitted
Land status: Alabama state park
Nearest town: Huntsville

Fees and permits: Day-use fee
Schedule: Year-round, 7 a.m.–sunset
Maps: USGS Dugout Valley, Fort Payne, AL; *DeLorme: Alabama Atlas & Gazetteer*, page 21 G8; state park trail maps available for free at country store
Trail contact: DeSoto State Park, 7104 DeSoto Pkwy. NE, Fort Payne, AL 35967; (256) 845-0051; www.alapark.com/desotoresort

Finding the trailhead: From Fort Payne on I-59 at exit 218, head east on Glenn Boulevard SW / Pine Ridge Road SW 1 mile and turn left onto Gault Avenue South. Travel 1.1 miles and turn right onto Fifth Street. Travel 0.4 mile and turn left onto Wallace Avenue NE. Follow Wallace Avenue NE 2 miles and turn left onto CR 89 / DeSoto Parkway NE. Travel 5.7 miles. At the DeSoto State Park Country Store, turn right into the picnic area then make an immediate left. In 0.2 mile you will arrive at the tennis courts. If the gate to the pool parking lot is not closed, turn right here and park at the swimming pool building. If it is closed, park at the tennis courts. GPS: N34 30.069' / W85 38.057'

The Hike

This 1.9-mile hike on the DeSoto Scout Trail, or DST, spotlights a much different side of DeSoto State Park than you find on the Falls Loop trail. The trail takes you high above rocky bluffs that were formed by the West Fork of Little River thousands of years ago for a view of the roaring rapids below. The path then meanders to a beautiful waterfall, Indian Falls (which you will visit twice), before it quickly ducks down to river level for a deafening view of the river itself.

Now, keep in mind that even a river of this size is seasonal, but unlike many smaller creeks and streams, there will most always be a flow of water through its channel. In dry seasons the river can be quite low, with not much of a flow at all. The best time to see the real character of the West Fork is to visit the park late fall to late spring

The West Fork of Little River rushes by the trail.

when the rains really kick it up. Fall also has the added benefit of the hardwoods coming to life and lining the trail with amazing autumn colors.

While the full DeSoto Scout Trail extends well beyond the borders of the state park (16 miles to be exact), the entire length of this trip is within its boundaries. DeSoto State Park, as with most of the state parks in Alabama, was built by the Civilian Conservation Corps (CCC) in the 1930s. You will see an example of their handiwork a half mile into the hike when you come to a large trail shelter overlooking the gorge.

The hike itself is moderately steep in some areas but not too difficult. Many sections of the trail are lined with rhododendron, mountain laurel, and azalea. The off-white blossoms and their sweet fragrance fill the air in late spring, usually peaking by the third week of May. The trail is marked with paint blazes: blue for the Pool Loop approach trail, lime green for the Cabin Trail, and yellow for the DeSoto Scout Trail itself. Additionally you will see a few yellow wooden signs marked with red DST lettering.

Your hike begins at the state park's pool. During the summer you can park here in the large paved lot. During the off-season vehicle access is prohibited (the lot is chained off), so instead park a few dozen yards away at the tennis courts. The blue Pool Loop Trail begins on the left side (north) of the pool's parking lot as you are looking at the pool. A brown post with a hiker logo on it leads the way into the woods here. This section of the Pool Loop is a very pretty 0.25-mile walk through a "tunnel" of azalea, rhododendron, and holly and follows the banks of Sharp's Creek as it tumbles into the river. After a good rain you will see, and hear, some really nice cascades and small falls.

Almost 0.5 mile into the trip, the trail splits off onto the yellow-blazed DST for a short trek to an old trail shelter built by the CCC in the 1930s. The shelter is perched high atop a bluff overlooking West Fork of Little River's gorge. It is a beautiful view and a great place to just sit and relax in the shade of the building. The best views come late fall through winter when the foliage is down.

From here the trail heads back to the intersection with the Pool Loop Trail and follows the yellow blazes downhill to just above the river. You will have great views of the river gorge and rapids below, and at about 1 mile into the walk, you will come to Indian Falls. When the water is flowing, this is an impressive 50-foot cascade. There are two short side trails you can take here to view the waterfall. You can either head downhill about 200 feet or so to the river's edge and view the falls from the bottom up, or walk straight ahead 50 feet to stand next to the falls and the rock shelter it has created. Either way, be very careful on the slippery rocks.

The trail itself climbs about 30 feet to the west (your right) up some railroad tie stairs and takes you over the top of the falls. From here the trail heads downhill to the banks of the river, one of the most beautiful sections of the hike when the river is full and the blue-green waters are rushing through narrow channels around boulders. Be sure to check out the bluffs and rock shelters to your right as you walk this section.

After taking in the river, the DST comes to a Y. The right fork starts taking you back uphill to the lime-green-blazed Cabin Trail, where you will be walking behind the park's beautifully restored cabins with some nice gorge views, before it rejoins the DST and takes you back to your vehicle.

When hiking the DeSoto Scout Trail, be sure to keep your eyes to the sky for hawks that soar above the canyon looking for their next meal. And watch for lizards darting in and out of the rocks, which are also inhabited by snakes including the northern black racer, northern cottonmouth, and timber rattlesnake.

Miles and Directions

0.0   Start from either the parking lot at the tennis courts or the pool house. If starting at the tennis courts, head to the east a short 100 to 200 feet toward the pool house parking lot. From the pool house parking lot, head to the north toward the woods. You will see a brown sign with a hiker logo on it. Duck into the woods here. The trail has blue blazes and travels through thick "caves" of azalea, rhododendron, and holly.

0.2   The trail appears to Y. Turn to the right (northeast); straight is a dead-end game trail. Just after the turn, cross a short bridge over Sharp's Creek.

0.3   The trail passes a nice cascade in the stream to the right (southwest) and heads downhill on wooden railroad tie steps. In less than 0.1 mile, pass an impressive rock shelter on the left (east). The pool house can be seen through the trees uphill to your right.

0.4   Come to the intersection of the DeSoto Scout Trail and the Blue Trail. The Blue Trail continues off to the right (west). The DST is blazed in yellow, with an occasional yellow-and-red DST sign hung on a tree. Follow the yellow blazes of the DST to the left (east).

0.5   Pass a nice view high above the West Fork of Little River and its canyon to the east. In less than 0.1 mile, arrive at a CCC Trail Shelter with an impressive view of the canyon and river below. Turn around here and head back to the Blue Trail / DeSoto Scout Trail intersection you passed at mile 0.4.

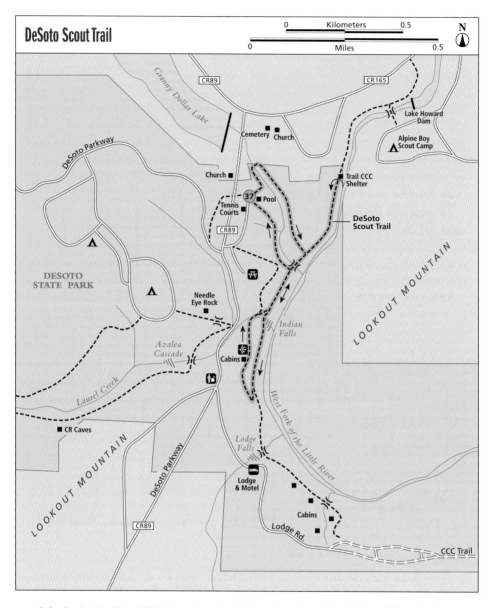

0.6 Back at the Blue/DST intersection, turn left (west) and head steeply downhill on the joined Blue/DST (the path is blazed both blue and yellow here).

0.7 At the bottom of the hill, cross a 20-foot bridge over Sharp's Creek. Following the bridge, the Blue Trail heads uphill to the right (northwest); the DST turns left (southwest). Turn left onto the yellow-blazed DST. In 100 feet climb down some stone stairs. The path is narrow, with a mix of dirt and rock footing. You will be walking above the river with excellent views to your left (east).

0.8 Pass a connector trail to the park's CCC Pavilion on the right (north). In less than 0.1 mile, there is an excellent view of the river and rapids on the left (south).

0.9 Come to a crossroad. Straight is a 200-foot walk that takes you next to Indian Falls; right (south) is a 100-foot walk to the banks of the river and the bottom of Indian Falls. Turn right (north) and climb several railroad tie stairs. At the top turn left (west) onto the DST. In less than 0.1 mile, cross Indian Falls on a 50-foot-long bridge. Just past the bridge, come to a Y. This is where the loop will rejoin. Take the left fork and follow the yellow blazes steeply downhill. You will now be walking next to the river with great views, but be careful, the rocks can be slippery.

1.2 Walk past some impressive bluffs and rock shelters on the right (west). Come to a Y. The yellow DST heads off on the left to the southeast. Take the right fork and head uphill to the south on the unmarked trail. In 200 yards the Violet Trail comes in on the left. Continue to the right (north). This is now the lime-green-blazed Cabin Trail. You will now be walking on top of the bluffs you just passed.

1.4 Pass behind cabins. There are a few nice views here.

1.5 Rejoin the DST at mile 0.9. Follow the yellow blazes back to mile 0.7.

1.7 The blue-blazed Pool Loop Trail will be on your left (northwest). Turn left here onto the Pool Loop. There is a steep drop to your right along this narrow trail.

1.8 Come to chain-link fence next to the pool building. Follow it around to the left (north) back to the pool parking lot.

1.9 Arrive back at the parking lot.

Hiking Information

Local Information

Alabama Mountain Lakes Tourist Association, 402 Sherman St., Decatur, AL 35602; (800) 648-5381; www.northalabama.org

Local Events/Attractions

The World's Longest Yard Sale, Gadsden. This is the southern end of the 93-mile-long yard sale that features over 1,000 vendors in north Alabama. Held annually the first weekend in August.

Lodging

DeSoto State Park Campground, 7104 DeSoto Pkwy. NE, Fort Payne; (256) 845-5075; www.alapark.com/desotoresort/camping. Improved and primitive campsites.

Restaurants

DeSoto State Park Mountain Inn, 7104 DeSoto Pkwy. NE, Fort Payne; www.alapark.com/desotoresort/%20restaurant. Breakfast is served 7–10 a.m., lunch 11:30 a.m.–2 p.m., dinner 5–8 p.m.

Hike Tours

DeSoto State Park Campground, 7104 DeSoto Pkwy. NE, Fort Payne; (256) 845-5075; http://alapark.com/desotoresort/Nature%20Programs%20&%20Events. DeSoto State Park, along with its many partners including Jacksonville State University and Little River Canyon National Preserve, hosts many educational programs and hikes. Visit the website for schedule.

THE ALABAMA TRAILS COMMISSION

Throughout this edition I have remarked how Alabama has become a hiking destination, not only for residents of the state but also for hikers and backpackers from around the country and the world. This is due in great part to the amazing work being done by hundreds of volunteer trail builders across the state.

Up until recently, these volunteers went about their work quietly, cutting and maintaining trails without much in the way of thanks and more importantly, without a voice in the state government or financial backing. Recently, that all changed.

On February 16, 2010, seeing the whirlwind of trail groups that had arisen in the state and realizing that outdoor recreation such as hiking, paddling, and horseback riding was becoming an income stream for the state (ecotourism), the Alabama House voted to establish a new commission to help organize and guide the trail groups. The Alabama Trails Commission was signed into law soon after by Governor Bob Riley.

Stakeholders including proponents of river trails, birding trails, walking trails, hiking trails, equestrian trails, off-road vehicle trails, and mountain bike and road bike trails needed vision, coordination, and an established voice. The answer was the Alabama Trails Commission.

Where there is intense development, there tends to be intense overlap of purpose. The Alabama Trails Commission was established to foster communication among all the trail constituents to balance their efforts wisely and in chosen directions—an initiative to replace the scattershot approach that had previously seen uncoordinated approaches wither and disappear. The commission has given unification to all of Alabama's trail stakeholders.

Since its inception, the commission has mapped out and pursued a path toward a realm of large-scale projects impossible until now. It has begun an initiative to create a web-based portal for the various trail stakeholders in the state; it has held meetings of the Alabama Trails Conference; it has identified a roster of must-do initiatives to make Alabama's standing commensurate with its natural resources; and it has created a funding arm to sustain its endeavors.

The Alabama Trails Commission is a vital effort to institutionalize best practices in the establishment of Alabama trails, the distribution of information about its endeavors, and the means to support such important ventures in the long term.

38 Falls Loop

This loop trail is located in DeSoto State Park and uses three trails to take you to some impressive waterfalls and geologic features. The trails and their namesake falls (Lost Falls, Laurel Falls, and Azalea Cascade) are simply beautiful as they cascade over jagged rock walls. The trails also take you past rock outcroppings, bluffs, and a few rock shelters, and near Azalea Cascade, you'll be walking through walls of beautiful azaleas, rhododendrons, and mountain laurel.

Start: Lost Falls Trailhead on CR 618 (DeSoto Parkway)
Distance: 3.1-mile lollipop
Hiking time: About 2 hours
Difficulty: Moderate due to climbs
Trail surface: Dirt and rock
Best seasons: Year-round
Other trail users: None
Canine compatibility: Leashed dogs permitted
Land status: Alabama state park

Nearest town: Huntsville
Fees and permits: None
Schedule: Year-round, 7 a.m.–sunset
Maps: USGS Dugout Valley, Fort Payne, AL; *DeLorme: Alabama Atlas & Gazetteer*, page 21 G8; park trail maps available for free at country store
Trail contact: DeSoto State Park, 7104 DeSoto Pkwy. NE, Fort Payne, AL 35967; (256) 845-0051; www.alapark.com/desotoresort

Finding the trailhead: From Fort Payne on I-59 at exit 218, head east on Glenn Boulevard SW / Pine Ridge Road SW 1 mile and turn left onto Gault Avenue South. Travel 1.1 miles and turn right onto Fifth Street. Travel 0.4 mile and turn left onto Wallace Avenue NE. Follow Wallace Avenue NE 2 miles and turn left onto CR 89 / DeSoto Parkway NE. Travel 5.7 miles and turn left onto DeSoto Parkway. In 1.2 miles the parking area will be on the right and clearly marked. The trailhead is across the road to the south. GPS: N34 30.069' / W85 38.057'

The Hike

DeSoto State Park is packed with breathtaking water features. Several waterfalls can be found here as well as the churning waters of the West Fork of Little River. Add to the mix lush forests and colorful wildflowers, and you can understand why the park is known as the "Home of Mother Nature."

The Falls Loop Trail takes you to three of those beautiful falls using their namesake trails: Lost Falls, Laurel Falls, and Azalea Cascade. There is great news for hikers: Since the last edition, damage from past major ice storms and more recent tornados along these trails has been cleared, and the paths are hikeable once again and beautiful. Each is now clearly marked with paint blazes on trees or on the rock trail bed: orange for Laurel Falls, red for Azalea Cascade, and blue for Lost Falls. You will still see remnants of the damage from these storms, mainly downed trees, along sections of the hike. They make great reminders of the power of nature.

A view of Lost Falls

The hike begins at the Lost Falls Trailhead, a gravel parking lot off of CR 618. It is a nice large parking area with ample room for twenty-plus cars. There is a nice restroom here as well. The trail begins across the road from the parking lot to the south. Two bike trails also come in here: the Family Bike Trail from the north behind the restroom, and the Never Never Land Loop across the road next to the Laurel Falls Trail to the west.

The hike is rated moderate due to some climbs, especially following the junction of the Azalea Cascade and Laurel Falls Trails, but don't let this stop you. These are short climbs. The remainder of the hike is fairly easy over relatively flat, but rocky, terrain.

The hike begins by using the orange-blazed Laurel Falls Trail, which is a National Recreational Trail. This is a nice dirt and rock footpath through stands of pines and hardwoods. The first waterfall, Lost Falls, is about 0.5 mile into the hike. This makes it easy for those of you who don't want to hike the entire loop. You can simply park and take a quick out-and-back to this waterfall. It is an impressive 50-foot-or-so cascade tumbling down two tiers of rock. To get to the falls, the orange trail splits to the east and south; a small carved rock on the ground marks the short trail to the falls, which is also blazed in orange. Once you visit the falls, you can either retrace your steps back to where you were or turn right (west) and follow this side trail a short 50 feet back to the main trail.

Of course, there needs to be a word of warning: The bluffs around the falls are tall, slippery, and dangerous. Use extreme caution around any of the waterfalls.

The trail then ambles along until it heads behind the campground, where things get a bit rockier (you will be climbing through some stone cuts), and it finally intersects with the red-blazed Azalea Cascade Trail. This aptly named path is lined with thick, tall azalea bushes that are beautiful in the spring when they bloom. The red trail leads you right to the stream and the cascade.

Shortly after Azalea Cascade we join the blue-blazed Lost Falls Trail (formerly known as CR Caves). After a rugged little climb from the stream, you will be walking alongside a bluff on your left. Keep a lookout for rock shelters in the bluffs carved by the elements thousands of years ago. This is the section where you will see the most damage from recent tornados, but the path is clear. Somewhere along this trail there is a side path where you can see Laurel Falls from the opposite side, but I wasn't able to find it. Maybe you can when you visit. You will, however, come up to a short trail

THE CCC IN ALABAMA

In the depths of the Great Depression, President Franklin D. Roosevelt enacted a new program that would spur the economy by creating a virtual army of young men to bolster the nation's infrastructure as well as build exciting new places of recreation for the public. They were the Civilian Conservation Corps, or CCC.

The program would employ over 500,000 men in their late teens to early twenties, to build dams, state parks, and more. In exchange for their work, the government provided food, clothing, shelter, and $30 a month in pay, with $25 of that sent home to their families.

The amazing work of the CCC can be seen throughout the state parks of Alabama, like the massive stone fire tower atop Cheaha Mountain or the beautiful lodge at Monte Sano State Park. In his book *The Civilian Conservation Corps in Alabama*, Robert Pasquill says that the program employed 20,000 men in the state between 1933 and 1942, creating thirteen state forests and seven state parks.

You can see the CCC in action in Alabama with rare historic movies (see appendix B, "Further Reading," for URLs).

that leads to the opposite side of Lost Falls for a really great view of the rock shelter it careens over before the trail links back up with the Laurel Falls Trail and heads back to the trailhead.

Miles and Directions

0.0 Start from the parking lot on CR 618. Cross the road to the south and you will see the Lost Falls Trailhead clearly marked. As you enter the woods, there is a sign that points to the Never Never Land Bike Trail to the right (west) and the Laurel Falls Trail to the south. Follow the orange blazes of the Laurel Falls Trail. The path throughout is a combination of dirt and rock bed. It is wide here, about 4 feet, with plenty of pine trees.

0.1 Cross a wide stream. The canopy opens, with some grassy edging along the sides of the trail. The first signs of past damage from ice storms and tornados will be seen, with many downed trees, but the path is clear.

0.4 The trail is a large flat rock bed. Come to a Y. The right fork (south) is the blue-blazed Lost Falls Trail, which will be used for the return trip. Take the left fork (southeast) and continue on the orange-blazed Laurel Falls Trail.

0.5 Come to a Y. A small carved sign on the ground marks the short trail that leads to Lost Falls. The Laurel Falls Trail splits here to the left (east) and right (south). Take a right and hike down to Lost Falls. Be careful on the bluffs around the falls! They are slippery and can be dangerous. When done, turn around and head back to the Y. At the Y turn right (east) to continue on the main orange-blazed trail.

0.8 Cross a wide stream. There's a nice cascade here.

0.9 The orange/silver-blazed Campground Trail comes in from the left (north). Continue straight, following the orange blazes. The trail bed starts turning more rocky.

1.2 Another carved stone on the ground marks the short side trail to Laurel Falls. Turn right here onto the unmarked trail to visit the falls in less than 50 feet. Again, be careful on the slippery rocks. When done, turn around and head back to the Laurel Falls Trail. Turn right (northeast) and continue on the orange-blazed trail.

1.4 The Campground Trail comes in from the left (north). Continue following the orange blazes to the right (east).

1.5 Pass rock outcroppings on the right. Follow the trail around them past the campground on the left. Walking behind the campground, the trail climbs through cuts in outcroppings. In less than 0.1 mile, come to a Y. The orange trail heads to the left; the red-blazed Azalea Cascade Trail heads to the south. Turn right onto the Azalea Cascade Trail.

1.6 Come to a T intersection. The trail heads left and right (east and west). Turn right and continue following the red blazes. This area is thick with azalea and rhododendron. In less than 0.1 mile, arrive at Azalea Cascade. Cross the stream and falls over a bridge and come to a T intersection on the other side. The blue-blazed Lost Falls Trail heads left and right. Turn right (south) onto the blue-blazed trail. The trail heads uphill past rock outcroppings and rock shelters on the left (east). The path is a rock bed at this point.

1.8 The outcroppings end. The trail levels out and is a dirt footpath again. Evidence of past severe storms is very noticeable through here.

2.4 A short, 30-foot side trail to the right (north) leads to the opposite side of Lost Falls. Continue to the south, following the blue blazes.

Falls Loop

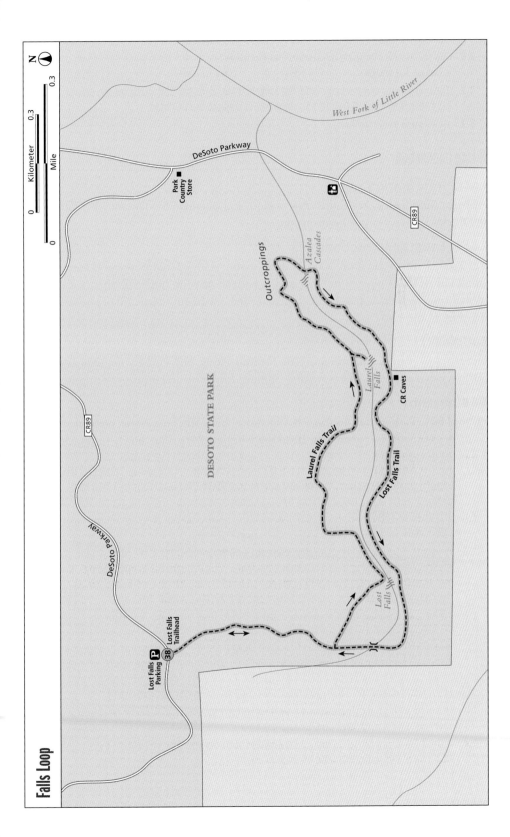

2.6 The trail travels alongside the stream that forms the falls on the right. Cross the stream on a unique log bridge.

2.7 The trail follows along a long, wide, flat rock. In a few yards the trail intersects the orange Lost Falls Trail. Turn left (north) and retrace your steps to the trailhead.

3.1 Arrive back at the trailhead.

Hiking Information

Local Information

Alabama Mountain Lakes Tourist Association, 402 Sherman St., Decatur, AL 35602; (800) 648-5381; www.northalabama.org

Local Events/Attractions

411 Twin Drive-In and Grill, 300 CR 265, Centre; (256) 927-2855; www.411drivein .com. The 411 first opened in 1953, and as with all drive-in movie theaters, has had its share of tough times, but it is now thriving and one of only a handful of remaining drive-ins in the state.

Lodging

DeSoto State Park Campground, 7104 DeSoto Pkwy. NE, Fort Payne; (256) 845-5075; www.alapark.com/desotoresort/camping. Improved and primitive campsites.

Restaurants

DeSoto State Park Mountain Inn, 7104 DeSoto Pkwy. NE, Fort Payne; www.alapark .com/desotoresort/%20restaurant. Breakfast is served 7–10 a.m., lunch 11:30 a.m.– 2 p.m., dinner 5–8 p.m.

39 Beaver Pond Loop

Take a different view of the Little River Canyon National Preserve on this 1.4-mile trail. The Beaver Pond Loop is a perfect hike for you and your family, especially younger children who couldn't make the tougher climbs found in the canyon itself. The trail gives you a chance to explore a beautiful hardwood and pine forest with creeks, moss-covered footpaths, and an amazing little ecosystem created by beavers.

Start: Trailhead on CR 176 (Little River Canyon Scenic Parkway)

Distance: 1.4-mile lollipop

Hiking time: About 1 hour

Difficulty: Easy over flat dirt paths and bridges

Trail surface: Dirt with some rock

Best seasons: Year-round

Other trail users: None

Canine compatibility: Leashed dogs permitted

Land status: National preserve

Nearest town: Fort Payne

Fees and permits: None

Schedule: Year-round, sunrise to sunset

Maps: USGS Fort Payne, AL; *DeLorme: Alabama Atlas & Gazetteer*, page 27 A7

Trail contact: Little River Canyon National Preserve, 4322 Little River Trail NE, Ste. 100, Fort Payne, AL 35967; (256) 845-9605; www.nps.gov/liri

Finding the trailhead: From Fort Payne at the intersection of AL 35 and US 11, take Fifth Street southeast 0.4 mile and turn left onto Wallace Avenue NE / AL 35 South. Travel 7.3 miles. Turn right onto AL 176 / Little River Canyon Parkway. Travel 1.3 miles (you will pass the Little River Canyon and Lynn Overlooks on the left). The parking lot and trailhead will be on the right. GPS: N34 23.003' / W85 37.752'

The Hike

So there we were, my wife and I, driving along heading to Little River Canyon to do research for another hike. I was looking forward to getting back to the canyon, but I'll be honest, I wasn't looking forward to the steep 0.75-mile climb down the canyon wall to the river and the subsequent climb back up.

We turned onto Little River Canyon Parkway, passed the Little River Canyon Overlook and the Lynn Overlook, and then we saw it—a trail kiosk. I had never noticed it before. So we pulled into the parking lot and, lo and behold, there was a trail: the Beaver Pond Loop. Turns out that this is a really nice 1.4-mile lollipop loop—just a walk in the woods if you will, but a great little place to take your kids or for you birders a good place to break out the binoculars.

The trail is located on the plateau above the canyon so you won't have any canyon views here, but what it does give you is a serene walk through a wetland habitat forest with wildflowers like yellow false foxglove and pale-spike lobelia and trees like bitternut, pignut, and shagbark. The trail is especially pretty in spring and early summer when azaleas are in full bloom, forest grasses and ferns are deep green, and sections of the footpath have a deep, soft green bed of moss.

The Beaver Pond Loop's namesake

If you walk the trail at the right time of year, wild blueberries will be found growing alongside it. Most of the time you would be discouraged from picking the berries, but not this time. On the Little River Canyon website, the National Park Service actually says to feel free and have a snack as you walk.

The trail eventually leads you to its namesake beaver dam. Beavers build these dams to stem the flow of running water so that they can raise their families. The pond that is formed actually creates a more active ecosystem than before the dam was built, becoming an excellent habitat for many species of wildlife.

Several different types of birds make the pond their home, like wood ducks, dark-eyed juncos, towhees, nuthatches, and a wide variety of woodpeckers and sapsuckers. Catfish have also found a home here along with salamanders, and, of course, an abundance of mammals frequent the pond, including white-tailed deer, foxes, and raccoons. Being in a wetland, you may come across a snake or two like cottonmouth or water moccasin. If you see one, stop, wait a moment, and it should move along. Remember, all wildlife and plants in the park are federally protected, so do not harm them in any way. There is a short boardwalk here that leads up to the pond, with an observation deck and benches that overlook it and the dam.

For the most part the trail follows a dirt footpath. There are a couple of sections that travel over flat rock and the moss trail bed I mentioned earlier. You will cross over four creeks on some nice footbridges. One of the prettiest is at mile 0.4. As always, keep in mind that water flows in the creek and pond are seasonal and could be low or nonexistent during droughts or the heat of summer. The trail sports several benches as well, just in case you want to take a break and enjoy the forest.

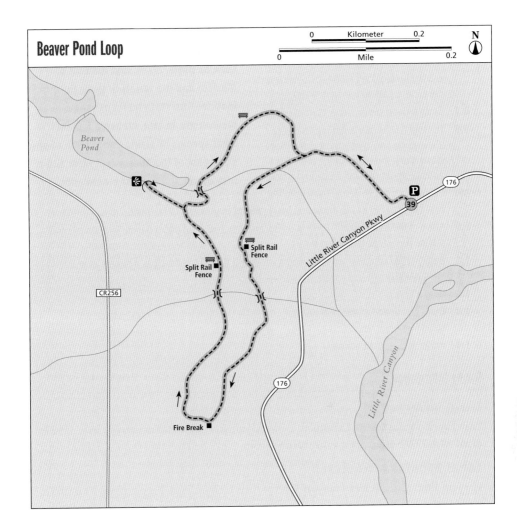

Beaver Pond Loop

Oh, and by the way, we did end up revisiting and hiking down into the canyon on the Eberhart Trail. Yes, it's still there, and yes, it is still steep.

Miles and Directions

0.0 Start from the parking lot / trailhead off of AL 176 / Little River Canyon Scenic Parkway (it is located just past the second overlook on the parkway, Lynn Overlook, on the right). The parking lot is gravel, with a kiosk and map. There is room for about fifteen cars here. Start by heading southwest on the dirt footpath, with a good mix of hardwoods and pines. The trail is level the entire length. There are no blazes.

0.2 Come to a sign that reads "Beaver Pond Overlook ½ mile" (arrow pointing to right [north]) / "Beaver Pond Loop" (arrow pointing to left [west]). Head to the left and cross a creek over a nice 15- to 20-foot bridge. The forest is thick with pines here.

0.3 The canopy opens up a bit. Pass a zigzag split-rail fence on the left and a bench.

0.4 Cross a creek over a 20-foot bridge. In the spring the green moss is very pretty here.

0.6 A trail comes in from the left (south). This is a fire break; don't follow it. Continue on the current path to the right (west).

0.7 Cross a deep creek over a 10-foot bridge.

0.8 The trail travels over a flat rock base for a few yards. Very pretty, thick green moss grows along the edges of the path. Pass another zigzag split-rail fence and a bench.

0.9 Come to a Y. A sign points the way to the Beaver Pond. Follow the arrow and head straight (northwest) to the pond.

1.0 Arrive at the Beaver Pond. There is an observation deck here and a bench. Turn around and retrace your steps to the last Y.

1.1 Back at the last Y, turn left and head east. In less than 0.1 mile, cross a stream over a short bridge.

1.2 Pass a bench.

1.3 Come to the end of the loop you started at mile 0.2. Turn left (north) and retrace your steps to the trailhead.

1.4 Arrive back at the trailhead.

▶ Because of Alabama's warm and wet weather; the number of water features such as rivers, lakes, and the Gulf of Mexico; and the variety of geologic features, the state has remarkable biodiversity. In fact, Alabama has the most species of plants and wildlife of any state east of the Mississippi River and is fifth overall in the most biodiversity.

Hiking Information

Local Information

Fort Payne Chamber of Commerce, 300 Gault Ave. North, Fort Payne, AL 35967; (256) 845-2741; www.fortpaynechamber.com

Local Events/Attractions

Canyon Fest, Little River Canyon Interpretive Center, Fort Payne; (256) 782-5697; www.jsu.edu/epic. Held the first Saturday of November, Canyon Fest celebrates the natural beauty, history, and recreation of the largest canyon east of the Mississippi with a good dose of activities for the kids, food, and music.

Lodging

DeSoto State Park Campground, 7104 DeSoto Pkwy. NE, Fort Payne; (256) 845-5075; www.alapark.com/desotoresort/camping. Improved and primitive campsites.

Restaurants

DeSoto State Park Mountain Inn, 7104 DeSoto Pkwy. NE, Fort Payne; www.alapark .com/desotoresort/%20restaurant. Breakfast is served 7–10 a.m., lunch 11:30 a.m.– 2 p.m., dinner 5–8 p.m.

Organizations

Little River Canyon Interpretive Center, 4322 Little River Trail NE, Fort Payne, AL; (256) 845-3548; www.epic.jsu.edu

40 Cave Mountain Loop

The Cave Mountain Loop is an amazing little hike packed into a small tract of land on the southwest side of Lake Guntersville at the Tennessee Valley Authority (TVA) dam. This TVA trail is only 1.4 miles in length but is highlighted with nice views of the lake, a beautiful and rare tupelo gum swamp, towering rock bluffs, and a cave that was once mined for saltpeter for gun powder during the Civil War.

Start: Trailhead on CR 50 / Snow Road
Distance: 1.4-mile lollipop
Hiking time: About 2 hours
Difficulty: Moderate to difficult due to steep inclines
Trail surface: Dirt and rock footpath, some rock scrambling
Best seasons: Year-round
Other trail users: Cavers
Canine compatibility: Leashed dogs permitted
Land status: TVA small wild area
Nearest town: Guntersville

Fees and permits: None
Schedule: Year-round, sunrise to sunset
Maps: USGS Guntersville Dam, AL; *DeLorme: Alabama Atlas & Gazetteer*, page 19 H9
Trail contact: Tennessee Valley Authority Reservation, PO Box 1010, Muscle Shoals, AL 35662; (256) 386-2601; www.tva.gov
Special considerations: The cave can be dangerous. You can enter the first 100 to 150 feet; after that special permits are required and you must be an experienced caver. Contact the TVA for more information.

Finding the trailhead: From Guntersville at the intersection of US 431 and AL 69, take AL 69 south 6.1 miles. Turn right onto CR 240 / Union Grove Road. Travel 2.3 miles and turn right onto CR 50 / Snow Road. Travel 2.7 miles. The parking lot and trailhead will be on the left. There is a yellow steel pole gate here, gravel parking area, and enough room for at least 20 cars. GPS: N34 25.116' / W86 24.276'

The Hike

I really don't like clichés, but in this case I'll make an exception: Good things do come in small packages, especially when you're talking about the Cave Mountain Loop.

This hike is located in a small tract of land owned and managed by the Tennessee Valley Authority (TVA) just southwest of Lake Guntersville and Guntersville Dam. The tract is one of thirty-one small wild areas managed by the TVA. These areas are the result of a project started by the agency in 1976, the National Heritage Project. With the support of the Nature Conservancy, the project was designed to conduct studies on how to protect threatened and endangered species of wildlife and plant life in environmentally sensitive sites. Cave Mountain is one of those.

The property itself is small in size, only 34 acres, but within its boundaries there is a wealth of natural beauty to explore. The Cave Mountain Loop meanders around the top of the trail's namesake mountain using a generally rocky path along the north side and the ridge. All along the route you will see oak, basswood, hickory, eastern

The cave of the Cave Mountain Loop is located right alongside the trail. It's sad that graffiti "artists" were also here.

red cedar, yellow poplar, common persimmon, and sugar maple trees, to name only a few. Depending on the season, you will see many wildflowers along the path and on top of the rocks surrounding it. Some of the flowers you will see include jack-in-the-pulpit and verbena.

As you wind around to the north side of the mountain, the path drops down to follow the banks of a beautiful, wide tupelo swamp. This is a prime area to view wildlife, including white-tailed deer and wood ducks. It's not uncommon to see box turtles lining up on logs sunning themselves, and in the evening you'll be treated to a chorus of frog song.

The trail along the swamp is a dirt path and narrow, maybe 1 to 1½ feet wide in many spots. That's because it is wedged between the swamp and a massive rock bluff. It is an impressive rock formation, with water seeping down its face after rain. It is here that you come to the standout feature of the trip and the one that everyone wants to see, the cave itself.

Trust me, you won't have to search for the cave. It's right next to the trail and has the quintessential cave entrance: a semicircle opening with a flat floor. It's sad that people have to ruin the image by painting graffiti on the entrance wall.

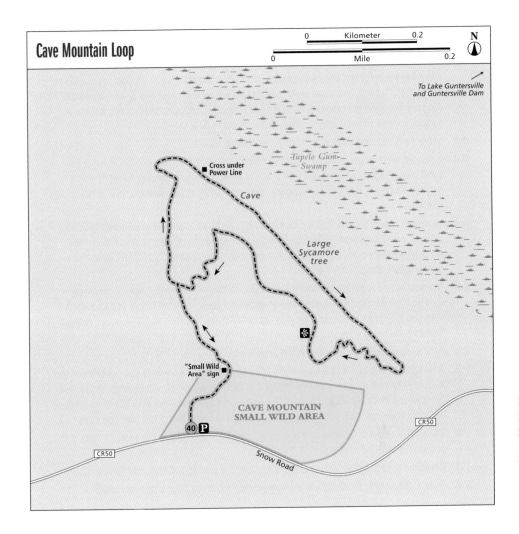

The cave was once a water channel, which created the opening over the centuries. Prior to the Civil War, the cave had an enormous bat population, which turned out to be their own undoing. Bat droppings, or guano, contain traces of potassium nitrate, better known as saltpeter, which is a prime ingredient in gun powder. During the war the Long Hollow Nitre Works came in and began mining the cave for the crystallized chemical. The mine operated twenty-four hours a day, bringing over 1,000 pounds of the mineral per day, but the human presence drove the bats out and they never returned.

The most important thing to remember when visiting the cave is that it goes straight into the mountain 300 feet or so, then after that there is a vertical drop that should only be attempted by trained cavers (spelunkers) and climbers. It is very dangerous! Also keep in mind that the floor can be very slippery during wet weather, so use caution when entering. There is adequate daylight for you to see for the first 100 to 150 feet or so, but after that a flashlight is required.

Miles and Directions

0.0 Start from the trailhead / parking lot on CR 50 / Snow Road to the northeast. A kiosk here has a large map of the route and photos of some of the plants and reptiles you could see on the trek. The trail has large white paint blazes and at this point is a 3- to 4-foot-wide dirt path but soon becomes rocky as it heads through rock outcroppings and boulders. Several species of trees are identified throughout the hike.

0.2 Some trees not only have white blazes, but orange as well.

0.3 A double white blaze indicates a left (northwest) turn in the trail. It looks like the trail continues straight but dead-ends in a few hundred feet. Turn left and head downhill through the rocks. You will see a power line tower and get your first glimpse of the tupelo swamp below.

0.4 Come to a T intersection. Turn right (northeast) and head under the power line tower. You will now be walking next to the tupelo swamp on your left (northeast). Watch for turtles sunning themselves on logs. The trail narrows here to only about 1 1/2 feet wide. There are no blazes through this section.

0.5 The narrow trail is wedged between the swamp to the left (northeast) and an impressive rock bluff on the right that towers above you. Water seeps down the face. In less than 0.1 mile, you will come to the cave on your right carved into the rock wall. The blazes resume following the cave.

0.6 Pass a large sycamore tree on the left (northeast).

0.9 The trail makes a turn to the west at double white blazes. The climb to the top of the ridge from here is through rock outcroppings and is fairly steep. CR 50 will be seen to your left (southwest). Plenty of wildflowers dot the path in the spring. In less than 0.1 mile, come to a double blaze and turn left (west). Start getting your first views of the lake and dam.

1.0 The path is now a dirt and rock mix, with good views of the lake to the east. The trail levels out as it follows the ridgeline.

1.3 Come to an intersection with the approach trail that started the loop. Turn left (south).

1.4 Pass a "Small Wild Area" sign. In a few hundred feet, arrive back at the trailhead.

Hiking Information

Local Information

Marshall County Convention and Visitors Bureau, PO Box 711, 200 Gunter Ave., Guntersville, AL 35976; (800) 582-6282; www.marshallcountycvb.com

Restaurants

Pine Crest Dining Room, Lake Guntersville State Park, 1155 Lodge Dr., Guntersville; (800) 548-4553. Great menu options, great food, all at reasonable prices.

41 Waterfall Trail

The Waterfall Trail at Lake Guntersville State Park is a favorite of many hikers. Its short distance and, of course, its namesake waterfall (which is seasonal) makes it a nice outing for individuals and families, especially in the spring and fall after a good rainfall. Sadly, multiple tornado strikes in 2011 have virtually defoliated the upper portion of the trail, but it is still one worth walking.

Start: Trailhead on Aubrey Carr Scenic Drive
Distance: 1.6-mile lollipop
Hiking time: About 1.5 hours
Difficulty: Easy to moderate with a hill climb
Trail surface: Dirt and rock
Best seasons: Oct–May
Other trail users: None
Canine compatibility: Leashed dogs permitted
Land status: State park

Nearest town: Guntersville
Fees and permits: Day-use fee per car
Schedule: Year-round, sunrise to sunset
Maps: USGS Columbus City, AL; *DeLorme: Alabama Atlas & Gazetteer*, page 26 A2; free trail maps available at camp store
Trail contact: Lake Guntersville State Park, 7966 AL 227, Guntersville 35976; (256) 571-5455; www.alapark.com/LakeGuntersville

Finding the trailhead: From Guntersville at the intersection of US 431 and AL 227, take AL 227 south 6.6 miles. Turn left onto Aubrey Carr Scenic Drive. Travel 0.2 mile and turn left to stay on Aubrey Carr Scenic Drive. Travel another 0.2 mile. The trailhead will be on the right. The parking lot is gravel, with room for 7 cars. GPS: N34 23.095' / W86 12.374'

The Hike

Just after dawn on April 27, 2011, what the National Weather Service classified as an EF-2 tornado swept across the town of Guntersville. The main area in the path of the storm (that only lasted four minutes) was Lake Guntersville State Park. When the storm had passed, the park had major damage. Cleanup in the area was estimated to be at $2.5 million. In seconds the lodge and campground were severely damaged and over 5,000 trees were snapped like matchsticks; 65 percent of those were near the park's golf course.

The good news, however, is that the trails were quickly reopened after the storm, due to the hard work of state employees and volunteers. A couple years later I revisited the park to hike the trails for this edition of the book and found it back in operation and almost back to normal. The sad part, however, is that not everything is recovering so quickly, including some of the hiking trails where the recovery will take years to take hold. One of those trails where you can still see the damage is along the Waterfall Trail.

The trail has always been one of my favorites, and it was a sad experience re-hiking it. The northern part of the trail looked more like an area where a nuclear bomb went off than the thick hardwood forest I had remembered. But as I walked

The trees are trying to make a comeback on the Waterfall Loop.

the trail, the waterfall was still very pretty tumbling over the rocks after a good rain, and the damage served as a backdrop reminding me of the power of Mother Nature. After walking it the trail was still a favorite and a fun, educational hike for individuals and families.

The trail begins at a trailhead along Aubrey Carr Scenic Highway. There is a small yellow post here that is a fee kiosk. The park requests a small day-use fee per car, with all proceeds going to trail maintenance, so please make sure you pay. The trail is a 3- to 4-foot-wide gravel footpath at the outset, then becomes more of a packed clay and rock bed. It is marked with white paint blazes. Right at the trailhead you will see the orange-blazed Moonshine Trail coming in from the left (west) and an un-blazed connector trail to the right.

The path has an easy to moderate grade as it meanders up the north side of the mountain, heading toward the golf course at the top. The beginning of the hike travels through a mixed forest that includes members of the beech family, like chestnut and upland willow oaks. Squirrels and woodchucks rummage here as well as white-tailed deer, and sometimes ring-necked pheasants may surprise you from the brush.

From early spring through fall, some wildflowers will be seen, including the lavender-leafed liatris, which blooms in early fall. You'll also find penstemon with leafy clusters of fifty or so lavender flowers. The smooth foxglove grows on the sides of white oak trees, bearing yellow flowers June through October.

The best time to hike this trail is from fall to spring when there has been a good rain. The trail crisscrosses a rocky stream three times, each crossing having a little taller cascade. The tumbling waters are beautiful, and in the fall the yellows and oranges of the unaffected hardwoods make the stream even more lovely.

Following the stream crossing, the canopy opens up due to the number of downed trees. On a summer day this can be one hot climb. Throughout this section you will see the power of Mother Nature. It is an amazing sight and an educational one as well, a good place to discuss weather with your children and what to do when severe weather strikes.

The trail continues up the mountain until it comes to within yards of the golf course. Here the Waterfall Trail ends. The Nature Trail comes in from the left (west) and heads north. The park's lodge (which has a great restaurant and spectacular views of the lake and surrounding mountains) can be reached by following the Nature Trail. Also here at the end of the Waterfall Trail is the connection with the blue-blazed Cascade Loop. Now, normally I would add this connection to the hike, but when

A NATURAL LIGHTNING ROD—YOU

While the odds of being struck by lightning while hiking are slim, you still need to know what to do if you find yourself caught in a lightning storm. Like the National Oceanic and Atmospheric Association says, no place is safe when a lightning storm is near.

The first thing to do is recognize what a thundercloud looks like. You may not be able to see it through a thick Alabama tree canopy, but a thundercloud (or cumulonimbus cloud) rises high into the atmosphere until it can't rise anymore and forms what is called an "anvil," a flattening of the cloud. You are more likely to see a cloud with a deep, dark bottom. A bad sign.

The best thing to do is get off the trail and seek shelter. If that's impossible and you're caught in the middle, quickly move to lower ground but away from water. If you have a metal frame pack or walking stick, put it down and leave it at least 100 feet away from you.

Reduce your strike potential by crouching down on the balls of your feet, keeping them close together, thus minimizing your connection to the ground. Be sure to cover your ears. And if you are hiking with a group, separate at least 20 feet apart from one another to avoid the risk of a multiple-victim strike.

And remember, even if it's a bright and sunny day, if you hear thunder the best bet is to cancel the hike for the day and head home or to shelter. Lightning can travel up to 10 miles, a real "bolt from the blue."

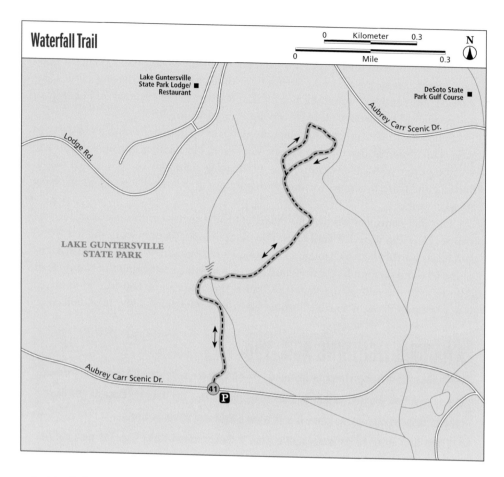

Waterfall Trail

I visited, the trail had virtually vanished. The hike described here uses an un-blazed connector trail to loop around and rejoin the Waterfall Trail for the return to the trailhead. Hopefully by the time you read this, the Cascade Loop will be back and well blazed. It's well worth the effort to add the additional 0.5 to 0.75 mile to see another waterfall and a view of the lake.

Remember that the stream is seasonal. It could be a torrent of water cascading down one day, a trickle the next.

Miles and Directions

0.0 Start at trailhead on Aubrey Carr Scenic Drive. To the north you will see the yellow fee kiosk. Just past the kiosk the orange-blazed Moonshine Trail comes in from the left (west) and an un-blazed connector trail from the right. Head north on the yellow-blazed Waterfall Trail (there is also a large vertical sign indicating that you're on the right trail in a dozen yards). The trail is a 3- to 4-foot-wide hard-packed clay and gravel footpath. There is a little canopy at this point but not for long. The first signs of the 2011 tornado can be seen here, with trees snapped off on either side of the trail.

0.2 Stream crossing. You will cross the stream again in less than 0.1 mile.

0.3 Another stream crossing. During times of rain a really nice waterfall cascades over the large rocks here. In less than 0.1 mile, pass the orange-blazed Old Still Trail on the right (south). Continue straight on the Waterfall Trail. The canopy really begins to thin out and is mostly nonexistent until you begin the return at the end of the loop. Because the trees are all laid out flat from the storms, you will be able to see the tops of all of the surrounding hills and other trails that you wouldn't normally see.

0.7 Pass the un-blazed connector trail to your right (east). This will be the south end of the loop.

0.8 The park's lodge, water tower, and golf course can be seen to the north. The Waterfall Trail ends here. The red-blazed Nature Trail comes in from the left (northwest) and bends to the north. The blue-blazed Cascade Loop Trail is to your right (southwest). Turn right onto the Cascade Loop.

0.9 Come to an un-blazed connector trail. At this point during my visit, the Cascade Loop had vanished (no more blazes or indications of a path). Hopefully when you read this, the trail will be back and you can use it for a longer loop. In the meantime, turn right (south) onto the connector trail.

1.0 Come to an intersection. Turn left (south) onto the Waterfall Trail and retrace your steps to the trailhead.

1.6 Arrive back at the trailhead.

Hiking Information

Local Information

Marshall County Convention and Visitors Bureau, PO Box 711, 200 Gunter Ave., Guntersville, AL 35976; (800) 582-6282; www.marshallcountycvb.com

Local Events/Attractions

Eagle Awareness Weekends, 7966 AL 227, Guntersville; (256) 571-5440. American bald eagles have made a huge comeback in Alabama, and each winter hundreds of visitors come to Lake Guntersville State Park to view the birds and attend dozens of presentations on the raptor. There are even special 5 a.m. treks to watch the eagles leave their nests and 4 p.m. return-to-roost watches. The event is held from January through the third weekend of February.

Restaurants

Pine Crest Dining Room, Lake Guntersville State Park, 1155 Lodge Dr., Guntersville; (800) 548-4553. Great menu options, great food, all at reasonable prices.

Hike Tours

Park rangers and volunteers hold regular guided Saturday morning hikes. Contact the park office for schedule.

42 Walls of Jericho

Described as one of Alabama's most beautiful destinations, the Walls of Jericho hike will take you past sinkholes and caves and across beautiful blue-green streams, culminating in a spectacular high-walled limestone canyon with breathtaking waterfalls.

Start: From the hiker trailhead on County Road 79

Distance: 6.4 miles out and back

Hiking time: About 5 hours (add at least an hour to explore).

Difficulty: Moderate out, strenuous back

Trail surface: Dirt and rock-strewn path, two stream fords

Best seasons: Spring and fall

Other trail users: None

Canine compatibility: Leashed dogs permitted

Land status: State wildlife management area

Nearest town: Hytop

Fees and permits: None

Schedule: Year-round, sunrise to sunset

Maps: USGS Hytop, AL; *DeLorme Alabama Atlas & Gazetteer,* page 20, A3; brochures available online www.outdooralabama.com/ outdoor-alabama/woj.pdf.

Trail contact: Alabama State Lands ADCNR, 64 N. Union St., Montgomery, AL 36130; (334) 242-3484; www.alabamaforeverwild.com
    Nature Conservancy, 4245 North Fairfax Drive, Suite 100, Arlington, VA 22203-1606; (800) 628-6860; www.nature.org

Finding the trailhead: From Scottsboro take AL 79 North for 26 miles. You will pass the Walls of Jericho Equestrian trailhead on the left. Just after that the hiker trailhead will be on the left. If you cross over into Tennessee, you've gone too far. GPS: N 34 58.62' / W 86 4.82'

The Hike

There are many words to describe the Walls of Jericho: Breathtaking, awe-inspiring, awesome—and they're all true. The name comes from a combination of the high-walled canyon that is the highlight of this trail and the nearby town of Jericho.

The state has pined for this piece of property for quite some time, not for its potential as a hiking destination, but for its ecological significance. Within the tract are the headwaters of the Paint Rock River. The river is home to more than one hundred species of fish and mussels, seventeen of which are on the Endangered Species List. A wide diversity of animal life can be found out of the water as well, including unique species of bats and rare birds like the cerulean warbler once believed to exist only in the Bankhead National Forest.

The land was once owned by Texas oilman Harry Lee Carter and his family. As soon as the Forever Wild program was established, the state began pursuing this property to preserve its unique and fragile environment. It wasn't until 2001, ten years after the formation of Forever Wild, that the Nature Conservancy convinced the family to sell. In turn, Forever Wild purchased the property from the Nature Conservancy to place it under state control and management.

The lower falls at the base of the Walls of Jericho.

Since it was purchased by the state, the Walls has become one of the most popular hiking destinations in Alabama, and it's no wonder. As you hike down the steep hillside into the canyon, the exposed limestone rocks provide an interesting fossil record and a look back in time.

Along the trail large sinkholes can be seen on either side of the path and a little farther on, a cave will be passed. The path is lined with yellow lady slippers and Dutchman's breeches to name a few of the plants you will encounter. In the crevasses of the canyon itself, beautiful red-tipped columbine peek out. Depressions in the terrain form bogs and stands of cane plants dot the landscape near them.

There are a few streams to contend with on this hike. The first is the beautiful blue-green waters of Hurricane Creek. Until recently hikers had to ford the stream, making it dangerous during times of high and fast water. Now, a single oak tree has been felled across the creek, one side planed to make a smooth walkway, a handrail attached to it to make crossing easier. Farther on you will cross Turkey Creek not once, but twice. No bridges here. Be ready to get a bit wet.

Shortly after the Hurricane Creek bridge, you will arrive at Clark Cemetery. One of the few gravestones engraved here indicates that the cemetery was established at least as early as 1835. Just to the left (west) of the cemetery is a large open field. This is a primitive camping area. A good idea would be to pack in your gear to spend a night. That would give you more time to explore what's to follow, but read on for precautions. Also remember that the area of the campsite is also the end of the equestrian trail.

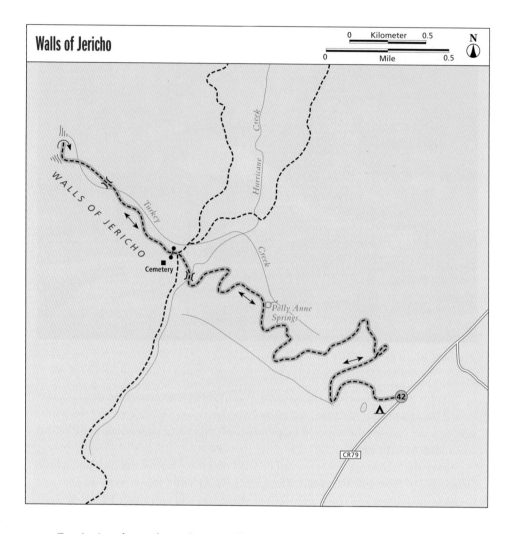

Continuing down the trail, you will start to notice rock walls rising above you, then after crossing Turkey Creek a second time, you will be at the base of the Walls of Jericho. Here waterfalls cascade down the rocks. A little rock scrambling will take you to the "bowl" of the canyon, and after climbing a vertical rock ledge, you will arrive at the end of the trip—a large cascade into a deep pool. The pool actually flows into the rocks. One of the waterfalls you pass after crossing the creek is the water from this pool.

While the Walls of Jericho is a spectacular hike, be sure to take precautions to be safe. First, this is a canyon and as such is prone to flash flooding during and after heavy rains. The rock climb to the upper pool is very steep and slippery creating potentially dangerous footing. And remember what goes down must come up. It is a very strenuous walk out of the canyon. Allow yourself plenty of time to get back to the trailhead. Be sure to pack plenty of water, snacks, and a lunch, and enjoy one of the true wonders of Alabama.

Miles and Directions

0.0 From the kiosk, cross the gravel equestrian trail and head west. An engraved wooden sign clearly points the direction. The trail is marked with red blazes.

0.2 The trail begins its big descent into the canyon as it bends to the southwest then to the north near a small creek.

0.6 Switchback down the hill for the next 0.2 mile.

0.9 The trail makes a long elbow as it heads from the northeast to southwest.

1.2 Cross the equestrian trail to the west. You will also cross a small creek in this area.

1.8 Pass through one of many stands of cane along the trail as it passes through small bogs. Also keep an eye out on both sides of the trail for sink holes and a large depression. At the bottom of this bowl is a narrow opening to a cave.

2.1 As the trail turns to the left (west), Hurricane Creek will be seen through the trees.

2.3 Follow the sign that reads "Foot Bridge." Shortly you will cross Hurricane Creek over a single log footbridge fitted with a handrail.

2.5 Rock hop across a small feeder creek to Hurricane Creek. Barbed-wire fence has been erected here to make a pathway for foot traffic and to keep equestrians and ATVs out. After crossing you will come to Clark Cemetery. To the left of the cemetery is a large open area, the Walls' campsite. Continue on the trail to the northwest.

2.7 The trail narrows as it follows the base of a large rock wall to the left. It is very slippery here so use caution. Turkey Creek can be seen cascading over the rocks to your right.

3.0 Ford across Turkey Creek. The canyon walls shoot up around you; the water will be cascading over the rocks to your left and a wide waterfall spills into the creek through the rock wall just up from that. After crossing, it's a small climb up a hill and then the full canyon comes into view. The waterfall coming through the rock wall is created by an upper fall at the top of the huge bowl that you are standing in. The water falls into a pool and disappears into the canyon, shooting out here. You will have to climb up the rock wall of the bowl to see the upper fall. It's a steep rock scramble and very slippery so again, use caution!

3.2 Arrive at the upper fall. Turn around here and return to the trailhead retracing your steps. Again remember, it is a very steep climb out so allow yourself plenty of time to return.

6.4 Return to the trailhead.

Hiking Information

Local Information

Alabama Mountain Lakes Tourist Association, 25062 North Street, PO Box 1075, Mooresville 35649; (800) 648-5381; www.northalabama.org.

Local Events/Attractions

Scottsboro-Jackson Heritage Center, 208 South Houston Street, Scottsboro 35768-0053; (256) 259-2122. A historical and cultural museum preserving the history of Jackson County from 8,000 BC to the 1930s. Exhibits include the "Sagetown" pioneer village and the 1868 Jackson Courthouse.

Restaurants

The Docks, 417 Ed Hembree Drive, Scottsboro; (256) 574-3074.

43 Monte Sano Nature Preserve Loop

A beautiful all-encompassing hike on the west side of Monte Sano Mountain, the Monte Sano Nature Preserve Loop takes in a little of everything. Along the route you will walk beside massive rock bluffs, cross many streams, walk through a field of wildflowers, pass a waterfall or two, and have great views of the huge Three Caves Quarry. The trail is moderately rugged, and after hiking the entire length, the last climb can be a challenge.

Start: Hikers' parking lot off Bankhead Parkway NE
Distance: 4.9-mile loop
Hiking time: 2.5–3 hours
Difficulty: Moderate to difficult due to length and some steep climbs near end of loop
Trail surface: Dirt and rock
Best seasons: Late fall–late spring
Other trail users: None
Canine compatibility: Leashed dogs permitted
Land status: Land trust property
Nearest town: Huntsville
Fees and permits: None; donation requested at trailhead lockbox
Schedule: Year-round, sunrise to sunset

Maps: USGS Huntsville, AL; *DeLorme: Alabama Atlas & Gazetteer,* page 19 D8; trail maps available online at the Land Trust of North Alabama website
Trail contact: Land Trust of North Alabama, 2707 Artie St. SW, Ste. 6, Huntsville, AL 35805; (256) 534-5263; www.landtrust nal.org
Special considerations: To help protect the trails from erosion, the Land Trust asks that you do not hike the trails after rain. Wait a few days after rain for the trails to dry before heading out. It is OK to hike if the ground is frozen, but when the temperatures go above freezing again, wait a day or two for the trails to dry out.

Finding the trailhead: From Huntsville on I-565 at exit 21, head south on Maysville Road NE 1.4 miles and turn left onto Pratt Avenue NE. Travel 1.4 miles. The parking lot and trailhead will be on your right and well marked. GPS: N34 44.610' / W86 32.640'

The Hike

Through the years the mountain area around Huntsville has seen its share of business and residential development, posing a threat to forests along Round Top and Monte Sano Mountains. For a time Monte Sano State Park was the only oasis of preservation. All that changed when a group of volunteers formed the Huntsville Land Trust (now known as the Land Trust of North Alabama). Their objective: to preserve nature in Madison County. Through contributions and land donations, several preserves were established to not only protect beautiful natural settings, but also provide amazing recreational opportunities for hikers.

The largest and most popular of the trust's sanctuaries is Monte Sano Nature Preserve. With land purchases and donations plus the land that makes up Monte Sano

The Waterline Trail portion of this hike is slightly elevated and rocky.

This waterfall on the Fagen Springs Trail is something to see in late winter and early spring when it runs full.

State Park, most of the forested hillside of Monte Sano Mountain has been protected from further development.

I can't say enough about the excellent job the Land Trust and its volunteers have done with building and maintaining trails on their properties. Each one highlights a piece of the preserve's rugged beauty. The trail described here, what I cleverly call the Monte Sano Nature Preserve Loop, traces the west side of Monte Sano Mountain by using several different trails. There are plenty of opportunities for you to create your own loop of exploration, but the one I describe here visits a good many of the preserve's standout features.

With only a few exceptions, the trails are well blazed with metallic diamond markers labeled with HLT (Huntsville Land Trust) and the trail name. The first section of the route, known as the Bluffline Trail, travels along the base of massive limestone bluffs. The trail crosses several creeks and passes two nice cascades. Remember that many streams are seasonal. The best time to catch a good flow is late fall to late spring.

I have changed things up a bit since the last edition. After the Bluffline Trail we now use the Annandale Trail to go to the Waterline Trail. This is an interesting little trail with some rock features, and it actually leaves the preserve and cuts through the state park for most of its length.

Annandale then meets up with the Waterline Trail at a creek crossing, where there is a nice cascade after good rains. The trail is so-named because sections of a water main that were used during the 1950s for the city of Huntsville run through here. Sections of the pipe are exposed for you to see.

At the intersection of the Waterline and Alms House Trails is the Three Caves Loop. The loop is a 0.2-mile trail around the quarry that gives you excellent views of the caves that were once mined for limestone. There are several steel fences here that you can stand by and look down into the quarry, but this is a dangerous place. Heed the warning signs and keep children, and yourself, away from the edges of the steep and deep cliffs. Also on the loop you will pass a road that leads directly to the caves. Do *not* go to the caves! Entry is by permission only.

The Alms House Trail levels things out for a bit, though the path is rocky for the most part. On this section you will pass the foundation of an old spring-house. This stone structure was once used as an early form of refrigeration, using the spring that ran beneath it to cool meats and vegetables.

▶ The city of Huntsville stepped from its cotton-based economy to being a leader in high-tech industry when Dr. Wernher von Braun and his team of rocket scientists came to the city to get the US space program literally off the ground. His successes included the building of the first American rocket to send a satellite in space (the Jupiter C), the Redstone rocket that sent the nation's first man into space, and, of course, the Saturn V that sent men to the moon. Needless to say, Huntsville is known as the Rocket City.

On the final stretch to the parking lot, we use a short stretch of the Wagon Trail to visit a beautiful wide stream and the Fagen Springs Trail to pass an impressive water-fall (again, remember that flows are seasonal). The final stretch uses the Alms House Trail once again, taking you steeply uphill to the trailhead. This last section has few markers, so read the mile-by-mile description below and keep your eyes peeled for the trail bed.

Miles and Directions

0.0 Start from the parking lot on Pratt Avenue NE. A sign here indicates where to enter the trail to the northeast. In 100 feet come to a sign that shows the direction of the Bluffline and Old Railroad Bed Trails (the signs are carved wood with red lettering). Turn to the right (southeast). The trail is not blazed at this point, but it is a 2- to 3-foot-wide dirt and rock footpath. The trail has a dense canopy with many pines. In less than 0.1 mile, pass a short side trail to an education pavilion on the right (south).

0.1 Diamond-shaped "HLT Bluffline" markers begin, tacked to trees. The Old Railroad Bed Trail comes in from the right (south). Continue straight (east) on the Bluffline Trail.

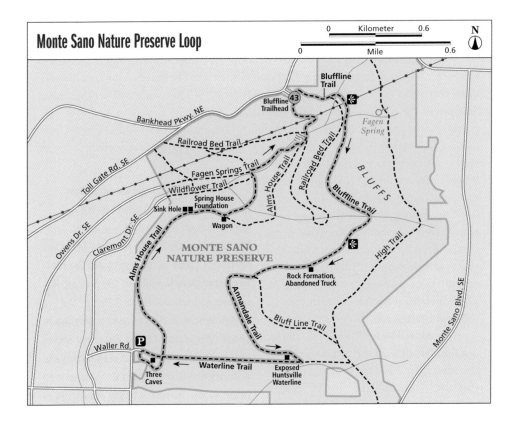

Monte Sano Nature Preserve Loop

0   Kilometer   0.6

0   Mile   0.6

N

0.2   Cross a stream, with nice cascade when it is flowing. The trail widens to a 4-foot-wide clay and dirt path.

0.3   Cross a power line. There are views of the surrounding mountains and valley (the giant Saturn V that stands at the Space and Rocket Center can be seen in the distance). In less than 0.1 mile, cross a stream (this one is wide and fast after a good rain). There is a bench here. The trail's namesake bluffs begin on the left.

0.4   Cross a small creek.

0.5   Cross an intermittent stream.

0.7   The trail bed is a mix of rock and dirt and can be deep in mud after rain (see "special considerations"). There are cedars and pines through here with a swift-flowing stream downhill to the right.

0.8   Cross a small creek, followed in less than 0.1 mile by a wider rocky stream crossing.

1.0   Good view of the bluff on the left.

1.1   Cross a creek.

1.2   A discarded rusty truck is downhill on the right. The bluff continues on the left (southeast). There are some interesting rock formations here, including an outcropping that has been etched by the elements, making it look like the rocks have been stacked.

1.4 The Wagon Trail comes in from the right (north). Continue straight on the Bluffline Trail (there is a directional sign here). In less than 0.1 mile, come to a Y. The Bluffline Trail heads uphill to the left (southeast). Turn right (southwest) onto the Annandale Trail; the trail is now blazed with diamond-shaped "MSSP Annandale Trail" markers (MSSP stands for Monte Sano State Park). The trail is mostly dirt and can be very boggy after rain. It is enclosed and has more hardwoods here.

1.6 Cross a stream.

1.9 The trail has a deep gully in it that can fill knee-deep with water after a good rain. In a few hundred yards, pass a whitish gray bluff and outcroppings on the left, with plenty of wildflowers growing from the tops in the spring. The trail is back in the preserve and out of the state park.

2.0 Come to a bench and a set of log stairs. At the bottom turn right (southwest) onto the Waterline Trail. The trail is elevated, almost like a railroad bed. The trail bed is narrow (1½ feet) and mostly rock. There are several areas along the trail that have steep drop-offs to the left (south).

2.1 The old Huntsville water line can be seen popping out of the ground on the left.

2.3 The Young Kennedy Trail comes in from the right (north); continue straight on the Waterline Trail. The trail becomes less rocky, mostly dirt bed.

2.6 Pass a sign warning you that you are approaching Three Caves, with dangerous bluffs, and to keep your children away from the edge. In a few yards come to a Y at a sign pointing the way to the Three Caves Loop, Waterline Trail, and Alms House Trail. Continue straight (west) on the Three Caves Loop.

2.8 Come to a gravel parking lot. Walk along the east side of the lot to a kiosk. Next to the kiosk is a set of railroad tie stairs. Head up these stairs to continue the loop to the west. In a few yards cross a gravel road. *Do not turn down the road and go to the caves!* Special permission is required. Continue straight across the road to the south and continue following the loop.

3.0 The Cave Loop ends back at the Y at mile 2.6. Continue straight to the north on the Alms House Trail. The trail is very rocky, with several intermittent stream crossings.

3.2 The trail follows a flat rock bed, then climbs through some rocks.

3.4 The Alms House–Wagon Trail Connector comes in from the right (east). Continue straight (north) on the Alms House Trail.

3.6 Cross a creek.

3.7 Pass the Sink Hole Trail on the left (north). There is a small sinkhole between the two trails. Continue straight (east) on the Alms House Trail. In a few yards pass the springhouse foundation on the left (south).

3.9 Come to the intersection of the Wagon and Alms House Trails. Turn left (northeast) onto the Wagon Trail.

4.0 Cross a wide stream.

4.1 Pass the Wildflower Trail on the right (east). Continue straight on the Wagon Trail. In less than 0.1 mile, cross a wide rocky stream. Just after crossing, start climbing uphill on the rocky slope and in a few yards turn right (east) onto the Fagen Springs Trail. The path is not well defined here, so keep your eyes peeled.

4.2 Cross Fagen Springs over a bridge. Nice waterfall to the right (south).

4.3 Cross the spring again over a 20-foot bridge. Come to an intersection. Turn left (east) onto the Fagen Springs / Wildflower Trail. (A sign here points the way to Toll Gate Road, Railroad Bed, and Owens Drive.)

4.5 Pass a very rocky area of the stream. There is a nice waterfall here. The trail markers are virtually gone through this section. Keep your head up and watch for a green sign with a yellow arrow pointing the way on a tree. In a few yards come to a T intersection with the Alms House Trail. Turn left (northeast) onto the Alms House Trail. In less than 0.1 mile, come to a T intersection with the Railroad Bed Trail. Turn left (northwest), heading toward the falls. (***FYI:*** A sign here says to take a right, but it appears to be backwards. Take the left. After the sign, cross the stream again.)

4.7 Cross a power line. There is a beautiful, fragrant wildflower glade here in the spring. Start a long, steady, rocky uphill climb.

4.8 A trail comes in on the right (northeast). It looks like the trail should go straight, but it doesn't. It dead-ends. Turn right onto the unmarked trail, which is still the Alms House Trail. (There are some markers in a few yards, but they are for those heading in the opposite direction.) Very steep climb here over rocks.

4.9 Arrive back at the trailhead.

Hiking Information

Local Information

Huntsville / Madison County Convention and Visitors Bureau, 500 Church St., Ste. 1, Huntsville, AL 35801; (256) 551-2230; www.huntsville.org

Local Events/Attractions

Burritt on the Mountain, 3101 Burritt Dr., Huntsville; (256) 536-2882; www.burritt onthemountain.com. Take a trip back in time to the 1800s in the home and grounds of the eccentric Dr. Burritt.

Lodging

Monte Sano State Park Campground, 5105 Nolen Ave., Huntsville; (256) 534-6589; www.alapark.com/montesano. Improved and primitive campsites.

Restaurants

Blue Plate Cafe, 3210 Governors Dr., Huntsville; (256) 533-8808; www.blueplate cafe.com. Classic Southern food like Mom (or Grandma) used to make.

44 South Plateau Loop

An enjoyable walk around the summit of Monte Sano Mountain, the South Plateau Loop is a 3.5-mile hike past a few intermittent streams with nice cascades when they are flowing and rustic CCC shelters to rest at and take in the views. And speaking of views, the highlight of the trip is O'Shaughnessy Point. The point is a rock outcropping with wonderful views of the valley below, just a great place to simply sit and enjoy your surroundings.

Start: Hikers' parking lot off of Nolen Drive
Distance: 3.5-mile loop
Hiking time: About 1.5 hours
Difficulty: Easy to moderate due to distance
Trail surface: Dirt footpath, some rock or gravel road
Best seasons: Year-round
Other trail users: Cyclists, joggers
Canine compatibility: Leashed dogs permitted
Land status: Alabama state park

Nearest town: Huntsville
Fees and permits: Day-use fee (under 6 free)
Schedule: Year-round, 7 a.m.–sunset
Maps: USGS Huntsville, AL; *DeLorme: Alabama Atlas & Gazetteer*, page 19 D8; free trail maps available at park office
Trail contact: Monte Sano State Park, 5105 Nolen Ave., Huntsville, AL 35801; (256) 534-3757; www.alapark.com/montesano

Finding the trailhead: From Huntsville on I-565 take exit 21, Maysville Road NE. Head south on Maysville Road NE 1.4 miles and turn left onto Pratt Avenue NE. Travel 2.7 miles and turn right onto Fearn Street NE. Travel 0.7 mile and turn left onto Nolen Avenue SE. Follow Nolen Avenue SE 0.7 mile to the entrance gate, where you'll pay your day-use fee. Continue straight on Nolen Avenue SE 0.4 mile. Come to a Y in the road and take the right fork. The hikers' parking lot will be immediately on your right. GPS: N34 44.619' / W86 30.670'

The Hike

Once again we pay a visit to Monte Sano State Park, which is located on the outskirts of Huntsville high atop its namesake mountain. Monte Sano Mountain is a limestone formation jutting over 1,400 feet above sea level. The mountain was formed some 65 to 150 million years ago when the entire region, then under a vast ocean, was thrust upward. The receding ocean left behind much of the marine life to fossilize, which created the limestone formations of the area.

This geologic period, known as the Pennsylvanian age, also left behind large outcroppings of rock that can be seen around the flat plateau of the mountain. These outcroppings and bluffs are what form the route of this hike, the South Plateau Loop.

The trail will take you around the flat plateau within 30 to 50 feet of the bluffs, with some good views of the surrounding mountains and valleys. Several short side trails lead to the bluffs for these overlooks, but heed the warnings: These are dangerous high bluffs, so use extreme caution.

Cyclists and hikers enjoy the view from O'Shaughnessy Point.

Besides geologic history, Monte Sano has some interesting, and more recent, history. *Monte sano* is a Latin term that means "mountain of health." In the early 1800s, with outbreaks of yellow fever, cholera, and malaria ever increasing, this mountain became a refuge for ailing patients because of the crisp, cool mountain air and clear mountain streams.

In 1827 Dr. Thomas Fearn established a colony here for these people. Fearn constructed a large ornate house for himself and his family, complete with stables and smokehouse. The colony flourished until the advent of the Civil War, when Union soldiers moved through and laid the settlement virtually in ruin. According to reports from the time, "the smokehouse was pilfered by the Yankee Soldiers of its bacon, shoulders, and jowls, but they failed to locate the hams concealed in the cellar."

Following the war, the area was rebuilt and began to flourish with the establishment of the Monte Sano Hotel. Tourists began flocking to the mountain until the Great Depression arrived in the 1930s. President Franklin Roosevelt's Civilian Conservation Corps (CCC) arrived in 1935, and the rebuilding process began yet again. Cabins, picnic areas, horse barns, trails, roadways, and a public lodge were all completed by 1938, and Monte Sano State Park was born.

The South Plateau Loop is an easy, flat 3.5-mile hike over a wide dirt path. The trail crosses several seasonal creeks as it makes its way around the south side of the mountain. There are several bluffs along this section of the trail; the better views, however, come as you walk the eastern side of the mountain and at O'Shaughnessy Point. Here you will find a bench and a beautiful panoramic view down into a valley known as the Big Cove.

The point was named for Colonel James O'Shaughnessy from Dublin, Ireland, who came to the region to supervise the construction of a trunk railroad line from Brunswick, Georgia, to St. Louis, Missouri, that would pass through Huntsville. He also helped supervise the building of the Monte Sano Hotel.

Colonel O'Shaughnessy purchased an estate on Monte Sano Mountain to house his many guests, but he was not lucky when it came to being a home owner. The Fearn Mansion that he purchased was once the centerpiece of the sanitarium that Dr. Fearn established on the mountain to bring patients to the clean, crisp air of the countryside. In 1890, not long after the colonel purchased the mansion, it was destroyed by fire. So, he rebuilt his home, this time in a spectacular Queen Anne style, with rich wood paneling, ornate fireplaces, and large wraparound porches. However, a few short years after its construction, fire destroyed this home as well. According to park officials, archeologists return to this area regularly to try to locate the remains of this home and establish more of the history that Colonel O'Shaughnessy brought to Monte Sano.

The trail is dotted with rest shelters. These are nice covered buildings where you can sit and take a break. Also, several other trails crisscross the path and head back to the trailhead, making it easy to cut the trip short, a blessing if you have small children and you need to get back.

Along the trail you might see several species of wildlife, including bobcat, white-tailed deer, opossum, skunk, and woodchuck. As for vegetation, the trail passes through forests of red and silver maple and birch trees. From early spring to the beginning of summer, wildflowers such as violets and catchfly will be found blooming.

Miles and Directions

0.0 Start from the hikers' parking lot to the southwest. A sign here shows mileages and blaze colors for the South Plateau Loop (white blazed), Fire Tower Trail (red blazed), and North Plateau Loop (blue blazed). In just a few feet, come to an intersection. The South Plateau Loop heads straight and to the left. Continue straight and follow the white blazes. The trail is a wide 5-foot dirt path.

0.2 Come to a Y. The Fire Tower Trail heads off to the left. Continue to follow the white blazes to the right (south).

0.5 Cross a stream over a 20-foot-long bridge. When the stream is flowing, there is a nice cascade here.

0.6 Cross a stream over a 10-foot-long bridge.

0.9 Come to a rickety old bridge over an intermittent stream and boggy area. It's best to stay off it and walk around the area on the right. Just past the bridge there are some views through the trees of the valley and farms below to the right (southwest).

South Plateau Loop

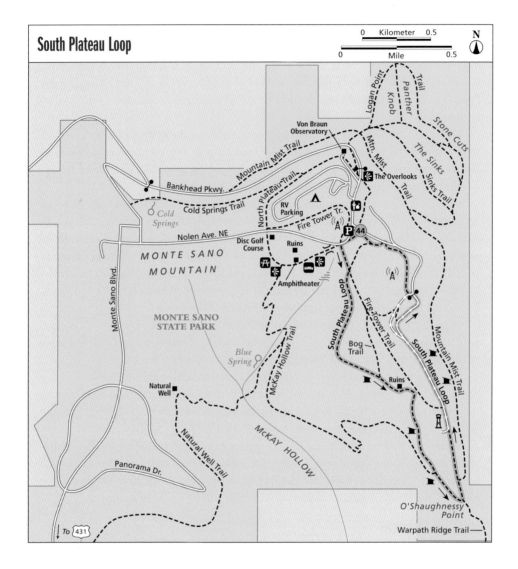

1.0 Pass a nice covered trail shelter. Just after the shelter there are some outcroppings on the right (southwest).

1.1 The Bog Trail comes in from the left (northeast). There are also two benches here. Continue straight (southeast) and follow the white blazes.

1.2 Come to a Y. The red-blazed Fire Tower Trail comes in from the left. Take the right fork to the south and continue following the white blazes.

1.3 Views to the right (southwest).

1.4 Pass a trail shelter.

1.6 The McKay Hollow Trail comes in from the right (there is also a trail shelter here). Continue to the south on the white-blazed trail.

1.7 A short, 100-foot trail to the right (southwest) takes you to a bluff.

1.8 Continue straight (southeast) on the white-blazed trail. There are more views just after the intersection.

1.9 Arrive at O'Shaughnessy Point, with a great view. This is followed by a Y intersection. The Warpath Ridge Bike Trail continues straight to the south; turn left (north) and continue on the South Plateau Loop. In a few feet the Mountain Mist Trail will be passed on the right.

2.1 Pass a trail shelter and view.

2.3 Pass a bluff with a view on the right (east). In less than 0.1 mile, the dirt path merges with a gravel road that comes in from the left (a sign here reads "Gravel Road"). Continue to follow the white blazes to the north.

2.4 The Fire Tower Trail enters from the left. Continue straight (north), following the white blazes.

2.6 Pass a trail shelter.

2.7 The gravel road turns to the left; continue to follow the white blazes to the north. The trail is a wide dirt footpath again.

2.9 Pass a trail shelter.

3.0 Pass cabins on the right. The trail crosses a paved road to the northwest.

3.1 Pass a cell tower, cross under a set of power lines, and cross a gravel road to the north.

3.3 In less than 0.1 mile, come to a Y. Continue to follow the white blazes to the west. In 100 feet cross a short bridge over an intermittent creek.

3.5 Arrive back at the trailhead.

Hiking Information

Local Information

Huntsville / Madison County Convention and Visitors Bureau, 500 Church St., Ste. 1, Huntsville, AL 35801; (256) 551-2230; www.huntsville.org

Local Events/Attractions

Von Braun Astronomical Observatory, PO Box 1142, Huntsville 35807; (256) 539-0316; www.vbas.org. An added bonus at Monte Sano State Park, the Von Braun Observatory was built in the 1950s by the famed rocket scientist. The Von Braun Astronomical Society holds educational programs every Saturday night on a space-related subject, then, weather permitting, members invite you to look through their telescopes at the night sky. Admission is charged.

Lodging

Monte Sano State Park Campground, 5105 Nolen Ave., Huntsville; (256) 534-6589; www.alapark.com/montesano. Improved and primitive campsites.

Restaurants

Ol Heidelberg, 6125 University Dr., Huntsville; (256) 922-0556; www.olheidelberg .com. Serving authentic German food since 1972.

45 North Plateau Loop

Another easy hike, this one travels around the northern plateau of Monte Sano Mountain. Once again, the trails are wide, well maintained, and cross several nice seasonal creeks. The highlight of this trip includes a short side trail to a beautiful 70-foot waterfall at the end of the picnic area. There are several nice overlooks and a chance to see the handiwork of the Civilian Conservation Corps from 1935.

Start: Kiosk on the south side of the hikers' parking lot
Distance: 1.9-mile loop
Hiking time: About 1 hour
Difficulty: Easy on a level path around the rim of Monte Sano Mountain
Trail surface: Dirt
Best seasons: Fall–spring
Other trail users: Cyclists
Canine compatibility: Leashed dogs permitted

Land status: State park
Nearest town: Huntsville
Fees and permits: Day-use fee (under 6 free)
Schedule: Year-round, 7 a.m.–sunset
Maps: USGS Huntsville, AL; *DeLorme: Alabama Atlas & Gazetteer,* page 19 D8; free trail maps available at park office.
Trail contact: Monte Sano State Park, 5105 Nolen Ave., Huntsville, AL 35801; (256) 534-3757; www.alapark.com/montesano

Finding the trailhead: From Huntsville on I-565 take exit 21, Maysville Road NE. Head south on Maysville Road NE 1.4 miles and turn left onto Pratt Avenue NE. Travel 2.7 miles and turn right onto Fearn Street NE. Travel 0.7 mile and turn left onto Nolen Avenue SE. Follow Nolen Avenue SE 0.7 mile to the entrance gate, where you'll pay your day-use fee. Continue straight on Nolen Avenue SE 0.4 mile. Come to a Y in the road and take the right fork. The hikers' parking lot will be immediately on your right. GPS: N34 44.637' / W86 30.676'

The Hike

While the South Plateau Loop focuses more on the geology of the mountains, with wonderful views from high bluffs, the North Plateau Loop shows more of the history of Monte Sano State Park but still provides nice views of the surrounding valleys and mountains and a waterfall.

Monte sano is a Latin term that means "mountain of health." In the early 1800s, with outbreaks of yellow fever, cholera, and malaria ever increasing, this mountain became a refuge for ailing patients because of the crisp, cool mountain air and clear mountain streams.

In 1827 Dr. Thomas Fearn established a colony here on Monte Sano for the victims of these epidemics. The lavish facility flourished until the advent of the Civil War, when Union soldiers made their way south and laid the complex in ruin.

Following the Civil War, the area was rebuilt. The Monte Sano Hotel was constructed and the region flourished once again with tourists to the mountain until the

A view from the trail into McKay Hollow

Great Depression arrived in the 1930s. President Franklin Roosevelt's Civilian Conservation Corps (CCC) arrived in 1935, and the rebuilding process began. Cabins, picnic areas, horse barns, trails, roadways, and a public lodge were all completed by 1938, and Monte Sano State Park was born. Because of all this construction, this section of the trail has been described as looking more like a city park than a state park, but how many city parks have waterfalls running through them?

The trail begins at the hikers' parking lot and loops the north plateau to the west. As it moves along a wonderful bluff, it passes a small creek and a nice waterfall. Traveling through a picnic area, evidence of the CCC influence is seen with the ruins of the Monte Sano Tavern. The tavern was built in 1937 but was destroyed by fire in 1947. This is one of the largest remains of CCC buildings in the state and is an excellent example of the stonemasonry of the corps.

Continuing on to the west, an amphitheater, also constructed by the CCC, will be seen. It is used for a variety of entertainment and educational programs. Just past the amphitheater, a beautiful 70-foot waterfall tumbles down the rocks and is a haven for artists painting and drawing any time of the year. As the trail loops around the plateau,

A butterfly going about his business on the North Plateau Loop

there are nice views of the rocky outcroppings known as The Sinks (where the Stone Cuts Trail travels) and Mills Hollow.

Finally, more recent Monte Sano history will be seen at the Von Braun Observatory. When Dr. Wernher von Braun came to Huntsville to head up the American space program and its new facility in Huntsville, he and his colleagues helped guide the building of this planetarium and observatory. Opened in 1956, the facility is operated by the Von Braun Astronomical Society. Von Braun and astronaut Alan Sheppard used to visit the facility to talk about the Apollo program. The first and second Saturday of each month, the society holds a meeting that the public is invited to attend. A view of the night sky, a lecture by prominent astronomers and NASA scientists, and, weather permitting, views through the telescopes are in store.

The hike is interesting and makes a good warm-up for the more difficult Stone Cuts Trail.

North Plateau Loop

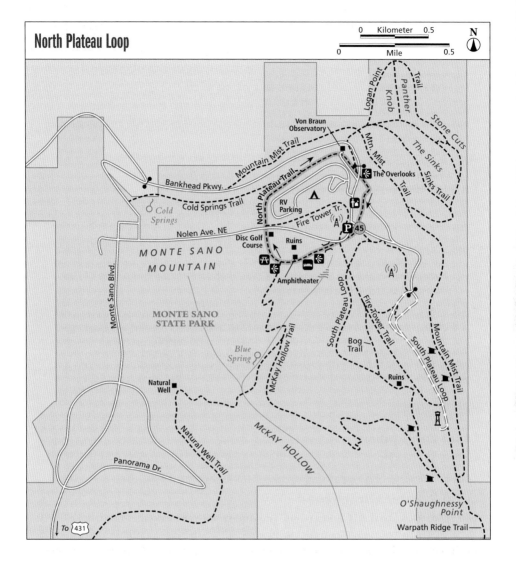

0   Kilometer   0.5

N

0   Mile   0.5

Von Braun Observatory

Mountain Mist Trail

Bankhead Pkwy.

Cold Springs Trail

North Plateau Trail

Cold Springs

Nolen Ave. NE

RV Parking

Fire Tower Tr.

The Overlooks

Mtn. Mist Trail

Stone Cuts

The Sinks

Sinks Trail

Logan Point

Panther Knob Trail

Disc Golf Course

Ruins

45

Amphitheater

MONTE SANO MOUNTAIN

Monte Sano Blvd.

MONTE SANO STATE PARK

Blue Spring

South Plateau Loop

McKay Hollow Trail

Natural Well

Fire Tower Trail

Bog Trail

Ruins

South Plateau Loop

Mountain Mist Trail

Natural Well Trail

Panorama Dr.

McKAY HOLLOW

To 431

O'Shaughnessy Point

Warpath Ridge Trail

Miles and Directions

0.0 Start at the hikers' parking lot to the south. Immediately after passing the kiosk, turn right onto the blue-blazed North Plateau Loop Trail. In 400 feet pass hole #10 of the disc golf course on the right.

0.1 Cross the red-blazed Fire Tower Trail.

0.2 Cross a runoff with a small cascade on a 30-foot footbridge.

0.3 Walk behind the lodge to the first overlook.

0.4 Pass the amphitheater on the right. In 50 feet walk through a picnic area. In less than 0.1 mile, cross a small creek.

0.5 Pass another overlook on the left. In 120 feet pass a CCC picnic pavilion on the left. The McKay Hollow Trail merges here from the right side of the pavilion. Continue to the right (northeast) on the blue trail. (*Option:* Head down the McKay Hollow Trail for a few short yards to view the waterfall. Be careful, it's steep and slippery.) In just over 100 feet, the trail leaves the picnic area and heads back into the woods.

0.7 Cross the disc golf course. In 50 feet cross the main park road at the entrance station.

0.8 Pass the red Fire Tower Trail on the right. You will also be passing the primitive campground on the right.

0.9 The trail meanders beneath the campground. Drop off into a ravine on the left. There is a nice little view here in winter.

1.0 Pass the Cold Springs Trail on the left.

1.1 The closest approach to the campground is on the right.

1.3 Pass Von Braun Observatory on the right.

1.5 Arrive at what looks like a T intersection, but the left turn is merely a game trail. Turn right (southeast) and continue on the North Plateau Loop. In 60 feet cross a road to reach the overlook parking lot and arrive at the overlook. In 150 feet the trail heads back into the woods on the south side of the parking lot.

1.7 Cross a paved road to the south.

1.8 Pass a picnic pavilion on the right and come to a trailer that at the time of this writing was being used as a temporary office to register campers. Walk around the left side of the trailer and pick up the blue blazes on the other side to the south.

1.9 Cross another paved road and arrive back at the hikers' parking lot.

Hiking Information

Local Information

Huntsville / Madison County Convention and Visitors Bureau, 500 Church St., Ste. 1, Huntsville, AL 35801; (256) 551-2230; www.huntsville.org

Local Events/Attractions

US Space and Rocket Center, One Tranquility Base, Huntsville; (800) 637-7223; www.rocketcenter.com. Crammed with over 1500 artifacts documenting America's space program from its earliest days to the present, with lots of interactive fun for kids.

Lodging

Monte Sano State Park Campground, 5105 Nolen Ave., Huntsville; (256) 534-6589; www.alapark.com/montesano. Improved and primitive campsites.

Restaurants

Another Broken Egg Cafe, 2722D Carl T. Jones Dr., Huntsville; (256) 883-2915; www.anotherbrokenegg.com

46 Lawson Branch Loop

The Lawson Branch Loop is a beautiful, easy walking Forever Wild trail in what is called the Shoal Creek Preserve. The highlight of the trip is water—lots of it. You will be treated to several beautiful cascades along the trail's namesake creek as well as a bit of Jones Branch and nice views of Indian Camp Creek as it flows into Shoal Creek and feeds Wilson Lake.

Start: Shoal Creek Preserve trailhead
Distance: 3.0-mile lollipop
Hiking time: 1.5–2 hours
Difficulty: Easy with a few climbs bordering moderate
Trail surface: Hard-packed dirt
Best seasons: Fall-spring
Other trail users: None
Canine compatibility: Leashed dogs permitted
Land status: State nature preserve
Nearest town: Florence
Fees and permits: None

Schedule: Year-round, sunrise to sunset
Maps: USGS Pruitton, AL; *DeLorme: Alabama Atlas & Gazetteer,* page 18 B7; trail maps available online at the Forever Wild website
Trail contact: Alabama State Lands ADCNR, 64 N. Union St., Montgomery, AL 36130; (334) 242-3484; www.alabamaforeverwild.com
Special considerations: Hunting is permitted on the property from fall through early spring. Please visit the Forever Wild website for dates and restrictions.

Finding the trailhead: From Florence at the intersection of US 72 (Florence Boulevard) and Darby Drive, head north on Darby Drive / Old Jackson Highway south 4.4 miles. Turn left onto CR 61 (Butler Creek Road) and travel 2.6 miles. A small sign is at the turn into the preserve on the right. Turn right and head down the gravel road 0.5 mile to the trailhead. GPS: N34 54.437' / W87 37.233'

The Hike

Tucked away in northwest Alabama just north of Florence is the 298-acre Shoal Creek Preserve. This beautiful water-feature-filled property once faced possible development, and it might have ended at that until grant money awarded to Forever Wild by the National Park Service's Land and Water Conservation Fund and the Alabama Department of Economic and Community Affairs, along with several financial and in-kind donations made by the city of Florence and Lauderdale County, put the property out of reach of developers. The property is now managed by Forever Wild.

The goal of acquiring this property was "to preserve natural plant and animal species and habitats while providing opportunities for hiking, horseback riding, fishing, hunting, canoeing, picnicking, bird watching, photography and nature study."

Since the acquisition 4.5 miles of trail have been created, including two hiking trails (this hike and the Jones Branch Loop) and a horseback–riding trail. The addition of these trails has made the preserve a popular place, thus fulfilling one of the state's

The state is serious about keeping equestrian and hiking trails separate.

goals for purchasing the tract. The trail system here was named a National Recreational Trail in 2012.

Like the Jones Branch Loop, the Lawson Branch Loop meanders through several different habitats including mature upland hardwood stands, scenic creek bottoms, and fallow fields. Along the 2.4-mile-long trail you will have a chance to see a beautiful stream, Lawson Branch. Along this section are some really nice cascades, including a horseshoe-shaped one near the end of the loop, and a nice view of the wide Indian Camp Creek from high atop a bluff as it flows into Shoal Creek and eventually Wilson Lake. The best time to take in the view is late fall or winter when the leaves are down.

As you walk the trail, you will have plenty of opportunities to view wildlife. Along the route you may spot white-tailed deer, quail, fox, and wild turkey. And there are plenty of other birds to spot as well, including wood ducks, hawks, and turkey vultures, not to mention a wide variety of songbirds.

The trail begins on the north side of the Shoal Creek Preserve parking lot, sharing the starting point with the preserve's horse trail and the Jones Branch Loop. This is a huge gravel parking area with ample room for fifty cars.

The path starts out as a wide gravel road but soon turns into a narrow, hard-packed dirt footpath, which it remains for the remainder of the hike. Only a few yards into

One of many cascades found along Lawson Creek

the hike, the horse trail splits off to the northeast and you will be on a hiking-only trail from here on out. Forever Wild was careful to place large orange signs warning equestrians not to use the trail at each intersection between the two paths.

The trail actually uses the west side of the Jones Branch Loop as an approach trail for 0.6 mile. The entire trail is well blazed, using single red paint blazes on trees along this stretch and an occasional yellow diamond marker tacked to a tree that reads "Lawson Branch Loop" with the image of a red blaze on it. Where the trail crosses the horse trail, you will find the crossing well marked on the opposite side so there is no confusion.

This first section is a nice walk in the woods, especially in the fall when the hardwoods blaze with color. Then you reach the junction with the Jones Branch Loop. Here you will cross Lawson Branch over a log footbridge with a handrail, and the actual Lawson Branch Loop begins. The blazes now turn to double red paint blazes. For a portion of the loop, you will be walking alongside the beautiful wide stream, passing several cascades including a really nice horseshoe of water tumbling over rocks. You will also be treated to excellent views of Indian Camp Creek as it merges with Shoal Creek from a high bluff. The best time for these views is in late fall and winter.

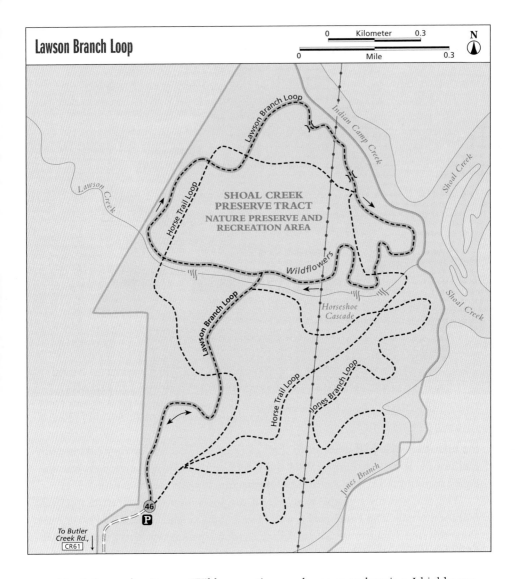

Don't forget that Forever Wild properties are also open to hunting. I highly suggest that you visit the Forever Wild website (www.alabamaforeverwild.com) for dates and additional information about hunting season. And if you do go out on a hike during hunting season, please remember to wear safety orange at all times.

Miles and Directions

0.0 Start at information kiosk to the north. The trail begins on the left side of the kiosk and immediately splits into two trails. The right is clearly marked for horses. The left is the beginning of the Lawson Branch Trail and the access trail for Jones Branch. Take the left trail, which begins as a wide dirt road.

0.2 The trail narrows to a 2-foot-wide dirt path.

0.4 Cross the horse trail to the north (there is a bench here).

0.5 You are walking next to a nice creek on the left.

0.6 Arrive at Lawson Branch, with great cascades on both sides. This is the intersection with the Jones Branch Loop (to the right). Continue straight to the north, crossing the branch over a felled tree with a flat planed side and handrail. On the other side come to a T intersection. Turn left onto the Lawson Branch Loop (to the right is the return trail). There are excellent views and access to the branch through this section. Blazes are now double red.

0.8 Cross the horse trail to the southwest. There is a yellow Lawson Branch sign here (with double red stripes).

1.2 Cross the horse trail to the east. In 250 feet cross the horse trail to the north.

1.4 Views of Indian Camp Creek on the left (best views in winter/early spring).

1.5 Cross a runoff over a short footbridge.

1.6 Cross a railroad tie footbridge over a runoff channel.

2.0 Come to a T intersection with the horse trail. Turn left onto the horse trail. In a few feet turn right (south) off the horse trail and continue on the double red-blazed Lawson Branch Trail. In 150 feet there will be a cascade to left with a short side trail to the creek.

2.1 Come to a pretty horseshoe cascade in the creek.

2.3 Cross a power line in a field of wildflowers in the spring. You will be walking alongside the creek once again.

2.4 Come to a Y intersection. The left fork takes you to the creek. Take the right fork to the west. In less than 0.1 mile, arrive at Lawson Branch. Cross Lawson Branch again over the log bridge to the south. Once across, continue straight to the southwest on the Lawson Branch Loop and retrace your steps to the trailhead. (*Option:* Turn left and finish the Jones Branch Loop to make a longer trek.)

3.0 Arrive back at the trailhead.

Hiking Information

Local Information

Alabama Mountain Lakes Tourist Association, 402 Sherman St., Decatur, AL 35602; (800) 648-5381; www.northalabama.org

Local Events/Attractions

Jack-O-Lantern Farm Market, 344 Garage Rd., Muscle Shoals; (256) 386-2335; www.jackolanternfarm.com. Shop for certified naturally grown fruits, vegetables, and hydroponically grown lettuce.

Restaurants

Singleton's Bar-B-Que, 4420 Huntsville Rd., Florence; (256) 760-0802

Hike Tours

Shoals Environmental Alliance, PO Box 699, Sheffield, AL 35660; http://sea.tiny webs.org. An organization dedicated to the protection of the natural resources of the Shoals area, the alliance holds informative hikes and events in the area.

47 Jones Branch Loop

The second of two great hiking trails in the Shoal Creek Preserve, the Jones Branch Loop is an easy walking 2.5-mile loop that will take you to the beautiful cascading waters of both Lawson and Jones Branches and some nice views of Shoal Creek. Sections of the trail are also lined with a rainbow of wildflowers from early spring to early summer.

Start: Shoal Creek Preserve trailhead
Distance: 2.5-mile loop
Hiking time: About 1.5-2 hours
Difficulty: Easy with a few climbs bordering moderate
Trail surface: Hard-packed dirt
Best seasons: Fall-spring
Other trail users: None
Canine compatibility: Leashed dogs permitted
Land status: State nature preserve
Nearest town: Florence
Fees and permits: None

Schedule: Year-round, sunrise to sunset
Maps: USGS Pruitton, AL; *DeLorme: Alabama Atlas & Gazetteer,* page 18 B7; trail maps available online at the Forever Wild website
Trail contact: Alabama State Lands ADCNR, 64 N. Union St., Montgomery, AL 36130; (334) 242-3484; www.alabamaforeverwild.com
Special considerations: Hunting is permitted on the property from fall through early spring. Please visit the Forever Wild website for dates and restrictions.

Finding the trailhead: From Florence at the intersection of US 72 (Florence Boulevard) and Darby Drive, head north on Darby Drive / Old Jackson Highway south 4.4 miles. Turn left onto CR 61 (Butler Creek Road) and travel 2.6 miles. A small sign is at the turn into the preserve on the right. Turn right and head down the gravel road 0.5 mile to the trailhead. GPS: N34 54.437' / W87 37.233'

The Hike

Only a few miles south of the Tennessee state line and just north of the city of Florence is a 298-acre tract of land called the Shoal Creek Preserve. The property, managed by the Alabama Forever Wild Program (Department of Conservation and Natural Resources), is a beautiful water-feature-filled property. Within its boundaries are two impressive streams, Lawson and Jones Branches, and a wide feeder creek into Wilson Lake, not to mention the tract's namesake, Shoal Creek.

The property was once facing development and would have been lost forever if not saved by grant money and generous donations from the city of Florence and Lauderdale County. That was in 2002. Today, three trails totaling 4.5 miles grace the property: a 2.1-mile-long horseback-riding trail and two hiking trails, the Lawson Branch Loop and this trail, the Jones Branch Loop.

As with the Lawson Branch Loop, the Jones Branch Loop winds its way through several different habitats, including mature upland hardwood stands, scenic creek

Trail amenities along the Jones Branch Loop include beautiful wildflowers.

bottoms, and fallow fields. And once again, as with the Lawson Branch, there are water features. Along this path you will take in a bit of Lawson Branch from the south side of the creek (whereas the Lawson Branch Loop follows the north side) and another wide, swift creek, Jones Branch, where the water sparkles as it tumbles over the rocky streambed. You will also get a few views of Shoal Creek itself—a big, wide creek, popular with boaters and anglers—from atop a bluff. The best time for the view is late fall or winter.

You will find many different varieties of mushrooms and fungi along the trail, including Judas ear and turkey tail. From spring to early summer, wildflowers such as deadnettle and shepherd's purse will be found blooming.

The trail begins on the north side of the Shoal Creek Preserve parking lot, a large gravel parking area with ample room for fifty cars. The path begins as a wide gravel road but soon turns into a narrow, hard-packed dirt footpath, which it remains for the remainder of the hike. This is also the beginning of the preserve's horse trail, but in only a few yards the horse trail branches off and from here on horses are not allowed on the trail. Although there are large orange signs warning equestrians not to use the trail, I did see some evidence that a few apparently couldn't read, but I didn't encounter any.

A cascade along Jones Branch is tinted green from the summer foliage.

The first 0.6 mile of the hike is also used as the approach trail for the Lawson Branch Loop. An option to consider is to make this a 4.3-mile hike by crossing Lawson Creek and completing the Lawson Branch Loop at mile 0.6 before returning to the intersection and finishing the Jones Branch Loop.

The trail is well blazed with red paint blazes on trees and an occasional yellow diamond marker tacked to a tree that reads "Jones Branch Loop" with the image of a single red blaze on it. Intersections, such as where the trail crosses the horse trail, are well marked on the opposite side from where you cross, so there is no confusion.

Don't forget that Forever Wild properties are also open to hunting. I highly suggest that you visit the Forever Wild website (www.alabamaforeverwild.com) for dates and additional information about hunting season. And if you do go out on a hike during hunting season, please remember to wear safety orange at all times.

Miles and Directions

0.0 Start at the information kiosk to the north. The trail begins on the left side of the kiosk and immediately splits into two trails. The right is clearly marked for horses. The left is the

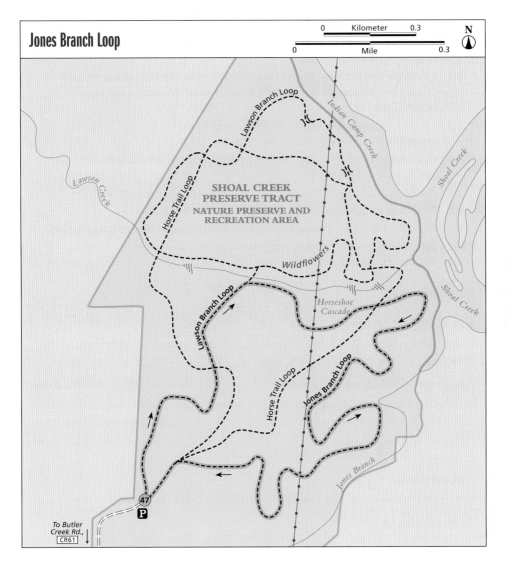

SHOAL CREEK
PRESERVE TRACT
NATURE PRESERVE AND
RECREATION AREA

Wildflowers

Horseshoe Cascade

To Butler Creek Rd., CR61

beginning of the Lawson Branch Loop and the access trail for Jones Branch Loop. Take the left trail, which begins as a wide dirt road.

0.2 The trail narrows to 2-foot-wide dirt path.

0.4 Cross the horse trail to the north (there is a bench here).

0.5 You are walking next to nice creek on the left.

0.6 Arrive at Lawson Branch, with some pretty cascades to the left. This is the intersection with the Lawson Branch Loop (straight ahead to the north). Do not cross the creek. Turn right onto the single red-blazed Jones Branch Loop, with excellent views and access to the branch through this section. Blazes are now double red. (*Option:* You can cross the creek and extend the trip by completing the Lawson Branch Loop and then finishing the Jones Branch Loop at this point.)

0.7 Turn left (south) onto an old dirt road. In 20 feet turn right (south) and continue on the Jones Branch Loop.

1.0 Cross the horse trail to the east.

1.1 Cross a dirt road to the east. On the other side, turn right (south) to continue the loop (there is a short game trail to the left that leads nowhere). In winter there are good views of Shoal Creek here.

1.5 The trail skirts the eastern edge of the power line as it heads to the south. The trail can be overgrown with grass but the path is discernible.

1.6 As you approach trees along the power line, the trail turns left (northeast) back into the woods (you will see the blaze).

1.9 The trail skirts the edge of the power line again on its east side. There are wildflowers here.

2.0 Cross under the power line to the west and head back into the woods.

2.3 Pass a dirt road, part of the equestrian trail, on the right. This last section is hard-packed clay.

2.5 Arrive back at the trailhead.

Hiking Information

Local Information
Alabama Mountain Lakes Tourist Association, 402 Sherman St., Decatur, AL 35602; (800) 648-5381; www.northalabama.org

Local Events/Attractions
Coon Dog Memorial Cemetery, 4945 Coon Dog Cemetery Rd., Tuscumbia; (256) 383-0783; www.coondogcemetery.com. In 1937 Ken Underwood buried his coon dog on this site. Since then over 180 coon dogs have been laid to rest here. There are picnic areas and a Labor Day celebration.

Restaurants
Riverside Restaurant, 111 E. Limestone, Florence; (256) 766-4436

Organizations
Shoals Environmental Alliance, PO Box 699, Sheffield, AL 35660; sea.tinywebs.org. An organization dedicated to the protection of the natural resources of the Shoals area, the alliance holds informative hikes and events in the area.

48 TVA Nature Trail

Take a walk through time along this set of historic trails on the banks of Pickwick Lake (Tennessee River) in northwestern Alabama. The footpath leads you through, and over, the handiwork of the Civilian Conservation Corps (CCC) from the mid-1930s and through the site of a town that was once a major shipping center, and you'll literally walk on water halfway across the lake on a restored railroad trestle.

Start: East side of the TVA Nature Trail parking lot
Distance: 2.7-mile lollipop
Hiking time: About 1.5 hours
Difficulty: Easy to moderate with some stair climbing
Trail surface: Dirt footpath, some stone stairs
Best seasons: Fall–spring
Other trail users: Joggers on paved road section
Canine compatibility: Leashed dogs permitted

Land status: Tennessee Valley Authority small wild area
Nearest town: Florence
Fees and permits: None
Schedule: Year-round, sunrise to sunset
Maps: USGS Florence, AL; *DeLorme: Alabama Atlas & Gazetteer*, page 17 C7
Trail contact: Tennessee Valley Authority, SB1H, PO Box 1010, Muscle Shoals, AL 35661; (256) 386-2543; www.tva.gov/river/recreation

---

Finding the trailhead: Start in Florence at the intersection of US 72 / US 43 and AL 133. Take AL 133 south 5 miles (you will cross Wilson Dam along the way). Turn right at the TVA Nature Trail sign onto Thunder Road. The parking lot is ahead in 500 feet. The trailhead is on the east side of the parking lot. GPS: N34 46.806' / W87 39.392'

The Hike

While I was in the Muscle Shoals / Florence area researching campsites for my book *Best Tent Camping: Alabama*, several people told me I should visit the trails at the Tennessee Valley Authority's Muscle Shoals Reservation for the next edition of *Hiking Alabama*. I did a quick drive through and saw a paved jogging trail. Figuring I was just overlooking something, I made a note to myself that I needed to come back and check it out in more detail. I'm glad I did.

The reservation sits on the southern banks of Pickwick Lake, which is formed by the TVA's Wilson Dam along the Tennessee River. The property is only 25 acres in size, and yes, they do have an extensive paved jogging trail, but hidden in the woods high above the lake are some really neat hiking trails that combine history with beautiful landscapes to make a great little day hike.

All in all there are 11 miles of trails at the reservation, each interconnecting to give you several choices from which to create your own loop. This loop, what is known in the area as the TVA Nature Trail Loop, begins at the large paved parking lot just off Wilson Dam Highway. There is plenty of parking for sixty-plus cars, and it's a good thing. This is one popular location for joggers, recreational walkers, and cyclists. Here

In early summer with thick foliage, the stone steps of the CCC trail resemble an old English garden.

you will find nice restrooms, water fountains, and an informative kiosk that explains a little bit about the wildlife and history of the area you are about to walk.

The reservation and the First Quarter Ravine Small Wild Area were set aside by the TVA to preserve the area's natural habitat and its cultural and historical features, including the remains of structures used by the US Army Corps of Engineers when building Wilson Dam between 1918 and 1925 and the work of the CCC in the 1930s.

The trail is not blazed, but the well-worn paths make it easy enough to follow. Directional signs are placed at intersections to make hiking the trail even easier.

For the most part the path is a narrow, 1 1/2- to 2-foot dirt and rock footpath. Along several climbs up hillsides, you will find yourself scampering up stone stairs. These stairs are some of the handiwork of the CCC, who helped build the recreational part of the reservation in the mid-1930s.

In the fall the mixed hardwood forest lights up the trail with fiery orange, yellow, and red colors. In the winter you may find yourself hiking in the stillness of freshly fallen snow. And from spring through summer the forest is lush green and thick. In some cases you may find the trail a bit overgrown, but it will still be passable. From spring through summer along several sections you will be treated to displays of wild-flowers like Dutchman's-breeches, cut-leaf toothwort, and purple phacelia.

No pun intended, but birders "flock" to the reservation in the spring and summer to catch the song of wood thrushes, Swainson's warblers, and yellow-billed cuckoos.

This trek is made up of several different trails, beginning with the Old First Quarters Trail. Along this short section you'll cross an old CCC bridge which partially uses local stones. You will also see more of their handiwork along a runoff next to the trail, where the banks are shored up with stone retaining walls and culverts.

Old First Quarters then intersects the Rockpile Trail, the main natural path running through the park. The trail was originally built by the CCC, and you will be walking up several sets of stone stairs they built in the mid-1930s as you climb high above the river. Along this section you will have some great panoramas of the river, pass the sandstone foundation of an old building built by the CCC, and view some of those wildflowers as you cross through a field under a power line.

The trail leaves the woods for a bit and uses the paved jogging road to take you to one of the highlights of the trip: a walk on water across the Tennessee River over a restored railroad trestle resurrected for just this purpose. The bridge was originally built and opened as a toll bridge and train crossing in 1840. In subsequent years it was severely damaged by two storms, burned by the Union army during the Civil War, then saw an engine and its cars crash through both decks of the double-decker span in 1892. Following the accident the catastrophes ended, and the bridge served as a successful river crossing until it was retired in 1992. The lower deck of the bridge was converted into a wood plank walkway, which this loop will take you on, to about a half mile across the river. The structure is the oldest river bridge in the state and one of the few remaining signs that the town of Southport once stood here. The town was established in 1813 and at the time was the greatest cotton town east of Memphis.

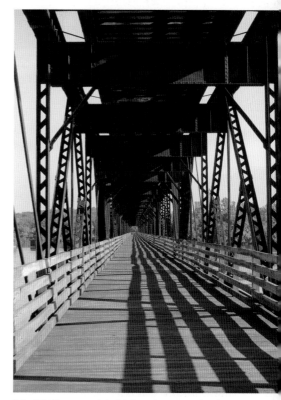

The TVA Nature Trail hike takes you a half mile across the Tennessee River over this historic repurposed railroad bridge.

Miles and Directions

0.0 Start on the east side of the parking lot. You will see the entrance to the paved Reservation Road Trail. Just a few feet in before the metal gate, turn left (north) onto the dirt Old First Quarters Trail (a sign here shows the way).

0.1 Cross an impressive CCC bridge. Come to a Y. The CCC Pavilion Trail is the right fork. Continue on the Old First Quarters Trail on the left to the northeast. You will be walking alongside a deep runoff or seasonal stream bed to the left. (***Option:*** Take the CCC Pavilion Trail to add 0.6 mile to the hike where it loops back onto the Rockpile Trail).

0.3 Pass a CCC retaining wall on the opposite side of the runoff. In 250 feet come to a T intersection with the Rockpile Trail. Turn left (southeast) onto the Rockpile Trail. In a few yards cross a 50-foot bridge over the runoff to the west and come to a Y. The Loop Trail is to the left and leads back to the parking lot. Take the right fork to the north and continue on the Rockpile Trail. In 50 feet Pickwick Lake and the Tennessee River will be in front of you. The trail makes a left turn and heads up stairs.

0.4 Come to the top of the stairs and the overlook. Walk around the left side of the building and pass another short stone structure. In 150 feet come to another Y. Take the right fork to the southwest and continue on the Rockpile Trail. You will be walking along a tall bluff.

0.5 Climb stairs uphill, with wildflowers lining the trail in season. In 200 feet a trail enters from the left (south). Continue straight (west). This is now the Southport Trail (a sign shows the way). There are nice lake views to your right.

0.6 A good view of the lake and the city of Florence as you walk under a power line. The trail is thick grass here with wildflowers. In less than 0.1 mile, climb down stairs (about 100 feet).

0.7 Come to the paved Reservation Road. Turn right onto the road to the southwest.

0.8 Pass a bench on the left. The Southport Historical Trail enters the woods to the right of the bench (you'll return to this point later). Continue south on the paved road.

0.9 Come to picnic tables on the right. There is a wide cut through the woods that leads uphill. Turn right (west) and follow the cut uphill.

1.0 Come out at a paved road. Turn right onto the road and head northwest.

1.1 Come to the old railroad bridge. Follow the bridge out across the lake.

1.4 Great views from the middle of the lake. Turn around and head back the way you came.

1.8 Back at the cut at mile 0.9, turn left and follow the cut back to Reservation Road. When you reach the road, turn left (north) onto the road.

2.0 Back at mile 0.8, turn right onto the Southport Historical Trail, heading uphill using wooden railroad tie and stone stairs. In 175 feet pass a short wooden fence on the left to keep you from falling into a shallow ravine. In a few feet come to a Y. Take the left fork to the northeast onto the Gunnery Hill Trail.

2.1 Come to a Y. Take the right fork.

2.2 Come to a T intersection with the Southport Historical Trail. Take the left fork and head down more stone steps. After the stairs, a seasonal stream will be on your right (nice cascades after rain).

2.5 Pass a large area of kudzu.

2.6 Come to a T intersection. There are two signs here: "Parking Left" and "Parking Right." Turn right (south) and continue on the Southport Historical Trail.

2.7 Arrive back at the parking lot.

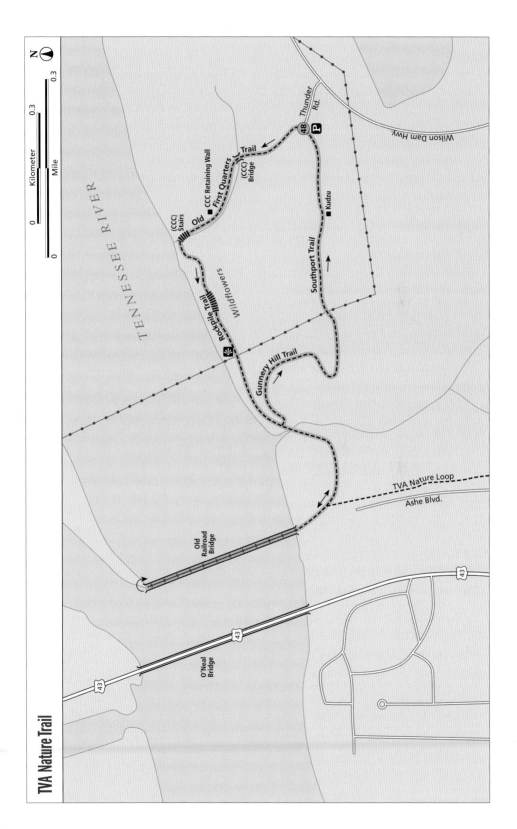

TVA Nature Trail

TENNESSEE RIVER

Old Railroad Bridge

O'Neal Bridge

(CCC) Stairs
Old
CCC Retaining Wall
First Quarters
(CCC) Bridge
Trail
48
P
Thunder Rd
Wilson Dam Hwy.

Rockpile Trail
Wildflowers
Southport Trail
Kudzu

Gunnery Hill Trail

TVA Nature Loop
Ashe Blvd.

43

N

0   Kilometer   0.3
0   Mile   0.3

Options

There are two nice options that can increase the length of the hike and add to the adventure. The first is to add the 0.6-mile Pavilion Trail that intersects with the Old First Quarters Trail. This trail takes you to a nice overlook and a CCC pavilion. The trail loops around until it ends at the Rockpile Trail just east of its intersection with the Old First Quarters.

The second option is to make a right at the intersection with the Rockpile Trail and add an almost 2-mile out-and-back to the trip. The turnaround for this option is at a waterfall near Wilson Dam.

Hiking Information

Local Information

Alabama Mountain Lakes Tourist Association, 402 Sherman St., Decatur, AL 35602; (800) 648–5381; www.northalabama.org

Local Events/Attractions

Alabama Music Hall of Fame, 617 US 72 West, Tuscumbia; (256) 381-4417; www .alamhof.org. The Alabama Music Hall of Fame celebrates the singers, songwriters, and musicians that hailed from the state like Nat King Cole, W. C. Handy, the Commodores, and Emmylou Harris.

Restaurants

Trowbridge's Ice Cream and Sandwich Shop, 316 N. Court St., Florence; (256) 764-1503. The story goes that dairyman Paul Trowbridge stopped in Florence in 1917 on the way to a dairy conference, fell in love with the town, and the rest is history, opening this restaurant that to this day serves up delicious homemade ice cream and sandwiches.

49 Cane Creek Canyon Nature Preserve

One of the most fascinating hikes in the state, Cane Creek Canyon Nature Preserve combines some of the most remarkable canyon scenery you'll find anywhere. Spectacular ancient rock shelters, waterfalls, and a rainbow of rare wildflowers await you on this hike.

Start: Parking lot next to Jim and Faye Lacefield's house
Distance: 4.0-mile multiloop
Hiking time: About 2 hours
Difficulty: Moderate with some steep inclines
Trail surface: Combination dirt, gravel, and rock paths
Best seasons: Fall–early summer
Other trail users: None
Canine compatibility: Leashed dogs permitted
Land status: Privately owned

Nearest town: Tuscumbia
Fees and permits: None
Schedule: Year-round, sunrise to sunset
Maps: USGS Frankfurt, Pride, AL; *DeLorme: Alabama Atlas & Gazetteer,* pages 16 F5 and 17 F6
Trail contacts: Jim and Faye Lacefield, 251 Loop Rd., Tuscumbia, AL 35674; (256) 381-6301; www.facebook.com/pages/Friends-of-Cane-Creek-Canyon-Nature-Preserve/126802417335447

Finding the trailhead: From Tuscumbia at the intersection of US 72 and Veterans Boulevard, take US 72 west 0.7 mile and turn left onto CR 65 / Frankfort Road. Travel 7.6 miles and turn right onto Loop Road. In 0.2 mile as Loop Road bends to the right, continue straight on a gravel road (a sign points the direction to the preserve). Travel 0.3 mile, passing an old poultry farm on the left and through a gate indicating the entrance to the preserve, until you come to a Spanish-influenced house. This is the Lacefields' home. You will see signs plainly indicating where to park. GPS: N34 37.332' / W87 47.668'

The Hike

In other hikes in this book, I've probably used the words "spectacular" and "beautiful" ad nauseam. But each hike has held something a little more "spectacular" than the last, making each special in its own right. So here we are, nearing the end of our journeys, and lo and behold . . .

In 1976 Jim and Faye Lacefield purchased a modest amount of property at what is now the south end of this preserve. They knew what the property to the north held and knew it had to be protected. The owner of the northern property, after opening it to logging, sold his 400 acres to the Lacefields in 2000, and Jim and Faye went to work.

▶ Alabama's state rock is marble. The largest concentration of the rock is a narrow belt that runs from the Coosa River to near Talladega. The marble is known around the world for its crystalline texture and brilliant whiteness. Since 1900, 30 million tons of marble have been quarried.

One of many falls and rock shelters at Cane Creek

Using abandoned logging roads and building their own footpaths to hard-to-access areas, the Lacefields have created a fascinating look at not only wildflowers and waterfalls, but also the distant past. Etched on the walls of this canyon is the geologic record of an ancient time dating back to when all of the continents were joined as one and known as Pangaea. This region was part of an ancient barrier island; evidence of its sand dunes is etched in the towering sandstone cliffs.

The actions of the creek and the environment over the ages molded this canyon, creating astounding rock shelters, many of which were used by Native Americans for refuge during the Mississippian period. Artifacts can still be found, but remember it is a federal crime to take any that you might find!

Almost immediately after heading out from the trailhead, you will come to the first of many rock shelters. This one features a tiered waterfall cascading down the overhanging rocks. But wait, there's more! Even more breathtaking rock shelters are on the way, including Tree Fern and wonderful views high above the canyon from The Point. In the distance you will be able to see mountains 6 miles away, with no trace of civilization between you and those peaks.

Another highlight is the Boulder Garden. Atop giant boulders grow grass and a multitude of wildflowers. Visitors flock to the preserve between mid-March and mid-May to see yellow lady's slippers, trout lily, and mountain laurel, to name only a few. Many rare species can be found here as well, such as the giant columbo.

And, of course, along most of the trip you will encounter Cane Creek itself, a beautiful blue-green creek that helps shape the preserve. Along its banks is a picnic area known as Linden Meadows, which makes a nice stop and a place where you can see periwinkles (small creek snails) by the hundreds along the creek banks, a sign of the purity of the water. But even so, the Lacefields make sure there is a jug of drinking water here as well as several other locations around the preserve in case you need to refill.

The trail described here is only a short subset of the myriad trails that wind their way through the preserve. Once you get your feet wet and experience the canyon, I'm sure you will be back again and again to travel deeper into the canyon to experience features like Karen and Johnson Falls, the Yellow Wood Falls Rock Shelter, and the impressive rock overhangs of Devil's Hollow.

When you arrive at the preserve, you will park next to the Lacefields' home. Please stop by their house and let them know of your hiking plans. Whether or not they are in, be sure to sign the register at the kiosk next to the parking lot. Jim and Faye are fantastic hosts. They'll give you an overview of what you'll see, and often if they have time will join you, taking you on a personal and unforgettable tour of the preserve.

There are five backcountry primitive campsites available on a first-come, first-served basis at the preserve. You must reserve a campsite at least two weeks in advance. Visit the preserve's Facebook page to download a registration form.

Miles and Directions

0.0 Start at the parking lot at the Lacefields' house. Take the dirt road 250 feet. A trail Ys to the right (west). Turn right here onto that trail. In a few feet you will pass a portable toilet on the left.

0.2 Arrive at Small Point. Pass three portable toilets and a campsite. A sign here points the direction of the Waterfall Trail. A series of stairs leads down the hill a short distance.

0.3 Come to a waterfall and rock shelter. Be very careful along the rim of the gorge! Follow the advice of the sign here that reads "Best View of Falls is on Rock Ledge Across Footbridge." Cross the narrow footbridge to the south and come to a Y. A sign here points to the left fork and the way to The Point and the Canyon Rim Trail. Take the left fork uphill (west). (**Option:** After crossing there is a short side trail that leads to the base of the falls).

0.4 Pass a bench on the right (good view of falls in late fall-winter). In 300 feet come to a T intersection at a wide dirt road. Take the right fork (a sign here reads "Canyon Rim Trail" and points the direction).

0.7 Come to a portable toilet and campsite. Turn to the right (northwest).

0.8 Arrive at The Point with its panoramic view. There are benches here and in late spring walls of mountain laurel. To the left (west) is a Y. The right fork is the Steep Trail. Take the left fork to the south on the Canyon Rim Trail. The trail turns into a narrow dirt and rock path, with nice views of valley below to your right.

0.9 Pass an overlook from an outcropping hanging out over the canyon. Be careful if you walk out! In less than 0.1 mile, pass another overlook.

1.1 Come to a T intersection. Turn right (southeast) onto the wide path, which is a dirt road covered with large gravel to protect it from washout. In 150 feet come to a Y. The left fork takes you back to the house. Take the right fork (southwest).

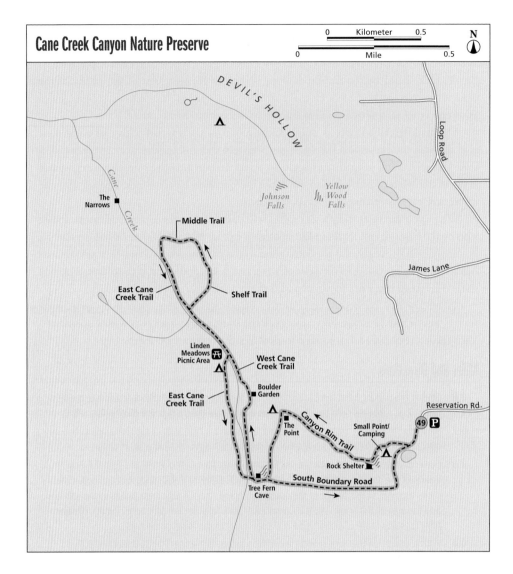

Cane Creek Canyon Nature Preserve

0   Kilometer   0.5

0   Mile   0.5

N

DEVIL'S HOLLOW

Loop Road

The Narrows

Cane Creek

Johnson Falls

Yellow Wood Falls

James Lane

Middle Trail

East Cane Creek Trail

Shelf Trail

Linden Meadows Picnic Area

West Cane Creek Trail

East Cane Creek Trail

Boulder Garden

Reservation Rd.

Canyon Rim Trail

The Point

Small Point/ Camping

49 P

Rock Shelter

South Boundary Road

Tree Fern Cave

1.2 Pass an old dirt road on the left. In a few feet you will pass a bench and pass through a metal gate. This is part of the South Boundary Road. In 100 feet arrive at the Tree Fern Cave Rock Shelter on the right. In 150 feet come to another Y. Take the right fork. A sign points the way to the main Cane Creek Trail.

1.3 Pass a bench and get your first look at Cane Creek.

1.4 Come to a Y. The West Cane Creek Trail is down the left fork to the west. Take the right fork. You are now on the East Cane Creek Trail. In 200 feet pass Big Azalea Footbridge on the left.

1.5 A short, 30-foot trail to the left leads to the cascades of Cane Creek.

1.6 A small trail leads off to the right (east). A sign indicates that this is the Boulder Garden. Turn right here and loop around the two big boulders and wildflowers until you come to a short side trail to the right (west) back to the East Cane Creek Trail.

1.7 Back on the East Cane Creek Trail, turn right onto the trail. In 250 feet pass a footbridge and Linden Garden Meadows on the left (west); continue straight to the northeast. There is a stand of bamboo growing here.

1.8 Come to a Y. To the left is the East Cane Creek Trail, to the right Waterfall Creek Bridge. Take the right fork to the northeast. You are on the south end of the Shelf Trail. Pass an informational sign: "Waterfall Creek Bridge 30 Yards, the Gap $\%_{10}$ of a Mile." In 30 yards cross the footbridge over a nice rocky stream.

2.2 The Shelf Trail continues straight to the north. Turn left (west) onto the Middle Trail.

2.3 Turn left (southeast) onto the East Cane Creek Trail.

2.4 Pass Quarry Bridge over Cane Creek on the right.

2.5 Pass Middle Bridge on the right.

2.6 Cross a creek over the Lower Waterfall Creek Footbridge.

2.7 Return to the Y at mile 1.8. Continue straight to the southwest. In a few yards turn right and cross Cane Creek over a stone and cement footbridge. Look for periwinkles in the stream. After crossing, you are at the Linden Meadows Picnic Area. There is a picnic table, shelter, and water in a jug here. Turn left (southwest) onto the West Cane Creek Trail. The trail is more enclosed and is a narrower dirt road on this side of the creek.

3.1 Cross Cane Creek again to the north over a footbridge. In just over 100 feet, come to a Y. The left fork takes you to the East Cane Creek Trail. Take the right fork onto the Southern Boundary Road.

3.4 Back at the intersection of the Boundary Road and Canyon Rim Trail, continue straight on the South Boundary Road. In 300 feet pass a wildflower patch to the right.

3.6 Pass a trail that leads back to the point on the left; continue straight to the east.

3.7 Arrive at a Y. The left fork is a "shortcut" back to the parking lot. It is rather steep. Take the right fork across a short footbridge over a creek.

3.8 Pass through a gate; a large wildflower field is to the right.

3.9 Pass a pretty little pond on the right. In less than 0.1 mile, arrive back at the first Y at the beginning of the hike. Continue straight toward the parking lot.

4.0 Arrive back at the parking lot/trailhead.

Hiking Information

Local Information

Alabama Mountain Lakes Tourist Association, 402 Sherman St., Decatur, AL 35602; (800) 648-5381; www.northalabama.org

Local Events/Attractions

Fame Recording Studio, 603 E. Avalon Ave., Muscle Shoals; (256) 381-0801; www .fame2.com. Take a tour and see artifacts from the studio that is credited with starting the Muscle Shoals Sound. Fame sold over 300 million records worldwide for stars such as Arthur Alexander, the Tams, and Etta James, and still records artists today.

Restaurants

Dale's, 1001 Mitchell Blvd., Florence; (256) 766-4961. The origin of the famous Dale's marinade, serving up delicious steaks and seafood.

50 Borden Creek (Trail 200)

This is a great hike for kids and adults alike through the Sipsey Wilderness. Sandstone cliffs tower above the trail, forming a canyon as the route travels along the Sipsey River and the trail's namesake creek. The hike gives you a chance to do a little spelunking through a 100-foot cave next to a waterfall.

Start: Sipsey Wilderness Recreational Area off Cranal Road (CR 60)
Distance: 2.8 miles point to point (requires shuttle)
Hiking time: About 2 hours
Difficulty: Easy over relatively flat footpath, moderate due to distance
Trail surface: Dirt and rock
Best seasons: Winter–late spring
Other trail users: None
Canine compatibility: Leashed dogs permitted
Land status: Wilderness
Nearest town: Moulton
Fees and permits: Day-use fee

Schedule: Year-round, sunrise to sunset
Maps: USGS Mount Hope, AL; *DeLorme: Alabama Atlas & Gazetteer,* page 23 B9 B10; trail maps available online at the Sipsey Wilderness Hiking Club website (www.sipseywilderness.org)
Trail contact: US Forest Service, 1070 AL 33, Double Springs, AL 35553; (205) 489-5111; www.fs.usda.gov/alabama
Special considerations: Hunting is permitted in the Sipsey Wilderness Area of William Bankhead National Forest, and trails are closed during certain times of the season. Visit the Forest Service website for dates and additional information.

Finding the trailhead: From Moulton at the intersection of AL 24 and AL 33, take AL 33 south 13.9 miles. Turn right onto CR 60 / Cranal Road. Travel 4 miles. The recreation area is well marked on the left side of the highway. GPS: N34 17.137' / W87 23.920'

The Hike

Most people don't think of Alabama as a wilderness retreat, but it is. As a matter of fact, the state has three designated wilderness areas: Cheaha Wilderness, with its 7,490 acres, lies in northeast Alabama near Cheaha State Park; the Dugger Mountain Wilderness, near Anniston, has 9,200 acres; and the largest tract is the Sipsey Wilderness, with over 24,000 acres—the third largest wilderness area in the United States east of the Mississippi.

Located in William Bankhead National Forest, the Sipsey Wilderness exemplifies all of the characteristics (and more) of the federal government's definition of wilderness: amazing landscapes and wildlife, an area untouched by humans, and an area that provides recreation and solitude. One of the best trails to experience all that the Sipsey has to offer is the Borden Creek Trail (Trail 200). Of all of the Sipsey's trails, Borden Creek draws together all of the wilderness's most attractive elements and does so along a footpath that's easy enough for the whole family, with the exception of very young children, to enjoy. Having said that, keep in mind that the uniqueness

The Borden Creek Trail takes you past many impressive bluffs and rock shelters.

of this trail and its relative ease of hiking also make it very popular. On any given weekend the trailhead is full. But don't let that deter you!

There are several things that make the Sipsey so special. The first is that it is the only area of old-growth oak forest remaining in Alabama. Along the trail you will also find magnificent specimens of magnolia, holly, hemlock, and cedar. This is also a prime wildflower region. Don't be surprised to see a lot of photographers along the trail, capturing images of yellow lady's slippers, shooting stars, yellow and white trilliums, and other flowers.

The Sipsey is also the home of amazing sandstone bluffs, towering canyon walls carved over the ages by the action of Borden Creek, the Sipsey River, and the many waterfalls hidden away throughout the forest. As a matter of fact, throughout this hike you will hear the sounds of water splashing down the tall canyon walls, the reason why this area is known as Land of a Thousand Waterfalls.

The trail itself ranges from a narrow, 2-foot-wide dirt path to a wide, 5-plus-foot-wide path. You will climb over a few rocks along the way, too.

You have three options when it comes to walking this trail. The first is a 2.8-mile point-to-point. This is a fairly easy walk over dirt and rock footpaths. It is the best choice if you are bringing children since it's shorter in length, being half the distance of the out-and-back version, but it will require you to have a shuttle vehicle waiting at the other end. You can start from either the Sipsey Wilderness Recreation Area or the Borden Creek Trailhead.

The other option is a 5.6-mile out-and-back. Of course, the length makes this more of a moderate hike and probably not good for young children.

The third option is to make it into an overnight backpacking trip and split the mileage up. There are numerous established campsites along the trail, either right next to the Sipsey River or Borden Creek or near an impressive rock shelter.

Along the trail you will be walking either alongside, or very near, the cold, clear waters of Borden Creek and the Sipsey River. Sandstone cliffs rise above both sides of the trail, some 100 feet high. The trail will make several stops at amazing rock shelters and waterfalls.

Just south of the Borden Creek Trailhead, you will come to what is known as the Fat Man's Squeeze, a 200-foot-long cave through the rocks that is aptly named. From the north side the cave is large enough to comfortably walk into; at the southern end you will know how it got its name, narrowing to about a foot wide. If you have to, you can crawl through the bottom of the opening, where it is wider. It is a very damp cave, if not downright wet, because at the opening on the north end is a 50-foot waterfall. Just a little something extra to add to the adventure.

Although the trails in the wilderness are not marked, except for signs that mark the trailheads and the occasional intersection, staying on this trail is fairly easy. Unlike the Sipsey Trail, which has several unmarked branch trails and game paths that sometimes lure hikers in the wrong direction, this path is well worn and the only side trails are short ones leading to the established campsites I mentioned earlier.

The two trailheads are quite different. The better of the two is the Sipsey River Recreation Area at the south end of the trail. This is a wide gravel parking lot with plenty of room for thirty to forty cars. There is an information kiosk here and a decent composting restroom, and this is where you pay your day-use fee. The directions given below begin at this trailhead.

The Borden Creek Trailhead at the north end of the trail is a narrow gravel cul-de-sac that can hold maybe ten cars. You can park along the side of the approach road, but it's narrow. There is no fee to park here. If you use this trailhead, simply reverse the directions below.

Miles and Directions

0.0 Start on the northwest side of the Sipsey Wilderness Picnic Area parking lot at the informational kiosk. A sign reading 200/209 (the trail numbers for the Borden and Sipsey Trails) points the direction. The trail is a well-worn and easy-to-follow dirt and rock footpath as it heads under the CR 60 bridge. You will have great views of the gorge and rocks of the Sipsey River on your left (west).

0.1 Come to a Y. Take the right fork (northeast).

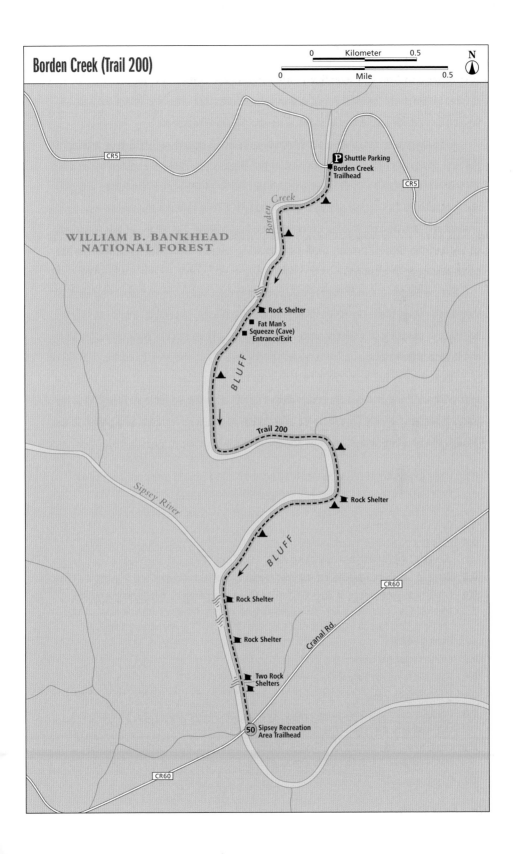

Borden Creek (Trail 200)

0   Kilometer   0.5
0   Mile   0.5

N

CR5

Shuttle Parking
Borden Creek
Trailhead

CR5

Borden Creek

WILLIAM B. BANKHEAD
NATIONAL FOREST

Rock Shelter

Fat Man's
Squeeze (Cave)
Entrance/Exit

BLUFF

Trail 200

Rock Shelter

Sipsey River

BLUFF

CR60

Rock Shelter

Cranal Rd.

Rock Shelter

Two Rock
Shelters

50 Sipsey Recreation
Area Trailhead

CR60

THE LAND OF A THOUSAND WATERFALLS

Located in Bankhead National Forest is a wilderness area that many feel offers the best hiking and backpacking experiences in the state—the Sipsey Wilderness.

The Sipsey was designated a wilderness area by Congress in 1975, thus making it the first designated wilderness area east of the Mississippi. Today the wilderness is over 24,000 acres in size. The soft limestone and sandstone of the region have given way over the centuries to the action of rivers and creeks that flow through the wilderness, most prominently Bee Branch, Borden Creek, and the Sipsey River. The action of this water has carved out the Sipsey, leaving behind an amazing canyon filled with rock shelters and caves waiting to be explored.

But the Sipsey is a work in progress, as those creeks and rivers continue their work as they tumble down the rocky walls. Hiking through the Sipsey, you will be treated to literally hundreds of cascades of different sizes—that's why the wilderness has been called the Land of a Thousand Waterfalls.

There are way too many trails in the Sipsey to tell you about here. It would require a separate book if you included the many "hidden" trails of Bankhead National Forest. Visit the Sipsey Wilderness Hiking Club for more information on trails, restrictions, and guided hikes through this amazing landscape (www.sipseywilderness.org).

0.2 Come to your first rock shelter with a waterfall. Continue straight under the shelter and come up on a second one. The trail swings under these shelters, then back on the riverbank.

0.3 Cross a runoff creek.

0.4 Pass a large bluff with a rock shelter on the right. In 100 feet pass another huge rock overhang/shelter with a seasonal waterfall.

0.5 Come to another Y. Take the left fork (northwest) to stay near the river.

0.6 Come to the confluence of Borden Creek and the Sipsey River. A sign marks the intersection with the Sipsey River Trail (#209) heading to the left (crosses river). There is a campsite here. Continue straight on the wide Borden Creek Trail. You are now walking above Borden Creek.

0.7 Cross a seasonal creek.

0.8 Pass a side trail to a campsite and the river on the left.

0.9 Cross a rocky creek.

1.0 Pass a shoal in the creek to your left. In 200 feet pass a campsite on the left. There is a nice bluff with shelters on the right.

1.1 Come to a Y. Take the left fork. There is another campsite here. Cross the creek to the northwest and in 100 feet cross a second creek.

1.2 Pass a campsite.

1.3 The trail comes to another nice creek. Hike straight across it and pick up the trail on the other side, where you will cross an unmarked trail that heads left and right (north and south). Continue straight to the west. In 200 feet pass another campsite.

1.4 The trail moves away from the bluffs and the forest opens up for a short distance.

1.7 Pass a large bluff on the right.

1.9 Pass a short side trail to a campsite on the right.

2.0 Cross an intermittent stream (there is a small waterfall here during times of rain).

2.1 The trail is slightly washed out and only about 6 inches wide for a few yards just before arriving at the cave.

2.2 Arrive at Fat Man's Squeeze. The cave is about 200 feet long, with a slight bend to it. Walk through the cave and on the other side there is a small waterfall. In less than 0.1 mile, pass a rock shelter on the right.

2.3 Pass a very big rock bluff on the right with seasonal falls.

2.4 Pass another campsite on the left.

2.6 Pass a side trail to a campsite and the creek on the left. Another big rock bluff is to the right.

2.7 Pass a short trail to another campsite on the left.

2.8 Arrive at the Borden Creek trailhead. (*Option:* You need to either have a shuttle vehicle waiting for you here or this is your turnaround point to head back to the Sipsey Wilderness Recreation Area.)

Hiking Information

Local Information
Lawrence County Alabama Chamber of Commerce, 12467 AL 157, Moulton, AL 35650; (256) 974-1658; www.lawrencealabama.com

Local Events/Attractions
Alabama Chicken and Egg Festival, Lions Club Fairgrounds, 455 School St., Moulton; (256) 905-0700; www.alabamachickenandeggfestival.com. Held annually the second weekend of April, this interactive agricultural festival features three stages of bands, arts and crafts, and plenty of chicken to eat prepared in a variety of ways.

Restaurants
Nesmith's Hamburgers, 14396 Court St., Moulton; (256) 974-9806. A Moulton staple since 1966. Great double cheeseburgers.

Hike Tours
Wild South, 11312 AL 33, Ste. 1, Moulton, AL 35650; (256) 974-6166; www.wild south.org. Not only is Wild South an amazing outdoor conservation organization, they also believe in sharing their knowledge of Bankhead National Forest with others and hold regular hikes.

Organizations
Sipsey Wilderness Hiking Club; www.sipseywilderness.org. Excellent website for information on the many trails of the Sipsey Wilderness and Bankhead National Forest.

North Region Honorable Mentions

Alabama's North Region gives you diverse hiking adventures, from panoramic views to breathtaking waterfalls at the geologic fall line. The following trails didn't make the top of our list, but while in the area, you may want to check them out. These hikes still provide interesting scenery and challenges. Let us know what you think about the selection. Maybe one should be upgraded to the A list, or maybe you know of a hidden gem that would make a good honorable mention.

K Eberhart Trail

Here's a fine, but difficult, 1.8-mile out-and-back hike to the bottom of the deepest canyon east of the Mississippi, Little River Canyon. This one isn't for anyone that's out of shape. It's a very steep climb down to the rocky banks of the Little River, which cut the sandstone rocks eons ago to create the canyon.

The trail is wide, sometimes 10 to 15 feet in places. About halfway down the canyon wall there is a bench and right behind it a small bluff where you will get a bird's-eye view of the canyon. (Be careful! These are high and dangerous bluffs.) The canyon walls continue to rise above you until you reach the bottom and the boiling blue-green waters of the river. When you reach the river, take the time to explore, especially a little to the north for a view of Grace's High Falls, a pencil thin waterfall. (Keep in mind the falls are seasonal.)

Just remember that it's a long, steep trip back up the canyon wall. Leave yourself plenty of time for the walk out. For more information visit Little River National Preserve online at www.nps.gov/liri/ or call (256) 845-9605. *DeLorme: Alabama Atlas & Gazetteer:* Page 27 A7.

L Point Rock Trail

Situated within a deep canyon near Lake Guntersville is Buck's Pocket State Park and the Point Rock Trail. This trail is a steep 2.2-mile out-and-back and rated difficult.

It begins at the park office and heads into the woods at the bottom of a ravine, where it climbs over huge boulders. Just before the trail turns to make the final push to the top of the mountain, a 70-foot-long cascade pops out of the boulders and then drops back into an underground channel known as the Big Sink. This is a seasonal stream, so the best time to view it would be late fall through early spring.

The trail makes its way to the top of Point Rock, a 285-foot-tall sandstone bluff that reaches an elevation of just over 900 feet. An outcropping popular with rock climbers drops off steeply here. The trail makes its way to the very edge of Point Rock, offering panoramic views of the canyon and its sandstone walls. Contact Buck's Pocket State Park by phone at (256) 659-2000 or visit online www.alapark.com/buckspocket/. *DeLorme: Alabama Atlas & Gazetteer:* Page 20 H3.

M Russell Cave National Monument

Situated near the borders of Alabama, Tennessee, and Georgia, Russell Cave National Monument has been operated by the National Park Service since 1962. The cave and surrounding landscape are said to hold the oldest and most complete archeological records of human existence in the eastern United States.

The Russell Cave Trail includes a 2-foot-wide asphalt path up the side of Montague Mountain to an elevation of about 1,300 feet. The steep trail weaves through stands of chinquapin, hickory, and chestnut. Deep-green moss clings to rocks along the trail. Wildflowers such as bluets and white rue anemones line the path. White-tailed deer are often seen darting in and out of the brush. The path becomes a boardwalk before arriving at the park's centerpiece—Russell Cave itself, a large limestone cave that has sheltered humans for more than 9,000 years.

The park hosts many events centered on the long, rich history of the cave throughout the year. Find out more by contacting Russell Cave National Monument at (256) 495-2672 or online at www.nps.gov/ruca. *DeLorme: Alabama Atlas & Gazetteer:* Page 20 A5.

N Stone Cuts Trail

The Stone Cuts Trail is a moderately difficult 3-mile lollipop loop at Monte Sano State Park in Huntsville. The draw to this trail is the deep erosional clefts that have been carved in limestone outcroppings, which the trail runs right through. The "cuts" in the rock have high walls, narrow corridors, and at least one cave chamber to walk through. Kids love climbing around in here, rock climbers love the high cliff walls, and small cave-like spaces in the rocks attract spelunkers. Find out more by visiting www.alapark.com/MonteSano/ or call (256) 534-3757. *DeLorme: Alabama Atlas & Gazetteer:* Page 19 D8.

The Stone Cuts Trail leads you straight into the limestone "cuts."

Appendix A: Clubs and Trail Groups

Alabama Birding Trail, www.alabamabirdingtrails.com

Alabama Hiking Trail Society, PO Box 231164, Montgomery, AL 36123; www .hikealabama.org

Alabama Scenic River Trail, 799 Ashley Dr., Madison, AL 35758; www.alabama scenicrivertrail.com

Alabama Trails Association, www.alabamatrailsasso.org

Anniston Outdoor Association, PO Box 2168, Anniston, AL 36202; www.anniston al.gov

Appalachian Trail Club of Alabama, PO Box 381842, Birmingham, AL 35238; www .birminghamal.org/places/appalachian-trail-club-of-alabama

Cahaba River Society, 2717 7th Ave. South #205, Birmingham, AL 35233; www .cahabariversociety.org

Cherokee Ridge Alpine Trail Association, PO Box 240503, Eclectic, AL 36024

Fresh Air Family, www.freshairfamily.org

Jacksonville State University Field School, www.jsu.edu/epic

Pinhoti Trail Alliance, www.pinhotitrailalliance.org

Shoals Environmental Alliance, PO Box 699, Sheffield, AL 3560; www.sea.tiny webs.org

Sierra Club of Alabama, www.alabama.sierraclub.org

Sipsey Wilderness Hiking Club, www.sipseywilderness.org

Vulcan Trail Association, PO Box 382754, Birmingham, AL 35238; www.vulcantrail association.ws

WildSouth, 11312 AL 33, Ste. 1, Moulton, AL 35650; (256) 974-6166; www.wild south.org

Appendix B: Further Reading

History

Pasquill, Robert, Jr. *The Civilian Conservation Corps in Alabama, 1933–1942: A Great and Lasting Good*. Tuscaloosa: University of Alabama Press, 2008.

US Department of the Interior. *Auburn Alabama: Remember When*. Washington, DC, 1935. Video of the CCC building Chewacla State Park. www.alapark.com/chewacla.

US Department of Interior. *Down Mobile Way*. Washington, DC, 1935. Video of the CCC building Gulf State Park and Little River State Forest. www.youtube.com/watch?v=N23Vpy6VTmw.

Natural History

Lacefield, Jim. *Lost Worlds in Alabama Rocks: A Guide*. Tuscaloosa: Alabama Geological Society, 2000.

Medina, Victor, and Barbara Medina. *Southern Appalachian Wildflowers*. Guilford, CT: Falcon Books, 2002.

Phillips, Doug, and Robert P. Falls. *Discovering Alabama Wetlands*. Tuscaloosa: University of Alabama Press, 2002.

Young, Beth Maynor, Rhett Johnson, and John C. Hall. *Longleaf, As Far as the Eye Can See: A New Vision of America's Richest Forest*. Chapel Hill: University of North Carolina Press, 2012.

Recreational

Cuhaj, Joe. *Best Tent Camping: Alabama*. Birmingham, AL: Menasha Ridge Press, 2012.

The Art of Hiking

When standing nose to nose with a mountain lion, you're probably not too concerned with the issue of ethical behavior in the wild. No doubt you're just terrified. But let's be honest. How often are you nose to nose with a mountain lion? For most of us, a hike into the "wild" means loading up the SUV with expensive gear and driving to a toileted trailhead. Sure, you can mourn how civilized we've become—how GPS units have replaced natural instinct and Gore-Tex stands in for true-grit—but the silly gadgets of civilization aside, we have plenty of reason to take pride in how we've matured. With survival now on the back burner, we've begun to understand that we have a responsibility to protect, no longer just conquer, our wild places: that they, not we, are at risk. So please, do what you can. The following section will help you understand better what it means to "do what you can" while still making the most of your hiking experience. Anyone can take a hike, but hiking safely and well is an art requiring preparation and proper equipment.

Trail Etiquette

Leave no trace. Always leave an area just like you found it—if not better than you found it. Avoid camping in fragile, alpine meadows and along the banks of streams and lakes. Use a camp stove versus building a wood fire. Pack up all of your trash and extra food. Bury human waste at least 100 feet from water sources under 6 to 8 inches of topsoil. Don't bathe with soap in a lake or stream—use prepackaged moistened towels to wipe off sweat and dirt, or bathe in the water without soap.

Stay on the trail. It's true, a path anywhere leads nowhere new, but purists will just have to get over it. Paths serve an important purpose; they limit impact on natural areas. Straying from a designated trail may seem innocent but it can cause damage to sensitive areas—damage that may take years to recover, if it can recover at all. Even simple shortcuts can be destructive. So, please, stay on the trail.

Leave no weeds. Noxious weeds tend to overtake other plants, which in turn affects animals and birds that depend on them for food. To minimize the spread of noxious weeds, hikers should regularly clean their boots, tents, packs, and hiking poles of mud and seeds. Also brush your dog to remove any weed seeds before heading off into a new area.

Keep your dog under control. You can buy a flexi-lead that allows your dog to go exploring along the trail, while allowing you the ability to reel him in should another hiker approach or should he decide to chase a rabbit. Always obey leash laws and be sure to bury your dog's waste or pack it in resealable plastic bags.

Respect other trail users. Often you're not the only one on the trail. With the rise in popularity of multiuse trails, you'll have to learn a new kind of respect, beyond the nod and "hello" approach you may be used to. First investigate whether you're on a multiuse trail, and assume the appropriate precautions. When you encounter motorized vehicles (ATVs, motorcycles, and 4WDs), be alert. Though they should always yield to the hiker, often they're going too fast or are too lost in the buzz of their engine to react to your presence. If you hear activity ahead, step off the trail just to be safe. Note that you're not likely to hear a mountain biker coming, so be prepared and know ahead of time whether you share the trail with them. Cyclists should always yield to hikers, but that's little comfort to the hiker. Be aware. When you approach horses or pack animals on the trail, always step quietly off the trail, preferably on the downhill side, and let them pass. If you're wearing a large backpack, it's often a good idea to sit down. To some animals, a hiker wearing a large backpack might appear threatening. Many national forests allow domesticated grazing, usually for sheep and cattle. Make sure your dog doesn't harass these animals, and respect ranchers' rights while you're enjoying yours.

Getting into Shape

Unless you want to be sore—and possibly have to shorten your trip or vacation—be sure to get in shape before a big hike. If you're terribly out of shape, start a walking program early, preferably eight weeks in advance. Start with a fifteen-minute walk during your lunch hour or after work and gradually increase your walking time to an hour. You should also increase your elevation gain. Walking briskly up hills really strengthens your leg muscles and gets your heart rate up. If you work in a storied office building, take the stairs instead of the elevator. If you prefer going to a gym, walk the treadmill or use a stair machine. You can further increase your strength and endurance by walking with a loaded backpack. Stationary exercises you might consider are squats, leg lifts, sit-ups, and push-ups. Other good ways to get in shape include biking, running, aerobics, and, of course, short hikes. Stretching before and after a hike keeps muscles flexible and helps avoid injuries.

Preparedness

It's been said that failing to plan means planning to fail. So do take the necessary time to plan your trip. Whether going on a short day hike or an extended backpack trip, always prepare for the worst. Simply remembering to pack a copy of the U.S. Army Survival Manual is not preparedness. Although it's not a bad idea if you plan on entering truly wild places, it's merely the tourniquet answer to a problem. You need to do your best to prevent the problem from arising in the first place. In order to survive— and to stay reasonably comfortable—you need to concern yourself with the basics: water, food, and shelter. Don't go on a hike without having these bases covered. And don't go on a hike expecting to find these items in the woods.

Water. Even in frigid conditions, you need at least two quarts of water a day to function efficiently. Add heat and taxing terrain and you can bump that figure up to one gallon. That's simply a base to work from—your metabolism and your level of conditioning can raise or lower that amount. Unless you know your level, assume that you need one gallon of water a day. Now, where do you plan on getting the water?

Preferably not from natural water sources. These sources can be loaded with intestinal disturbers, such as bacteria, viruses, and fertilizers. Giardia lamblia, the most common of these disturbers, is a protozoan parasite that lives part of its life cycle as a cyst in water sources. The parasite spreads when mammals defecate in water sources. Once ingested, Giardia can induce cramping, diarrhea, vomiting, and fatigue within two days to two weeks after ingestion. Giardiasis is treatable with prescription drugs. If you believe you've contracted giardiasis, see a doctor immediately.

Treating water. The best and easiest solution to avoid polluted water is to carry your water with you. Yet, depending on the nature of your hike and the duration, this may not be an option—one gallon of water weighs eight-and-a-half pounds. In that case, you'll need to look into treating water. Regardless of which method you choose, you should always carry some water with you in case of an emergency. Save this reserve until you absolutely need it.

There are three methods of treating water: boiling, chemical treatment, and filtering. If you boil water, it's recommended that you do so for ten to fifteen minutes. This is often impractical because you're forced to exhaust a great deal of your fuel supply. You can opt for chemical treatment, which will kill Giardia but will not take care of other chemical pollutants. Another drawback to chemical treatments is the unpleasant taste of the water after it's treated. You can remedy this by adding powdered drink mix to the water. Filters are the preferred method for treating water. Many filters remove Giardia, organic and inorganic contaminants, and don't leave an aftertaste. Water filters are far from perfect as they can easily become clogged or leak if a gasket wears out. It's always a good idea to carry a backup supply of chemical treatment tablets in case your filter decides to quit on you.

Food. If we're talking about survival, you can go days without food, as long as you have water. But we're also talking about comfort. Try to avoid foods that are high in sugar and fat like candy bars and potato chips. These food types are harder to digest and are low in nutritional value. Instead, bring along foods that are easy to pack, nutritious, and high in energy (e.g., bagels, nutrition bars, dehydrated fruit, gorp, and jerky). If you are on an overnight trip, easy-to-fix dinners include rice mixes with dehydrated potatoes, corn, pasta with cheese sauce, and soup mixes. For a tasty breakfast, you can fix hot oatmeal with brown sugar and reconstituted milk powder topped off with banana chips. If you like a hot drink in the morning, bring along herbal tea bags or hot chocolate. If you are a coffee junkie, you can purchase coffee that is packaged like tea bags. You can prepackage all of your meals in heavy-duty resealable plastic bags to keep food from spilling in your pack. These bags can be reused to pack out trash.

Shelter. The type of shelter you choose depends less on the conditions than on your tolerance for discomfort. Shelter comes in many forms—tent, tarp, lean-to, bivy sack, cabin, cave, etc. If you're camping in the desert, a bivy sack may suffice, but if you're above the treeline and a storm is approaching, a better choice is a three- or four-season tent. Tents are the logical and most popular choice for most backpackers as they're lightweight and packable—and you can rest assured that you always have shelter from the elements. Before you leave on your trip, anticipate what the weather and terrain will be like and plan for the type of shelter that will work best for your comfort level (see Equipment later in this section).

Finding a campsite. If there are established campsites, stick to those. If not, start looking for a campsite early—around 3:30 or 4:00 p.m. Stop at the first decent site you see. Depending on the area, it could be a long time before you find another suitable location. Pitch your camp in an area that's level. Make sure the area is at least 200 feet from fragile areas like lakeshores, meadows, and stream banks. And try to avoid areas thick in underbrush, as they can harbor insects and provide cover for approaching animals.

If you are camping in stormy, rainy weather, look for a rock outcrop or a shelter in the trees to keep the wind from blowing your tent all night. Be sure that you don't camp under trees with dead limbs that might break off on top of you. Also, try to find an area that has an absorbent surface, such as sandy soil or forest duff. This, in addition to camping on a surface with a slight angle, will provide better drainage. By all means, don't dig trenches to provide drainage around your tent—remember you're practicing zero-impact camping.

If you're in bear country, steer clear of creekbeds or animal paths. If you see any signs of a bear's presence (i.e., scat, footprints), relocate. You'll need to find a campsite near a tall tree where you can hang your food and other items that may attract bears such as deodorant, toothpaste, or soap. Carry a lightweight nylon rope with which to hang your food. As a rule, you should hang your food at least 20 feet from the ground and 5 feet away from the tree trunk. You can put food and other items in a waterproof stuff sack and tie one end of the rope to the stuff sack. To get the other end of the rope over the tree branch, tie a good size rock to it, and gently toss the rock over the tree branch. Pull the stuff sack up until it reaches the top of the branch and tie it off securely. Don't hang your food near your tent! If possible, hang your food at least 100 feet away from your campsite. Alternatives to hanging your food are bear-proof plastic tubes and metal bear boxes.

Lastly, think of comfort. Lie down on the ground where you intend to sleep and see if it's a good fit. For morning warmth (and a nice view to wake up to), have your tent face east.

First Aid

I know you're tough, but get 10 miles into the woods and develop a blister and you'll wish you had carried that first-aid kit. Face it, it's just plain good sense. Many companies produce lightweight, compact first-aid kits. Just make sure yours contains at least the following:

- ❑ Ace bandage
- ❑ adhesive bandages
- ❑ antacid tablets
- ❑ antibacterial wipes
- ❑ antihistamine

- ❏ aspirin
- ❏ Betadine solution
- ❏ first-aid book
- ❏ moleskin or duct tape
- ❏ plastic gloves
- ❏ scissors
- ❏ sterile cotton tip applicators
- ❏ sterile gauze and dressings
- ❏ syrup of ipecac (to induce vomiting)
- ❏ thermometer
- ❏ triple-antibiotic ointment
- ❏ tweezers
- ❏ white surgical tape
- ❏ wire splint

Here are a few tips for dealing with and hopefully preventing certain ailments.

Sunburn. Take along sunscreen or sun block, protective clothing, and a wide-brimmed hat. If you do get a sunburn, treat the area with aloe vera gel, and protect the area from further sun exposure. At higher elevations, the sun's radiation can be particularly damaging to skin. Remember that your eyes are vulnerable to this radiation as well. Sunglasses can be a good way to prevent headaches and permanent eye damage from the sun, especially in places where light-colored rock or patches of snow reflect light up in your face.

Blisters. Be prepared to take care of these hike-spoilers by carrying moleskin (a lightly padded adhesive), gauze and tape, or adhesive bandages. An effective way to apply moleskin is to cut out a circle of moleskin and remove the center—like a doughnut—and place it over the blistered area. Cutting the center out will reduce the pressure applied to the sensitive skin. Other products can help you combat blisters. Some are applied to suspicious hot spots before a blister forms to help decrease friction to that area, while others are applied to the blister after it has popped to help prevent further irritation.

Insect bites and stings. You can treat most insect bites and stings by applying hydrocortisone 1% cream topically and taking a pain medication such as ibuprofen or acetaminophen to reduce swelling. If you forgot to pack these items, a cold compress or a paste of mud and ashes can sometimes assuage the itching and discomfort. Remove any stingers by using tweezers or scraping the area with your fingernail or a knife blade. Don't pinch the area as you'll only spread the venom.

Some hikers are highly sensitive to bites and stings and may have a serious allergic reaction that can be life threatening. Symptoms of such a reaction can include wheezing, an asthmatic attack, and shock. The treatment for this severe type of reaction is epinephrine. If you know that you are sensitive to bites and stings, carry a pre-packaged kit of epinephrine, which can be obtained only by prescription from your doctor.

Ticks. Ticks can carry diseases such as Rocky Mountain spotted fever and Lyme disease. The best defense is, of course, prevention. If you know you're going to be hiking through an area littered with ticks, wear long pants and a long sleeved shirt. You can apply a permethrin repellent to your clothing and a Deet repellent to exposed skin. At the end of your hike, do a spot check for ticks (and insects in general). If you do find a tick, grab the head of the tick firmly—with a pair of tweezers if you have them—and gently pull it away from the skin with a twisting motion. Sometimes the mouth parts linger, embedded in your skin. If this happens, try to remove them with a disinfected needle. Clean the affected area with an antibacterial cleanser and then apply triple antibiotic ointment. Monitor the area for a few days. If irritation persists or a white spot develops, see a doctor for possible infection.

Poison ivy, oak, and sumac. These skin irritants can be found most anywhere in North America and come in the form of a bush or a vine, having leaflets in groups of three, five, seven, or nine. Learn how to spot the plants. The oil they secrete can cause an allergic reaction in the form of blisters, usually about twelve hours after exposure. The itchy rash can last from ten days to several weeks. The best defense against these irritants is to wear clothing that covers the arms, legs and torso. For summer, zip-off cargo pants come in handy. There are also nonprescription lotions you can apply to exposed skin that guard against the effects of poison ivy/oak/sumac and can be washed off with soap and water. If you think you were in contact with the plants, after hiking (or even on the trail during longer hikes) wash with soap and water. Taking a hot shower with soap after you return home from your hike will also help to remove any lingering oil from your skin. Should you contract a rash from any of these plants, use an antihistamine to reduce the itching. If the rash is localized, create a light bleach/water wash to dry up the area. If the rash has spread, either tough it out or see your doctor about getting a dose of cortisone (available both orally and by injection).

Snakebites. Snakebites are rare in North America. Unless startled or provoked, the majority of snakes will not bite. If you are wise to their habitats and keep a careful eye on the trail, you should be just fine. When stepping over logs, first step on the log, making sure you can see what's on the other side before stepping down. Though your chances of being struck are slim, it's wise to know what to do in the event you are.

If a nonpoisonous snake bites you, allow the wound to bleed a small amount and then cleanse the wounded area with a Betadine solution (10% povidone iodine). Rinse the wound with clean water (preferably) or fresh urine (it might sound ugly, but it's sterile). Once the area is clean, cover it with triple antibiotic ointment and a clean bandage. Remember, most residual damage from snakebites, poisonous or otherwise, comes from infection, not the snake's venom. Keep the area as clean as possible and get medical attention immediately.

If somebody in your party is bitten by a poisonous snake, follow these steps:

1. Calm the patient.

2. Remove jewelry, watches, and restrictive clothing, and immobilize the affected limb. Do not elevate the injury. Medical opinions vary on whether the area should be lower or level with the heart, but the consensus is that it should not be above it.

3. Make a note of the circumference of the limb at the bite site and at various points above the site as well. This will help you monitor swelling.

4. Evacuate your victim. Ideally he should be carried out to minimize movement. If the victim appears to be doing okay, he can walk. Stop and rest frequently, and if the swelling appears to be spreading or the patient's symptoms increase, change your plan and find a way to get your patient transported.

5. If you are waiting for rescue, make sure to keep your patient comfortable and hydrated (unless he begins vomiting).

Snakebite treatment is rife with old-fashioned remedies: You used to be told to cut and suck the venom out of the bite site or to use a suction cup extractor for the same purpose; applying an electric shock to the area was even in vogue for a while. Do not do any of these things. Do not apply ice, do not give your patient painkillers, and do not apply a tourniquet. All you really want to do is keep your patient calm and get help. If you're alone and have to hike out, don't run—you'll only increase the flow of blood throughout your system. Instead, walk calmly.

Dehydration. Have you ever hiked in hot weather and had a roaring headache and felt fatigued after only a few miles? More than likely you were dehydrated. Symptoms of dehydration include fatigue, headache, and decreased coordination and judgment. When you are hiking, your body's rate of fluid loss depends on the outside temperature, humidity, altitude, and your activity level. On average, a hiker walking in warm weather will lose four liters of fluid a day. That fluid loss is easily replaced by normal consumption of liquids and food. However, if a hiker is walking briskly in hot, dry weather and hauling a heavy pack, he or she can lose one to three liters of water an hour. It's important to always carry plenty of water and to stop often and drink fluids regularly, even if you aren't thirsty.

Heat exhaustion is the result of a loss of large amounts of electrolytes and often occurs if a hiker is dehydrated and has been under heavy exertion. Common symptoms of heat exhaustion include cramping, exhaustion, fatigue, lightheadedness, and nausea. You can treat heat exhaustion by getting out of the sun and drinking an electrolyte solution made up of one teaspoon of salt and one tablespoon of sugar dissolved in a liter of water. Drink this solution slowly over a period of one hour. Drinking plenty of fluids (preferably an electrolyte solution/sports drink) can prevent heat exhaustion. Avoid hiking during the hottest parts of the day, and wear breathable clothing, a wide-brimmed hat, and sunglasses.

Hypothermia is one of the biggest dangers in the backcountry, especially for day hikers in the summertime. That may sound strange, but imagine starting out on a hike in midsummer when it's sunny and 80 degrees out. You're clad in nylon shorts and a cotton T-shirt. About halfway through your hike, the sky begins to cloud up, and in the next hour a light drizzle begins to fall and the wind starts to pick up. Before you know it, you are soaking wet and shivering—the perfect recipe for hypothermia. More advanced signs include decreased coordination, slurred speech, and blurred vision. When a victim's temperature falls below 92 degrees, the blood pressure and pulse plummet, possibly leading to coma and death.

To avoid hypothermia, always bring a windproof/rainproof shell, a fleece jacket, long underwear made of a breathable, synthetic fiber, gloves, and hat when you are hiking in the mountains. Learn to adjust your clothing layers based on the temperature. If you are climbing uphill at a moderate pace you will stay warm, but when you stop for a break you'll become cold quickly, unless you add more layers of clothing.

If a hiker is showing advanced signs of hypothermia, dress him or her in dry clothes and make sure he or she is wearing a hat and gloves. Place the person in a sleeping bag in a tent or shelter that will protect him or her from the wind and other elements. Give the person warm fluids to drink and keep him awake.

Frostbite. When the mercury dips below 32 degrees, your extremities begin to chill. If a persistent chill attacks a localized area, say, your hands or your toes, the circulatory system reacts by cutting off blood flow to the affected area—the idea being to protect and preserve the body's overall temperature. And so it's death by attrition for the affected area. Ice crystals start to form from the water in the cells of the neglected tissue. Deprived of heat, nourishment, and now water, the tissue literally starves. This is frostbite.

Prevention is your best defense against this situation. Most prone to frostbite are your face, hands, and feet, so protect these areas well. Wool is the traditional material of choice because it provides ample air space for insulation and draws moisture away from the skin. Synthetic fabrics, however, have made great strides in the cold weather clothing market. Do your research. A pair of light silk liners under your regular gloves is a good trick for keeping warm. They afford some additional warmth, but more importantly they'll allow you to remove your mitts for tedious work without exposing the skin.

If your feet or hands start to feel cold or numb due to the elements, warm them as quickly as possible. Place cold hands under your armpits or bury them in your crotch. If your feet are cold, change your socks. If there's plenty of room in your boots, add another pair of socks. Do remember, though, that constricting your feet in tight boots can restrict blood flow and actually make your feet colder more quickly. Your socks need to have breathing room if they're going to be effective. Dead air provides insulation. If your face is cold, place your warm hands over your face, or simply wear a head stocking.

Should your skin go numb and start to appear white and waxy, chances are you've got or are developing frostbite. Don't try to thaw the area unless you can maintain the warmth. In other words, don't stop to warm up your frostbitten feet only to head back on the trail. You'll do more damage than good. Tests have shown that hikers who walked on thawed feet did more harm, and endured more pain, than hikers who left the affected areas alone. Do your best to get out of the cold entirely and seek medical attention—which usually consists of performing a rapid rewarming in water for twenty to thirty minutes.

The overall objective in preventing both hypothermia and frostbite is to keep the body's core warm. Protect key areas where heat escapes, like the top of the head, and maintain the proper nutrition level. Foods that are high in calories aid the body in producing heat. Never smoke or drink when you're in situations where the cold is threatening. By affecting blood flow, these activities ultimately cool the body's core temperature.

Altitude sickness (AMS). High lofty peaks, clear alpine lakes, and vast mountain views beckon hikers to the high country. But those who like to venture high may become victims of altitude sickness (also known as Acute Mountain Sickness—AMS). Altitude sickness is your body's reaction to insufficient oxygen in the blood due to decreased barometric pressure. While some hikers may feel lightheaded, nauseous, and experience shortness of breath at 7,000 feet, others may not experience these symptoms until they reach 10,000 feet or higher.

Slowing your ascent to high places and giving your body a chance to acclimatize to the higher elevations can prevent altitude sickness. For example, if you live at sea level and are planning a weeklong backpacking trip to elevations between 7,000 and 12,000 feet, start by staying below 7,000 feet for one night, then move to between 7,000 and 10,000 feet for another night or two. Avoid strenuous exertion and alcohol to give your body a chance to adjust to the new altitude. It's also important to eat light food and drink plenty of nonalcoholic fluids, preferably water. Loss of appetite at altitude is common, but you must eat!

Most hikers who experience mild to moderate AMS develop a headache and/or nausea, grow lethargic, and have problems sleeping. The treatment for AMS is simple: stop heading uphill. Keep eating and drinking water and take meds for the headache. You actually need to take more breaths at altitude than at sea level, so breathe a little faster without hyperventilating. If symptoms don't improve over twenty-four to forty-eight hours, descend. Once a victim descends about 2,000 to 3,000 feet, his signs will usually begin to diminish.

Severe AMS comes in two forms: High Altitude Pulmonary Edema (HAPE) and High Altitude Cerebral Edema (HACE). HAPE, an accumulation of fluid in the lungs, can occur above 8,000 feet. Symptoms include rapid heart rate, shortness of breath at rest, AMS symptoms, dry cough developing into a wet cough, gurgling sounds, flu-like or bronchitis symptoms, and lack of muscle coordination. HAPE is life threatening so descend immediately, at least 2,000 to 4,000 feet. HACE usually occurs above 12,000 feet but sometimes occurs above 10,000 feet. Symptoms are similar to HAPE but also include seizures, hallucinations, paralysis, and vision disturbances. Descend immediately—HACE is also life threatening.

Hantavirus Pulmonary Syndrome (HPS). Deer mice spread the virus that causes HPS, and humans contract it from breathing it in, usually when they've disturbed an area with dust and mice feces from nests or surfaces with mice droppings or urine. Exposure to large numbers of rodents and their feces or urine presents the greatest risk. As hikers, we sometimes enter old buildings, and often deer mice live in these places. We may not be around long enough to be exposed, but do be aware of this disease. About half the people who develop HPS die. Symptoms are flu-like and appear about two to three weeks after exposure. After initial symptoms, a dry cough and shortness of breath follow. Breathing is difficult. If you even think you might have HPS, see a doctor immediately!

Natural Hazards

Besides tripping over a rock or tree root on the trail, there are some real hazards to be aware of while hiking. Even if where you're hiking doesn't have the plethora of poisonous snakes and plants, insects, and grizzly bears found in other parts of the United States, there are a few weather conditions and predators you may need to take into account.

Lightning. Thunderstorms build over the mountains almost every day during the summer. Lightning is generated by thunderheads and can strike without warning, even several miles away from the nearest overhead cloud. The best rule of thumb is to start leaving exposed peaks, ridges, and canyon rims by about noon. This time can vary a little depending on storm buildup. Keep an eye on cloud formation and don't underestimate how fast a storm can build. The bigger they get, the more likely a thunderstorm will happen. Lightning takes the path of least resistance, so if you're the high point, it might choose you. Ducking under a rock overhang is dangerous as you form the shortest path between the rock and ground. If you dash below treeline, avoid standing under the only or the tallest tree. If you are caught above treeline, stay away from anything metal you might be carrying, Move down off the ridge slightly to a low, treeless point and squat until the storm passes. If you have an insulating pad, squat on it. Avoid having both your hands and feet touching the ground at once and never lay flat. If you hear a buzzing sound or feel your hair standing on end, move quickly as an electrical charge is building up.

Flash floods. On July 31, 1976, a torrential downpour unleashed by a thunderstorm dumped tons of water into the Big Thompson watershed near Estes Park. Within hours, a wall of water moved down the narrow canyon killing 139 people and causing more than $30 million in property damage. The spooky thing about flash floods, especially in western canyons, is that they can appear out of nowhere from a storm many miles away. While hiking or driving in canyons, keep an eye on the weather. Always climb to safety if danger threatens. Flash floods usually subside quickly, so be patient and don't cross a swollen stream.

Bears. Most of the United States (outside of the Pacific Northwest and parts of the Northern Rockies) does not have a grizzly bear population, although some rumors exist about sightings where there should be none. Black bears are plentiful, however. Here are some tips in case you and a bear scare each other. Most of all, avoid surprising a bear. Talk or sing where visibility or hearing are limited, such as along a rushing creek or in thick brush. In grizzly country especially, carry bear spray in a holster on your pack belt where you can quickly grab it. While hiking, watch for bear tracks (five toes), droppings (sizable with leaves, partly digested berries, seeds, and/or animal fur), or rocks and roots along the trail that show signs of being dug up (this could be a bear looking for bugs to eat). Keep a clean camp, hang food or use bearproof storage containers, and don't sleep in the clothes you wore while cooking. Be especially careful to avoid getting between a mother and her cubs. In late summer and fall bears are busy eating to fatten up for winter, so be extra careful around berry bushes and oakbrush. If you do encounter a bear, move away slowly while facing the bear, talk softly, and avoid direct eye contact. Give the bear room to escape. Since bears are very curious, it might stand upright to get a better whiff of you, and it may even charge you to try to intimidate you. Try to stay calm. If a black bear attacks you, fight back with anything you have handy. If a grizzly bear attacks you, your best option is to "play dead" by lying face down on the ground and covering the back of your neck and head with your hands. Unleashed dogs have been known to come running back to their owners with a bear close behind. Keep your dog on a leash or leave it at home.

Mountain lions. Mountain lions appear to be getting more comfortable around humans as long as deer (their favorite prey) are in an area with adequate cover. Usually elusive and quiet, lions rarely attack people. If you meet a lion, give it a chance to escape. Stay calm and talk firmly to it. Back away slowly while facing the lion. If you run, you'll only encourage the cat to chase you. Make yourself look large by opening a jacket, if you have one, or waving your hiking poles. If the lion behaves aggressively throw stones, sticks, or whatever you can while remaining tall. If a lion does attack, fight for your life with anything you can grab.

Moose. Because moose have very few natural predators, they don't fear humans like other animals. You might find moose in sagebrush and wetter areas of willow, aspen, and pine, or in beaver habitats. Mothers with calves, as well as bulls during mating season, can be particularly aggressive. If a moose threatens you, back away slowly and talk calmly to it. Keep your pets away from moose.

Other considerations. Hunting is a popular sport in the United States, especially during rifle season in October and November. Hiking is still enjoyable in those months in many areas, so just take a few precautions. First, learn when the different hunting seasons start and end in the area in which you'll be hiking. During this time frame, be sure to wear at least a blaze orange hat, and possibly put an orange vest over your pack. Don't be surprised to see hunters in camo outfits carrying bows or rifles around during their season. If you would feel more comfortable without hunters around, hike in national parks and monuments or state and local parks where hunting is not allowed.

Navigation

Whether you are going on a short hike in a familiar area or planning a weeklong backpack trip, you should always be equipped with the proper navigational equipment—at the very least a detailed map and a sturdy compass.

Maps. There are many different types of maps available to help you find your way on the trail. Easiest to find are Forest Service maps and BLM (Bureau of Land Management) maps. These maps tend to cover large areas, so be sure they are detailed enough for your particular trip. You can also obtain National Park maps as well as high quality maps from private companies and trail groups. These maps can be obtained either from outdoor stores or ranger stations.

U.S. Geological Survey topographic maps are particularly popular with hikers—especially serious backcountry hikers. These maps contain the standard map symbols such as roads, lakes, and rivers, as well as contour lines that show the details of the trail terrain like ridges, valleys, passes, and mountain peaks. The 7.5-minute series (1 inch on the map equals approximately 0.4 mile on the ground) provides the closest inspection avail-

This red buckeye brightens the Peavine Falls Loop.

able. USGS maps are available by mail (U.S. Geological Survey, Map Distribution Branch, PO Box 25286, Denver, CO 80225), or at mapping.usgs.gov/esic/to_order.html.

If you want to check out the high-tech world of maps, you can purchase topographic maps on CD-ROM. These software-mapping programs let you select a route on your computer, print it out, then take it with you on the trail. Some software mapping programs let you insert symbols and labels, download waypoints from a GPS unit, and export the maps to other software programs.

The art of map reading is a skill that you can develop by first practicing in an area you are familiar with. To begin, orient the map so the map is lined up in the correct direction (i.e. north on the map is lined up with true north). Next, familiarize yourself with the map symbols and try and match them up with terrain features around you such as a high ridge, mountain peak, river, or lake. If you are practicing with a USGS map, notice the contour lines. On gentler terrain these contour lines are spaced farther apart, and on steeper terrain they are closer together. Pick a short loop trail, and stop frequently to check your position on the map. As you practice map reading, you'll learn how to anticipate a steep section on the trail or a good place to take a rest break, and so on.

Compasses. First off, the sun is not a substitute for a compass. So, what kind of compass should you have? Here are some characteristics you should look for: a rectangular base with detailed scales, a liquid-filled housing, protective housing, a sighting line on the mirror, luminous alignment and back-bearing arrows, a luminous north-seeking arrow, and a well-defined bezel ring.

You can learn compass basics by reading the detailed instructions included with your compass. If you want to fine-tune your compass skills, sign up for an orienteering class or purchase a book on compass reading. Once you've learned the basic skills of using a compass, remember to practice these skills before you head into the backcountry.

If you are a klutz at using a compass, you may be interested in checking out the technical wizardry of the GPS (Global Positioning System) device. The GPS was developed by the Pentagon and works off twenty-four NAVSTAR satellites, which were designed to guide missiles to their targets. A GPS device is a handheld unit that calculates your latitude and longitude with the easy press of a button. The Department of Defense used to scramble the satellite signals a bit to prevent civilians (and spies!) from getting extremely accurate readings, but that practice was discontinued in May 2000, and GPS units now provide nearly pinpoint accuracy (within 30 to 60 feet).

There are many different types of GPS units available and they range in price from $100 to $400. In general, all GPS units have a display screen and keypad where you input information. In addition to acting as a compass, the unit allows you to plot your route, easily retrace your path, track your travelling speed, find the mileage between waypoints, and calculate the total mileage of your route.

Before you purchase a GPS unit, keep in mind that these devices don't pick up signals indoors, in heavily wooded areas, on mountain peaks, or in deep valleys. Also, batteries can wear out or other technical problems can develop. A GPS unit should be used in conjunction with a map and compass, not in place of those items.

Pedometers. A pedometer is a small, clip-on unit with a digital display that calculates your hiking distance in miles or kilometers based on your walking stride. Some units also calculate the calories you burn and your total hiking time. Pedometers are available at most large outdoor stores and range in price from $20 to $40.

Trip Planning

Planning your hiking adventure begins with letting a friend or relative know your trip itinerary so they can call for help if you don't return at your scheduled time. Your next task is to make sure you are outfitted to experience the risks and rewards of the trail. This section highlights gear and clothing you may want to take with you to get the most out of your hike.

Day Hikes

❑ bear repellent spray (if hiking in grizzly country)
❑ camera
❑ compass/GPS unit
❑ pedometer
❑ daypack
❑ first-aid kit
❑ food
❑ guidebook
❑ headlamp/flashlight with extra batteries and bulbs
❑ hat
❑ insect repellent
❑ knife/multipurpose tool
❑ map
❑ matches in waterproof container and fire starter
❑ fleece jacket
❑ rain gear
❑ space blanket
❑ sunglasses
❑ sunscreen
❑ swimsuit and/or fishing gear (if hiking to a lake)
❑ watch
❑ water
❑ water bottles/water hydration system

Overnight Trip

- ❑ backpack and waterproof rain cover
- ❑ backpacker's trowel
- ❑ bandanna
- ❑ bear repellent spray (if hiking in grizzly country)
- ❑ bear bell
- ❑ biodegradable soap
- ❑ pot scrubber
- ❑ collapsible water container (2–3 gallon capacity)
- ❑ clothing—extra wool socks, shirt and shorts
- ❑ cook set/utensils
- ❑ ditty bags to store gear
- ❑ extra plastic resealable bags
- ❑ gaiters
- ❑ garbage bag
- ❑ ground cloth
- ❑ journal/pen
- ❑ nylon rope to hang food
- ❑ long underwear
- ❑ permit (if required)
- ❑ rain jacket and pants
- ❑ sandals to wear around camp and to ford streams
- ❑ sleeping bag
- ❑ waterproof stuff sack
- ❑ sleeping pad
- ❑ small bath towel
- ❑ stove and fuel
- ❑ tent
- ❑ toiletry items
- ❑ water filter
- ❑ whistle

Equipment

With the outdoor market currently flooded with products, many of which are pure gimmickry, it seems impossible to both differentiate and choose. Do I really need a tropical-fish-lined collapsible shower? (No, you don't.) The only defense against the maddening quantity of items thrust in your face is to think practically—and to do so before you go shopping. The worst buys are impulsive buys. Since most name brands will differ only slightly in quality, it's best to know what you're looking for in terms of function. Buy only what you need. You will, don't forget, be carrying what you've bought on your back. Here are some things to keep in mind before you go shopping.

Clothes. Clothing is your armor against Mother Nature's little surprises. Hikers should be prepared for any possibility, especially when hiking in mountainous areas. Adequate rain protection and extra layers of clothing are a good idea. In summer, a wide-brimmed hat can help keep the sun at bay. In the winter months the first layer you'll want to wear is a "wicking" layer of long underwear that keeps perspiration away from your skin. Wear long underwear made from synthetic fibers that wick moisture away from the skin and draw it toward the next layer of clothing, where it then evaporates. Avoid wearing long underwear made of cotton as it is slow to dry and keeps moisture next to your skin.

The second layer you'll wear is the "insulating" layer. Aside from keeping you warm, this layer needs to "breathe" so you stay dry while hiking. A fabric that provides insulation and dries quickly is fleece. It's interesting to note that this one-of-a-kind fabric is made out of recycled plastic. Purchasing a zip-up jacket made of this material is highly recommended.

The last line of layering defense is the "shell" layer. You'll need some type of waterproof, windproof, breathable jacket that will fit over all of your other layers. It should have a large hood that fits over a hat. You'll also need a good pair of rain pants made from a similar waterproof, breathable fabric. Some Gore-Tex jackets cost as much as $500, but you should know that there are more affordable fabrics out there that work just as well.

Now that you've learned the basics of layering, you can't forget to protect your hands and face. In cold, windy, or rainy weather you'll need a hat made of wool or fleece and insulated, waterproof gloves that will keep your hands warm and toasty. As mentioned earlier, buying an additional pair of light silk liners to wear under your regular gloves is a good idea.

Footwear. If you have any extra money to spend on your trip, put that money into boots or trail shoes. Poor shoes will bring a hike to a halt faster than anything else. To avoid this annoyance, buy shoes that provide support and are lightweight and flexible. A lightweight hiking boot is better than a heavy, leather mountaineering boot for most day hikes and backpacking. Trail running shoes provide a little extra cushion and are made in a high-top style that many people wear for hiking. These running shoes are lighter, more flexible, and more breathable than hiking boots. If you know you'll be hiking in wet weather often, purchase boots or shoes with a Gore-Tex liner, which will help keep your feet dry.

When buying your boots, be sure to wear the same type of socks you'll be wearing on the trail. If the boots you're buying are for cold weather hiking, try the boots on while wearing two pairs of socks. Speaking of socks, a good cold weather sock combination is to wear a thinner sock made of wool or polypropylene covered by a heavier outer sock made of wool or a synthetic/wool mix. The inner sock protects the foot from the rubbing effects of the outer sock and prevents blisters. Many outdoor stores have some type of ramp to simulate hiking uphill and downhill. Be sure to take advantage of this test, as toe-jamming boot fronts can be very painful and debilitating on the downhill trek.

Once you've purchased your footwear, be sure to break them in before you hit the trail. New footwear is often stiff and needs to be stretched and molded to your foot.

Hiking poles. Hiking poles help with balance, and more importantly take pressure off your knees. The ones with shock absorbers are easier on your elbows and knees. Some poles even come with a camera attachment to be used as a monopod. And heaven forbid you meet a mountain lion, bear, or unfriendly dog, the poles can make you look a lot bigger.

Backpacks. No matter what type of hiking you do you'll need a pack of some sort to carry the basic trail essentials. There are a variety of backpacks on the market, but let's first discuss what you intend to use it for. Day hikes or overnight trips?

If you plan on doing a day hike, a daypack should have some of the following characteristics: a padded hip belt that's at least 2 inches in diameter (avoid packs with only a small nylon piece of webbing for a hip belt); a chest strap (the chest strap helps stabilize the pack against your body); external pockets to carry water and other items that you want easy access to; an internal pocket to hold keys, a knife, a wallet, and other miscellaneous items; an external lashing system to hold a jacket; and, if you so desire, a hydration pocket for carrying a hydration system (which consists of a water bladder with an attachable drinking hose).

For short hikes, some hikers like to use a fanny pack to store just a camera, food, a compass, a map, and other trail essentials. Most fanny packs have pockets for two water bottles and a padded hip belt.

If you intend to do an extended, overnight trip, there are multiple considerations. First off, you need to decide what kind of framed pack you want. There are two backpack types for backpacking: the internal frame and the external frame. An internal frame pack rests closer to your body, making it more stable and easier to balance when hiking over rough terrain. An external frame pack is just that, an aluminum frame attached to the exterior of the pack. Some hikers consider an external frame pack to be better for long backpack trips because it distributes the pack weight better and allows you to carry heavier loads. It's often easier to pack, and your gear is more accessible. It also offers better back ventilation in hot weather.

The most critical measurement for fitting a pack is torso length. The pack needs to rest evenly on your hips without sagging. A good pack will come in two or three sizes and have straps and hip belts that are adjustable according to your body size and characteristics.

When you purchase a backpack, go to an outdoor store with salespeople who are knowledgeable in how to properly fit a pack. Once the pack is fitted for you, load the pack with the amount of weight you plan on taking on the trail. The weight of the pack should be distributed evenly and you should be able to swing your arms and walk briskly without feeling out of balance. Another good technique for evaluating a pack is to walk up and down stairs and make quick turns to the right and to the left to be sure the pack doesn't feel out of balance. Other features that are nice to have on a backpack include a removable day pack or fanny pack, external pockets for extra water, and extra lash points to attach a jacket or other items.

Sleeping bags and pads. Sleeping bags are rated by temperature. You can purchase a bag made with synthetic insulation, or you can buy a goose down bag. Goose down bags are more expensive, but they have a higher insulating capacity by weight and will keep their loft longer. You'll want to purchase a bag with a temperature rating that fits the time of year and conditions you are most likely to camp in. One caveat: The techno-standard for temperature ratings is far from perfect. Ratings vary from manufacturer to manufacturer, so to protect yourself you should purchase a bag rated 10 to 15 degrees below the temperature you expect to be camping in. Synthetic bags are more resistant to water than down bags, but many down bags are now made with a Gore-Tex shell that helps to repel water. Down bags are also more compressible than synthetic bags and take up less room in your pack, which is an important consideration if you are planning a multiday backpack trip. Features to look for in a sleeping bag include a mummy style bag, a hood you can cinch down around your head in cold weather, and draft tubes along the zippers that help keep heat in and drafts out.

You'll also want a sleeping pad to provide insulation and padding from the cold ground. There are different types of sleeping pads available, from the more expensive self-inflating air mattresses to the less expensive closed-cell foam pads. Self-inflating air mattresses are usually heavier than closed-cell foam mattresses and are prone to punctures.

Tents. The tent is your home away from home while on the trail. It provides protection from wind, rain, snow, and insects. A three-season tent is a good choice for backpacking and can range in price from $100 to $500. These lightweight and versatile tents provide protection in all types of weather, except heavy snowstorms or high winds, and range in weight from four to eight pounds. Look for a tent that's easy to set up and will easily fit two people with gear. Dome type tents usually offer more headroom and places to store gear. Other handy tent features include a vestibule where you can store wet boots and backpacks. Some nice-to-have items in a tent include interior pockets to store small items and lashing points to hang a clothesline. Most three-season tents also come with stakes so you can secure the tent in high winds. Before you purchase a tent, set it up and take it down a few times to be sure it is easy to handle. Also, sit inside the tent and make sure it has enough room for you and your gear.

Cell phones. Many hikers are carrying their cell phones into the backcountry these days in case of emergency. That's fine and good, but please know that cell phone coverage is often poor to nonexistent in valleys, canyons, and thick forest. More importantly people have started to call for help because they're tired or lost. Let's go back to being prepared. You are responsible for yourself in the backcountry. Use your brain to avoid problems, and if you do encounter one, first use your brain to try to correct the situation. Only use your cell phone, if it works, in true emergencies. If it doesn't work down low in a valley, try hiking to a high point where you might get reception.

Hiking with Children

Hiking with children isn't a matter of how many miles you can cover or how much elevation gain you make in a day; it's about seeing and experiencing nature through their eyes.

Kids like to explore and have fun. They like to stop and point out bugs and plants, look under rocks, jump in puddles, and throw sticks. If you're taking a toddler or young child on a hike, start with a trail that you're familiar with. Trails that have interesting things for kids, like piles of leaves to play in or a small stream to wade through during the summer, will make the hike much more enjoyable for them and will keep them from getting bored.

You can keep your child's attention if you have a strategy before starting on the trail. Using games is not only an effective way to keep a child's attention, it's also a great way to teach him or her about nature. Quiz children on the names of plants and animals. Pick up a family-friendly outdoor hobby like Geocaching (www.geocaching.com) or Letterboxing (www.atlasquest.com), both of which combine the outdoors, clue-solving, and treasure hunting. If your children are old enough, let them carry their own daypack filled with snacks and water. So that you are sure to go at their pace and not yours, let them lead the way. Playing follow the leader works particularly well when you have a group of children. Have each child take a turn at being the leader.

With children, a lot of clothing is key. The only thing predictable about weather is that it will change. Especially in mountainous areas, weather can change dramatically in a very short time. Always bring extra clothing for children, regardless of the season. In the winter, have your children wear wool socks, and warm layers such as long underwear, a fleece jacket and hat, wool mittens, and good rain gear. It's not a bad idea to have these along in late fall and early spring as well. Good footwear is also important. A sturdy pair of high top tennis shoes or lightweight hiking boots are the best bet for little ones. If you're hiking in the summer near a lake or stream, bring along a pair of old sneakers that your child can put on when he wants to go exploring in the water. Remember when you're near any type of water, always watch your child at all times. Also, keep a close eye on teething toddlers who may decide a rock or leaf of poison oak is an interesting item to put in their mouth.

From spring through fall, you'll want your kids to wear a wide-brimmed hat to keep their face, head, and ears protected from the hot sun. Also, make sure your children wear sunscreen at all times. Choose a brand without Paba—children have sensitive skin and may have an allergic reaction to sunscreen that contains Paba. If you are hiking with a child younger than six months, don't use sunscreen or insect repellent. Instead, be sure that their head, face, neck, and ears are protected from the sun with a wide-brimmed hat, and that all other skin exposed to the sun is protected with the appropriate clothing.

Remember that food is fun. Kids like snacks so it's important to bring a lot of munchies for the trail. Stopping often for snack breaks is a fun way to keep the trail interesting. Raisins, apples, granola bars, crackers and cheese, cereal, and trail mix all make great snacks. Also, a few of their favorite candy treats can go a long way toward heading off a fit of fussing. If your child is old enough to carry her own backpack, let him or her fill it with some lightweight "comfort" items such as a doll, a small stuffed animal, or a little toy (you'll have to draw the line at bringing the ten-pound Tonka truck). If your kids don't like drinking water, you can bring some powdered drink mix or a juice box.

Avoid poorly designed child-carrying packs—you don't want to break your back carrying your child. Most child-carrying backpacks designed to hold a forty-pound child will contain a large carrying pocket to hold diapers and other items. Some have an optional rain/sun hood.

Hiking with Your Dog

Bringing your furry friend with you is always more fun than leaving him behind. Our canine pals make great trail buddies because they never complain and always make good company. Hiking with your dog can be a rewarding experience, especially if you plan ahead.

Getting your dog in shape. Before you plan outdoor adventures with your dog, make sure he's in shape for the trail. Getting your dog into shape takes the same discipline as getting yourself into shape, but luckily, your dog can get in shape with you. Take your dog with you on your daily runs or walks. If there is a park near your house, hit a tennis ball or play Frisbee with your dog.

Swimming is also an excellent way to get your dog into shape. If there is a lake or river near where you live and your dog likes the water, have him retrieve a tennis ball or stick. Gradually build your dog's stamina up over a two- to three-month period. A good rule of thumb is to assume that your dog will travel twice as far as you will on the trail. If you plan on doing a 5-mile hike, be sure your dog is in shape for a 10-mile hike.

Training your dog for the trail. Before you go on your first hiking adventure with your dog, be sure he has a firm grasp on the basics of canine etiquette and behavior. Make sure he can sit, lie down, stay, and come. One of the most important commands you can teach your canine pal is to "come" under any situation. It's easy for your friend's nose to lead him astray or possibly get lost. Another helpful command is the "get behind" command. When you're on a hiking trail that's narrow, you can have your dog follow behind you when other trail users approach. Nothing is more bothersome than an enthusiastic dog that runs back and forth on the trail and disrupts the peace of the trail for others—or, worse, jumps up on other hikers and gets them muddy. When you see other trail users approaching you on the trail, give them the right of way by quietly stepping off the trail and making your dog lie down and stay until they pass.

Equipment. The most critical pieces of equipment you can invest in for your dog are proper identification and a sturdy leash. Flexi-leads work well for hiking because they give your dog more freedom to explore but still leave you in control. Make sure your dog has identification that includes your name and address and a number for your veterinarian. Other forms of identification for your dog include a tattoo or a microchip. You should consult your veterinarian for more information on these last two options.

The next piece of equipment you'll want to consider is a pack for your dog. By no means should you hold all of your dog's essentials in your pack—let him carry his own gear! Dogs that are in good shape can carry 30 to 40 percent of their own weight.

Most packs are fitted by a dog's weight and girth measurement. Companies that make dog packs generally include guidelines to help you pick out the size that's right for your dog. Some characteristics to look for when purchasing a pack for your dog include a harness that contains two padded girth straps, a padded chest strap, leash attachments, removable saddle bags, internal water bladders, and external gear cords.

You can introduce your dog to the pack by first placing the empty pack on his back and letting him wear it around the yard. Keep an eye on him during this first introduction. He may decide to chew through the straps if you aren't watching him closely. Once he learns to treat the pack as an object of fun and not a foreign enemy, fill the pack evenly on both sides with a few ounces of dog food in resealable plastic bags. Have your dog wear his pack on your daily walks for a period of two to three weeks. Each week add a little more weight to the pack until your dog will accept carrying the maximum amount of weight he can carry.

You can also purchase collapsible water and dog food bowls for your dog. These bowls are lightweight and can easily be stashed into your pack or your dog's. If you are hiking on rocky terrain or in the snow, you can purchase footwear for your dog that will protect his feet from cuts and bruises.

Always carry plastic bags to remove feces from the trail. It is a courtesy to other trail users and helps protect local wildlife.

The following is a list of items to bring when you take your dog hiking: collapsible water bowls, a comb, a collar and a leash, dog food, plastic bags for feces, a dog pack, flea/tick powder, paw protection, water, and a first-aid kit that contains eye ointment, tweezers, scissors, stretchy foot wrap, gauze, antibacterial wash, sterile cotton tip applicators, antibiotic ointment, and cotton wrap.

First aid for your dog. Your dog is just as prone—if not more prone—to getting in trouble on the trail as you are, so be prepared. Here's a rundown of the more likely misfortunes that might befall your little friend.

Bees and wasps. If a bee or wasp stings your dog, remove the stinger with a pair of tweezers and place a mudpack or a cloth dipped in cold water over the affected area.

Porcupines. One good reason to keep your dog on a leash is to prevent it from getting a nose full of porcupine quills. You may be able to remove the quills with pliers, but a veterinarian is the best person to do this nasty job because most dogs need to be sedated.

Heat stroke. Avoid hiking with your dog in really hot weather. Dogs with heat stroke will pant excessively, lie down and refuse to get up, and become lethargic and disoriented. If your dog shows any of these signs on the trail, have him lie down in the shade. If you are near a stream, pour cool water over your dog's entire body to help bring his body temperature back to normal.

Heartworm. Dogs get heartworms from mosquitoes which carry the disease in the prime mosquito months of July and August. Giving your dog a monthly pill prescribed by your veterinarian easily prevents this condition.

Plant pitfalls. One of the biggest plant hazards for dogs on the trail is foxtails. Foxtails are pointed grass seed heads that bury themselves in your friend's fur, between his toes, and even get in his ear canal. If left unattended, these nasty seeds can work their way under the skin and cause abscesses and other problems. If you have a long-haired dog, consider trimming the hair between his toes and giving him a summer haircut to help prevent foxtails from attaching to his fur. After every hike, always look over your dog for these seeds—especially between his toes and his ears.

Other plant hazards include burrs, thorns, thistles, and poison oak. If you find any burrs or thistles on your dog, remove them as soon as possible before they become an unmanageable mat. Thorns can pierce a dog's foot and cause a great deal of pain. If you see that your dog is lame, stop and check his feet for thorns. Dogs are immune to poison oak but they can pick up the sticky, oily substance from the plant and transfer it to you.

Protect those paws. Be sure to keep your dog's nails trimmed so he avoids getting soft tissue or joint injuries. If your dog slows and refuses to go on, check to see that his paws aren't torn or worn. You can protect your dog's paws from trail hazards such as sharp gravel, foxtails, lava scree, and thorns by purchasing dog boots.

Sunburn. If your dog has light skin he is an easy target for sunburn on his nose and other exposed skin areas. You can apply a nontoxic sunscreen to exposed skin areas that will help protect him from overexposure to the sun.

Ticks and fleas. Ticks can easily give your dog Lyme disease, as well as other diseases. Before you hit the trail, treat your dog with a flea and tick spray or powder. You can also ask your veterinarian about a once-a-month pour-on treatment that repels fleas and ticks.

Mosquitoes and deer flies. These little flying machines can do a job on your dog's snout and ears. Best bet is to spray your dog with fly repellent for horses to discourage both pests.

Giardia. Dogs can get giardia, which results in diarrhea. It is usually not debilitating, but it's definitely messy. A vaccine against giardia is available.

Mushrooms. Make sure your dog doesn't sample mushrooms along the trail. They could be poisonous to him, but he doesn't know that.

When you are finally ready to hit the trail with your dog, keep in mind that national parks and many wilderness areas do not allow dogs on trails. Your best bet is to hike in national forests, BLM lands, and state parks. Always call ahead to see what the restrictions are.

Hike Index

Alligator Alley (HM), 79

Bald Rock / Doug Ghee Boardwalk Trail (HM), 201

Beaver Pond Loop, 217

Bell/CCC Trail, 88

Blue Trail, 41

BMRR–Ike Maston Loop, 173

Borden Creek (Trail 200), 272

Cane Creek Canyon Nature Preserve, 267

Cave Mountain Loop, 221

Cemetery Loop Trail, 69

Centennial / Jeff Friend Trail, 26

Chewacla State Park Loop, 118

Chinnabee Silent Trail, 150

Conecuh Trail (HM), 134

Confederate Memorial Park Nature Trail, 197

Cotton Bayou Trail, 36

Deadening Trail (HM), 202

DeSoto Scout Trail, 205

Doug Ghee Boardwalk Trail to Bald Rock (HM), 201

Eberhart Trail (HM), 278

Eufaula Wildlife Refuge Nature Trail (HM), 133

Falls Loop, 211

Five Runs Loop, 102

Fort Toulouse / Fort Jackson Loop, 97

Frank Jackson State Park (HM), 133

Gator Lake Trail, 31

Gazebo Trail, 83

Geneva State Forest (HM), 133

Historic Blakeley State Park, 58

Horseshoe Bend Nature Trail, 141

Hugh Branyon Backcountry Trail (HM), 79

Ike Maston–BMRR Loop, 173

Jeff Friend / Centennial Trail, 26

Jones Branch Loop, 256

Lawson Branch Loop, 251

Maggie's Glen Loop, 159

Monte Sano Nature Preserve Loop, 234

Muddy Creek Interpretive Trail, 64

Nellie Pond Loop, 108

North Plateau Loop, 246

Nubbin Creek Trail, 146

Old St Stephens Historical Park, 93

Overlook Loop, 129

Peavine Falls Loop, 168

Perdido River Trail, 46

Perry Lake Loop, 113

Pine Beach Trail, 21

Point Rock Trail (HM), 278

Pulpit Rock Trail, 155

Quarry Trail, 183

Rock Garden Trail (HM), 201

Russell Cave National Monument (HM), 279

Smith Mountain Loop, 137

South Plateau Loop, 241

Splinter Hill Bog, 74

Stone Cuts Trail (HM), 279

Tannehill Ironworks Historic Trail, 192

Trails of Gulf State Park (HM), 79

Treetop Trail, 164

Tunnel Falls Loop, 178

Turkey Creek Loop, 188

TVA Nature Trail, 264

Village Point Park Preserve, 53

Walls of Jericho, 230

Waterfall Trail, 225

Weeks Bay Nature Trail, 15

Wood Duck Trail, 123

(HM) = Honorable Mention

Sidebar Index

Alabama Trails Commission, The, 210

Alabama's First Long Path: The Pinhoti Trail, 152

Alabama's Long Trails, 48

Bama Firsts, 161

Biodiversity, 220

Cahaba Lily, 117

CCC in Alabama, The, 213

Creamy Chicken and Rice, 140

Eastern Indigo Snake, The, 112

Huntsville, the Rocket City, 237

Iron and Steel, 173

Jubilee!, 55

Just the Facts . . . about Alabama, 17

Keeping Alabama Forever Wild—Again, 126

Land of a Thousand Waterfalls, The, 276

Marble, Alabama State Rock, 267

Mardi Gras, 64

Natural Lightning Rod—You, A, 227

Trail Teriyaki Chicken, 87

Watch Your Step, 132

The Ike Maston-BMRR Loop Trail takes you to the beautiful mission style architecture of the Redding Mine Hoist House.

About the Author

Joe Cuhaj grew up in Mahwah, New Jersey, near Harriman / Bear Mountain State Parks. It is here, near where the first sections of the Appalachian Trail were built, that his love of hiking and the outdoors began. After high school Joe enlisted in the US Navy, where he met his wife, Maggie. The two moved to her hometown, Mobile, Alabama, and now live on the Eastern Shore of Mobile Bay in Daphne.

Joe spent many years in radio broadcasting before changing careers, becoming a software programmer for a local company where he still works by day. By night Joe is an author and freelance writer, having penned three other books, *Paddling Alabama* (FalconGuides), *Baseball in Mobile,* and *Best Tent Camping: Alabama*. He has also written many articles for magazines and online publications on a wide variety of topics ranging from the environment to political issues to the media.

Joe Cuhaj at the summit of Smith Mountain (Hike 23).

The forest is lush and green along the TVA Nature Trail.

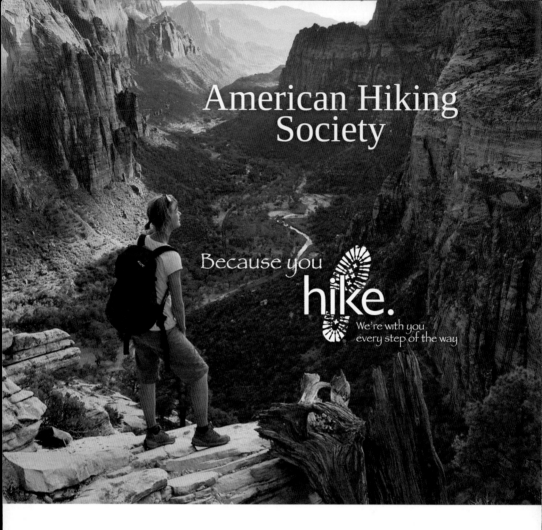

American Hiking Society

Because you

hike.
We're with you
every step of the way

As a national voice for hikers, **American Hiking Society** works every day:

- Building and maintaining hiking trails
- Educating and supporting hikers by providing information and resources
- Supporting hiking and trail organizations nationwide
- Speaking for hikers in the halls of Congress and with federal land managers

Whether you're a casual hiker or a seasoned backpacker, become a member of American Hiking Society and join the national hiking community! You'll enjoy great member benefits and help preserve the nation's hiking trails, so tomorrow's hike is even better than today's. We invite you to join us now!

American Hiking Society